WORKERS AND COMMUNISTS
IN FRANCE

Workers and Communists

in France

From Popular Front to Eurocommunism

GEORGE ROSS

UNIVERSITY OF CALIFORNIA PRESS

BERKELEY · LOS ANGELES · LONDON

Library of Congress Cataloging in Publication Data

Ross, George, 1940–
   Workers and Communists in France. From Popular Front to Eurocommunism.
   Bibliography: p.
   Includes index.
   1. Parti communiste français—History.
  2. Confédération générale du travail—History.
  I. Title.
  JN3007.C6R67   324.244075   80-26532
  ISBN 0-520-04075-9

University of California Press
Berkeley and Los Angeles, California
University of California Press, Ltd. London, England

1 2 3 4 5 6 7 8 9

CONTENTS

ACKNOWLEDGMENTS

The most important source of inspiration for this study came from its subjects themselves—the workers and Communists of France. At three particular moments—during May-June 1968, during the "Eurocommunization" of the mid-1970s, and during the strange events surrounding the French elections of 1978—French workers and Communists led me to think that there existed a story worth telling, and that I might be able to tell it. The dedication, intelligence and probity of my friends in France, especially those in and around the CGT and PCF, continue to teach me more than archives and libraries ever could. Because they are presently working with all of their energy to change things, I will not risk their efforts, even in a minor way, by thanking them by name. My heart and my hopes, in addition to my deep gratitude, go out to them.

Two great teachers—and friends—also inspired me and provided immense encouragement, in addition to unattainable role models, for this work. Ralph Miliband and Barrington Moore, Jr., each in his own way, prodded me onwards while demonstrating what the vocation of an intellectual could be. The Harvard University Center for European Studies provided me with a precious milieu, marked by intellectual energy, tolerance and unselfish comradeship, in which to think and work. Stanley Hoffman (who read an earlier draft of this study) and Abby Collins, along with other friends make Harvard, CES happen. I join a very large chorus in expressing my gratitude to them. Jane Jenson has been a collaborator in all ways, intellectually, first of all, in the mechanical tasks of producing a book, and, finally, in making life rich and coherent enough to do the work which we both believe important. Friends and colleagues of the Brandeis University Sociology Department have, over the years, granted me the rare gift of complete intellectual liberty and allowed me to live and work in an atmosphere of generosity and civility.

Material support has come from a number of places. Without a Fellowship in 1978-1979 from the German Marshall Fund of the United States, which allowed me to work in France relieved of teaching responsibilities, this project would never have been completed. The GMF's help gave me space to write and do research, to be sure, but also to reflect and explore. This book is only the first result of such generosity. The Sachar Fund at Brandeis and the Dean of Social Sciences at Carleton University in Ottawa, Canada, also helped out financially as did, earlier, the Center for International Affairs at Harvard University.

Errors of fact and interpretation, along with any other forms of general wrong-headedness, are my own doing.

INTRODUCTION

It is characteristic of modern trade-union movements—those which emerged from the twin crucibles of the Great Depression and the immediate post-World War II periods—that they face in two directions. Unions exist to defend the material interests of all or part of the wage-labor force in their societies. But however differently unions have defined these tasks in different places, rarely, in the modern period, have they been content with self-definitions which restricted their activities to the market place alone. The advanced capitalism of "post-war settlements"—a term which refers to the socioeconomic equilibria struck in the immediate post-1945 period—has not allowed this. Complex networks of representative democracy, highly developed patterns of coordination between major social actors (producer groups in particular), plus state interventions in the accumulation process itself have made strictly market-centered trade unionism little more than a myth from the golden past. Everywhere unions have explicit programs for shaping and changing national economic and social processes which dictate the mobilization of political resources for implementation. Everywhere unions are involved in attempting to influence the electoral behavior of their rank and file. Everywhere unions define the aggregation and specification of their memberships' political interests as part of their tasks. In short, union involvement in politics, over and above union activities in the labor market, is a universal fact of social life.

There are very great variations between different union movements in the ways in which they do participate in their national political processes, however. Some unions, primarily but not exclusively the "business unionism" of North American, attempt to intervene politically as pressure groups and voting blocs without open affiliation with a political party. Most other unions focus much of their political attention through affiliation with political parties. If direct union-party affiliation is very common, however, the nature of such affiliation also varies greatly. Two general types of affiliation predominate. First, there is the social democratic type, roughly associated with union movements and political parties which grew to maturity in the years of the Socialist Second International. Party-union ties of a social democratic kind share one general characteristic—both the union and the party maintain primary autonomy in deciding their own strategies in their respective spheres. Thus unions, for their own reasons, decide on their labor market and political strategies, while the party decides on politics. In the case of social democratic union-party complexes, then, relationships of mutual influence between union and party are relationships of rough equality. Exchanges between them go in both directions so that generalizations about whether party or union will be determinant in any given situation are hazardous.

The second type of affiliation is that which developed in the Third International/Communist tradition. In the Third International/Communist model of union-party relationships the weight of the political party in determining trade union strategy and goals has tended to be vastly greater than in the social democratic type. The historical reasons for this are obvious. One of the major failures which Lenin and the other founders of the Communist International in the 1920s attributed to earlier socialist movements was the growing domination of the concerns of "reformist" trade unions—ever more bound up in complex networks of collaboration with capitalists and the capitalist state—over revolutionary political parties. Lenin's discussion of working-class "spontaneity" and trade unionism in *What is to be Done?* is eloquent and uncompromising on this point. Left to their own resorts, unions would become a vehicle for bourgeois ideology among the working class. What was needed was the intervention of "professional revolutionaries" in the unfolding of labor-market and other union struggles to bring revolutionary class consciousness to the workers "from without." When Communists approached the task of organization building in the aftermath of the Bolshevik revolution, they therefore chose what they believed to be a corrective course to protect the revolutionary integrity of their movement by rather dramatically increasing the strategic subordination of affiliated union movements to Communist Parties.[1]

The work which follows is a case study of union-party relationships of this Third International/Communist type. It examines the modern ties between the French *Confédération Générale du Travail* (CGT) and the *Parti Communiste Français* (PCF). The PCF has not always dominated the CGT. In fact, predominant Communist power within the Confederation dates only from the immediate post-World War II years. Since then, however, the facts of PCF power over the CGT have been clear and consis-

---

1. Lenin's articles and speeches on unionism, including relevant passages from *What is to be Done?*, discussion of unions in the Soviet Union and the Third International, have been collected in *Lenin on Trade Unions* (1970). See also Bernard Badie, *Stratégie de la grève* (1976) for a discussion of France and Leninist views on unions.

tent. Despite the fact that there has been a studied attempt to maintain an equitable division of posts between Communists and non-Communists on the CGT *Bureau Confédéral*, the Confederation's highest executive body, the two post-1947 leaders of the CGT, Benoît Frachon and Georges Séguy, were both members of the PCF *Bureau Politique* (BP). And more often than not they have had *Bureau Confédéral* colleagues who were either BP members or members of the PCF Central Committee. In addition, for the most part the non-Communists on the *Bureau Confédéral* have shared a clear "class point of view" with their Communist colleagues, having been coopted to the *Bureau Confédéral* primarily because of this. The next highest regular deliberative levels of the CGT—the *Commission Executive* (CE), composed of members elected by the CGT Congress, and the *Comité Confédéral National* (CCN), composed of the Secretaries-General of the CGT's constituent organizations (industrial federations and geographical unions)—have consistently been overwhelmingly Communist in membership. At present, for example, the CE elected at the Fortieth Congress in 1978 is 80 percent Communist, and the percentage of Communists on the CCN is even higher. The triannual Congress, which is the legal repository of long-term strategic decision-making for the CGT, has been attended, over the years, by delegates from constituent unions, the vast majority of whom have been members of the PCF. The Secretaries-General of the CGT's industrial federations have been almost universally Communist, with a liberal sprinkling among them of members of the party Central Committee and even, on occasion, members of the *Bureau Politique*. The major CGT publication, *La Vie Ouvrière*, was run in 1981 by a member of the CGT *Bureau Confédéral*, Henri Krasucki, who was also a member of the PCF *Bureau Politique*. Thus the fact that only a minority of CGT members at large (20–30 percent, depending upon the period) are PCF members ought not to be misleading. The CGT organization is run by Communists, who virtually monopolize its critical middle levels. And Communists, whether officals or simple *militants*, are the life blood and vitality of the Confederation. It is the statutory duty of ordinary Communists to belong to and be active within trade unions—the CGT when possible—at their place of work, which means that a substantial part of the PCF's membership is involved in the CGT. At the very least, little can happen within the CGT of which Communists do not approve. And, as our examination of the CGT's modern history will demonstrate, the shaping hand of Communists in CGT behavior is much greater than mere approval.

The CGT's own denial of any connection with political parties—let alone the PCF—is in large part ritual, then, as the CGT's behavior amply indicates. Such ritual is, of course, connected with a long tradition in France. The 1906 *Charte d'Amiens*, one of the CGT's founding documents, declared that while the CGT should be class oriented and revolutionary, it should also be non-partisan. Like all rituals, however, the CGT's claim of non-partisanship is not a complete mystification. To note that Communists predominate in the CGT organization and in its decision-making does not necessarily imply that the CGT will follow PCF lines, whatever they might be. In fact, the Communists in the modern CGT present themselves publicly as trade unionists, claiming that their party affiliation is a separate and unrelated matter. While generally this is a somewhat jesuitical argument, it does contain a modicum of serious content. The CGT is a labor "mass organization" whose success at maintaining itself and deepening its influence depends on its ability to defend the material interests of its members and sympathizers. Since the Confederation must attempt to reach as broad a working-class audience as possible, if only to protect its preeminent but not inevitable place as part of the broader pluralistic French labor movement, it must, Communist control or not, avoid overly partisan positions in order to speak to its target constituency.

The problematic which forms the core of this project is given by these two apparently contradictory claims on the CGT. The modern CGT is dominated by the PCF, and one can reasonably assume both that this domination is not gratuitous and that its purpose is ultimately partisan. On the other hand the CGT, to survive and thrive, must be a labor mass organization able to transcend partisan issues. PCF members have been in a position to determine the orientations of the modern CGT. Yet because the CGT can only be useful politically if it is simultaneously successful as a mass organization in mobilizing workers far beyond the perimeters of political fidelity to the PCF, the PCF cannot simply use the CGT as a direct action arm for PCF politics. The PCF needs and cherishes the CGT as its *central* instrument for cultivating and mobilizing working-class support for its goals. Yet the instrument can perform these tasks *only* if it behaves in a very different way from the party itself. With this in mind it becomes immediately clear that the PCF, as a political party, is likely to have one strategy, while the CGT is likely to have a different one, appropriate to its status as a mass organization. The strategic subordination of union to party, which we have posited as the distinguishing characteristic of Third International/Communist unionism, is likely to be achieved by arrangements of strategic *complementarity*, rather than strategic uniformity. The union will elaborate its own strategy in ways which will ultimately contribute to the advancement of the party's strategy. Our task, then, is to document for the modern period the ways in which the CGT has resolved the contradictory claims on its action, party affiliation and mass-organizational appeal, in terms which make its positions ultimately complementary to those of the PCF's. To do so we will have to examine CGT strategy, party strategy, and the exact nature of their ultimately complementary relationships.

Studying CGT-PCF relationships, as they have evolved in the post-World War II period, has another dimension to it, over and above the obviously relevant task of analyzing a particular manifestation of the more general pattern of trade-union–political rapport in modern capitalism. Western European Communism has been widely studied of late, primarily because of the interesting and difficult-to-understand processes of Euro-communization which the Italian, Spanish and French parties have been undergoing.[2] Alas, widely studied does not mean well studied! Much of the modern work on Western European Communism suffers from narrowness of conception.[3] Inquiry has been directed, almost exclusively, towards the areas of general strategy and foreign policy. Students of strategy have tried to discern what European Communists want to do, what kinds of policies they desire to promote, how they foresee attaining their new goals. More globally, the questions asked are "Are they really democratic?"—with "democratic" often meaning "safe"—or, from a very different political vantage point, "Are they now social democratic?" The foreign-policy specialists want to assess the likely impact of new Communist behavior on existing patterns of international relations. Here the questions are "Have they really changed?" and "Is the new European Communism good or bad for the United States (or NATO, the EEC, or the Russians)?"

Focus on strategy and international politics is not necessarily wrong. The problem is, rather, that looking only at strategy and foreign policy makes full understanding of Western European Communism difficult. Communist parties, even modern parties touched by Eurocommunism, are not parties like the others. In fact, Communist *parties*, strictly speaking, are only a part—albeit the central part—of complex sociopolitical *formations*. In all major Western European cases, for example, the party itself is the strategic head and nervous system of a whole corpus of organizations, all designed, in different ways, to prompt large numbers of people to share points of view and take actions which will advance general Communist goals. And in each of these cases Communist influence over organized labor is the keystone of Communist efforts to mobilize mass support. Thus we are not only studying the important problem of trade-union–political relationships in a particular type of situation, we are also attempting to

2. Probably the best sources to get to the heart of Eurocommunization are those of the parties themselves. In English, see the interview with Giorgio Napolitano, in E. Hobsbawm, *The Italian Road to Socialism* (1977) and Santiago Carrillo, *Eurocommunism and the State* (1977). On the French party see Jean Kanapa, "Les caractéristiques de l'eurocommunisme," in *Recherches Internationales* (March-April 1976) and Georges Marchais' report to the important PCF Twenty-second Congress, in *Cahiers du Communisme* (February 1976), reprinted in PCF, *Le socialisme pour la France* (1976). See also, on a more theoretical plane, the PCF's *Traité d'économie politique* (*le capitalisme monopoliste d'état*). For a brief approach to the PCF's flirtation with Eurocommunism, see George Ross, "The End of the Bolshevik Dream," in Carl Boggs and David Plotke, ed., *The Politics of Eurocommunism* (1980).

3. Perhaps the best collection of serious work on the PCF and PCI which attempts to transcend the strategic and foreign policy biases is D. L. M. Blackmer and S. Tarrow, eds., *Communism in Italy and France* (1975).

begin redressing the balance in the study of Western European Communism by treating the Communist phenomenon in its full scope.

To this point we have only opened our discussion, of course. Simply detailing the facts of PCF power in the CGT tells us little except that Communists are powerful in the CGT. More generally, asserting that the CGT-PCF relations are exemplary of the union-party relations created in the Third International/Communist tradition tells us little about these relations. Simple examination of what the PCF itself is doing will therefore tell us little, a priori, about what the CGT is doing at the same time. Thus far we only know that these relations and the use of PCF power in the CGT will be primarily concerned with resolving a contradiction between partisan goals and mass appeal. The PCF needs its connections with the CGT to generate working-class political support, to socialize workers politically to hold visions of the world congruent with the party's goals. On the other hand, the CGT has to be effective in the labor market and not allow overt politics to diminish its capacities to make a mass trade-union appeal to French workers. Attempting to resolve this contradiction at different points in the development of French post-war capitalism is likely to have created different forms of the union-party relationship, even within the general limit of PCF control over the CGT.

The form of union-party relationship decided upon by the CGT and PCF at any given time is almost certain to fall somewhere between two obvious limits. Extreme politicization of union activity in support of party political goals, other things being equal, is likely to cripple the union's ability to make a credible mass appeal to workers, many of whom will disagree with the politics in question, feel that politicization should not be part of the union's activities, or be apolitical altogether. At the other extreme, a strictly labor-market–centered unionism which avoids politics will not shape working-class political options and attitudes in the ways desired by the PCF and therefore will waste using the political opportunity which PCF influence over the CGT presents. Between these two extremes, however, there exist a number of possible formulations of union-party relationships. "Transmission beltism," in which the party conceives of the union as a quasi-direct conduit for mobilizing workers around party political goals, is one classic formulation from Third International/Communist union traditions. It is characteristic of the transmission-belt form to find the party using its influence over the union to translate day-to-day political purposes into union activity. The primary frame of union reference in transmission-belt periods becomes, therefore, the rhythms of political life, which are imposed by the party on the union. What is important about this is the subordination to politics of the rhythms of the labor market, which have their own autonomy and which are the primary frame of reference for most ordinary unions. Transmission-belt–union politics may be moderate or radical, cautious or reckless. What matters is less the content of the politics directly imposed upon union life by the party, than the fact of this imposition.

Another basic form of union-party ties is what we will call "relative autonomy." Here the party recognizes that the dynamics of the labor market ought to be the primary focus of labor mass-organizational activity. Strategic subordination of the union to broader Communist goals persists in the relative autonomy model, but it is formulated in a very different way. The developing shape of events in the labor market allows any union, of whatever political leanings, a broad range of choice between strategic and tactical options, any one of which may be plausibly congruent with the task of defending the interests of the rank and file. The relative autonomy form recognizes this. What characterizes the behavior of a relatively autonomous Communist-influenced union is that, after consideration of all of the possible union options given in a specific labor-market situation, it will choose that option which is most likely to further Communist political goals.

Both the transmission-belt and the relative-autonomy forms of union-party ties involve union subordination to party strategy, the first directly and the second indirectly. One could also envisage a third type of tie, therefore, perhaps labelled "union autonomy." In this form the party might decide that the best use of its influence over the union would be to set up two different strategic poles of activity, one in the party, the other in the union, without the latter being subordinate to the former. This form of union-party tie would depart from classical Leninist views on the use of mass organizations by positing strategic decentralization. The union would pursue change-oriented goals of its own, set by itself. The party would do likewise. The task of promoting party-union complementarity would then become one of coordination between equals moving on separate fronts towards a common goal rather than subordination of union to party strategy. While such strategic polycentrism is not habitual in Third International/Communist union-party relationships, it is at least theoretically conceivable.

It would be unduly abstract to discuss possible types of union-party relationships without raising the issue of the actual *strategic context* of such relationships. The CGT and PCF did not develop different divisions of labor between them simply for reasons of principle. They did so in order to facilitate the achievement of specific goals in French society. Our focus will be not only on what kind of union-party relationships came to exist, their mechanisms and their shape, but, more importantly, on what these relationships were *for*. How the party explains the world theoretically, what alliances it may be pursuing, what kinds of mass mobilization it desires, what policies it advocates for the present and future, how the party hopes to model working-class understanding of the socioeconomic environment—all of these will change with changes in party perspectives and in the context which the party faces. To the degree to which such concerns become those of the union, the content and goals of union behavior will be affected. The union itself must specify its own strategy, which will be separate in important ways from that of the party, and this will change in time as well.

This study, therefore, examines historically the evolution of PCF-CGT relationships in the modern period, focusing both on the general forms of these relationships and on the specific strategic and tactical content with which party and union filled in these forms. Part One traces party-union relations in the Stalin-Thorez era, beginning with the consolidation of PCF influence over the CGT, through the transmission-belt use of this influence following World War II, to the beginnings of a shift towards relative autonomy in the mid-1950s. Part Two discusses the development of CGT-PCF ties in the Fifth Republic to May-June 1968, roughly the definitional years of CGT relative autonomy. Part Three examines the contradictory development of CGT relative autonomy in the historical context of PCF Eurocommunization in the period from the late 1960s through the disastrous electoral failure of March 1978. The conclusion is a more general consideration of the profound crisis for the CGT and the PCF which was opened by the 1978 electoral catastrophe.

PART ONE

The PCF and French Labor from the Popular Front to the Cold War

The roots of working-class radicalism in France lie deep in the complexities of French social history, which are far beyond the scope of this work. As France industrialized, workers progressively became a class apart from broader French society. To an extent uncommon in other Western capitalist societies, French workers were not successfully persuaded to share important elite values and perceptions about the growth of capitalism. Nor were the workers' self-generated understandings of their situation generally congruent with the aims of French elites.

The new industrial working class in France faced a unique form of bourgeois society. The general culture of bourgeois elite groups in France was exclusivist and elitist, for reasons which stretched back to the *ancien régime* and to the social dealings between France's nascent bourgeoisie and aristocratic upper classes. In nineteenth-century bourgeois France, status and prestige were granted because of the possession of certain kinds of cultivation which distinguished one from the masses. The accumulation of capital was a necessary, but not sufficient, condition for this cultivation. In this cultural setting workers found little to bind them to bourgeois France. Bourgeois culture was what workers did not have, by definition. In addition, channels of access to the cultural accoutrements necessary for bourgeois social legitimacy were completely closed to lower-class groups. It was not surprising, then, that French workers responded to this exclusion by seeking collective virtue in working-class culture, rather than individual inferiority within bourgeois culture.

French capitalism might have been able to afford anti-bourgeois attitudes in workers if workers could have been persuaded to hold political values functional to the prospering of French capitalism. Alas, the instability of French liberal institutions in the nineteenth century was such that throughout much of the critical formative period of the French working class even French bourgeois groups, those who had most to gain from ensuring the hegemony of liberal parliamentarism over French workers, were rarely more than lukewarm in their own commitment to liberal, let alone democratic, ideals. However inaccurate in its historical detail, Karl Marx's *18th Brumaire of Louis Bonaparte* provides a vivid picture of French elite groups divided among themselves about how much, and what kind of, liberalism and democracy they could afford. Marx was correct in stressing deep bourgeois fears in nineteenth-century France that the lower orders might makes claims on politics which French capitalism could not pay were these orders to be allowed to take liberalism too seriously. Even in the formally democratic politics of the "stalemate society" Third Republic, elite political forces ranged from openly anti-democratic to ambivalent about granting any real political power to the lower classes.[1]

The pre-1914 economic experiences of French workers were similar to those in politics. The growth of French capitalism was such that over long periods in the nineteenth century relatively small industrial units, often family firms, were prominent. Within such firms industrial relations were highly conflictual. Entrepreneurs insisted upon, and developed highly articulate defenses of, managerial prerogatives of an unlimited sort, often in exchange for the alleged benefits of paternalism. In effect, such employers denied their workers any right to a voice in determining conditions of work and remuneration. In such a context, many workers, fed by myths depicting an equitable artisanal order in the past and memories of glorious days of revolutionary protest, viewed the advance of capitalism as reversible through struggle. Such attitudes draw strong support from a long-standing French socialist tradition—beginning with the "conspiracy of equals" in the Great Revolution, and extending through Proudhon, Fourier, Louis Blanc, and August Blanqui. Furthermore, peasants entering the industrial work force brought with them a strong rural anti-capitalism built on the deep economic distress of peasant smallholding in nineteenth-century France.

By the turn of the twentieth century French working-class radicalism was flourishing. Revolutionary syndicalism, with its stress on change at the point of production and its disdain for politics and politicians, was one vocal strain of this radicalism.[2] Guesdist Marxism, political and statist, was another. Both traditions were to mark the French labor movement far into the future. Also present were more moderate reformist strains, in both union and political spheres. By the pre-World War I years these varied forms of radicalism had found their ways into a French Socialist party

1. See Stanley Hoffman's essay "Paradoxes of the French Political Community" in S. Hoffman, et al., *In Search of France* (1964).

2. Val Lorwin, *The French Labor Movement* (1954), part I; Georges Lefranc, *Le syndical-isme français* (1965), p. 28; and Bernard Moss, *The Origins of the French Labor Movement* (1976).

—the SFIO (*Section Française de l'Internationale Ouvrière*)—and a radical union movement—the CGT (*Confédération Générale du Travail*). Both of these bodies were strong, if volatile, coalitions of reformists and *révolutionnaires*.

The Painful Childhood of French Leninism

The existence of working-class cultural solidarity and political radicalism in nineteenth-century France does not in itself account for the success of Marxism-Leninism later on. In other societies, similar situations evolved in quite different ways. The transformation of nineteenth-century working-class radicalism into twentieth-century social democratic "revisionism," with its acceptance of liberal parliamentarist rules of the game seems to have been the general trend, to which France proved an exception. Moderate tendencies in France did move in a "revisionist" direction in the twentieth century. But alongside these tendencies there also emerged a Communist Party with a strong working-class base. Elsewhere among western capitalist societies only Italy developed in broadly similar ways. Why?

The uniqueness of twentieth-century French labor history begins with World War I. The Great War was a shattering experience for the French Left. Moderate Left and trade-union groups did not resist the war and enthusiastically participated in a nationalist *Union Sacrée* against the Germans.[3] A small number of Leftist rebels did oppose the war and made connections with their counterparts in other countries at Zimmerwald and elsewhere. But they existed in isolation as long as the French working class was carried away by nationalist fervor. However, as the war turned into an immensely costly, drawn-out bloodbath, especially for French workers, the continued identification of moderate labor elites with the war effort created a growing chasm between them and the labor rank and file, both those in the factories and those on the front lines.[4] As a result, radicals who had opposed the war from the beginning began to find a constituency which agreed with their case. Peace groups flourished. Toward the end of the war actual mutinies occurred. Events such as the Russian October and other European risings deepened the gap between French "labor statesmen" and their usual base. In essence, the war's effects caused the precarious unity between reformists and revolutionaries on the French Left to dissolve.

In the immediate aftermath of the war forces of the political and trade-union Left, inspired by the Soviet example, emerged in favor of the formation of a "new type" political party and union movement. Some were immediately attracted to the Third International in 1919. Other Left forces,

3. Georges Lefranc, *Le mouvement sous la Troisième République* (1967), pp. 95–99.
4. Lorwin, p. 58.

less strongly pro-Bolshevik, were sufficiently opposed to the "labor statesmen" to join the pro-Bolsheviks in struggle against them. Moderate labor leaders like Léon Jouhaux emerged from the war promoting new approaches in labor politics involving economic planning and a labor *politique de présence* in or near governments. Such tame talk by moderates deepened division in the first two post-war years, which were characterized by great turbulence in the labor market, large numbers of strikes, and increasing resort to repression on the part of governments and employers.[5]

Eventually the radical-moderate conflict led to schism both for the political Left and for French trade unionism. At Tours, in December 1920, the SFIO lost a majority of its members to the Left, which seceded to form the new *Parti Communiste Français*.[6] The *Confédération Générale du Travail* split at its Lille Congress in June 1921. The old CGT, led by the moderates, remained in business, but in bitter competition with a new revolutionary rival, the *Confédération Générale du Travail Unitaire* (CGTU), which took with it an important part of CGT membership. A new type of revolutionary labor movement had been founded in France.[7]

The splits of 1920–1921 did not guarantee Leninist success in France, however. The PCF and CGTU both fell upon hard times very quickly. In the PCF the greater the insistence by Leninists on the need for a "new type" of revolutionary party, the more opponents of such notions were frightened away. Early support of the Soviet Union and then controversy over Moscow's Twenty-One Conditions for adherence to the Third International led to substantial expulsions and departures. A membership of 130,000 at Tours in 1920 fell to 55,000 by 1923.[8] In 1924 the "Bolshevization" of the party began in earnest, involving restructuring the organization around factory cells (a radical departure in the history of the French Left, since the SFIO had traditionally been built around geographical sections), and this caused further attrition. The departure soon thereafter of Trotsky's French sympathizers led to further conflict. The beginnings of Stalinization, with the imposition of top-down leadership and authority patterns modelled on Soviet practices, further "purified" the PCF and the CGTU.

In the short space of a decade, lively debate and discussion about theory and strategy on rank-and-file level in the PCF was replaced by the unification of decision-making in the hands of a small group of leaders, and eventually in those of the Secretary-General, Maurice Thorez. The primary task

5. Lorwin, pp. 53–54; Lefranc, *3e République*, pp. 222–237.

6. See Annie Kriegel, *Aux origines du communisme français*. (1964), esp. vol. II, parts 1 and 2, and her extensive bibliography; plus Robert Wohl, *French Communism in the Making* (1966).

7. Lefranc, *3e République*, pp. 256–260; Jean-Louis Robert, *La scission syndicale, 1914–1921* (1977).

8. Jacques Fauvet, *Histoire du Parti communiste français*, vol. I (1964), p. 57.

of rank-and-file Communists became the enthusiastic ratification and execution of policies in whose definition they had no real part. Organizational change also brought with it strategic change. In the years after 1927, the "class-against-class" period in the history of the Comintern, everyone to the Right of the PCF was adjudged to be part of a bourgeois plot. Isolation inevitably followed from this, as did an internal "state of siege" mentality. The PCF quickly became a small band of only the most faithful, convinced and committed.[9]

The CGTU, totally dominated by the PCF, experienced the same traumas. When the organizational and political implications of membership in the Third International became clear, the CGTU lost most of its original non-Bolshevik supporters, most importantly, the revolutionary syndicalists.[10] The CGTU's ineptness as a trade union—which followed from its new revolutionary position, especially in the "class-against-class" years—was its main problem, however. It became a caricature of a Leninist "transmission-belt" front organization. It superimposed inappropriate political slogans upon labor-market conflicts with no regard for the rhythms of the labor market. It attempted to command strikes, without sufficient consideration of the desires of the union rank and file. It vilified labor groups which did not agree with its positions and behavior. All of this cost it much of its following.[11] The effects of the CGTU's sectarianism were multiplied by the climate prevailing in French industrial relations in the twenties and early thirties. It was not a good time for union activity, and this was particularly true in those industrial areas and sectors of the work force where the CGTU had originally been strongest.[12]

After an auspicious start, then, Marxism-Leninism failed to become a major force in France, at least in the period prior to 1934. By the early 1930s the PCF had become little more than a political sect. Its membership fell from 50,000 in 1928 to 29,000 in 1933, with circulation of *L'Humanité*, the party's paper, declining commensurately.[13] By its own admission, in

9. Daniel Brower, *The New Jacobins* (1969), ch. 1 on "Bolshevization"; and Wohl, *French Communism*, for the earlier period.

10. Under pressure from the French, Lenin himself exempted the CGTU from some of the more stringent conditions for membership in the Profintern—the Comintern's trade-union wing. In particular the CGTU was allowed to proclaim itself an "independent" trade union, in order to adhere to the letter, if not the spirit, of the Amiens Charter; see Jean Charles, "Les débuts de l'Internationale syndicale rouge," in *Cahiers de l'Institut Maurice Thorez*, nos. 25–26 and 28 (1978). See also André Barjonet, *La CGT* (1968), pp. 23–23; Henry Ehrmann, *French Labor from Popular Front to Liberation* (1947), ch. 2; Georges Lasserre, *Le syndicalisme ouvrier en France* (1965), vol. II, p. 61.

11. Lucien Rioux, *Où en est le syndicalisme?* (1967), p. 29; Lefranc, *Le syndicalisme français*, p. 67.

12. Brower, ch. 1; Antoine Prost, *La CGT à l'époque du Front populaire* (1964), pp. 33–34; Lefranc, *Le syndicalisme français*, part III; Ehrmann, *French Labor*, pp. 25–27.

13. Brower, p. 15; Annie Kriegel, "Le Parti communiste français sous la Troisième République: évolution de ses effectifs," *Revue Française de Science Politique* (February 1966).

1934 the party had only 450 functioning factory cells, and this was probably an inflated figure.[14] The CGTU's claimed membership—again probably an exaggeration—had declined from 431,000 in 1926 to 264,000 in 1934.[15] The period prior to 1934 was not a total loss for French Communism, of course. The compression of membership, Bolshevization, and Stalinization did create an organizational infrastructure staffed by hardened, totally dedicated *cadres*. Indeed, in the light of time, the political generation of Communists who lived through these hard moments set a tone and established habits which have marked the PCF and CGT to this day. Up to the early 1930s, however, French Communism clearly had failed to build a mass political and trade-union base. This failure left a significant opening for "reformist" and other non-Communist tendencies on the French Left to establish a new hegemony over the French working class. That they were unable to do this is one of the most important facts in French labor history.

Pre-World War I Left politics and trade unionism in France were firmly based on specific kinds of workers—those who possessed craft skills and those in the public-service sector of the economy. Beginning in 1918, however, the semi-skilled factory worker in the private sector of the economy emerged as the major constituent of the French work force. And perhaps the most important fact about these semi-skilled mass-production operatives was that they were not organized into the labor movement.[16] One reason for this was that French employers ferociously resisted their attempts at organization. Another reason was that the sociology of such workers was significantly different from that of the categories forming the traditional bases of working-class movements in France. Because of their rural origins, the nature of their work situation (fragmented tasks, repetitious procedures), and their powerlessness in the face of an externally imposed, complex, and machine-oriented organization of production, such workers needed much more bureaucratic forms of organization than any French labor union or party seemed prepared to provide. Craftsmen and public-service workers had been able to build and carry on their own organizations. Semi-skilled operatives were much less able to do so. They needed *encadrement*.[17]

14. Brower; Prost, p. 131; R. Alloyer, "Nos forces dans les entreprises," *Cahiers du Bolchevisme* (Feb. 1, 1934), p. 180 ff.

15. Prost, p. 35.

16. Ehrmann, *French Labor*, claims that except for short periods (1918–1920, for example) no successful trade-union inroads were made among these groups of workers, so that no more than 6.3 percent of semi-skilled operatives were organized prior to the coming of the Popular Front.

17. Michel Collinet, *L'ouvrièr français, esprit du syndicalisme* (1951), pp. 46, 167, 200; Serge Mallet, *La nouvelle classe ouvrière* (1963), Introduction. See also Daniel Mothé, *Militant chez Renault* (1965) and *Journal d'un ouvrier* (1959).

If semi-skilled workers remained basically unorganized well in to the 1930s, they were nonetheless "organizable." Most of the factors which accounted for working-class culture and radicalism in the pre-1914 period had intensified. In larger mass-production firms, where most such workers were found, the traditional labor-repressive practices of the French *patronat* were carried to new extremes, strongly complemented by militant anti-unionism. Anyone who has ever wandered through the streets of Boulogne-Billancourt has sensed the degree of residential ostracism to which Parisian mass-production workers were subject. The insular and class-specific life styles of such workers marked the entire Paris industrial *banlieue*. Moreover, nothing had happened to change the cultural situation of French workers, no new avenues for the acquisition of bourgeois culture had opened up. Although the task of organizing such workers was difficult, then, the raw materials of oppression and resentment were there. The key question for much of subsequent French political and labor history was which of the several tendencies on the French Left would "get to" such workers first.

In the event, the PCF and CGTU were able to benefit from a unique organizational vacuum for building Communist labor strength. All of the other conceivable candidates for approaching mass-production workers defaulted. By the inter-war period revolutionary syndicalism had lost much of its energy. Moreover, the anti-bureaucratic predilections of the remaining revolutionary syndicalists made them singularly ill-equipped to deal with the problems of factory operatives. The factory operatives' defense had to be coordinated from outside, their understanding of the industrial situation mediated by organizational interpreters. Revolutionary syndicalists did not believe in such things.[18] On the other end of the French labor spectrum, the "reformist" wing of the French labor movement also disqualified itself. Beginning in World War I the "reformist" CGT had turned away from aggressive organizational tactics. The CGT's postwar concerns were primarily political—obtaining reforms such as economic planning, social legislation, nationalizations—not by mass-membership pressure, but by a *politique de présence*, lobbying and bargaining with political parties.[19] This strategy reflected the CGT's rank and file, mainly public-sector and state workers, whose interests could be promoted by such political means.[20] Moreover, such workers were among the most moderate in the work force, both in their political views and in their positions on struggle in the labor market. The task of organizing mass-production operatives involved big risks, considerable resources and, above all, a commitment to

18. Collinet, *Esprit*; and Mallet, *Nouvelle classe*, pp. 29–34.

19. Lefranc, *Le syndicalisme français*, part II; Collinet, *Esprit*, ch. IV; Jean Bruhat and Marc Piolot, *La CGT, esquisse d'une histoire* (1966), p. 94 ff; Ehrmann, *French Labor*, p. 23 ff.

20. See Prost, ch. IV; Collinet, *Esprit*, p. 67 ff.

direct industrial action. The CGT of the early 1930s was not eager to provide any of these things.

Adolescence and Its Trials—the Popular Front and After

Before the great shift in French Left politics of the mid-1930s, it looked very much as if the PCF had also thrown away its chance for acquiring the working-class base which it needed to become a serious political formation. True, the CGTU had met with some success among mass-production workers in the private sector of the economy in the twenties, particularly in metallurgy, building, and chemicals. In time, however, PCF and CGTU sectarianism had severely limited such success. By the early 1930s the CGTU's toehold in these strategic areas seemed to be disappearing. The semi-skilled factory operatives simply went unorganized. The CGTU remained in approximately the right place to appeal to them. But the rigid organizational behavior and intransigent Leftist line of the PCF and CGTU rendered them both ineffective and isolated.

The Popular Front years changed all this. The political threat of Fascism, plus the economic effects of the Great Depression, led to a profound realignment of the French political and trade-union Left.[21] Popular mobilization from below literally forced the CGT and the CGTU to collaborate in anti-fascist demonstrations in February 1934. The PCF, caught momentarily between a powerful move towards Left unity from below and its international commitment to the "class-against-class" line (which ruled out collaboration with the "right-wing social democrats"), took its problem to the Comintern itself.[22] And the Comintern, partly because of French pressure but also because of a shift in Soviet foreign policy, legislated a drastic change in the strategy of the international Communist movement. "Class against class" gave way to the "United Front against Fascism."[23] Parallel change on the French non-Communist Left (the SFIO had spent much of the twenties and early thirties being more anti-Communist than socialist) aided Socialist-Communist collaboration. In July 1934 the PCF and SFIO signed a formal unity-in-action pact. For the first time in fifteen years, the French Left was officially united. And for the first time in its history, the PCF was not isolated. The effects were

21. Lorwin, p. 69; Lefranc, *Troisième République*, p. 317; Claude Willard, ed., *Front populaire* (1972).

22. Brower, ch. II. See also Georgi Dimitrov, *United Front Against Fascism* (1935), a compendium of Dimitrov's speeches to the Seventh Comintern Congress in August 1935 where the line shift, which had already been in effect in the PCF for some time, became general Comintern policy.

23. See Fauvet, *Histoire du PCF (1964)*, vol. I, pp. 247, 275; PCF, *Histoire du Pcf (manuel)*, (1964), ch. VI; Claude Willard, ed., *Front populaire*, ch. 2; Brower, ch. 1, 2. On international questions, see Fernando Claudin, *La crise du mouvement communiste* (1973), vol. I, ch. IV, V.

dramatic. Communists suddenly acquired a national legitimacy which they had never before had. The "United Front against Fascism" line transformed them into devoted Republicans, Jacobins—protectors of France's national heritage against the barbarians. Almost overnight, hopes for *le grand soir* were filed away. The Red Flag and the *Tricouleur* marched together.

Unity on the political Left was followed by unity in the union movement. In labor, however, the popular *élan* of the Popular Front years went beyond treaties of cooperation between different organizations. The CGT and the CGTU began negotiating the formation of a single labor organization in 1935, culminating in the official reunification of the CGT in early 1936. To win unity, the Communist-dominated CGTU gave in on all of the major conditions set by the reformist CGT. It abandoned dual union tactics and merged its organizations with those of the CGT. It also agreed that there should be no organized "fractions" within the unified CGT, thereby theoretically abandoning open PCF activity. Henceforth the CGT and its constituent unions were to be formally independent of political parties, while trade-union officials were to hold no political offices.[24]

Popular mobilization and United Front politics did not stop there, however. The Popular Front electoral alliance of Communists, Socialists, and Radicals swept to electoral victory in the spring of 1936.[25] The Léon Blum government which was formed as a result (without Communist ministers, but with Communist parliamentary support) had to face almost immediately the massed energy of the French working class. In May and June of 1936 French workers "sat down" en masse for changes which had been denied them for too long. The largest strike wave in French history to that point was ended in June, but only after the momentous Matignon agreements had been negotiated between the state, employers, and unions. The strikers won large concessions at Matignon, which were followed by a substantial round of major social reform legislated by the Popular Front government.[26] The forty-hour week, paid vacations, and several social-welfare progams were among the measures taken.

United Frontism led to the PCF's integration into mainstream French politics, a change which had large payoffs indeed. By the end of 1937 the PCF had 302,000 members, four times as many as it had had at the beginning of 1936 and ten times as many as in 1933.[27] The PCF's press suddenly bloomed. And the number of PCF factory cells, perhaps the critical indi-

24. Bruhat and Piolot, p. 128. Collinet, *Esprit*, p. 98; Prost, pp. 36–37.

25. Brower, ch. V; Louis Bodin and Jean Touchard, *Front populaire* (1961); Jacques Danos and Marcel Gibelin, *Juin 1936* (1952); Georges Lefranc, *Juin 1936*; Georges Lefranc, *Le Front populaire* (1969).

26. Ehrmann, *French Labor*, p. 40; Prost, ch. III; Lefranc, *Juin 1936*; Henri Prouteau, *Les occupations d'usines en Italie et en France* (1946); Salomon Schwartz, *Les occupations d'usines en France de mai et juin 1936* (1947).

27. Brower, pp. 195–197.

cator of French Communist health, grew from 450 in 1934 to 4000 in late 1937.[28] This last figure also indicated startling changes in the balance of forces in organized labor. In the Popular Front mobilization, and especially in the labor-market uprising of 1936, literally millions of hitherto non-unionized workers moved into the reunified CGT. From a membership of one million in early 1936, the CGT ballooned to 5.3 million by the end of 1937.[29] What happened, in fact, was that the French union movement caught up with changes in the structure of the French working class with a vengeance, massively organizing, for the first time, workers in the mass production sectors of the economy. What looked, at first glance, however, to be the triumph of the reunified CGT was really a giant step forward for the PCF. The bulk of this huge rank-and-file enlistment into the labor movement occurred in precisely those areas of the work force where ex-CGTU militants were strongest and old-line reformist CGT organizers weakest. The situation developed in such as way as to allow the PCF to play the one strong card which the party had dealt itself in the otherwise barren period of Bolshevization and Stalinization which had preceded the Popular Front. The thousands of true believers who had stayed with the PCF and CGTU through the "class-against-class" period became steeled and hardened "professional revolutionaries," ready, able, and willing to accomplish the kind of organizational tasks which the Popular Front union wave demanded. Thus not far beneath the surface of this great CGT growth lay a power struggle between ex-reformist CGTers and former CGTUers. In this struggle over who would organize the new unionists under whose wing, former CGTUers had an overwhelming advantage. The old-line CGTers had dismantled much of the organizing equipment and lost most of their taste for *encadrement* during their flirtation with pressure-group politics. Moreover, their union home was far away from those areas of the work force which unionized in the Popular Front. The CGTUers, in contrast, had numbers of dedicated organizers in the right place, with the right skills, at the right time.

The former CGTUers did agree to a great many concessions in order to merge the CGTU with the CGT. But they did not give up their primary loyalty to the PCF. They still considered their most important task to be organizing workers into unions which would, in turn, further the aims of the PCF. The only real difference made by the reunification was that Communist unionists worked for their goals within the CGT, rather than outside it. Their new position gave Communist organizers new legitimacy and access to workers which the earlier split in the labor movement had closed off. Although the necessity of preserving unity did place some constraints

---

28. Lefranc, *Le syndicalisme français*, ch. VII; Jean-Daniel Reynaud, *Les syndicats en France* (1975), p. 90; Collinet, *Esprit*, p. 98; Brower, p. 58; Prost, p. 130.
29. Prost, p. 51.

on Communist union activity, the result, given the climate of the Popular Front years, was predictable. Because ex-CGTUers were better union organizers than the old CGTers, and because they were better placed in the work force to make fruitful contact with the explosion of rank-and-file energy which occurred, most of the semi-skilled factory operatives who connected with the labor movement moved into unions which were dominated by ex-CGTU militants. Communist power within the labor movement expanded greatly as a result.[30] Beyond those areas where the PCF already had significant union power (metals, chemicals, building), Communist unionists took over union federations in new sectors (textiles, wood fabrication, leather work) and moved to control of important CGT departmental unions (the CGT's geographical, as opposed to occupational organizations, the successors of the *Bourses du Travail*).[31] While such dramatic changes did not yet place the PCF in a position of hegemony over organized labor in Fance, they did represent a giant stride in that direction.

Barriers to Maturity—the Onset of World War II

Events of the late 1930s demonstrated that the Popular Front successes of the PCF, substantial though they were, were anything but definitive. By 1937 the Popular Front had begun to disintegrate. A series of profound differences between the PCF and the Socialists cracked, and finally sundered, the tenuous political alliance which had promised so much in the mid-1930s. The Léon Blum government turned to orthodox financial policies after the 1936 strikes in ways which ate away the gains which French workers had won by so spectacularly occupying French factories. The government failed to follow the foreign policy which the PCF desired, particularly around the Spanish Civil War, when Blum's "non-intervention" stance further sealed the doom of the Spanish Republicans. This was also the time of the grotesque, surrealistic Moscow Trials, in which Stalin, with war clearly on the horizon, purged his party of the remaining Old Bolsheviks and most of the military high command.[32] The PCF's unswerving support of the Soviet Secretary-General's actions did not increase its standing in France, and its attitudes provided an ideal platform for its enemies to launch anti-Communist crusades. Despite all of this, the PCF, while doing its best to persuade its coalition partners to change their positions, desperately tried to hold the Popular Front together (even proposing that PCF Ministers join the government). Nonetheless, divided by discord, abandoned by the masses, and confronted by a veritable onslaught from the political Right and the *patronat*, the Popular Front went to its doom in January 1938, having long since lost any creative energy. Stung by the

30. Ibid., p. 56 ff.
31. Claudin, *La crise*, vol. I, chs. 4, 5.
32. Fauvet, vol. I, ch. 4; PCF, *Histoire du PCF*, ch. 8.

events of the mid-1930s and animated with an overdriven desire for political revenge ("rather Hitler than Léon Blum"), important parts of the French bourgeoisie staggered towards the capitulation of 1940 and Vichy. The once-united Left, in a world which it had ceased to understand, reverted to older habits of internecine warfare. Disagreement over Munich was the point of no return. The PCF's opposition to Munich led it once again into a political wilderness of isolation.[33]

Events in the labor movement followed those in the political world. By late 1938 inflation had wiped out most of the gains of 1936–37. On top of this, the end of the Popular Front gave French employers a green light to roll back most of the concessions made under duress in the Matignon period. The CGT predictably divided about how to respond to the new situation. PCF labor leaders advocated a labor-market offensive, while the more moderate old-line CGTers around Léon Jouhaux were more cautious. This led, in November, 1938, to a round of militant strikes in PCF-dominated industrial areas to protest governmental decrees which suspended the operation of many Popular Front reforms. The militancy of the strikers was met by the more-than-equal determination of government and employers using repression and lockouts.[34] The strikes were soundly defeated and led to incipient schism in the CGT. At the same time the CGT's labor-market failure demoralized its union rank and file. Deep controversies over foreign policy complicated the CGT's debates. Battered by Spain, Munich and the Czech crisis, the old-line CGT leadership around Jouhaux stood an uneasy pacifist middle ground between the PCF-exCGTU's strong antifascist positions and the Right-Wing *Syndicats* group's pro-appeasement line.[35] Internal political conflict and growing weakness in the labor market led to a precipitous decline in CGT membership—from 5.3 million in 1937 to 2.5 million in 1939.[36] And the bulk of the decline was in those areas where the PCF's union strength had exploded in 1936.

In such conditions, the Nazi-Soviet pact of 1939 proved the last straw. Along with the rest of the Third International, the PCF abruptly shifted towards "revolutionary defeatism." To this day the logic of this shift remains incomprehensible except to those who believe that unthinking loyalty to the diplomatic goals of the Soviet Union was more important even than the domestic survival of the PCF. "Revolutionary defeatism" resembled the "class-against-class" period. From one day to the next the PCF decided that the impending war was an "imperialist" affair in which neither side would be worthy of support. Hitlerism and the western democracies were

33. Brower, pp. 226–230; Ehrmann, *French Labor*, pp. 15–120, 182, 204, 217; Lorwin, p. 83.
34. Prost, p. 47; Bruhat and Piolot, pp. 102–103; Ehrmann, *French Labor*, pp. 107–110.
35. Brower, p. 230.
36. Ehrmann, *French Labor*, p. 148; Bruhat and Piolot, p. 168.

equated. The task of French workers was to refuse participation, to say "a pox on all your houses," in the imminent conflict. At a moment when almost all groups in France, of whatever political stripe, saw the necessity to prepare for war, "revolutionary defeatism" was a disastrous provocation. With Communists treating all non-Communists as class enemies, with Communist unionists promoting strikes and industrial sabotage against war mobilization, "revolutionary defeatism" created a unified front against the PCF, one moreover which could generate considerable popular support. Forces of the Right had long awaited such an opportunity to rid France of the Bolshevik menace.Forces of the non-Communist Left and Center could not countenance Communist efforts to undermine national preparation for the coming onslaught. The results were predictable. The Daladier government seized the occasion to expel PCF deputies from Parliament and legally dissolve the PCF. In September 1939 the non-Communist leadership in the CGT followed the government's lead, once again reading the Communists out of the CGT.

From the vantage point of 1940 nothing could have seemed less certain than that Leninism would survive to become the major form of French working-class radicalism. The PCF's great successes of the Popular Front years, both in politics and in organized labor, were deeply menaced. The PCF was once again a pariah, attacked by enemies within the labor movement and the political Right. Its former Popular Front allies joined in the anti-Communist offensive. The French business class undertook tactics to root out Communism once and for all. The party's social base shrank drastically. Isolated and cast out of the national community (which it had only recently joined by dint of its strategic shift in the mid-1930s), the PCF was forced underground in disarray. The party's response to the defeat of June 1940 demonstrated its impossible position. When Maurice Thorez, *fils du peuple* and party Secretary-General (who had studiously promoted his own cult of personality throughout the 1930s), was mobilized for the war effort, he deserted, on Stalin's orders, turning up soon thereafter in Moscow. Then, as the terrifying reality of German occupation imposed itself on the French, the PCF's Paris leadership (under Jacques Duclos) set about trying to deal with the Nazis so that *L'Humanité* might reappear with German permission—an act which even party *cadres* outside Paris could not understand. In short, the party's line was suicidal. After the defeat, and the installation of the Vichy regime, dedicated, as it was, to the eradication of Communism, the very survival of Leninism in France was questionable. In 1940 the issue of how the French Communist Party would deploy a Communist-dominated labor mass organization was moot. The real question was whether the PCF would ever again be anything more than a small Leftist sect or, indeed, whether it would survive at all.

The Legacy of Two Decades

Pre-World War II French Communism was haunted by the Bolshevik dream. The Soviet party had succeeded in making a revolution. If the French party organized itself in the same basic way, if it adopted the same theoretical perspectives on the development of capitalism, if it held the same ideas about how capitalism could be transformed, then it, too, might succeed. What would such success be, in fact? The answer was simple—a reproduction of the Soviet model. Thus, in its youth, the French party thoroughly Stalinized itself organizationally. "Democratic" centralism gave way in the PCF to centralism *tout court*. An analogous process occurred in the Communist International. Stalin's victory in the Soviet Union brought a strategic shift in the Comintern towards the "Socialism in One Country" line. From the late 1920s all the constituent parties of the International were charged with the task of protecting and preserving the Soviet experiment. For the PCF, which rapidly became one of the most loyal and subservient members of the International, this meant relegating national goals for change to second place in its hierarchy of concerns. This change in priorities was reinforced by parallel changes in the organization of the International itself. Under Stalin, debate between national parties to reach a strategic consensus on the line to be followed by the world Communist movement (which was Lenin's ideal) was replaced by Soviet domination. By the 1930s the Comintern had become an instrument for the implementation of Soviet foreign policies. Organizationally the change also meant that the Russians increasingly gained hegemonic power over the internal lives of Communist parties. At the very moment when the Secretary-General of the PCF came to dominate the workings of French Communism, Stalin, through the Comintern, increasingly came to dominate the Secretary-General of the PCF. By the end of the 1930s all of these processes had culminated in the maturing PCF. Internally, the party was fully Stalinized—and, it must be said, quite proud of the fact. Internationally, the PCF was strategically subordinate to the Comintern, or in any event, to Stalin's foreign policy, as the disaster after 1939 demonstrated so tragically.

As the PCF settled into organizational patterns, it came to acquire a certain theoretical baggage as well. The basic intellectual model for the PCF's analysis of the world was Lenin's *Imperialism*, as elaborated in Soviet writings and in the dicta of the International. Advanced capitalism was in the throes of its final crisis, in which the revolutionary working class would ultimately unify under Communist leadership. In this terminal crisis intermediary social groups which had tended, historically, to shift their allegiances back and forth from the working class to the bourgeoisie (usually siding with the latter in crises which threatened order) would finally line up with the workers. When the working class, led by its vanguard party, had constructed a solid coalition in which peasants and *petits bourgeois* followed their lead, a revolutionary situation would ensue. Growing polarization along these lines would make a revolutionary insurrection possible. The success of such an insurrection would then allow the creation of a new social order modelled on the Soviet Union. After the working class, guided by the PCF, had "seized power," the "party of the working class" would set up a one-party "dictatorship of the proletariat," through which the bourgeois state would be "smashed"—along with counter-revolutionary elements, bourgeois and otherwise. At the same time the PCF would proceed to create social and political institutions patterned directly on the Soviet model—centralized economic planning, state ownership of the means of production, distribution and exchange, collectivization of agriculture, and so on.

From its inception, of course, the PCF conceived of itself in Leninist terms, as a collective of professional revolutionaries whose task it was to intervene in various social processes (in particular those in which the working class was enmeshed) to hasten the kind of class polarization which its theoretical vision foresaw. To begin with, the PCF taught whomever was willing to learn that there was only *one* working class in France—that ethnic, occupational, regional or religious differences were profoundly less important to workers than the common bonds of the proletarian condition which united them. Beyond this, the PCF promoted the notion that the interest—immediate and longer term—of this *one* working class were specifiable. The PCF's most important class-forming lesson followed from this: the one French working class needed a vanguard, the PCF, to understand working-class problems, the dynamics of imperialism, the needs of the international workers' movement, and, above all, to specify working-class interests.

The major problem in all of this was that inter-war France was not declining Tsarist Russia. Whereas Russia on the eve of revolution was a society riven by contradictions and falling apart at the seams, twentieth-century capitalist France, with all of its problems, was nonetheless relatively well integrated. And even if, by some incredible social miracle, inter-war France had collapsed into revolutionary chaos, the kind of revolutionary regime of which French Communists dreamed would have been totally inappropriate to France. The neo-Bolshevik scenario adopted by the PCF was, then, little more than a fantasy. Not that the PCF's efforts went unrewarded, of course. The party's appeals resonated in certain sectors of the French working class, especially in the mid-1930s. And the party was able to attract large numbers of dedicated members and *cadres* who sincerely believed that a revolutionary transformation of French society was the only way out of a harsh and exploitative capitalism. The problem was that the party's appeals, and its successes, had natural limits, beyond which they produced solid hostility.

On top of everything, the development of French social classes did not conform to the PCF's theories. In some very abstract sense there *was* one working class in France, but the abstraction was at a very high level. Divisions within the working class were very real, and they had definite behavioral consequences, whatever the PCF thought. Communists could attract support from mass-production sectors of the work force (that is, when the party was sufficiently able to tone down its sectarianism to talk sense to them) and could also touch deep reflexes in certain traditionally far-Left rural areas. Beyond this, however, new categories of "middle class" people were emerging to fit the professional, technical and bureaucratic needs of a new advanced capitalist order beginning to burst through in France. Thus an old intermediary strata—peasants and *petit bourgeois*—were threatened by change, newer ones arose which seemed, initially, to be the beneficiaries of such change. In fact, just beneath the surface of crisis-ridden inter-war France, French class structure was becoming more complex, rather than simpler and more polarized. Most important, such new social strata were to prove new havens for the social democratic reformism which the PCF in the inter-war period so desperately wanted to destroy.

Sociological considerations provided only one key to understanding the persistence of social democratic reformism in France. One form of cultural solidarity which united perhaps a majority of the French—even segments of the working class—was belief in the principles and forms of democracy. France, after all, was the country of 1789, 1848, of the Commune, and of successive bourgeois democratic republics. It was also a society in which democratic changes had been won by repeated struggle conducted by coalitions of workers and middle-class groups. Even if it was evident in the inter-war period that certain sectors of the French ruling class pledged only the most formal allegiance to this great national heritage, the heritage ran deep nonetheless. In its activities the PCF could insist all it wanted that "bourgeois democracy" was a sham, *la France Républicaine* was very real. Thus, try as it might to expose "bourgeois democracy" by contrasting it with the "proletarian democracy" which, the PCF claimed, existed in the Soviet Union, the party ran up against a stone wall as soon as it reached out beyond its own working-class constituencies. In general, then, however conscious many Frenchmen were that Republican institutions, as they existed, talked more democracy than they produced, they were also aware of the drastic shortfall between promise and performance in the "proletarian democracy" so much vaunted by the PCF. Here it was a question of simple cost-benefit analysis. While the PCF was quite successful at persuading important fractions of the working class, beginning in the 1930s, that the benefits of proletarian democracy outweighed its costs, other groups of workers and the critical middle strata reached different conclusions. However imperfect, French democracy had some important virtues. And its very existence made it theoretically possible for some of the imperfections to be removed through further struggle. Against these considerations people weighed what they knew of the Soviet Union: one-party rule, the lack of elementary civil liberties, the repression by force of any open political disagreement, periodic bloody purges, the elevation of Stalin to demigod status, and so on. To many Frenchmen, then, the price to be paid for the "proletarian democracy" advocated by the PCF was much too high.

The young PCF in the interwar years rapidly accumulated a series of political liabilities. The strategic shift to United Frontism in the middle 1930s momentarily opened up new paths to success for the party, however, even if the shift was motivated as much by Soviet diplomatic aims as by considerations of French reality. The fact of the matter behind such success was that the PCF, while abandoning neither its neo-Bolshevik theory and rhetoric nor its Stalinized internal-organizational life, had begun to practice a radical reformist politics somewhat more in touch with the realities of French society. The party did not give up its goal of the socialist transformation of France. Rather it adjusted its strategic vision to focus on promoting Left-Center alliance politics dedicated to enacting structural reforms which might, hopefully, break the back of French capitalism. In the process the party was able somewhat to lower the immense barriers which separated it from the rest of French society and politics. It became, for the moment, a national party with its share in France's Jacobin heritage. This "nationalization" process, in turn, gave it access to broad new constituencies. In the inter-war period, however, the PCF was too close to its neo-Bolshevism and too tightly entangled with the Comintern to institutionalize the lessons of the Popular Front into a genuinely coherent, genuinely French strategy for socialist change. Eurocommunism was very far away. No more eloquent evidence for this exists than the party's behavior after the 1939 Nazi-Soviet pact.

United Front reformism, 1930s style, was riven with profound contradictions. The PCF wanted allies. Yet its behavior towards these allies tended to undermine the likelihood of successful coalition. This was so because the PCF fully intended to use the political and social contiguity of any concluded alliances to organize sizeable portions of its allies' rank-and-file support out from under its leadership and into the PCF's own fold (a practice which was graphically illustrated by the behavior of PCF unionists in the CGT after reunification in 1935). The PCF wanted allies, in part, in order to *use* them, undermine their strength and, ultimately, to discard them. Since other forces on the French Left and Center were quite aware of this, the PCF found it difficult to make firm United Front friendships. Knowledge of the PCF's longer term intentions did nothing to assuage the wariness of allies either. Here the PCF's continuing "insurrectionary" rhetoric, its Manichaean theoretical views which allowed of only *one* vanguard party, the PCF, and its espousal of the Soviet model were strong deterrents to groups well aware of the fates which the "party of the working class" reserved for them in a Soviet-model "dictatorship of the proletariat."

The PCF also geared its domestic goals tightly to the objectives of Soviet

foreign policy, a practice which made United Frontism even more complicated in the 1930s. Because of its devotion to Soviet diplomacy, the PCF
was obliged to pursue two separate strategic and tactical lines simultaneously. One the one hand it had its domestic strategy, United Front or
other. On the other hand it attempted to use its domestic influence over
other political forces to shape the international posture of France in ways
which would further Soviet international goals. And, because of the exaggerated loyalty of the PCF to the Comintern, the goal of supporting Soviet
foreign policy took evident pride of place. All of this placed actual and
potential United Front allies in a doubly unpleasant situation. If they
decided to collaborate with the PCF they risked being swallowed up by the
Communists domestically, while at the same time being manipulated into
serving the international purposes of the Soviet Union.

As of 1939 all of these dilemmas must have seemed irrelevant, since the
PCF seemed bent on destroying itself and undermining its own working-
class support. But, with the benefit of hindsight, we know that it was just
this set of dilemmas which was to beset the immediate post–World War II
PCF. It is to this troubled era in the PCF's history, with particular reference to the relationship between French Communism and French workers
as mediated by the party's labor mass organizations, that we must now
turn.

Chapter 2

TRANSMISSION BELT FOR A UNITED FRONT: THE CGT FROM RESISTANCE TO 1947

Resistance, Liberation and the Return of United Frontism

Hitler played an important role in reversing the disastrous course upon which the PCF had set itself in 1939. When he unleashed his Blitzkrieg toward the East, PCF "revolutionary defeatism"—which had come quite close to defeating the PCF once and for all—came to an end. The Soviet Union desperately needed an alliance with the Western democracies to stave off the Nazi attack. This need, in turn, led the Comintern to decree a return to the "United Front against Fascism" policy. For the PCF this meant a return to a Popular Front strategy not unlike that which it had pursued in the mid-1930s. And, as in the 1930s, for a brief few years United Frontism was to pay great dividends for the party. Immediately after the war the party's radical reformism played a key role in promoting the most important moment of social reform in modern French history. Its United Front position also enabled the party to grow and prosper. Most important, the post-Liberation period provided the openings necessary for the PCF to establish a firm and permanent hold over the *Confédération Générale du Travail*. In these years, then, the long story of party-mass–organization relationships which is the central focus of our essay actually begins.

The PCF's Resistance slogan, "for a politics of unity of the working class and union of the French nation,"[1] revealed quite clearly the two goals of the PCF's post-1941 strategy. The party pledged itself to work towards the formation of a national Resistance front which would include itself, the

---

1. PCF, *Histoire du PCF*, p. 419; François Hincker, "La classe ouvrière et la nation dans le Résistance," in Germaine Willard et al., *De la guerre à la Libération* (1972); Claude Angeli and Paul Gillet, *Debout partisans!* (1970); Stéphane Courtois, *Le PCF pendant la guerre* (1979).

rest of the Left and any bourgeois forces willing to join the struggle. At the same time within this broad front the party hoped to develop unity-in-action on the political Left and in the labor movement which would ultimately enhance its own fortunes. A successful, broadly-based Resistance movement would hasten the defeat of the Nazis, cement Allied unity and, with luck, ensure an independent postwar France, all results which would serve Soviet foreign policy well. Domestically a Resistance front committed to serious postwar reforms might begin to undermine bourgeois power. And, if all went well, the PCF would be able to build a solid hegemonic base within the Left through its Resistance and immediate postwar activities.

The PCF's hopes for the Resistance and the reality of the Resistance situation did not altogether coincide, however. Because of the party's earlier devotion to "revolutionary defeatism" it had been unavailable at the most important moment in the development of Resistance, its beginning. While the PCF was denouncing "imperialist war," General de Gaulle, starting with his 1940 London speech proclaiming that "France had lost a battle, it had not lost the war," had begun building a bourgeois and nationalist anti-Nazi movement.[2] Because of this the PCF was never able to claim undisputed leadership in the Resistance front. It also meant that the Resistance front was to be riven by complicated jockeying for position. In fact, all of the actors in this Resistance struggle had "hidden agenda" for the postwar world. Everyone knew, for example, that the PCF intended to use the Resistance to strengthen its own position. And the PCF knew that everyone else intended to use the Resistance to prevent this from happening. The Gaullists (or at least the core of political support behind General de Gaulle) wanted to use Resistance nationalism to create a new and different French state while keeping social reform from getting out of hand after the war. The Left in the Resistance, to varying degrees, desired progressive reform. However, forces just to the immediate Right of the PCF—the Socialists, Christian Democrats (the *Mouvement Républicain Populaire* (MRP), as French Christian Democracy came to be called) and what remained of the Radicals—wanted to keep the PCF from gaining hegemony over the reforming wing of the Resistance, and to do so were willing to ally with the Gaullists.

As Liberation approached, the PCF had become the most important, best organized and most coherent arm of the domestic Resistance (the Gaullists being based outside France). By the party's courage and intelligence, it had won an important place in the coalition of forces which would reorder France after Liberation. In the process it had attracted large num-

---

2. This contradiction is, of course, the product of the PCF's subservience to Soviet foreign policy in the 1939–1941 period. In turn, there can be no question but that the important strategic option to return to United Frontism in 1941 was dictated by Soviet foreign-policy concerns, however well it was to work out for the PCF domestically. See Fernando Claudin, *La crise du mouvement communiste*, vol. I, pp. 372 ff.

bers of new members, while building new strength in key areas, especially in the labor movement (the clandestine CGT reunified again in 1943 as part of the Resistance front).[3] The entire Resistance coalition agreed on the need to use the immediate postwar period to eliminate those political and social flaws which had led to June 1940 and then to Vichy. Within this consensus, the PCF's aim was to pin down its Resistance colleagues to a specific program of changes (a Resistance "Common Program," to use more current vocabulary). To this end, during the last months of the Resistance it worked feverishly to animate the *Conseil National de la Résistance* (CNR)[4] and to commit the CNR to a list of concrete reforms to be enacted after Liberation (the CNR program appeared in March, 1944). If the PCF could hold its Resistance partners to the letter of the CNR program, it might be able to promote the implementation of an impressive number of changes—income redistribution, social-welfare programs, nationalizations, new political institutions, new rights for workers in economic life.[5] The enactment of the CNR program, or even of large parts of it, would almost certainly benefit the Left politically and, if things worked out as the PCF desired, the PCF within the Left. The job of making this happen would not be easy, however. The unity of the Resistance front, such as it was, was forged by war. Once the war ended, most of the impetus for unity and much of the desire for change could evaporate.

Governmental Communism: 1944–1945

The PCF

The PCF was on its very best behavior after Liberation in 1944. Despite its military presence throughout France, it agreed to lay down its arms in November under the slogan "One State, One Police, One Army" and went to work to finish winning the war. It accepted ministries in General de Gaulle's provisional government and its share of seats in the Consultative Assembly. And from its different bastions of influence it did its best to keep the CNR and its program alive. In the words of Maurice Thorez, the CNR program represented "the sum of aspirations common to diverse patriotic forces . . . whose applications would consolidate . . . the front of democratic and national forces, weaken the *grande bourgeoisie* and rein-

3. See André Tollet, *La classe ouvrière dans la Résistance* (1960); and Hincker, in G. Willard.

4. *L'année politique, 1944–1945*, p. 8 ff. The CNR was composed of delegates from three main groups: trade unions (CFTC, CGT), anti-Vichy political parties, Resistance groups. Thus PCF strength in the CNR followed not only from official PCF representation on the CNR, but also from PCF power within the *Front national* and *Franc tireur* Resistance groups and within the CGT.

5. *L'année politique, 1944–45*, p. 8. PCF, *Histoire du PCF*, pp. 442, 471–472. See also Jacques Fauvet, *Histoire du Parti Communiste Français*, (1965), vol. II; and William Graham, *The French Socialists and Tripartism* (1967), p. 117 ff; *L'année politique, 1944–45*, pp. 289, 340–341, 470.

force the authority and prestige of the working class and the Communist Party." Communist moderation, patriotism and statesmanlike behavior were means to keep the peace within the Resistance coalition. Keeping such peace, in turn, was one way in which the PCF sought to promote the post-war social reforms which would shift the balance of power in France from Right to Left.

The entire Resistance front was agreed that some change was necessary. How much change, and of what, were rather more contentious issues. Everyone agreed that property belonging to open collaborators (Renault, the press) should be nationalized,[6] and that a new social security system, plus the introduction of works committees giving unions and workers new power on the shop floor of large firms were necessary. Here the CNR program went much further, but the governing coalition ceased agreeing. General de Gaulle and many of his supporters saw little need for further change, while the PCF desired much more extensive nationalizations and social reforms. Using the governmental and mass-organizational resources (among labor, peasants, women, etc.) it could muster, plus whatever allies were available, the PCF prodded for broader structural changes, not always successfully.[7] The same situation prevailed in discussions of new political arrangements. Everyone agreed that new political institutions had to be set up, but there agreement ceased. General de Gaulle leaned towards Presidentialism and institutional barriers to what he feared would be undue party political power. The PCF's basic position, in contrast, was that new institutions should "break down the barriers which block the creative initiative of the masses."[8] To begin with, this meant a completely sovereign Constituent Assembly to succeed the Liberation Consultative Assembly. It also meant trying to get France out of its "provisional" status as rapidly as possible—i.e., create a new constitutional order—in order to maximize the electoral returns to the Left of the progressive climate which the Resistance had created. Ultimately, the PCF took a position of thorough democracy on the question of new institutions. It wanted a unicameral legislature, to which governments would be directly responsible without "checks and balances." And it desired a system of proportional electoral representation which would translate the electoral preferences of the French as directly as possible into the composition of this legislature. On all of these issues, controversy was rife.[9]

The PCF presented its reformism in this period with great care. As Jacques Duclos was eager to announce, the social and political measures which the PCF favored were not "socialistic."[10] Rather, the party was

6. *L'année politique, 1944–45*, p. 71.
7. Ibid., pp. 71–84.
8. PCF, *Histoire du PCF*, p. 460.
9. *L'année politique, 1944–45*, pp. 355–256, 288–289.
10. Georgette Elgey, *La république des illusions* (1965), p. 34.

aiding the "progressive forces" in power to translate the aims of the
Resistance for the "democratization" of French society.[11] And the PCF,
when necessary, was extremely hard on anyone who suggested actions
which, by going beyond the CNR Program and its goals of "democratization," might risk dividing the "front of national forces" upon whose consolidation the PCF had spent so much time, energy and ingenuity.[12]

This said, the PCF did intend to prod the Resistance coalition to promote
reforms which would remove power and influence from "the trusts" and
the political Right. And removing power from certain hands meant
reassigning it to others. To a great extent the PCF saw opening up of new
areas of democratic control in France as an avenue to increased PCF influence. Electorally, for example, the PCF was, in the immediate postwar
months, the largest party in France. Institutions which would allow this
electoral strength to be translated into a maximum of parliamentary
strength would increase PCF power. This, in turn, would give the PCF the
governmental clout to promote reforms which, it felt, would further increase its mass support. The party had a similar perspective on social
reform. Transferring power from the trusts to the people, as the CNR Program proposed, raised the issue of how the people were to be represented in
new arrangements. In the new public sector, for example, the PCF favored
nationalized firms in which boards of directors would be tripartite, appointed by the government, consumers and the workers in the firm. Formally this might seem unthreatening, but it could be, and was, used to
"stack" the boards of certain newly nationalized industries towards the
PCF (with the government and consumer groups appointing fellow
travellers, and the workers, whose choice was made through their unions,
voting for CGT candidates, at a moment when the CGT was rapidly
becoming Communist-dominated).[13] Where such a situation could be promoted, the resources of the industry in question could then be biased
towards further promoting PCF strength. The social security system—as
modified by Communist Minister Ambroise Croizat in 1945—seemed in-
nocuous enough on the face of it. Administrative *caisses* were elected by
workers, who thereby gained control over the administration of the social
security system. However, the electoral system gave unions the right to
nominate slates of candidates, a situation which once again gave the CGT
new opportunities to politically socialize the rank and file in the elections
themselves, plus the added benefit of domination over the social security

11. See PCF, *Histoire du PCF*, p. 445, for Maurice Thorez' statement to the PCF Central
Committee in January 1945 on the centrality of the CNR program.

12. PCF, *Histoire du PCF*, pp. 445, 442.

13. Elgey, *Illusions*, p. 16; Georges Lefranc, *Les expériences syndicales en France, 1939 à
1950* (1950), p. 329. On the *Comités d'entreprise* see Maurice Combe, *L'alibi, vingt ans d'expérience d'un comité central d'entreprise* (1969); Maurice Montluclard, *La dynamique des
comités d'entreprise* (1963); Emile James, *Les comités d'entreprise* (1945). See also François
Billoux, *Quand nous étions ministres* (1972), esp. Parts 2, 3.

system. The *Comités d'entreprise* (works committees) likewise redesigned by a PCF Minister in 1945, gave the CGT similar new opportunities.

The PCF's strategy was complex, therefore. It wanted to hold the Resistance coalition together as long as possible in order to implement the CNR program to the full. To do this the party had to be moderate and conciliatory. Simultaneously, however, the party hoped to use the progressive postwar climate to serve its own political ends, an intention which, the party knew, would eventually disaggregate the Resistance coalition along Left-Center lines. While the PCF wanted to put the moment of decisive conflict off as long as possible, it did realize that such conflict was inevitable. The Gaullists and probably the Christian Democrats would eventually balk at further reforms rather than moving forward in the directions the PCF desired. With this in mind the party was deeply concerned simultaneously to promote narrower unity among Left Resistance forces.[14]

The list of PCF actions taken to cement working unity with the Socialists after Liberation is long. A Socialist-Communist *Comité d'Entente*, established in 1944, met with regularity for over a year, occasionally leading to common positions between the two parties.[15] It became particularly influential on electoral issues, although the PCF's success in lining up the SFIO behind its own positions was limited.[16] Then in June, 1945, the PCF Central Committee published a "Charter of Unity" which proposed a fusion of the two parties in a new *parti ouvrier français*.[17] The 1945 PCF Congress seconded this and suggested a series of less drastic steps towards "organic" unity which might be taken in the interim.[18] The SFIO was cool to all of this, but the PCF took comfort from the fact that anti-Communist initiatives by Léon Blum and Daniel Mayer within the SFIO were blocked by the SFIO left wing.[19] Next, the *Délégation des Gauches* (an ad hoc grouping promoted by the PCF and CGT and composed of the CGT, PCF, SFIO, Radicals, and representatives from the League for Human Rights) proposed a full Popular Front electoral coalition for the fall 1945 elections, to no avail.[20] As long as the Socialists had other options, in this case the perpetuation of a broader multi-party coalition, they wanted no part of a new Popular Front.

14. PCF, *Histoire du PCF*, p. 449. *L'année politique, 1944–45*, p. 479; Graham, p. 97; PCF, *Histoire du PCF*, pp. 461–462.

15. *L'année politique, 1944–45*, p. 94.

16. Ibid., pp. 60, 202.

17. *L'Humanité*, 12 June 1945; *L'année politique, 1944–45*, p. 479; Graham, p. 97; PCF *Histoire du PCF*, pp. 461–462.

18. Proposed were twice-monthly meetings between the two party leaderships, departmental and local organizations to coordinate unified actions, common positions in the government and assemblies, common propaganda in the country, and collaboration between the Socialist and Communist press. cf. PCF, *Histoire du PCF*, p. 468.

19. See Léon Blum's pamphlet, *Le problème de l'unité* (1945); *L'année politique, 1944–45*, p. 230; Graham, p. 98; PCF, *Histoire du PCF*, p. 468.

20. *L'année politique, 1944–45*, p. 289.

Signs of trouble for the PCF scenario began to appear in the fall of 1945. After the November elections—in which the Left emerged very strong—the PCF Central Committee proposed a genuine Popular Front government (Communists, Socialists, Radicals) to the SFIO.[21] The SFIO refused, insisting instead on Christian Democratic participation in any new coalition. The MRP, in turn, insisted that General de Gaulle be appointed Prime Minister. The PCF eventually fell back to a moderate position, refusing, in its words, "the politics of all or nothing" (instead bargaining for important ministries).[22] Nonetheless a pattern had been set. The PCF had failed to promote workable Left unity to prepare for the obvious eventuality of the collapse of the Resistance coalition. The SFIO had discovered a way out by insisting upon *tripartisme* rather than a left-wing Popular Front. In addition the Christian Democrats were rapidly moving to the Right. Making the best of a bad situation for the moment, the PCF began to attack General de Gaulle as the figure behind which the French bourgeoisie was regrouping.[23] Then General de Gaulle abruptly took his leave at the beginning of 1946, in disgust with *la politique des partis*. At this point a good deal of Gaullist support shifted to the MRP, which likewise became the target of PCF hostility. To the PCF the "reactionaries were right behind the Resistants" in the MRP. The logic of events was sharpening conflict in postwar France.[24]

The CGT

The PCF's Resistance and postwar United Frontism involved much more than the complicated alliance politics which we have just described. The party knew that Communist strength in government and Parliament would not be enough to persuade reluctant allies to do things which they really did not want to do. Mass mobilization from outside the formal political system was necessary to supplement the PCF's political activities. And, while the PCF had a number of ways of prompting mass mobilization, by far its most important resource was the organized labor movement, the CGT in particular. The problem was that the PCF's control over the CGT had its limits. The party had built considerable power within the CGT in the Popular Front period. But actual domination of the CGT had eluded the PCF during these years, while catastrophic PCF policies after 1939 plus the unpleasant turn of events of the late 1930s had undermined many of the party's earlier gains. Thus the question of post-Liberation Communist mo-

21. PCF, *Histoire du PCF*, p. 474; Graham, p. 116.

22. PCF, *Histoire du PCF*, p. 474; Graham, pp. 122–123; *L'année politique, 1944–45*, p. 343.

23. Graham, pp. 86–89.

24. PCF. *Histoire du PCF*, pp. 462–465. See *L'Humanité*, 4, 12, 19 April 1946, for a series of articles on *laïcité* by the PCF *Bureau Politique*. Stress on *laïcité* was one tactic to split Socialists from Christian Democrats. Alfred Rieber, *Stalin and the French Communist Party* (1962), p. 58. Elgey, *Illusions*, p. 66.

bilization of organized labor was a complicated one. The party desired to reassert its power and consolidate its hegemony over the CGT. At the same time it hoped to deploy the CGT as an extra-political source of pressure on governments to further PCF political aims. Using the CGT for quasi-partisan purposes was bound to create opposition within the Confederation from the many non-Communists in the organization. Trying to take over the CGT would reinforce opposition from the same sources. Much depended, of course, on the skill with which the PCF pursued these two goals. As we will see, however, the party approached them with a handicap of sorts, its tendency to treat mass organizations like the CGT as direct transmission belts for party lines.

Consolidating a Mass Organization—Whatever else happened in the Resistance and post-Liberation years, the PCF took one giant step forward by consolidating its hold over the major segment of French organized labor, the CGT. The degree to which power within the CGT shifted in these years becomes clear from a few figures. By 1946 Communists had come to hold positions of control over twenty-one key CGT federations (including the virtual totality of federations in mass-production industry), as against only ten in 1939 (with the corresponding figures for non-Communist federations, which were most often in less central areas of the economy, dropping from twenty in 1939 to nine in 1946).[25] And by 1946 the

---

25. According to Georges Lefranc, *1939 à 1950*, p. 197, Communist and non-Communist strength by Federations in the CGT stood as follows in 1945. Federations with an asterisk were taken over by the PCF in the period from 1939 to 1945, primarily from 1942–1945.

CGT Federations as of 1945

Communist Dominated	*Non-Communist*
Agricultural laborers	
Woodworking	
Building trades	Functionaries
Metal workers	
*Railroad workers	
*Transport workers	
*State laborers	Tobacco workers
Textile workers	
	Municipal
*Garment workers	
*Entertainers	
*Food workers	
(Alimentation)	Pharmaceutical workers
	Sailors
	Port and dock workers
	(later shifted also)
*Commercial travellers	
(Voyageurs de commerce)	
	Printing (Livre)
	Employees (Employés)
Chemical workers	
Paper/cardboard workers	
*Miners	

party had come to control four-fifths of the CGT's departmental unions.[26]

Why did this shift in the CGT occur? The events of wartime were clearly one essential reason. The prominent Resistance roles of Communists—both outside and within the labor movement—were undeniable. Communists were in the forefront of domestic struggle against the Germans and against Vichy's corporatist designs on French unionism. Communist Resistance strategy included a large component of industrial action, strikes, sabotage, mass demonstrations and so on. And with the reunification of the CGT in 1943 and the general posture of the unified CGT in favor of Resistance activities, Communist unionists acquired key new avenues of access to the French working class. The fact that Communist unionists "put their bodies on the Resistance line" in itself may have shifted the balance towards Communists in some unions (railroads, for example). The war not only allowed Communists to assume new positions of influence in CGT unions, it also eliminated the Communists' most tenacious union enemies. The CGT right wing, in particular the whole *Syndicats* group led by René Bélin, was compromised beyond reprieve by its support of the Vichy regime and its labor policies.[27] At Liberation, legally-sanctioned purge committees (complemented by unofficial and often PCF-controlled purge groups within specific unions) worked a wholesale removal of trade-union collaborators from the CGT. The "Capocci-Jayat" purge officially excluded some 300 CGT leaders from further union activity, while unofficial purges may have eliminated many times this number.[28] In the climate of the times, it was not only open collaborators who were targeted. Anyone who could be assigned a degree of responsibility for the events of the late 1930s (pacifists and partisans of Munich, for example) was fair game, a fact which PCF unionists exploited to the hilt.[29]

The PCF's major adversary in the struggle for control over the CGT was the reformist "Center" group around Léon Jouhaux which had dominated the Confederation in the inter-war period. The war had its effects on this group as well. Léon Jouhaux himself, perhaps the most powerful figure in

---

CGT Federations as of 1945 *(continued)*	
Communist Dominated	*Non-Communist*
Lighting (Eclairage)	
Skin and leather workers	
	Jewelry workers
*Coiffeurs	
*Hat workers	
Glass workers	

26. Michel Collinet, *Esprit*, p. 133.

27. Georges Lefranc, *Le mouvement syndical en France, de la Libération aux événements de mai–juin 1968* (1969), pp. 14–15.

28. Hedvicq Stolvitzer, *La scission de le CGT* (1957), pp. 6–8. Also Lefranc, *1939–1950*, p. 138.

29. Stolvitzer, p. 46; Rieber, pp. 179–187.

French trade unionism in the years between the wars, was captured and deported by the Germans, not to return until well into 1945. Since Jouhaux was a union strategist of great astuteness and, above all, a genuine working-class hero around whom non-Communist elements in the CGT might have rallied, his temporary absence at a critical juncture was very important. In addition, many of the ablest young CGT Center leaders—people like Robert Lacoste and Christian Pineau—were propelled by the Resistance from union life into politics.[30] Beyond this, however, the virtual dissolution of the CGT right wing because of its *Vichisme* left the CGT Center without an essential political counterweight to the PCF in internal CGT struggle.

By far the most important reason for the PCF gains in the CGT was organizational, however. The period immediately after Liberation saw a tremendous influx of new CGT members. From a figure of 1.5 million members in 1939 the Confederation shot to a record high of six million in 1946. The CGT, along with the rest of the French Left, benefited from the vast outpouring of popular desire for change created by the Resistance. In this situation, several million new CGTers had to be organized into unions. Once again, as in the Popular Front period, the spoils of power in the CGT went to the faction best prepared to carry out this organizational task. As the war ended the Communist Party stood alone among groups connected to labor in possessing large numbers of organizational militants either present within, or available to move into, the CGT. Sociological factors accentuated the PCF's advantage. The Center faction was strongest in the civil servant/white-collar sectors of the workforce, where active *encadrement* was neither customary, nor particularly necessary. The Center, therefore, had little tradition of organizational development, few organizers and a diminished understanding of the need for *encadrement*. In contrast, the PCF power base in organized labor had, from the beginning, been in the private sector of the economy, with heavy stress on mass-production industry. And the PCF had long understood that mass-production workers needed *encadrement* to maintain unions. Thus, yet again as in the mid-30s CGT Centrists were in the wrong place to capitalize on CGT growth, while PCF unionists were in the right place, at the right time, with the right kind of organizers.[31]

Most often, when the PCF gained sufficient rank-and-file influence within a CGT federation to risk moving for power, it began to isolate potential centers of opposition. Usually this involved changing the offical federation leadership and the structure of union institutions to ensure continuing PCF control. The railroad workers' union was typical. In prewar years

---

30. To see how and why this happened to one man, read Christian Pineau's war memoirs, *La simple vérité* (1961).

31. Stolvitzer, p. 53; Lefranc, *1939–1950*, p. 159.

the *Cheminot* Federation had been structured around a factional truce among its membership. A system of "parity" had been established to allow both PCF and non-PCF factions to share in making Federation decisions. The war shifted the internal balance towards the PCF. In the postwar period, then, the PCF ended the "parity" system (which it had used to its advantage earlier) in favor of "true trade-union democracy" where the entire membership could choose "the best from within itself to lead it, regardless of faction."[32] In essence, the postwar environment gave the PCF the votes to promote institutional change in the *Cheminot* Federation democratically. And the result of this democratic change was the removal of non-Communists from effective leadership positions.

The CGT was a confederation of union federations and departmental unions. Its statutory legislative body was the CGT Congress, composed of delegates from federations and departmental unions. The Congress officially decided strategy and elected the CGT's executive bodies, the relatively large *Commission Administrative* (which met briefly several times per year) and the *Bureau Confédéral*, the day-to-day executive of the Confederation. The shift in power at rank-and-file level therefore not only meant that the PCF came to control federations and departmental unions, it meant also that, through these bodies, Communist unionists could control the CGT Congress and its elected executive bodies. Although the PCF had no hesitation in simply taking over federations and departmental unions, it approached the question of who was to run the Confederation itself with more delicacy. The CGT was a mass organization, and mass organizations were supposed to represent the masses and not be simply party fronts. Thus some discussion and difference had to be allowed in the CGT's highest instances since the postwar CGT had large numbers of non-Communists in its fold. This consideration was all the more important because several important federations within the CGT did not fall to PCF control during these years, primarily civil servants, but also the very large teachers' union and the powerful *Fédération du Livre*. The imposition by the PCF of a monocolor Confederal leadership and program would have been a red flag to such organizations, who might even consider secession. In this light the party's willingness to allow a "pluralistic" leadership structure at the Confederal level becomes comprehensible. The postwar *Bureau Confédéral* was thus equally divided between the PCF-Benoît Frachon faction and the Léon Jouhaux-Center group.

The CGT was, of course, not all of French organized labor, only its biggest morsel. For the PCF to maximize working-class mobilization in favor of its United Front politics, unity-in-action across the entire spectrum of union organizations around the CGT was desirable. Thus Communists

---

32. Cheminots, Fédération Nationale des, CGT, *Les cheminots dans l'histoire sociale de la France* (1967), p. 206.

within the CGT prodded the Confederation to promote unity agreements with other labor groups. First on the list to be wooed was the *Confédération Française des Travailleurs Chrétiens* (CFTC), the Catholic labor front (which believed in social harmony and therefore was chronically prone, in the CGT's eyes, to class collaboration). The CGT and CFTC had worked closely during the Resistance (a *Comité d'Entente* to coordinate action between the two Confederations existed well into 1945).[33] In early 1945, the CGT leadership proposed "organic" unity to the CFTC, in which the CFTC would join the CGT to promote the program of the *Conseil National de la Résistance*. The CFTC was to be given places in the CGT's Confederal leadership commensurate with its numerical strength.[34] The CFTC declined, and that was the end of the story. A different story, with a similar ending, surrounded the CGT's immediate postwar attempts to organize *cadres* (administrators) into the CGT. White-collar administrative workers in the private sector of the economy were separated from other workers by deep status barriers and, to a degree, by their functions within firms. The post-Liberation period was marked by a struggle between the CGT *cadre* union and the autonomous *Confédération Générale des Cadres* (CGC) for the loyalty of *cadres*. The CGT had essentially lost to the CGC by mid-1945.[35] The failure was important. *Cadres* were a small, but growing, segment of the workforce whose "upwardly mobile" social perspectives might have been counteracted by inclusion in the CGT. Moreover, the CGC, as an autonomous, non-affiliated "category" union was a dangerous precedent. Other occupational groups might be tempted to go this route in the future (the teachers did so in 1947–1948).

The CGT's failures with the CFTC and the CGC were serious. To begin with, they limited the CGT's mobilizing power, and the PCF needed all of the labor mobilization it could muster. But the issue was more profound even than this. The PCF wanted the CFTC within the CGT so that Catholic workers might be pried away from the "non-struggle," anti-Communist attitudes of the Church. The CFTC leadership knew this, and was aware of the deepening power of the PCF in the CGT. Fear of Communism essentially forced the CFTC to keep its distance.[36] And open anti-Communism

33. *Le Monde*, 15 June 1945.

34. Benoît Frachon, *Au rythme des jours* (1967), vol. I, p. 119 ff. Frachon's two-volume *mémoires*, really an edited collection of Frachon's speeches and articles over the years, is an invaluable source of documentation for our period as well as a complete exposure to the talents and character of France's most important modern trade-union figure. See also CFTC, *Unité syndicale ou unité d'action?*

35. Lefranc, *1944–1968*, pp. 16–17.

36. Once it became clear that the CFTC understood quite well what was at issue, the CGT had little choice but to admit failure. In *La Vie Ouvrière* of December 1945, Benoît Frachon wrote that the CFTC seemed determined to maintain the "division" of the working class "camouflaging it under the slightly ridiculous term of trade-union pluralism." Moreover, continued Frachon, the CFTC was in reality an instrument of the Church and the MRP. Since the

was one of the CGC's main organizing tools in keeping *cadres* out of the CGT. More generally, by 1946 the PCF's moves to turn the CGT into its privileged labor mass organization had created deep resentment, especially among displaced non-Communist forces within the CGT. This resentment, fueled by the transmission-belt use which the PCF made of the CGT to carry out its United Frontist political strategy, in the context of developing Cold War, was to lead to crisis.

The CGT's Role in the United Front Political Economy—The PCF set two major tasks for the CGT in the immediate postwar years. First, the Confederation was to support postwar governments—as long as there continued to be some possibility for change coming from them—as a loyal component of the Resistance coalition dedicated to implementing the CNR program. Then, given such broad CGT support for postwar governments, the Confederation was to use its mass organizational resources to push such governments to work the maximum amount of change. The party undoubtedly saw these two tasks as complementary at the time. In retrospect, however, they look mutually exclusive.

"Produce, produce," and "Work hard first, then ask for concessions," were the CGT leadership's basic slogans during these years. The PCF's official history indicates what the party felt about this: "to produce is at one and the same time a national duty and a class duty. By producing more the working class can prevent the trusts from carrying out their plan to isolate and subvert democracy in order to promote their politics of reaction."[37] To the PCF, then, the CGT's main job after Liberation was to "win the battle of production." The Confederation ought to promote labor productivity and discipline for economic reconstruction.

Telling the workers to work as hard as they could and not complain might have seemed, at first sight, a strange strategy for a union movement whose commitment to class struggle long predated any Communist presence within it. Yet there was a logic in this strategy. In the period between Liberation and the end of the war, "producing" was absolutely necessary to defeat the Germans. Yet even at this point, and certainly later, this was not the only reason why the PCF and CGT pushed production so assiduously. The deeper reasons were political.

The Resistance coalition was based on a cross-class social alliance, including workers, peasants and urban middle strata. In such an alliance, workers, its most radical and class-conscious members, had to assume primary responsibility for maintaining unity. Thus working-class action in the labor market which aimed only at bettering the situation of workers at

---

division which the CFTC seemed determined to maintain weakened the power of workers to fight for their interests, according to Frachon, nothing remained for the CGT but to try and organize Catholic workers out from underneath their CFTC "misleaders." Benoît Frachon in *La Vie Ouvrière*, 20 December 1945.

37. PCF, *Histoire du PCF*, p. 458; also Frachon, vol I, p. 60 ff.

the expense of other social groups could have been deeply divisive and might well have led to the alienation of middle-class elements and peasants who might otherwise have favored postwar changes. The CGT therefore had to be mature enough to be moderate. The postwar economic situation underlined this position. The war had left France devastated. Production was way down, communications totally disrupted, mass privation and economic chaos never very far away. Militant working-class action which disregarded broader national needs might well lead to economic collapse. Such behavior, dangerous enough economically, would be even more dangerous politically. For the moment, the Right was discredited. Should progressive forces, the working class in the first instance, act in selfish ways, middle-class elements in the Resistance coalition might well shift their allegiance towards the Right, destroying any prospect of further change and giving the Right a new lease on life.

The "battle for production" strategy had other, more ideological, uses as well. The battle was carried on amid incessant publicity which pointed out that, as in the war itself, so in the postwar period, the working class and its allies were the only true patriots. Along with this lesson, the French were also informed that the struggle for production was being conducted not only against abstract economic difficulties, but also against the economic consequences of the treason of French business and the political Right.[38] In all this there was an implicit threat as well. The battle for production was to prove in part that the PCF and CGT could discipline the entire French working class. This meant also that party and union might lead the entire French working class into battle *against* any government which strayed too far from the behavior which they desired.

And so the battle for production was engaged. In the oft-cited phrase of Maurice Thorez, "the strike is a weapon of the trusts [i.e., the monopolies]." The PCF and CGT carried out a vigorous anti-strike line well into the postwar period (until springtime 1947, to be exact). Whenever strike movements actually threatened, as they did from time to time, the PCF and CGT brought out all their big guns to block them. In one well-publicized instance in mid-1945, when miners in the Bethune area began to stop work, both Maurice Thorez and Benoît Frachon, the party's political and trade union leaders, backed by all of the PCF's and CGT's power in the mining sector, moved in to stop the movement. Thorez's address to the miners was memorable:

> To produce, to mine coal, is today the highest form of your class duty. . . .Produce to preserve, to reinforce the unity of the working class with the middle classes, the peasants . . . to insure the life of the country, to make possible the moral and cultural renaissance of France. . . .

38. Frachon, vol. I, p. 60 ff. "Il faut gagner la bataille de la production" (November 1944).

Yesterday, our arms were sabotage and armed action against the enemy. Today that arm is production, to frustrate the plans of the reactionaries, to manifest your class solidarity towards the workers in other areas whose work depends upon your efforts. . . .The slightest weakness on your part will aid the campaigns of the enemies of the people against you, against the working class, against nationalizations, against democracy, against France.[39]

One ought not to overlook the undoubted fact that French workers were, in general, quite sensitive to such appeals. But it was the PCF and, above all, the CGT, which kept the battle for production issues in front of them. And not without great effect. *There were no major strike movements in France from 1944 to May 1947.*[40]

It was, of course, neither possible nor desirable for the PCF and CGT to prevent the expression of all working-class discontent. But whenever unforeseen rank-and-file dissatisfaction did emerge, every attempt was made to limit it and shape its consequences. When railroad workers grew disgruntled in 1945, for example, the CGT *Cheminot* Federation (Communist-dominated by this point) did allow a strike to occur, but a peculiar strike, in fact. Railroad workers whose tasks did not involve actually running trains went out, while the trains continued to go and come.[41] Production was thus not interrupted, but a protest was registered against the government. And when discontent among civil servants developed in late 1945, the PCF and CGT went to great lengths to prevent it from becoming a serious movement (here the PCF had much less union power than with railroad workers). Finally, after a good deal of political pressuring by all of the Left to persuade General de Gaulle to make some concessions, a two-hour strike action did occur. Two hours' less work by civil servants did not disrupt much, however. In both cases mentioned, and in other less important instances, the PCF and CGT tactic was clear. Discontent was turned to symbolic public demonstrations to serve primarily as safety valves for the workers concerned.[42]

In all this PCF and CGT leaders were not naive. Patriotic propaganda and clever conflict management by themselves could not ensure self-denial on the part of the French working class. The government was controlling wages in these years, and the party knew that unless workers were persuaded that the government was dealing with their problems in a just way they would not fight any battle of production and might strike, even against the will of their union leaders. Something more than exhortation

39. Cited in Lefranc, *1944–1968*, p. 30. See also pp. 29–31; *Le Monde*, July 18–19, 1945; PCF, *Histoire du PCF*, p. 469; Maurice Thorez, *Oeuvres choisies* (1966), vol. II, p. 371.

40. Jean-Louis Guglielmi and Michelle Perrot, *Salaires et revendications sociales en France*, 1944–1953 (1953), p. 23.

41. Cheminots, pp. 203, 207.

42. *Le Monde*, 14 December 1945.

was needed to ensure working-class cooperation—the "goods had to be delivered" to the workers. "Delivering the goods" was all the more important to the PCF given Communist attempts to consolidate control in the CGT during this period. If Communist unionists could not defend the living standards of the CGT rank and file then the entire process of mass-organizational consolidation might be compromised.

The party and Communist CGTers had hopes that government policies would solve this problem, at least partially. Economic recovery, once underway, would allow rising real wages. Sensible government measures to limit price rises were needed. Thus the key policy issue lay in creating mechanisms which would tie wages to the cost of living while preventing business from passing on wage increases to consumers. A whole complex of new directive powers of the government over the economy, which came to be known as *dirigisme*, was seen as one answer. Beyond *dirigisme*, the nationalization of important industries and economic planning might also help.[43] However, a rigid system of wage and price control from above did not guarantee that working-class discontent could be anticipated and dealt with justly. Movements from below might emerge either because of the clumsiness of such a system or because of the unwillingness of politicians to use it in good faith. More important, any strict method of administrative control over the labor market might cut out the trade unions, especially the CGT. This, in turn, would be dangerous for the PCF in its efforts at building hegemony over the CGT. Whatever else occurred, the CGT had to be given the space to exercise its central union function of fighting in a credible, public way for the material interests of its membership.[44]

This dilemma was solved by redefining the CGT's tactics for protecting the material situation of its rank and file. Instead of open class war and direct action against employers and government, the CGT shifted emphasis to public pressure on the government for wage and other necessary concessions. When the situation warranted, or when pressed by rank-and-file discontent, the CGT publicly spoke to the government to obtain concessions, instead of promoting strike movements. This allowed the CGT to demonstrate to its members that they were indeed being protected by their unions. And it also served as a source of outside leverage for PCF ministers to move reluctant colleagues off center on questions of economic policy.

The CGT's role in the PCF's postwar United Frontism extended beyond the simple provision of labor discipline. The Confederation was also deployed in active direct political conflict in support of PCF positions. As Benoît Frachon noted in an address to the 1946 CGT Congress, "the fact is . . . that if they [workers] do not concern themselves with politics, politics will concern itself with them . . . and not in their favor. . . .We have

43. Guglielmi and Perrot, pp. 14, 18–19, 46–47, 52, 61.
44. Jean-Claude Casanova, *La position des syndicats français dans l'économie politique* (1956), p. 9.

therefore intervened to combat the reactionaries. . . ."[45] To Communist unionists, the CGT had every right and reason to throw its weight into the political balance to pressure governments towards progressive solutions.[46] And, of course, such progressive solutions were usually those which the PCF was advocating, but having difficulty obtaining, within the government. In May 1945, for example, the CGT publicly took a stand in favor of nationalizing the remainder of the coal mines, gas and electricity, and credit.[47] In November of the same year the CGT produced a plan to reform the Ministry of Industry (about which the PCF was very concerned) and again demanded that gas and electricity be nationalized.[48] Then in December the CGT pressured to nationalize the banks.

The CGT's political life in this period was not exhausted by pressure group action. In early 1945 the Confederal Bureau encouraged CGT militants to stand in municipal elections as Resistance candidates, in defiance of long-standing CGT customs.[49] And, at this point, in even greater defiance of CGT custom, the Confederation began to take open stands on pressing electoral questions. In June 1945, the Confederal Bureau came out in favor of a position similar to that of the PCF's on the election of a new Constituent Assembly to replace the Consultative Assembly.[50] Later, when de Gaulle proposed a referendum on the Constituent Assembly question, plus elections to the new Assembly, the Confederal Committee voted to support the same positions as the PCF.[51]

On occasion the CGT embarked upon political initiatives which seemed independent of the PCF positions. Usually what was really happening was that the CGT was taking actions which the PCF favored but which it could not itself openly take. The CGT was acting as a complement to the PCF. In the controversy of summer 1945 about the Constituent Assembly and how it was to be elected, the CGT, on its own, called for an assembly of the left wing of the Resistance coalition to work out a unified position. Delegates from the PCF, SFIO, Radicals and the League for Human Rights were invited to the CGT headquarters to discuss the issues. Few missed noticing that this CGT-promoted *Délégation des Gauches* was an embryonic United Front alliance.[52] After an initial meeting which voted in favor of

45. Benoît Frachon, in *L'Humanité*, April 9, 1946.

46. Benoît Frachon, in *Libération*, August 8, 1945.

47. *Le Monde*, 25, 28 May 1945.

48. *Combat*, 29 November 1945; *Le Monde*, 20 March 1945.

49. Lefranc, *1944–1968*, p. 23; *Le Monde*, 30 March 1945.

50. *Le Monde*, 15 June 1945; *L'année politique 1944–1945*, p. 250.

51. *Le Peuple*, 8 July 1945; *L'année politique 1944–1945*, pp. 288–289, 355–356.

52. In August the CGT Administrative Committee (CA) called for a meeting of "progressive forces" (PCF, SFIO, Radicals) to discuss strategy (*Libération*, 8 August 1945). In October it called for a "Rassemblement des Gauches" (PCF, SFIO, Radicals, *Ligue des droits de l'homme* plus trade unions) (*Le Monde*, 28–29 October 1945). In December 1945 such a meeting occurred to rejuvenate the CNR program, with little real success (*L'Humanité*, 12 December 1945). See also *L'année politique 1944–1945*, p. 287; Graham, pp. 105–108.

remonstrating with General de Gaulle about his proposed electoral procedures (unsuccessfully), the *Délégation* met again to urge the creation of
an actual Popular Front electoral alliance (which the Socialists refused to
accept).[53]

The Limits of Governmental Communism: to May 1947

By 1946 the PCF's United Front scenario was beginning to run into trouble. The complex interrelationships between the party's goals on the
political and trade-union levels left significant tactical openings for the party's opponents. The PCF wanted to use its resources to promote reforms. It
hoped that this in turn would create a political situation which would real-
locate resources to the Left, and to itself within the Left, in a cumulative
way. On the other hand, all of the PCF's Resistance partners (and most
especially those farthest to the Right) had a strong interest in persuading
the PCF to discipline the working class, through the CGT, in exchange for
as little as possible of the change which the PCF wanted. For the non-
Communist Left it was a question of promoting a limited amount of
reform in France without benefiting the PCF. For the Center and Center-
Right it was a question simply of using the PCF to rebuild French
capitalism in exchange for nothing at all. The PCF's position was most
delicate, then. It had to be moderate enough politically not to cut itself off
from its allies, particularly those closest to it with whom the party hoped to
construct a new Popular Front. On the other hand, if the party were too
moderate it would become a prisoner of its governmental partners, to be
used for purposes very different from its own. Mass pressure from outside,
from the CGT in particular, was the PCF's main weapon to "soften up" its
allies and protect its political integrity. Again, however, too much pressure
from outside might break up the fragile Resistance coalition. And any too-
overt politicization of the CGT would cause trouble for the PCF on the
trade-union front. Finally, whatever went on on the level of high politics,
Communist unionists had to protect the living standards of the CGT rank
and file.

The PCF: Popular Front or Crisis?

By 1946 Resistance euphoria had largely disappeared. General de
Gaulle's departure in January was seen by the PCF as a victory, but it raised
new problems as well. The General had been an important pivot in post-
Liberation politics. Behind him the MRP, and to a lesser extent the SFIO,
had been able to hide to avoid the difficult issue of collaboration with the
Communists. With de Gaulle gone the issue could no longer be avoided.
The MRP would clearly find collaboration with the PCF impossible sooner

53. *L'année politique 1944-1945*, pp. 299, 467.

or later, sooner if the rapid flocking of the more opportunistic Gaullists into the Christian Democrat fold was any indication. The Socialist Party, upon which all of the PCF's United Front hopes really fell, was deeply divided about how to deal with the Communists and how far to the Left to move politically, squeezed in the middle of pressure from its Left and Right. It could choose to govern in a Popular Front with the PCF, at the risk of entrapment in the PCF's strategy of ever greater change and ever larger PCF power. Or it could form a coalition with the MRP in an anti-Communist Third Force alliance, at the risk of burying forever its own reformist credentials and the profound popular desire for change created by the Resistance.

By this point the situation had been further complicated by the beginnings of the Cold War.[54] The PCF's domestic United Frontism was designed, as usual, to be congruent with Soviet diplomatic goals. The Russian strategy after Liberation had been to perpetuate cooperation between the erstwhile wartime allies into the postwar period. The Yalta agreements were not strong enough, however, to withstand the massive political changes which the post-war period brought, especially in Eastern Europe. The United States was growing exceedingly wary of what it perceived to be Soviet expansionism and its response was to promote the fortification, literally and ideologically, of those parts of Europe which might thereby be threatened. Because of this, additional weight was placed on the PCF's United Frontism. Preventing France from falling into an emerging bloc of U.S.-oriented nations, as well as withholding French cooperation from American schemes in the rest of Western Europe (in particular in those zones of Germany occupied by the Western powers), became vital PCF objectives. Without French participation, American plans might well be frustrated. Thus the stakes involved in French Communist politics grew exponentially with the Cold War.

In this context, the PCF had no choice but to hold to the course which it had set from the war's end. It continued to use its governmental position to promote further reform, and not without success. In the spring of 1946 the social security system was broadened and democratized, largely because of the activities of the PCF Minister Ambroise Croizat (an ex-CGTer). Croizat also vastly extended the powers of the *comités d'entreprise* and those of the *délégués du personnel*.[55] Maurice Thorez himself, as Minister of State, promoted a drastic recasting of the law regarding certain categories of peasants (the *statuts* governing *fermage* and *métayage*—renting and share-cropping). And Thorez was instrumental in legislating an entirely new system of regulations for civil-service careers. New nationalizations also occurred, largely because of Communist pressure. In the spring of

54. Elgey, *Illusions*, p. 118 speaks of secret government talks with the U.S. behind the back of PCF ministers.

55. PCF, *Histoire du PCF*, p. 482; *L'année politique 1946*, pp. 81–82.

1946 gas and electricity were finally nationalized, with PCF Minister Marcel Paul playing a leading role.[56] Paul, another ex-CGTer known for his ferocious devotion to the PCF, made certain that the workers and unions within gas and electricity—particularly the CGT—acquired large new prerogatives and powers. Insurance was nationalized, as were those coal mines which remained in private ownership.[57] In coal, August Lecoeur, Communist Under-Secretary to Marcel Paul (and another ex-CGTer) succeeded remarkably well in stacking the Board of Directors of the northern coal mines to create a PCF majority (virtually guaranteeing PCF control over the resources of the Board). Charles Tillon (former head of the *Francs-Tireurs Populaires*, the PCF's Resistance military wing) used his power as Minister of Armaments to do similar things in nationalized sectors of France's arms industry, particularly aviation.

Despite these undoubted successes, the political situation grew more and more ominous. The PCF-SFIO-MRP tripartite governing alliance proved tenacious. The PCF could not move the Socialists towards a Popular Front, no matter what it did.[58] The SFIO was willing to side with the PCF in the first 1946 Constitutional campaign (the proposed Constitution called for a strong Assembly regime) but the Constitution was rejected by the electorate.[59] A new Constituent Assembly then had to be elected, and in this campaign the SFIO studiously avoided collaboration with the PCF. A new tripartite government emerged from this, headed by Georges Bidault, the MRP leader.[60] No progress was made towards Popular Front-type arrangements for the fall 1946 elections and constitutional referenda either. And in the interim the PCF-SFIO *Comité d'Entente* ceased to exist.

The SFIO's reluctance to contemplate a new Popular Front, and the durability of *tripartisme* were tempered with some more promising signs, however. General de Gaulle's departure from the scene was brief. He returned in 1946 with his famous *discours de Bayeux* which laid the foundations for a new Gaullist movement in opposition to the *régime des partis* of the emerging Fourth Republic (the Gaullist *Rassemblement du Peuple Français* was formed officially in 1947). This gave the PCF something it had theretofore lacked, a tangible right-wing foil. With a threat from the Right, the PCF's pressure for Left union might meet with more success. And at the SFIO 1946 Congress the Left overthrew the leadership, as a result of which the party apparatus fell into the hands of a group of Leftish "Young Turks," led by Guy Mollet, who professed an interest in united action with the PCF.

Political crisis fell upon the new Fourth Republic as soon as it was set up,

56. *L'année politique 1946*, p. 63; Graham, p. 148.
57. *L'année politique 1946*, pp. 81–83, 92.
58. Ibid., pp. 8–9; Graham, p. 148.
59. Graham, pp. 156–157.
60. *L'année politique 1946*, p. 123.

however. By the November 1946 electoral period the MRP had clearly decided to force the Socialists' hands by pushing for an end to *tripartisme* and for a Socialist-Christian Democrat alliance. The SFIO was thereby placed in a vise. The PCF responded by pulling out all the stops to promote a Popular Front. The relative success of the PCF at the November elections (it was again the largest party in France in terms of votes) led it to propose that Maurice Thorez be designated Prime Minister.[61] At the same time it proposed a common Left governmental program.[62] And it was at this point that Maurice Thorez gave his now-famous interview to the *London Times* positing the possibility of a peaceful, national "French road to socialism."[63] The new National Assembly refused to elect Thorez, but the SFIO officially supported his candidacy.[64] However, by this point nothing was resolvable. The MRP refused to consider the PCF's demand for major ministerial posts. But Guy Mollet publicly pledged that the SFIO would not take part in any anti-Communist governing coalition.[65] *Tripartisme* was dead, but nothing existed to replace it. The only way out, for the moment, was the constitution of an all-Socialist government under Léon Blum, marking the first time that the PCF had been out of power since 1944. But it was only a matter of a few weeks before the PCF was back in power, this time as part of an all-party National Government (early 1947) headed by a Socialist, Paul Ramadier.

The CGT: Contradictions in the United Front Political Economy

By early 1947 rumor had it that dissension existed in the PCF *Bureau Politique* about the wisdom of continuing United Frontism. Thorez and Jacques Duclos were allegedly the principal figures for going ahead on the United Front path. André Marty and Benoît Frachon were the doubters.[66] André Marty was a perennial BP dissenter with a long history of sectarianism, willing to advocate extreme militancy even at the risk of isolating the PCF.[67] Benoît Frachon, in contrast, was no sectarian. He was the PCF's leading trade unionist, the architect of the party's success in the CGT and a man with a deep sense of the climate prevailing among rank-and-file workers. And he sensed coming trouble on the labor front.

By 1946 it had become clear that the living standards of French workers were not rising in a manner commensurate with the effort workers were making in the battle for production.[68] The new *dirigiste* political economy

61. Graham, p. 227.
62. Ibid., pp. 227, 234–236; *L'Humanité*, 28 November 1946.
63. *Times* (London), 18 November 1946; Graham, p. 234.
64. *L'année politique 1946*, p. 281.
65. PCF, *Histoire du PCF*, p. 489.
66. Fauvet, vol. II, p. 180.
67. See André Marty, *L'affaire Marty* (1955).
68. Guglielmi and Perrot, p. 32.

was not enough to achieve reconstruction with justice. The CGT's position that labor discipline was essential to promote social change became progressively harder to maintain in the shorter run when workers' situations deteriorated. It was far easier for workers to understand that they were being "had." As for who was "having" them, there was a choice of conclusions. Either the PCF and CGT leaderships were directly, or they, in turn, were being had by the bosses. Neither conclusion boded well for the CGT.

The CGT leadership faced a dilemma. For its own reasons and because of the PCF's line, it wanted to continue the battle for production. However, in circumstances of declining working-class living standards, a climate of hostility to labor discipline was almost certain to develop at the rank-and-file level. Since the CGT, even controlled by the PCF, suffered from the classic weaknesses of French unionism—underorganization, weak finances, and undermanning at all levels—it would have been hard put either to decree labor discipline from the top or to prevent the emergence of sudden movements from below which might overwhelm both militants and leadership.[69] The development of distance between the goals of the CGT's leadership and the desires of its rank and file also created openings for minority attempts to ignite rank-and-file unhappiness from below. And there existed no lack of trade-union *gauchistes* (the PCF's term) eager to exploit such openings.[70]

Such dangers were not abstract. In January 1946 a wildcat strike exploded in the Paris printing industry, fomented by anarchists within a union (the *Fédération du Livre*) where the PCF was weak.[71] The CGT leadership publicly opposed the strike, pointing out that the press workers were already well paid and that their movement threatened the government's economic policies. The Federation leadership then tried to settle things by imposing Confederal arbitration on the strikers, only to be denounced for meddling. In response the PCF Minister of Labor, Ambroise Croizat, accused the strikers on the radio of having worked harder for collaborationist newspapers than they had since Liberation. This initiative, which was not appreciated by the strikers, was then followed by a denunciation of the strike leaders as Trotskyists by the CGT Confederal Bureau.[72] The wildcat only lasted six days (during which the PCF newspapers *L'Humanité* and *Ce Soir* broke the strike), but it marked a turning point. Then in the summer of 1946 the post-office workers exploded. When rank-and-file discontent reached alarming proportions, the CGT postal-workers union called a

69. Most analysts stress this point and it is obvious from even a cursory overview of French labor history.

70. In 1946 the *Confédération Nationale du Travail*, a revolutionary syndicalist split-off of the CGT led by Pierre Monatte, was formed. There was also a renaissance of French Trotskyism in these years.

71. Lefranc, *1944–1968*, p. 31; Fauvet, vol. II, p. 177; *L'année politique 1946*, pp. 22–23.

72. Michel Branciard, *Société française et luttes de classe* (1967, 1978), vol. 2, p. 147.

short "warning" strike to clear the air. The safety valve tactic did not work, however. The warning action triggered an extended wildcat in several different cities, in part because of the actions of Trotskyist groups.[73] The movement became a full-fledged rebellion against the official CGT when wildcat leaders set up a National Strike Committee which cut off the Federation leadership from the rebellious rank and file.[74] The then Minister of Finances, Robert Schumann (an MRP leader with quick reflexes for embarrassing the PCF), proceeded at this point to recognize the rebel strike committee to settle the strike.[75] Other movements then occurred among railroad workers and civil servants. PCF accusations about the sordid work of *gréviculteurs* did little to help.[76] Tension between PCF and anti-PCF elements in many unions reached a flash point.[77]

The CGT was determined to continue its battle for production.[78] Faced with a deteriorating rank-and-file climate, however, it had no choice but to begin pressing governments much more vigorously for concessions. In spring 1946, then, the CGT initiated a massive campaign for wage increases.[79] First came a "Week of National Action for a General Wage Raise" in May, consisting mainly of mass demonstrations.[80] By June the campaign had become generalized agitation for a twenty-five percent raise, price controls, limitations on profits, and repression of black market activities.[81] By this point, the campaign had acquired a number of purposes, among them calming rank-and-file unrest, prying economic concessions from the PCF's reluctant allies in the government, and promoting PCF electoral chances (the PCF adopted the CGT's demands as part of its electoral platform).[82] In the short run, it met with success. After the election the PCF made concession to the CGT's demands a condition for its participation in a new tripartite government.[83] All of this finally led to a national wage conference in Paris which proposed substantial raises.[84]

The gains won at this so-called *Palais Royal* conference quickly disappeared in inflation. The CGT was then obliged to become even more vocal, beginning to demand an end to government wage control and a return to direct collective bargaining. It achieved a minor success in early 1947, when

73. Gérard Dehove, "Le mouvement ouvrier et la politique syndicale," in *La France Économique de 1939 à 1946*, p. 1582.

74. Lefranc, *1944–1968*, p. 34; Branciard, pp. 147–148; *L'année politique 1946*, p. 218.

75. *L'Humanité*, 13 August 1946; Stolvitzer, pp. 63–65.

76. Benoît Frachon in *L'Humanité*, 7 August 1946; also *Au rythme des jours*, vol. I, p. 158.

77. Branciard, p. 148; *L'année politique 1946*, p. 232.

78. Guglielmi and Perrot, p. 60.

79. This campaign itself may have had electoralist goals, in addition to its demands.

80. *L'Humanité*, 25 May 1946.

81. *Le Monde*, 1 June 1946.

82. Rieber, p. 294.

83. *L'année politique 1946*, p. 143.

84. Ibid., pp. 154–155; PCF, *Histoire du PCF*, p. 478.

the government consented to allow collective bargaining over working conditions, but wages were still to be determined administratively. In response the CGT began to demand the institution of a minimum standard of living, tying wages automatically to the cost of living,[85] (the beginning of a long CGT campaign for escalator clauses which would keep wages up with inflation levels). Still, workers faced blocked wages and rising prices. The Blum government tried a brief and spectacular program of price controls, which had momentary effects but quickly failed.[86] By late January 1947, Benoît Frachon was lecturing the government publicly and ominously about the possibility of strikes.

By springtime 1947 the CGT was caught in a difficult bind. CGT leaders could measure the depth of rank-and-file discontent and were forced to heighten pressure on the government for concessions which amounted to a basic change in the government's economic priorities (the *minimum vital*, the end of political wage setting, a return to collective bargaining). The CGT argued that only by such a change could workers be persuaded to continue the battle for production. To support such arguments, however, the CGT had to mobilize its rank and file. It intended this mobilization to fall far short of actual strike action. However, if the government did not move in the right directions, the effects of CGT mobilization, plus deepening rank-and-file dissatisfaction, could well lead to strike movements which the CGT could not control. A moment of truth was approaching.

The CGT: Resistance to Communist Power

The immediate postwar period revealed two major problems in the relationship between the PCF and CGT. The first has just been examined, the difficulties created for the CGT as a trade union caused by its subordination to PCF political goals. Using the CGT as a direct transmission belt for Communist politics, even if this policy dictated trade-union moderation, was bound to lead the CGT into a crisis with its rank and file. The second problem was simpler to understand. PCF efforts to "take over" control of the CGT created great resentment among non-Communist unionists.[87] Inevitably, the two problems intersected. The "politicization" of the CGT provided union opponents of the PCF with the arguments which they needed to organize resistance to PCF takeover.

Social democracy was a traditional ideology in sectors of the CGT, particularly in white-collar unions (civil servants, public-sector workers) which remained most free of PCF influence after the postwar shift in power. But even in many of the unions which the PCF had been able to

85. *L'année politique 1946*, p. 168; *Le Monde*, 26 June 1946; *L'année politique 1946*, pp. 179–189; PCF, *Histoire du PCF*, p. 478.

86. *Le Monde*, 14 September 1946; *Combat*, 19 September 1946.

87. Guglielmi and Perrot, p. 71.

take over outright, strong pockets of Socialist support persisted. While it was quite unlikely by 1946 that anti-Communist factions could regain control in the federations and departmental unions which the PCF had already conquered, other possibilities for anti-Communist action existed. Unions which the PCF did not control could secede from the CGT, for example. Or anti-Communist groups in PCF-controlled unions could form factions for "dual union" activities. Both things occurred.

The development of anti-Communist resistance within the CGT coincided directly with Communist political manipulation of the CGT. Trouble began with the March 1945 decision to encourage CGT members to stand in municipal elections. The CGT's zealous promotion of the CNR program, as well as its role in energizing the *Délégation des Gauches* in later 1945 increased resentment. The CGT's decision to replicate the PCF's stands on constitutional questions in the fall of 1945 deepened dissent.[88] In December 1945 more Communist/non-Communist fighting occurred over a Confederal decision about granting autonomy to the CGT's former North African union affiliates.[89] And throughout 1946 repeated Confederal position-taking on various constitutional issues made the rifts more profound.

Anti-Communist forces in the CGT coalesced formally in late 1945 around a journal called *Résistance Ouvrière*, which soon changed its name to *Force Ouvrière*. *Force Ouvrière* (FO) rapidly became an organization which moved to challenge to PCF leadership at the 1946 Confederal Congress. Here Benoît Frachon defended the CGT's acts vigorously, asserting that they had provided key support for the "alliance of democratic forces" needed to change France and that the CGT had a solemn duty to "go to the defense of menaced Republican liberties."[90] *Force Ouvrière* countered with an appeal to the Amiens Charter which had firmly established CGT independence of political parties, claiming that the CGT's post-Liberation politics amounted to a betrayal of CGT traditions. Frachon's response was quick and to the point. French unions had never been strictly apolitical. Workers had class interests which had political implications. What FO claimed to be a tradition was a myth. What neither FO nor Benoît Frachon broached openly, however, was that *Force Ouvrière*'s objection was not to *any* "politicization" of the CGT, since the CGT had always been an important part of the French Left, but to "politicization" on the side of the PCF.

Important constitutional issues exacerbated conflict at the 1946 Congress. The Frachon-PCF majority proposed to change the ways in which delegates would be elected to future Congresses. The old system allowed

88. *Le Monde*, 6 April 1946.
89. *New York Herald Tribune*, international edition, 26 March 1946.
90. CGT, *Congrès national de la CGT 1946*, *L'Humanité*, 9 April 1946; *L'année politique 1946*, p. 116.

each federation and departmental union, large or small, a similar number of delegates, a procedure which gave smaller unions voting power at Congresses which far outweighed their real membership strength. The new proposal advocated allotting Congress delegates to unions proportionally to the size of their memberships. Since the PCF controlled almost all of the large CGT federations and departmental unions, the proposed amendment, once enacted, would virtually guarantee the PCF's control over the Congress, and hence over the CGT executive bodies (the *Commission Administrative*, the Confederal Committee and the Confederal Bureau). *Force Ouvrière* resisted the change, tooth and nail, but to no avail. From this point it was clear to the FO leaders that challenging the PCF influence within the CGT would be nearly impossible. Although the PCF did not force its advantage in elections to the Confederal executive bodies at the Congress (a substantial minority of non-Communists were elected both to the Administrative Committee and the Confederal Bureau), it was amply clear that non-Communist representation at the CGT's highest levels persisted at Communist sufferance, primarily to serve Communist aims.[91]

The controversy was carried on amid misunderstanding. As we have seen, the PCF's politicization of the CGT during this period was hardly sectarian, if inept from the point of view of the CGT rank and file. The real issue was simply the PCF's rapid takeover of the CGT unions, and not the politics which the CGT followed. Indeed, it is doubtful whether FO would have behaved much differently, had it been in control of the CGT during this period, than had the new PCF leadership. Communist control in itself was the divisive question, and not what the Communists had done with control. The Cold War was beginning, however, and with it deepening divisions between the Communist and non-Communist portions of the French Left, both in politics and in union life. And American pressure was being applied not only to non-Communist political parties, but also to non-Communists in the labor movement. New divisions in the CGT, and perhaps a new period of "dual unionism,"were clearly written in the cards.

Conclusion: the Contradictions Come Together

The Renault works at Boulogne-Billancourt was the symbol of industrial France. France's largest factory (with more than 30,000 workers), it was the nerve center of the French automobile industry and the pilot plant in the vast Parisian manufacturing complex. Historically, whatever happened between workers and employers at Billancourt spread very quickly thereafter to other Paris metal-working firms and often spread throughout the entire country. Renault Billancourt was also a CGT stronghold (fifty percent of its workers were CGT members), and the Renault CGT was strongly Com-

91. CGT, *Congrès national, 1946*, p. 62; *L'année politique 1946*, pp. 116–117.

munist.[92] For these reasons what happened at Billancourt in the spring of 1947 was critical both for the PCF and for the political economy of postwar France.

Since Louis Renault had been a notorious collaborator, Renault had been nationalized in 1945. For two years thereafter the CGT had stopped at nothing to make the Renault nationalization a success, a shining symbol of United Front reformism.[93] According to an important PCF spokesman, writing at the time, "nationalizations . . . involve a profound change in the economic and social structure of the country." The PCF and CGT had to fight "to enlarge their scope, to ensure that they are real, and to prevent them being sabotaged."[94] Carrying on this fight at Renault, the CGT had promoted the battle for production and de-emphasized wage demands more vigorously there than anywhere else in the country. By early 1947 Renault, along with the rest of the automobile sector, had begun to experience the working-class dissatisfaction which followed from such politics.

Isolated work-stoppages began at Billancourt in January of 1947, mainly around localized demands for bonuses (which was one way for firms to circumvent the general wage blockage).[95] Renault workers saw their pay stagnating, even in comparison to wages in many of the smaller sub-contracting shops in and around Billancourt. In February a wildcat occurred in the neighboring Citroën factory in Paris, ending in a twenty-five percent raise, an event which whetted Renault appetites. Generalizing discontent, plus the obvious determination of the CGT at Renault to block any push for major wage revisions, provided ideal openings for the organization of anti-CGT *gauchiste* caucuses in the plant. By early spring several such caucuses existed, one being the *Union Communiste*, organized in the Collas sector of the plant, which openly sought to promote wildcat action against the wishes of the CGT.

The situation at Billancourt began to heat up on April 23, 1947, when an assembly of workers from Departments 6 and 18 called a strike for April 25. On that day both departments went out, but CGT hostility to the action kept it isolated. The *Union Communiste* then set up a wildcat strike committee to make connections with workers in the rest of the plant (more often than not, through other *gauchiste* caucuses).[96] On Monday April 28 the dam burst. Strikes broke out all over the factory and by the end of the

92. Philippe Fallachon, "Les grèves de la Régie Renault en 1947," in *Le Mouvement Social*, no. 81 (October–December 1972), pp. 113–114.

93. André Tiano and Michel Rocard, *L'expérience française du syndicalisme ouvrier* (1956), p. 186; Branciard, p. 148.

94. Fallachon, p. 113.

95. Stolvitzer, part III; Fallachon, p. 120.

96. Tiano and Rocard, p. 148; Fallachon, p. 122.

day 12,000 workers were out. The CGT desperately tried to beat the movement down. Strike leaders were called variously, "Gaullist-Trotskyite-Anarchists"[97] and "Hitlero-Trotskyite *provocateurs* in the pay of de Gaulle" (the words of Eugène Hénaff, Resistance hero and CGT leader at Renault).[98]

Nonetheless with half of the factory out on strike, the CGT had to trim its sails a bit and resort to the safety valve approach. To drown the wildcat in a larger, officially called, and limited action, the Renault CGT called a one-hour strike of its own for April 29, which was to be followed by mass meetings to air grievances. This tactic exploded in the CGT's face, however, when the CGT call triggered a plant-wide movement which escaped the CGT's control. From 12,000, the number of Renault workers on strike shot to 30,000, the totality of the Billancourt work force.[99] In response to this, the CGT was forced to shift positions yet again, coming out in favor of the strike, while at the same time desperately trying to promote negotiations with the Renault management which would limit the strike and its costs. Pierre Lefaucheux, the Renault President, proved willing to accept some of the CGT's demands. Unfortunately, when the CGT brought the management's concessions to the strikers, the strikers wanted much, much more.[100]

By May 2, the day when the strikers voted down the CGT's attempt at settlement, the Renault strike had become a political issue of immense importance. The unwillingness of the Renault management (prompted from behind the scenes by the Ministry of Labor) to grant large enough concessions to bring the workers back finally forced the CGT to face the painful choice to which the battle of production strategy had ultimately led. Under the watchful eye of the entire French working class, the Confederal leadership had either to disavow its membership at Renault or to challenge the government's economic policies. At this point, this was no choice at all. To have continued to oppose the Renault strikers would have meant risking PCF control over the CGT. The CGT therefore moved behind the strikers' demands.

The CGT's dramatic shift of position had enormous implications for the PCF. The party had no choice but to try and force deep changes in economic policy on the government. The PCF moved to support substantial wage increases at Renault, and this amounted to a renunciation of the government's general economic strategy. The crisis could not have happened at a worse moment, since the developing Cold War had already stretched relationships between the PCF and the other major governmental parties to the

97. Elgey, *Illusions*, p. 280.
98. *Une Semaine dans le Monde*, 3 May 1947.
99. *L'année politique 1947*, p. 66.
100. Tiano and Rocard, p. 137; Lefranc, *1944–1968*, p. 49.

breaking point. When the Cabinet met on economic policy it split between Communists and non-Communists, with the non-Communist majority favoring the continuation of the government's wage policies. Ramadier, the Prime Minister, then asked the National Assembly for a vote of confidence on the government's wage/price policies, putting the PCF in Parliament up against the wall. The party in government and Parliament had to choose between disavowing the Renault strikers and the CGT or voting against the government. Communist Ministers abstained on the vote and also refused to resign. They were then summarily removed from the government by the Prime Minister.[101]

In all of the complexity of the postwar situation, the PCF's political calculations came down to one specific question. When was PCF moderation in the pursuit of United Frontism likely to lead to the progress of the Left and when was it likely to play into the hands of anti-Communist forces? By May 1947 several problems had already strained the PCF's ties with its allies. On colonial and foreign policy the party had been courting disaster for some time. Socialists and Christian Democrats slid very easily into a reassertion of French imperialism. The horrible massacre of Algerians at Liberation had been just the beginning. Other rebels in North Africa were treated summarily, an atrocious bloodbath had been carried out in Madagascar and the long war in Indochina had begun, all while Communist Ministers sat in French governments.[102] And French foreign policy (in particular with regard to Germany) had begun to align itself with the Americans. However, the party stuck it out in various governments, using a number of tactics to save face in doing so.

That the PCF's actual departure from government came not on issues of colonial and foreign policy, but on wage and price questions was no accident. The situation following the Renault wildcat admitted of no temporization. The party's control over the CGT and its credibility to French workers was at stake. It could either give in to its governmental partners and risk undermining its strength in organized labor or it could side with the strikers and risk leaving the government. If a line was to be drawn beyond which the PCF would not go in its United Frontist moderation, it had to be drawn here. Beyond all of the compromises and maneuvers of the postwar years, the PCF knew it would either be "the party of the working class" or nothing at all.

After May 1947 the party did not abandon postwar United Frontism, at

101. Elgey, *Illusions*, pp. 277–288. It is clear that Ramadier and his non-Communist allies in the government had been looking for a pretext of this sort to get rid of PCF ministers. The Cold War was now in full force and all manner of fantasies about the intentions of the PCF were circulating. Jules Moch, Minister of the Interior, had gone so far as to prepare a response to a May Day PCF putsch which he thought was in the offing—although a more complete misunderstanding of the PCF's actual intentions could hardly have been imagined.

102. Graham, pp. 253, 257; *L'année politique 1947*, pp. 40, 48.

least for a while. On May 8 Maurice Thorez told the *New York Herald Tribune* that "we intend to work with the government for all measures in favor of the working class, although we are momentarily outside the government. And be sure to note that I say 'momentarily.' "[103] The PCF was out of the government, but little had really changed, in its eyes, in the French situation. A United Front outcome was still possible, although it now became necessary to pressure from outside government to make it happen.

What the PCF decided to do in the aftermath of its eviction from the government was to threaten economic disruption, primarily by using the CGT to promote working-class action, to force the government to change its policies and, hopefully, to allow the PCF to move back into the Cabinet. The party's plan was to let off the brake from working-class discontent, but only in a gradual way.[104] There was to be a slow escalation of CGT-promoted direct action which would progressively raise the economic costs to the government of excluding the PCF.[105] The primary focus of this new tactic was the SFIO. The party wanted to place the Socialists in a situation where they would have to choose between governing with the organized working class on its side—in a Popular Front with the PCF—or governing against the working class in alliance with the Right.[106] The PCF believed, and in normal circumstances its belief would have been accurate, that the SFIO, a fellow "Marxist Party," would be signing its political death warrant by governing with the Right.

What was strange about the moment was that circumstances *were* no longer normal, and everyone seemed to know this *except* the PCF. The Cold War was approaching a point of no return. Communists had been forced out of governments in Italy and Belgium during the same brief period, despite very great differences in domestic politics in both countries, and between both countries and France. That Ramadier had been under intense American pressure to fire the PCF ministers was a well-known fact. Western European nations were rapidly lining up behind American diplomatic strategies. The PCF chose to interpret all of these facts by denying that they were significant, perhaps because it had no other strategy to deploy except United Frontism. How long such an ostrich-like posture could be maintained was the question.

103. *Le Monde*, 9 May 1947.
104. Reference to all of the many strikes and other actions would be superfluous here. The reader need only consult *Le Monde* for the period to see what was happening. The railroad strike was rather typical and will perhaps bear more careful examination (see Cheminots, p. 213, and *Le Monde*, 8, 9 and 12 June 1947). The strike began as a rank-and-file protest against the food-supply problem, then was picked up and promoted by local unions where the PCF was particularly strong (in the Paris Red Belt primarily) and turned into a wage movement leading to a large public demonstration in Paris.
105. Frachon, vol. I, pp. 100–101, 114–115, 120–122.
106. Fauvet, vol. II, p. 98; André Barjonet, *La CGT* (1968), p. 49; Rieber, p. 351 plus the standard histories of the Fourth Republic (Julliard, Fauvet, Williams, etc.).

Chapter 3

THE COLD WAR YEARS: THE MASS ORGANIZATION AS TRANSMISSION BELT

The PCF's understanding of its situation after the eviction of Communist Ministers from government in May 1947 was wrong. The party believed that the Socialists within the government would be sensitive to a progressive escalation of working-class pressure and move towards a new United Front. This might have happened had France existed in isolation. But no Western European nation existed in isolation in the crucial months which announced the Cold War! The French government sought American economic aid (surely in part to resist PCF pressure) and the Marshall Plan was the result. The PCF was initially ambivalent about the Marshall Plan—Maurice Thorez announced that American aid would be acceptable if it came without strings. But by the autumn of 1947 the party understood that the Marshall Plan was meant as an economic life raft to save a non-Communist French government from drowning.

The Cold War and Marshall aid drastically restructured French politics. The PCF had theorized that there could exist only two alternatives in postwar France, rule by the Left in a new Popular Front, or rule by the Right and a return to the late 1930s. In 1947 a "third way" emerged. Former governmental partners of the PCF—the SFIO and MRP—began to present themselves as a "Third Force," defenders of the "democracy of the Free World" from "totalitarian Communism" to their Left and Gaullism to their Right. The new international situation, plus General de Gaulle's RPF, gave Socialists and Christian Democrats what they needed to legitimate their refusal to collaborate with the PCF. However contradictory this posture was to prove in the longer run, in the crisis of 1947 it suited the Third Force parties admirably. More important, it prompted them to move France squarely into the bloc of anti-Communist Western European nations being formed by the United States.

At this point the Russians stepped in. In October, at a secret meeting in Poland called to establish the Cominform, the PCF was called on the carpet for its "opportunist" strategy. Critics of the PCF (ironically, Milovan Djilas, the Yugoslav leader and later the strong critic of rule by the Communist "new class," was the most vocal) contended that the PCF had pursued United Frontism for too long and had, as a result, helped French capitalism and a French pro-American foreign policy to establish themselves. The PCF's strategy had led to an impasse: the Third Force parties had become enemies, their main goal being to resist Communism and promote American interests. Thus, not without considerable humiliation at the hands of the representatives of *partis frères*, the PCF was ordered to seek new approaches.[1] The October 1947 meeting gave the first indications of what these approaches were to be. In its self-criticism, the PCF Central Committee recognized its tardiness in perceiving the deterioration of the postwar situation and its underestimation of American influence.[2] Furthermore, it confessed that it had expected to win too much from its former Resistance partners by alliances at the top.[3] From this point on, the PCF's goal was open struggle against the "right-wing Socialists" who were fronting for the "men of the trusts" and for the "American imperialists." And the focus of this struggle was to be the "Marshallization" of France, the acceptance of which by the "right-wing Social Democrats" would involve the abandonment of French independence, increasing dependency on the Germans (the Americans were pushing for the consolidation of the western zones of Germany into a political and economic unit, with pressure for German rearmament clearly in the offing) and a deliberate policy of liquidating principal French industries.[4] In short, the Third Force parties were trying to mislead French workers ideologically and betray them economically.[5]

Since United Frontism was henceforth excluded (both by the Cominform and by the French domestic situation), the PCF had no choice, given its isolation, but to use mass mobilization as its major instrument of struggle. The Cominform's advice to the PCF had been to stop political maneuvering at the top and to rely on the masses. By acting vigorously, the party felt that it might have some chance to slow down, or halt, the development of the Cold War, perhaps by holding France out of the American camp. Success at this would be a decisive victory for the Cominform and for Soviet

1. Fauvet, vol. II, p. 198; *Le Monde*, 23 October 1947; *L'année politique 1947*, p. 192. See also Lilly Marcou, *Le Kominform* (1977), ch. 2.

2. *L'année politique 1947*, p. 215.

3. Maurice Thorez, in a self-criticism to the PCF Central Committee, cited in *Le Monde*, 30 October 1947.

4. This analysis is that of Jdanov, as elaborated by Benoît Frachon in *L'Humanité*, 12 October 1947, "Du Plan Monnet au Plan Marshall."

5. Frachon in *L'Humanité*, 4 November 1947.

foreign policy. Even if this proved impossible, however, relying on the masses might consolidate a degree of popular opposition to the policies of the Cold War and to the raging anti-Communism which justified them. Relying on the masses meant deploying Communist mass organizations and the PCF's most important mass organization was, of course, the *Confédération Générale du Travail*. The drastic shift in PCF strategy in the autumn of 1947 meant, then, an important new step in the relationship between the PCF and CGT.

The CGT to the Front Lines

Change Through Industrial Conflict?

Isolation rendered the PCF powerless to effect events in France through formal political processes. The party's organizational power within the French working class did give the PCF leverage to pressure for change from outside, however. In the new situation, then, the CGT was to gain a new role. In the fall of 1947 it became clear that the core of PCF action against the Cold War, at least initially, would be industrial. If the new Third Force coalition was vulnerable anywhere, it was vulnerable economically. France's dramatic economic situation meant the government's margin of maneuver was very narrow, despite the promise of Marshall aid. And it had laid itself open to an explosion of working-class anger by its inability to maintain a stable economy, the price of which was being paid primarily by French workers. Against the background of immediate postwar austerity (of which, as we have seen, the PCF and CGT had been central instigators) rampant inflation was eating away at working-class living standards. An eleven percent wage raise obtained in August 1947 by negotiations between the CGT and the *Conseil National du Patronat Français* was obliterated in a few weeks by rising prices.[6] The PCF could hope, then, that French workers would support decisive industrial action.

The logic of unleashing the CGT rank and file at this moment was compelling. The Marshall Plan was just taking shape and a demonstration of PCF industrial strength and governmental weakness might diminish the American Congress' eagerness to vote the funds needed.[7] Severe industrial conflict might also cause a governmental crisis in France. And even if neither of these things occurred, the government might be forced to resort to repression to deal with a large strike movement—provided the PCF's assessment of the extent of rank-and-file anger proved correct—and such a response might consolidate PCF hegemony over key segments of the working class. And, finally, a strike wave would put the PCF's opponents in the

6. *L'année politique 1947* is good reading on the severity of the economic situation; see also Guglielmi and Perrot, pp. 71 ff.

7. This was Jules Moch's hypothesis concerning the November strikes, and it makes much sense in the light of Jdanov's speech to the October Cominform meeting (see Lefranc, *1944-1968*, p. 64).

CGT, the *Force Ouvrière* group, in a difficult position. FO would have to choose whether to go along with the movement, which meant accepting the PCF's lead in the CGT *and* opposing the Third Force government, or to oppose it at the risk of undermining its credibility with the CGT rank and file.

Building towards industrial action began in earnest after the October 1947 municipal elections.[8] Local mobilization moves came first as the Paris region CGT opened an intensive campaign for wage raises[9]—the CGT federations of railroad workers, civil servants and post-office workers did the same, and "warning" strikes of short duration were promoted throughout France.[10] The November meeting of the CGT Confederal Committee unveiled the full scope of the Confederation's plans. A general manifesto of material grievances was to be submitted to *all* workers, unionized or not,[11] by means of a referendum conducted by the Confederation.

The CGT leadership's plans widened the internal rift in the Confederation. From the beginning of the mobilization process, Communist unionists incessantly attacked *Force Ouvrière*.[12] In turn, *Force Ouvrière* opposed the leadership's mobilization plans.[13] And, for the first time, *Force Ouvrière* convened publicly to organize factional activity to contest PCF leadership in the CGT.[14] At the Confederal Committee meeting which announced the referendum plans, FO denounced the forthcoming "political" strikes (from the vantage point of FO's own position favoring the Third Force government) and circulated a public statement against PCF tactics which was signed by an impressive list of union leaders.[15] It was thus virtually inevitable that strike movements and a split within the CGT would coincide.

Events broke even before the CGT had fully implemented its mobilization plans. On November 12, police, acting on orders from the new Gaullist mayor of Marseilles, broke up a CGT-organized protest against a rise in trolley fares. The arrest of several demonstrators prompted the CGT to call another protest in front of the Marseilles *Palais de Justice*. The police were

---

8. For the municipal elections, which were a major Gaullist victory, see *L'année politique 1947*, pp. 192–196.

9. *Le Monde*, 12, 13 October 1947; *L'année politique 1947*, p. 201.

10. *Le Monde*, 23 October 1947.

11. Reproduced by Frachon in "Les grandes grèves de novembre-décembre" in *Servir la France* (January 1948), and *Cahiers du Communisme* (November 1948).

12. *Le Monde*, 1 November 1947; Frachon in *L'Humanité*, 4 November 1947.

13. Dehove, "Le mouvement syndicale et la politique syndicale" in *La France Economique de 1946 à 1948*, p. 1206; *L'année politique 1947*, p. 223; Guglielmi and Perrot, pp. 77 ff.

14. *Le Monde*, 9, 10 November 1947; Stolvitzer, p. 57; Dehove, *1946 à 1948*, p. 1251; Guglielmi and Perrot, pp. 80, 91.

15. See *Le Populaire*, 13 November 1947. Included on the list were some who stayed with the CGT after the split, notably Louis Saillant (who later became the first President of the World Federation of Trade Unions), Alain le Léap (who became co-Secretary General of the CGT), and Edouard Ehni, leader of the influential *Fédération du Livre*.

called in again, and this time one protestor was killed.[16] By November 14, Marseilles was shut down by a general strike. Simultaneously the situation exploded in the North of France when Léon Delfosse, the PCF miners' leader, was fired from the Coal Board, leading to a miners' strike.[17] The occasion was seized by the CGT to begin its strike offensive. The Marseilles railroad strike became the core of a national rail shutdown spreading from railroad center to railroad center.[18] Next, PCF-dominated federations and departmental unions went out in force. On November 14 the Paris metals sector shut down (beginning at Renault), then the building trades, then gas and electricity, the Post Office and the docks. In very short order over two million workers were out.[19]

The PCF/CGT leadership did not hesitate to use top-down techniques to generalize the strike, where needed. At Oignies, in the northern mines, for example, the CGT apparatus precipitated action by simply refusing to give out safety equipment to men who appeared for work.[20] At Renault and other central points in the Paris metals sector the strike was decreed by the union leadership without consultation with the rank and file.[21] Similar reports came from the building trades and the Marseilles region.[22] In the northern mines the CGT used the Coal Board's motor pool to create flying squads of CGT commandos ready to beat back strikebreakers by force.[23] In Paris, the use of violence to sustain the strike was not uncommon.[24] As the strike wore on, CGT industrial sabotage and terror became more frequent.[25]

The use of such tactics did nothing to soothe wounds inside the Confederation. In many sectors *Force Ouvrière* dragged its feet, or even opposed the strike. In response PCF-CGT militants attacked the dissidents. Growing acrimony between the PCF majority and *Force Ouvrière* quite rapidly reached the top levels of the CGT. In later November the CGT Confederal Bureau (which was composed of a slight PCF majority and a strong old-line Center minority sympathetic, for the most part, to FO) met with the government, which was unwilling to make anything more than token concessions to the strikers. Since the strike had never been officially called on the Confederal level—although it was very definitely coordinated from there—the various CGT Federations were the bodies which had to accept

16. Elgey, *Illusions*, p. 361; *Le Monde*, 23 November 1947; *L'année politique 1947*, p. 222.
17. *Combat*, 18 November 1947; Elgey, *Illusions*, p. 342; *Le Monde*, 19 November 1947.
18. *Le Monde*, 14 November 1947; *L'année politique 1947*, p. 224.
19. *L'année politique 1947*, p. 224.
20. *Combat*, 18 November 1947.
21. *Combat*, 19 November 1947; Elgey, *Illusions*, p. 343.
22. Elgey, *Illusions*, p. 361; *Le Monde*, 23 November 1947.
23. *Le Figaro*, 4 December 1947.
24. Elgey, *Illusions*, pp. 343–351.
25. *Le Populaire*, 20 November 1947; *Le Monde*, 4 December 1947.

or reject the government's offer.[26] The Communist leadership of the CGT suggested, of course, that the federations should reject the concessions, and twenty did so (of which 18 were PCF-dominated). At this juncture, the five *Force Ouvrière* members of the Confederal Bureau, concluding that the PCF had decided to keep the strikers out no matter what the CGT minority thought, released a statement to the press which invited workers to demand secret ballots on the question of whether to return to work or not.[27] This led the PCF majority of the Confederal Bureau to decide that since a minority now opposed the strike the Bureau ought no longer to play a key role in strike coordinating. As a result, strike direction was delegated to a Strike Committee of those twenty federations actually carrying on the movement. With the change internal division at the top of the CGT passed the point of no return. The existence of the Strike Committee amounted to labelling the *Force Ouvrière* leadership as strikebreakers. And when FO began to urge strikers back to work, the label seemed merited.

The autumn 1947 strike therefore divided the CGT from top to bottom. Moreover, while the strike initially obtained a good deal of rank-and-file support, in the longer run it became evident that the PCF had over-estimated working-class combativeness. French workers were indeed unhappy about their situation. But they were not unhappy enough to carry on the extended industrial confrontation which the PCF wanted. Thus the government was eventually able to turn the tide, largely through repressive tactics. On November 28 it called up the army reserves, to use against the strikers, to be sure, but also to create an atmosphere of panic among the general public.[28] At the same time Jules Moch, Minister of the Interior (and chief anti-strike tactician), prevented municipal governments from using their treasuries to provide support for strikers. On November 29, the government introduced severe anti-strike legislation to Parliament, again to enhance public fear and anti-Communism.[29] On December 1, the CGT began pulling workers off Parisian electricity generators, an extreme move which threatened to bring all activity in Paris to a halt. The government responded by sending in the police, who broke picket lines by force, occupied the generators and allowed strikebreakers in to work. The success of this action encouraged the government to use troops to break the railroad strike.[30] After this, police and army intervention was generalized. Hundreds of workers were arrested and imprisoned.

The government's gamble on repression was successful. Public hysteria isolated the strikers. As this occurred, rank-and-file CGT militants tried to keep the action alive by extreme fervor and brute force (including

26. Lefranc, *1944–1968*, p. 51, pp. 56–58.

27. Frachon, *Cahiers du Communisme* (January 1948), p. 16.

28. *Le Monde*, 29 November 1947.

29. *Le Monde*, 30 November 1947; *L'année politique 1947*, pp. 224–225.

30. Cheminots, p. 218; Frachon, *Cahiers du Communisme* (January 1948), p. 12; *L'année politique 1947*, pp. 243–244.

sabotage), both of which alienated considerable support at the unions' base.[31] Progressively the strike was identified with the PCF, in the public's mind. Finally, amid fear, bitterness, fatigue, and hunger at the rank-and-file level, the Strike Committee called off the movement on December 9. The Committee's final communiqué underlined deep concern about the integrity of the CGT: "Trade union militants, we must persuade all the workers that they have a place in our ranks. . . ."[32] The strike had lost. What was important now for the PCF was not losing the working class base which it had so carefully consolidated since 1944!

None of the strike's demands were won. And the inevitable split with *Force Ouvrière* occurred in December. But things could have been worse for the CGT. The repressive response of the government to real working-class grievances had taught some workers that the Third Force was not likely to be sympathetic to working-class concerns.[33] And the strike had forced FO to choose between support of industrial action or support for the Third Force government. FO's choice of the latter, plus its espousal of the government's deflationary policies in the first half of 1948, meant that *Force Ouvrière* was unable to take much of the CGT's support away from it in the split. FO's main strength lay in those areas where the old-line CGT Center faction had been based, among civil servants. In critical industrial areas, and in many sectors even outside mass-production industry, the PCF-CGT held strong. FO emerged from the split as a rump faction, strong enough to make united working-class action difficult but nowhere near powerful enough to challenge PCF hegemony within organized labor. The major loss suffered in the split was not to FO. The *Fédération de l'Education Nationale* (FEN), the large union of teachers, decided to disaffiliate from the CGT and become autonomous.[34]

The failure of the 1947 strikes did not lead to any change in PCF strategy, however. "Relying on the masses" was still the line. And the masses were still to be produced by the CGT. By mid-1948 the CGT had begun gearing up for another round of militant industrial action. Short strikes in spring and summer were promoted to be greeted with immediate repressive measures by the government, an indication that the second round of "relying on the masses" would be quite as bitter as the first.[35] By early autumn

31. Elgey, *Illusions*, p. 361; Lefranc, *1939–1950*, p. 89; *Le Monde*, 29 November 1947.

32. Reprinted in *Une Semaine dans le Monde,* 13 December 1947.

33. Frachon, *Cahiers du Communisme*, January 1948, p. 28.

34. *L'année politique 1948*, p. 22; *Force Ouvrière* formally constituted itself as the CGT–FO in April 1948, see Force Ouvrière, "Comment et pourquoi se sont produites les scissions syndicales," *Force Ouvrière Informations* (1964); see also Lefranc, *1939–1950*, pp. 188 ff. On the FEN, see Didier Sapojnik, "La Fédération de l'Education Nationale dans l'Autonomie," in *Le Mouvement Social*, no. 92 (July-September 1975).

35. *Le Monde*, 15 March 1948; Branciard, vol. II, p. 167; *Le Monde*, 17 June 1948; *L'année politique 1948*, p. 97; Frachon, vol. I, pp. 302 ff.; *Le Peuple*, 27 February–4 March 1948; Guglielmi and Perrot, pp. 107–111.

the CGT was priming the strike pump in its strongest sectors, the railroads, Paris metallurgy and the coal mines.[36] The grievances advanced were a predictable mix: wages and hours, the government's economic policies, the Cold War and the alleged treason of "Marshallization."[37] The new confrontation was triggered by a series of governmental decrees in late September 1948 to reduce personnel in the nationalized sector of the economy by ten percent, install a much more rigorous system of work discipline and control over absenteeism in public industry, and make drastic changes in social security (which aimed partly at taking some power away from unions). The CGT seized upon these decrees as decisive evidence of the progress of "Marshallization," and began to mobilize the miners, who were the major target of the decrees, for battle. CGT agitation, which stressed the point that the "Lacoste decrees" were a frontal attack on nationalizations which had been won by long and hard working-class struggle, led to a referendum among all miners about the desirability of a strike.[38] The Confederation clearly was trying to avoid some of its earlier mistakes by not decreeing this strike from above. A vast majority of the miners who voted favored action, and the movement began on October 4.[39]

The CGT's tactics became clear almost immediately. The miners were to be the catalyst for a generalized strike. The Confederation began to push other critical sectors of the CGT rank and file to leave work once the miners' strike had begun en masse. This time the Confederation's calculations about rank-and-file discontent were dramatically wrong, however. In some areas, particularly the metals industries (where CGT strength was high), significant actions could not be prompted. The rank and file simply refused to listen to their union leadership. In other sectors membership support was halfhearted, not enough to build an extended strike. On the railroads, for example, the momentum which the CGT was able to generate was insufficient to overcome trade-union "pluralism," as both *Force Ouvrière* and the CFTC *Cheminot* Federations opposed the strike.[40] In the Lorraine iron and steel complex the government was able to play on union divisions to "buy off" non-CGT unionists with a quick settlement. The general movement which the CGT had hoped for did not develop. After a few days the miners stood alone on strike.

With the miners isolated, the CGT made another mistake. It decided to escalate the miners' strike to compensate for the weakness of other strikes. In response to alleged police brutality, the CGT called a twenty-four-hour

36. *Le Figaro*, 10 September 1948; *Le Monde*, 18, 21 September 1948; *L'année politique 1948*, pp. 166–167.

37. *Le Monde*, 18 September 1948.

38. *Le Peuple*, 28 October 1948; August Lecoeur, "La grève des mineurs," *Cahiers du Communisme* (February 1949).

39. *Le Monde*, 29 September, 4 October 1948; *L'année politique 1948*, p. 181.

40. *Le Monde*, 8, 9, and 14 October 1948.

suspension of mine security teams (groups of workers who kept the mines in working order during the strike).[41] The government then requisitioned these same crews, legally obliging them to stay on the job.[42] The CGT, in turn, called the crews out on an unlimited strike, an action which carried with it the threat of serious flooding in the mines, a longer-term disruption of coal production and an energy crisis for France.[43] The government very quickly sent troops in to occupy the mines. Jules Moch, again the government's anti-strike general, took to the airwaves to accuse the "Communized CGT" of trying "to block the U.S. from aiding Europe by provoking . . . the collapse of our economy," on "orders from the Cominform."[44] Later he went even further, connecting the strike to "Moscow Gold" by revealing information concerning the operations of PCF finances.[45]

What the CGT had intended to be a mass working-class action had very rapidly turned into a head-to-head slugging match between the PCF and the Third Force government. The situation promised little for the PCF and CGT, but this did not deter them from carrying things through to the bitter end. Internal divisions between miners emerged. In response to them, the CGT Miners' Federation resorted to muscle and sectarianism to keep the miners away from work.[46] Vilification of *Force Ouvrière* unionists reached new heights.[47] As the strike came to depend more and more upon the energy of the CGT apparatus and commandos (with the rank and file growing ever more tired and divided) the government resorted to greater repression. PCF–CGT officials on coal and railroad boards were fired.[48] CGT control over important local organizations (such as cooperatives) was broken[49] and family allowances to striking miners were reduced by decree.[50] Mine areas were occupied by troops (with the forcible removal of strikers from mine facilities) while port areas (where CGT dockers had been preventing the off-loading of foreign coal) were taken over by the army.[51]

41. *Le Monde*, 17–18 October, 22 and 26 October 1948; Frachon, vol. I, p. 324.

42. *Le Monde*, 19 October 1948.

43. *L'année politique 1948*, pp. 183–184.

44. *Le Monde*, 19 October 1948; *L'année politique 1948*, p. 182.

45. Lefranc, *1939–1950*, p. 216; *Le Monde*, 18 November 1948.

46. Branciard, vol. II, p. 169.

47. Elgey, *Illusions*, p. 400.

48. *Le Monde*, 31 October–1 November 1948.

49. Lefranc, *1939–1950*, p. 215; *Le Monde*, 7–8 November 1948. In particular, that of Beaumont-en-Artois which had provided much aid to strikers to that point.

50. *Combat*, 11 November 1948.

51. *Le Monde*, 30 October 1948. The clear intention of the government to crush the strike was so obvious that even John L. Lewis, not known as a friend of Communists, wrote to Léon Blum that Blum would be much better off "to put food into the shrunken stomachs of French miners rather than shooting American bullets into their undernourished bodies."

The determination of the PCF and CGT unionists was not enough to turn the strike around. The government won, by dint of anti-Communist ideological offensives, repression and the exhaustion of the miners.[52] On November 30, after fifty-six days, the CGT called off the strike. The government made no important concessions to the strikers' demands. Up through mid-November, 1041 arrests connected with the strike had been made, and many of those arrested were to stay in prison well into 1949;[53] 479 policemen were injured. After the end of the strike the management of *Charbonnages de France* moved to root out CGT power in the mines, firing some 3000 trade-union militants and strikers.[54] As a result, PCF strength among the miners was seriously and permanently impaired. The miners were not be be heard from as actors in industrial conflict for fifteen years.

"Relying on the masses" through industrial conflict was doomed from the start, based, as it was, on misunderstanding about the proper relationship between the PCF and its labor mass organization, the CGT. The PCF had every intention of using industrial conflict for political ends, of deploying the CGT directly as a transmission belt for PCF political goals. Yet the logic of such a strategy was not carried through to its conclusion. The CGT did not prepare workers for direct political action. Instead mobilization for the 1947–1948 confrontations focused mainly on the material grievances of the rank and file. The strikes which resulted were supported by workers because of their dissatisfaction with living conditions. What the PCF had hoped would turn into politically decisive industrial movements were developed by the CGT as ordinary strikes. The flaw in this approach became clear in the movements themselves. Workers were willing to strike to improve their material situations. However, when their strikes quickly became warfare between the PCF and the government, the workers backed down. They were willing to fight for higher wages and better working conditions, but they were not eager to be cannon fodder in a fight to the finish between Communists and the Third Force. Buried in the PCF's reliance-on-the-masses line at this point was, then, an assumption that the rhythms of the labor market and the problems of French politics coincided exactly, not only in time, but also in intensity. In effect PCF and CGT leaders were trying to use working-class discontent to achieve political ends *behind the backs of the workers themselves*. Because of this, relying on the masses could not work.

Do the Workers Want Peace?

The PCF clearly had to find means to alter the course of French Cold War politics other than industrial actions promoted by the CGT. Hoping

---

52. *Le Monde*, 28 November 1948.
53. *Le Monde*, 18 November 1948.
54. *Combat*, 1 December 1948; Elgey, *Illusions*, p. 403.

against logic, as the party had in 1947–1948, that the dynamics of protest in the labor market would magically coincide with the PCF's goals in the political sphere made little sense. In terms of the general structure of party-union relationships, two different paths out of the existing situation were conceivable. The first was retreat from transmission-belt policies by granting the CGT new autonomy in the labor market to pursue industrial protest in accordance with the Confederation's perception of the rank and file's immediate needs and interests, while leaving direct politics to the party. The second was making the CGT even more of a transmission belt, even more subordinate to PCF political tactics in its day-to-day union activities. It was the latter which party and union chose, with all of the risks to the CGT's integrity as a mass organization which this choice carried.

The failure of the 1948 strikes coincided with new developments in the Cold War which, as translated by the Cominform, made headlong CGT flight towards an extreme transmission-belt posture inevitable. From the economic focus of "Marshallization," the eyes of the PCF shifted towards the division of the world into military blocs. The Americans were consolidating a Western alliance and endowing it with vast military power. It fell to the PCF to do what it could to stop or hinder this consolidation. Thus from January 1949, in the words of the party's official history, "peace became the decisive question."[55] The PCF's April 1949 National Conference announced the change. According to Maurice Thorez, "war is neither ineluctable nor necessary . . . the relationship of forces has changed in the world. A considerable mass movement is developing against war. . . ."[56] Léon Mauvais added that the primary task of the party in new circumstances was to tie "peace issues to peoples' struggles for day-to-day needs."[57] In the same month, amid a great amount of international fanfaring, the "First World Congress of Partisans of Peace" was held in Paris, largely under PCF auspices, and presided over by Frédéric Joliot-Curie.[58]

The Peace Movement represented a very different tactical approach to the Cold War than the earlier industrial protest line. It banked on the hope that large numbers of French people, of all classes and persuasions, would be sensitive to the danger of war and respond to the agitation of peace-oriented mass organizations. The focus on the peace tactic was ideological, designed to influence the climate of ideas in France through propaganda. The desired results would follow when a sufficiently strong peace sentiment was aroused. Then, presumably, French governments would be forced by public opinion to move away from their pro-American foreign policy.

---

55. PCF, *Histoire du PCF*, p. 522; *L'Humanité*, 7, 10, 24, 25 February 1949.
56. PCF, *Histoire du PCF*, p. 524.
57. *L'année politique 1949*, p. 61; *Le Monde*, 4 April 1949.
58. PCF, *Histoire du PCF*, p. 524. See also Frédéric Joliot-Curie, *Cinq années de lutte pour la paix* (1954).

With the shift towards "peace," the CGT lost its pride of position as *the* central agency for implementing the PCF's anti-Cold War offensive. The PCF knew, however, that the peace movement would never amount to much unless it could mobilize a core of working-class support. Producing such support became the CGT's new task. The centrality of working-class peace action was clear from the outset. In March 1949, Thorez created a minor uproar in the National Assembly by announcing that the French working class would never fight against the Soviet Union. *L'Humanité* then asserted that the French working class would in no way consider itself bound by the North Atlantic treaty. Benoît Frachon, Secretary-General of the CGT, publicly proclaimed the same themes.[59] The reasons given for such arguments presaged the PCF's new line on working-class action. French workers would reject Cold War policies out of solidarity with fellow workers in nations where capitalist exploitation had been banished forever.[60] Secondly, the pro-war policies of the American and French governments were bound to increase working-class misery. In this domain, the party simply extended its "Marshallization" analysis. The consequence of French integration into a political and military bloc dominated by American imperialism would be the progressive sacrifice of French economic independence to the benefit of American capitalism. French industry would lose its autonomy and begin to decline, while French workers would become the objects of imperialist "superexploitation" which would enhance the profits of American monopolies. In short, the party predicted that the success of American capitalism, the presumed object of the Cold War, would be achieved at the cost of the under-development of France.

Using the CGT to produce anti-war action among French workers posed serious organizational problems for the Confederation, however. The PCF's contradictory use of the CGT in 1947–1948 to produce industrial conflict which the party hoped would lead to political change had failed dismally. But it had left the CGT a degree of latitude to act as a genuine trade-union mass organization. The peace line gave the CGT a new job, that of mobilizing its rank and file around issues of foreign policy, profoundly political in nature. This meant not only attempting to carry on as a union in the labor market, but also, and simultaneously, connecting labor-market issues in a day-to-day way with the diplomatic questions of the Cold War. Organizing workers against the war in Indochina, against NATO, against the Korean War, against German rearmament, against the production of war materials (to list only the most important campaigns to be undertaken) was vastly more complicated than organizing them to fight for higher wages and shorter hours. And connecting the two sets of issues in a way which made sense to ordinary workers escalated such complexity

59. *L'Humanité*, 17 March 1949.
60. Frachon, vol. I, p. 355.

immensely. The CGT could anticipate serious difficulties in carrying on labor-market activities in and for themselves, given trade-union pluralism, the aftermath of the 1947–1948 strikes, governmental and *patronal* hostility. On top of this the new burdens of the peace campaign would hardly improve the Confederation's position.

In fact, tacking peace issues onto day-to-day union activities proved impossible to do with any degree of success. From the onset of the peace tactic in 1949 the CGT leadership had a great deal of trouble persuading rank-and-file militants to subordinate economic struggle to peace questions.[61] What party and union made of this trouble indicated the course it had decided to take, however. The central theme in the party's ritual self-criticism at its 1950 Congress was that Communist work for peace and the PCF's work for the material interests of workers had not been successfully connected.[62] But François Billoux, speaking for the Thorez leadership, did not conclude from this that superimposing peace issues onto otherwise unrelated questions of working-class life was inappropriate. Rather he had harsh words to say to the Congress about PCF tendencies to subordinate the peace line to what he called "economism."[63]

The CGT tried, then. Throughout 1949 and 1950 efforts were devoted to internal debate among CGT *cadres* and militants for the purposes of peace mobilization. In almost all CGT departmental unions and federations one or another anti-war resolution was voted upon.[64] Reaching the working-class masses was the critical problem, however. Perhaps the most important way in which the message was carried to the masses was *via* the mass-signature petition campaign. In 1950 an immense amount of CGT energy was devoted to producing signatures on the Stockholm Appeal to outlaw the atom bomb (allegedly over fourteen million signatures were gathered in France altogether).[65] And in 1951 there were CGT petition campaigns for the Warsaw appeal for a Five Power Peace Conference (twelve million signatures alleged) and against German rearmament.[66] One of the highlights

61. Marshall Shulman, "Soviet Policy in Western Europe and the French Communist Party 1949–1952," (1959), p. 188.

62. Val Lorwin, p. 166.

63. PCF, *Histoire du PCF*, p. 528; *L'année politique 1950*, pp. 70–74.

64. See André Barjonet, *CGT*, p. 198, on the Schuman Plan. The resolutions passed were specifically geared to the industrial sector covered by the Federation. In late 1949, for example, a campaign against the production and transport of war materials was pushed within the metals and transport sectors. The initial stage of the campaign was the passage of Federation resolutions against such activities. The Metalworkers Federation, Aeronautics, Paris region engineers, and others passed anti-war resolutions of this sort during 1949. In another example, in 1950, after the Schuman Plan was proposed, the CGT called a National Conference of all CGT miners' and metalworkers' unions to discuss and pass resolutions about the relationship of the Plan to the government's Cold War policies and to pass new resolutions.

65. For the Stockholm appeal in the Fédération Nationale des Cheminots, see Cheminots, pp. 235–236; also PCF, *Histoire du PCF*, p. 530.

66. PCF, *Histoire du PCF*, p. 531.

of the 1951 CGT Congress was the awarding of prize trips to Hungary and the USSR to the CGTers who had collected the most signatures. And, as infrastructures for these various drives, *comités d'entreprise* and ad hoc Peace Committees on the shopfloor level were deployed.[67]

The Confederal leadership, taking Billoux's strictures against economism very seriously, insisted endlessly that peace issues and material demands be tied together in labor-market action.[68] To little avail, apparently.[69] In a 1951 *Cahiers du Communisme* article, Marcel Dufriche, an important CGT leader, complained that few real links between peace and material demands were being made. The CGT was raising both sets of issues, to be sure, but separately. Militants were sticking to regular trade unionism and shying away from the peace question because the rank and file was less interested in it. According to Dufriche, "while everyday reality is a powerful lever to develop united action against war policies, too often such action is being undertaken without ties to this reality."[70]

Alongside the CGT's apparent inability to make a mass connection around the peace issue occurred a rash of minority-based exemplary anti-war actions. When Maurice Thorez asked, with reference to the transport and handling of American war material by French workers, "Will the people of France accept the unloading and transshipment of these death machines?" he was answered by a rash of CGT-promoted commando actions against the manufacture, unloading, and transport of war materials, in particular those destined for Indochina.[71] Such actions were stronger and more frequent where the PCF core in CGT organizations was strongest (on the railroads and among dockers, for example).[72] In almost all of the ports of France in 1950 there were incidents in which dockers refused to load arms on ships headed for Vietnam.[73] *L'Affaire Henri Martin*, in which a Communist sailor (later imprisoned) led a shipboard mutiny against handling war materials, came to symbolize PCF/CGT anti-war militancy. There were also occasional acts of sabotage in arms production. Altogether, during the years 1949–1951 there were some 1500 work stop-

67. Frachon, vol. I, p. 437; *Le Peuple*, 7 February 1951.

68. *L'année politique 1950*, pp. 34–35; *Le Peuple*, 12 July 1950; CGT, *Congrès national, 1951*, pp. 15 ff.

69. On the railroads, the CGT official Federation history speaks of anti-CGT forces using the CGT's peace struggle as a means to divide workers in labor market struggles. Cf. Cheminots, p. 242.

70. Marcel Dufriche, "La lutte pour l'unité, après le Congrès de la CGT," *Cahiers du Communisme* (July 1951), p. 856.

71. Maurice Thorez, cited in Raymond Agosse, "Dockers en tête, la classe ouvrière poursuivra et élargira la lutte politique de masse contre la fabrication et le transport du matériel de guerre," in *Cahiers du Communisme* (November 1950); see also Maurice Thorez's report to the Twelfth PCF Congress, 1950, extracts in Thorez, *Oeuvres Choisies*, vol. II, p. 509 ff.

72. Cheminots, p. 237.

73. *L'année politique 1950*, pp. 9, 15; *Le Monde*, 19 January 1951.

pages and other actions to disorganize military production and transport.[74]
And almost all of these actions shared certain characteristics. They were
based on a small number of people (mainly Communists). They were
hyper-militant. And they were inevitably greeted by repression from the
authorities.

In time, the deteriorating dynamic of CGT peace tactics became clear.
Where it was a question of tacking peace issues onto trade-unionist labor-
market struggles, the tacking was done in a progressively more mechanical
way, without the in-depth preparation necessary to make such subtle connections comprehensible to the rank and file. Connected with this, CGT
peace actions tended to become less and less mass-based and more and
more *cadre* focused.[75] As the CGT's most dedicated activists shifted
towards symbolic anti-war activities, the Confederation began to neglect
the material problems of the CGT membership. In the always-delicate
balance between trade unionism and politics, weight shifted in strikingly
obvious ways towards politics.[76]

With the early 1950s, then, and because of the peace campaign, the CGT
apparatus began to turn in on itself. The programs and slogans of the CGT
as a mass organization grew more sectarian and less meaningful to the ordinary French worker. Locally, as the limited amount of organizational
energy available to the CGT was shifted from trade unionism to peace action, the CGT became a "peace committee" rather than a union.
Simultaneously, local CGT bodies tended to collapse into local PCF shop
cells.[77] Party and mass organization began de facto to merge, violating the
CGT's integrity as an association where workers of all political opinions
could expect to have their interests protected. Moreover, since France's
other major union confederations, *Force Ouvrière* and the CFTC, were on
the other side of the Cold War issues, the growing identification of the
CGT with the PCF—and both, in turn, with the broad goals of Soviet
foreign policy—had the effect of ruling out trade-union unity-in-action on
ordinary labor-market questions. By neglecting its union duties in the interests of Cold War politics, and by stressing just those issues which were
most likely to divide the CGT from other unions, the Confederation was
making a very large contribution to the paralysis of rank-and-file union life
in France. From this to the demoralization of the working-class rank and
file was not a very large step.

Unity, Disunity, Organizational Decline

The shift in CGT tactics towards peace coincided with the beginning of a

74. Barjonet, *CGT*, p. 129.
75. Ibid., p. 128; Lefranc, *1939–1950*, p. 128.
76. Shulman, p. 142; Barjonet, *CGT*, p. 128
77. Barjonet, *CGT*, p. 131; André Marty, *L'affaire Marty*, pp. 157–158.

disastrous and long decline in CGT membership.[78] By 1951 the CGT was down to about one-half of its peak 1946 membership strength; by 1955, one-third. Moreover, by 1951 the vast majority of French workers were no longer members of any trade union—CGT-affiliated or otherwise. The CGT maintained its relative strength among French workers—most of those who had ceased to be members of CGT unions were still willing to support the CGT in professional elections—but the drastic de-unionization of the French working class vastly increased uncertainty about its reactions to any given situation.[79] Thus as the Cold War reached its highest levels of intensity, the CGT grew too weak to order and promote strike actions, to maintain strikes if they occurred and even, in some cases, to end or prevent actions which the Confederation did not desire. At a critically important moment, then, the CGT was organizationally ill-prepared to act even to make the strike a credible sanction to employers, the bare minimum of effectiveness necessary for a trade union. The crucible of the Cold War therefore presented the French business class, only recently discredited by its wartime activities, with an ideal opportunity to impose its own rule in the labor market.

Theoretically, one path was open to the CGT to compensate for the decline of its organizational strength in these years, some form of unity-in-action with other unions. What the CGT could not be sure of accomplishing on its own might become possible if the CGT, FO and the CFTC could unite for industrial struggle. The enormous barrier which CGT peace activities presented to this we have already mentioned. Peace sectarianism was not the only thing blocking unity, however.

The CGT never stopped proclaiming its devotion to the cause of trade-union unity after the split of 1947. However, the CGT's approach to such unity made unity impossible. On a theoretical level, the CGT denied other union confederations a right to exist. To the CGT, there existed only one working class in France and, as a result, there should exist only one trade-

---

78. The CGT's own figures, which undoubtedly inflated real membership statistics, demonstrate this process as follows:

Year	Membership Cards Issued
1945	5,261,713
1946	5,857,786
1947	5,480,257
1948	4,079,943
1949	3,867,412
1950	3,393,800
1951	3,076,211
1952	2,505,357
1953	2,342,051
1954	2,132,642
1955	2,142,665

79. Tiano and Rocard, p. 146; Collinet, *Esprit*, p. 134.

union organization, the CGT. From this basic proposition, the CGT concluded that the final goal of any unity campaign could only be unity of all workers in the CGT—and the abolition of all other union organizations.[80] And from this basic proposition also followed the CGT's contention that the existence of trade-union organizations other than the CGT did not come from any legitimate divisions in the working class itself. Trade-union pluralism in France was caused by the ideological misleadership of workers by agents of the bourgeoisie. Behind *Force Ouvrière* lay the "right-wing social democrats," and behind the CFTC, the Catholic Church.[81]

Such a stance made unity agreement at the top very difficult to achieve, of course. Yet unity-in-action of some kind became ever more imperative as general trade-union support declined to France. The CGT's approach to the tactical question of unity-in-action was typical. If unity at the top was not likely, then the Confederation would push unity-in-action "from below," designing and initiating programs which might mobilize the rank and file of other unions to collaborate with the CGT. Since the major purpose of unity from below was to force other union leaderships to accept unity on the CGT's terms by seducing their rank and file out from underneath them, the main result of the tactic was that other union leaderships redoubled their efforts to keep their supporters from participating in CGT-promoted programs.

The question of unity-in-action reached a complete impasse. The CGT beckoned towards the FO rank and file with appeals for a "rally of misled workers" against the "accomplices of big capital."[82] The problem of unity became increasingly urgent after 1949 when the government finally began to relinquish administrative control over the labor market, opening the way to real collective bargaining.[83] The CGT decided to deal with this by appealing to unity with the CFTC, circumventing FO. The CFTC agreed that unity would be helpful, but refused to agree to any unity-in-action treaty unless *Force Ouvrière* joined in as well. FO ruled out unity with the CGT in principle (even when such unity might have, in the words of one observer, "obtained greater benefits for the working masses immediately").[84] *Force Ouvrière* equated the CGT with Moscow and, in the words of Robert Bothereau, an important FO leader, felt that "to bring a drop of water to its [the CGT's] mill . . ." was "to contribute to a movement to destroy the universe."[85] The anti-Communism of FO was also reinforced by realistic fears for its own organizational integrity. In the words of André Bergeron,

80. *Le Peuple*, 27 December 1947.

81. On the whole question of unity in this period, see Jean-Marie Lecler, "La position des centrales syndicales," (1966);Barjonet, *CGT*, part II, ch. 4.

82. Lecler, *La position*, p. 47.

83. *Le Peuple*, 3, 10 October 1949.

84. Lecler, *La position*, p. 47.

85. Lecler, *La position*, p. 43.

it is quite evident that they (the CGT) would give us all of the possible
and imaginable guarantees to get our signature on an agreement . . . . However, what then would happen would be that they
would find a way to call a meeting . . . or an assembly of workers . . .
to discuss a number of problems which go far beyond the positions
which had been initially agreed upon.[86]

Since no unity at the top could come from such animosity, however difficult the situation faced by French workers in the labor market, the CGT
relied ever more exclusively on its unity-in-action from below tactic, calling
for what it termed "Committees for Unity of Action" (CUA) at the shop
level.[87] The CUAs, to be set up by CGT militants, were meant to be shop-
level associations of workers of all opinions to promote local-level action.[88]
But the CUAs were unable to achieve much success. Bitterness on the part
of FO and the CFTC dating from the 1947–1948 period was still strong.[89]
And, to cite an important FO militant, the CUAs were usually marked by
"the desire of the CGT to impose its own objectives and methods on other
union organizations rather than to promote common actions by different
unions for common objectives."[90] In effect, the CGT activists in CUAs
were more concerned with pushing peace issues than with bread-and-butter
union issues. In general, the CGT considerably underestimated the attachment of rank-and-file followers of FO and the CFTC to their own unions.
In the best of circumstances, organizational attempts to circumvent profound hostility between union leaderships by prodding united action at the
base would have been delicate, demanding great subtlety on the part of
CGT militants. And if there was one quality which CGT militants lacked
during this difficult period, it was subtlety.[91]

The results of all this were amply visible in the labor market. The year
1949 was without significant trade-union industrial action, in part because
it was the first postwar year to see relative economic stability and some
prosperity. In the period following the new February 1950, legislation
allowing limited collective bargaining, a number of local strikes flickered
on and off, but the absence of trade-union unity prevented their generalization.[92] When the CGT attempted to prod or enlarge strikes on its own, the

86. Lecler, *La position*, p. 47.

87. *Le Peuple*, 10 January 1950.

88. Lecler, *La position*, p. 9.

89. Marcel Gibelin, "La division syndicale et l'unité d'action," in *Les Temps Modernes*,
no. 112–113, p. 1942.

90. Ibid., p. 1942.

91. The failure of the CUA's was finally acknowledged by Frachon at the 1953 CGT Congress. Lecler, *La position*, p. 9; Marcel Gibelin, in *L'Observateur*, 1 October 1953, p. 15.

92. See *Socialisme ou Barbarie*, no. 5–6, p. 152, for a description of the CGT's precipita-
tion of strikes by minority action. Also *Le Monde*, 23 February 1950; Lefranc, *1939–1950*, p.
232; *Le Populaire*, 4 March 1950.

rank and file did not follow.[93] And when industrial conflict did involve the CGT and other unions (not unified, but simultaneous) the eagerness of the CGT to extend strikes, when coupled with the moderation of other unions, allowed employers to end strikes by dividing the strikers. When the CGT tried to continue such strikes on its own, despite the collapse of other unions, the government and employers were only too willing to bring in the police to break the action.[94] Divide-and-rule became a useful employer tactic to limit strike damage, and most strikes were therefore settled very cheaply. And, if the union movement was hopelessly divided, employers were not. The *Conseil National du Patronat Français* (CNPF) took a strong position against the conclusion of any major collective bargaining agreements under the new bargaining laws, and none were in fact concluded.[95]

Working-class disunity was a gift to French capitalism. The CGT was not the only donor in these years, but its beneficence was considerable. Its attempts to politicize strikes continued into the early 1950s. In turn, this politicization allowed government and employers to label all CGT action, and by implication all strikes, as political. As the CGT grew weaker and more isolated, and as other branches of the union movement saw their mobilizing power decline, the French *patronat* felt free to return to the anti-labor policies which had marked its attitudes in the prewar years. After 1944 the French labor movement had been more powerful than at any point in the history of French capitalism. During the Cold War the whole atmosphere of French industrial relations changed, to the labor movement's detriment.

The Crisis of the Cold War: towards a Redefinition of Party-Union Relations?

For the PCF the 1950s were to be a nightmare, the worst part of which took place in the dark night of the Cold War. Of all the Communist parties outside the Socialist bloc, the PCF took Soviet guidelines for Cold War behavior most seriously. Its overzealous pursuit of Jdanovite socialist realism in cultural and intellectual realms was caricatural, and laid the foundations for the profound problems which the party was to have with intellectuals later.[96] And not only did the PCF wholeheartedly support the anti-Titoist

93. Lefranc, *1939–1950*, p. 232; *Le Monde*, 18 February 1950; *Le Monde*, 7 March 1950. These problems occurred in the decisively important Paris metals industries, the railroads, the mines and Paris transports, all areas where the CGT was strong.

94. Tiano and Rocard, p. 146.

95. *Le Peuple*, 5 April 1950. See Henry Ehrmann, *Organized Business in France* (1957), p. 439, for information on the attitudes on the CNPF.

96. See Dominique Desanti, *Les Staliniens* (1975); Pierre Daix, *J'ai cru au matin* (1976); Philippe Noirot, *La mémoire ouverte* (1976), all memoirs of this period. A good case could be made that one reason for the PCF's aberrant, and ultimately disastrous, reluctance to de-Stalinize after 1956 was that the party leadership remembered the years after 1950 when it had been obliged to live through a painful period of "de-Thorezization."

"show trials" in Eastern Europe which were carried on under Soviet auspices in the early 1950s (the Slansky trials in Czechoslovakia, the Gomulka trials in Poland, moves against Ann Pauker and Antonescu in Rumania, the trial of Janos Kadar in Hungary, to name only the most important), it managed to generate some quite unpleasant internal purges of its own in the Marty-Tillon *affaire* of 1952 and the Auguste Lecoeur incident a year later. In both cases, PCF leaders with strong Resistance records who might have been able to establish positions in the party independent from the Cominform, were purged. The paranoid mentality of an armed and besieged garrison came to prevail in inner-party life. French Communists responded to Cold War anti-Stalinism by proclaiming their desire to be the best Stalinists of all!

Worse still, the PCF had to face the storm of the early 1950s without strong leadership. Maurice Thorez suffered a serious stroke in late 1950 (from which he was never to recover fully) and he left France for nearly three years of treatment in the Soviet Union. Because the party's internal development had led it to extreme centralization around Thorez and his immediate coterie (his wife, Jeannette Vermeersch, had become a decisive figure in party life as well), justified by a full-blown cult of personality around *le fils du peuple*, the sudden absence of "Maurice" totally disrupted party decision-making. None of the second-rank leaders called to the fore during the years of Thorez's absence (including Jacques Duclos) succeeded in coordinating a party machine which had progressively become the private instrument of one man. Thus, at the very moment when the PCF most needed the guidance which it had come to expect from Thorez, such guidance was taken away. The irony in all this was striking. The PCF had become a thoroughly Stalinized party by 1950. However, at that very moment when it needed to defend itself as best it could in the only way it knew how, i.e., through Stalinist internal coordination, its own Stalin-figure was struck down. Confusion reigned, at considerable cost. And, since no one knew for sure that Thorez would ever return, such confusion compounded struggle over his succession between different strategic currents.[97]

The period after 1951 might have been quite different. The 1951 elections brought important changes. A new electoral law weakened the PCF's parliamentary power, and the Left in general lost ground at the polls. Gaullist gains made a threat from the Right credible for a time, but the Gaullists split over the issue of participation in or opposition to the Fourth Republic, with a number of Gaullists moving towards participation. In all this a parliamentary majority of the Right and Right-Center became numerically possible. Third Force governments were henceforth unworkable, therefore, and the Socialists were pushed into opposition. Ideally, the beginnings of a

97. Fauvet, *PCF Histoire*, ch. 3.

new Right-Left polarization of French politics might have made a new United Front initiative possible for the PCF. The Socialists were not about to abandon the quasi-religious anti-Communism which they had acquired after 1947, however, an attitude which was eventually to play a major role in destroying the Fourth Republic. The PCF, on the other hand, was not about to abandon its own form of religion at this point, its devotion to Soviet foreign policy goals. Thus the Left was to remain divided, and the PCF isolated. For the PCF, in 1951, the worst was yet to come.

The Crisis of 1952 and Its Aftermath

For party and union, the sad logic of transmission belts was about to play itself out to the full. Crisis began in early 1952 when the new Right-Center government of Antoine Pinay decided to forbid an annual demonstration by the PCF to commemorate the historic 1934 movements against fascism (which had been so important in leading to the Popular Front). The PCF's war cry at this time was anti-fascism, directed at the Gaullists. The government's ban was seen as a challenge to the PCF, and the party chose the CGT to respond. Claiming that the government was encouraging the rise of fascism, the CGT called a general strike in the Paris region for February 12, around the old slogan, "le fascisme ne passera pas."[98] Other unions did not perceive the fascist menace with the CGT's sense of urgency, however, and refused to support the Confederation's call, denouncing it as a political maneuver. The strike was a total failure, more a gathering of Communists in the labor movement than a mass movement, and those weak strike actions which did occur were repressed with ease.[99] The PCF and CGT cried victory nonetheless.

From a trade-union point of view everything was wrong with the February 12 strike. The economy was in a depressed state, creating the worst possible conditions for industrial action. And the strike was openly political, despite a crude attempt on the part of the CGT to tack material demands onto its "anti-fascist" slogans, a fact which ruled out any trade-union unity and limited potential support. Finally, the strike was decreed from the top by the CGT leadership at very short notice, with little or no advance preparation.[100] The CGT seemed to be losing touch with reality.

Reality slipped even further away in May. The PCF called a massive demonstration against the arrival of General Ridgway in Paris on May 28, 1952. The slogan for the day was *Ridgway la Peste*, a reference to charges that Ridgway had promoted bacteriological warfare during his Korean command. The government did not hesitate to try to break the demonstration by intimidation. On May 25, André Stil, editor of *L'Humanité*, was

98. *L'Humanité*, 31 January 1952; Branciard, vol. II, p. 183.

99. *L'année politique 1952*, p. 151.

100. Unir, *Histoire du PCF* (1962), vol. III, p. 73.

arrested and accused of undermining the morale of the armed services.[101] The Prefect of Paris banned the proposed demonstration. The PCF defied the ban and went ahead anyway. The demonstration turned into a rally of the party's most faithful—including a hard core of PCF streetfighting commandos armed with iron bars—and large numbers of police. The mixture was volatile, and conflict between protestors and police was violent. One demonstrator was killed, 718 were arrested and numerous representatives of the forces of order were hurt. The CGT called local strike movements to support the demostration, all of which failed. The government was clearly aware of the degree to which the PCF and CGT were isolated, and was determined to take advantage of this. Jacques Duclos, acting leader of the PCF, was arrested in his car on the day of the demonstration for "plotting against the internal security of the state" (this was the famous "pigeon" affair—the police found several pigeons in Duclos' car, the gift of a devoted comrade concerned that "Jacques" might dine well. The same pigeons became, in the government's version of the situation, vital cogs in the PCF's communications network). The next day police raided PCF and CGT offices all over France, looking for evidence to make the plot charges stick in court.[102] Further police raids continued in the weeks afterwards, with many CGT activists being arrested (including six CGT departmental leaders) on plot charges.[103]

In response to all this, the CGT called a day of strikes on June 4 to "liberate the prisoners." The circumstances of the strike call were the same as those on February 14. The labor market remained unfavorable for industrial action,[104] the strike was political in the extreme, ruling out unity with other groups, and it was decreed from the top with no prior preparation. What happened at Renault provides an illustration of the degree to which June 4 was a *cadre* action.[105] The powerful Renault CGT was unable to get the mass of Renault workers to move by normal trade-union means. Rather than give up, however, CGT militants simply shut off the electricity at Billancourt, forcing the rank and file to stop work, whatever they felt about the issues. *L'Humanité* once again cried victory. But the June 4 strikes were complete failures which even many faithful CGT militants refused to support.[106] That the CGT was in a desperate position was clear even to the CGT leadership. Benoît Frachon commented privately with reference to the PCF's public proclamation of success, "Victory . . . one or two more victories like this and there won't be any more CGT."

101. Elgey, *La république des contradictions* (1969), p. 70.
102. *Le Monde*, 1 June 1952; *L'Humanité*, 1 June 1952.
103. Frachon, vol. I, p. 506; Elgey, *Contradictions*, pp. 70–77.
104. Elgey, *Contradictions*, p. 70.
105. *Le Monde*, 6 June 1952; Unir, *PCF*, vol. III, p. 78; *Combat*, 5 June 1952; *L'année politique 1952*, pp. 40–41.
106. Unir, *PCF*, vol. III, p. 86.

The PCF was in a difficult position no matter what it did at this point, given the political climate in France and its own internal problems. The CGT had options, however. And the paroxysm of 1952 forced it to think about them seriously, a process which was the beginning of a profound reorientation in party-union relations. As early as June 7, 1952, *Le Monde* reported that the CGT leadership had decided to begin shifting away from politics and back towards "professional" demands.[107] At the June 1952 PCF Central Committee, Etienne Fajon indicated that the party was sensitive to the CGT's problems, criticizing the party press (a coded message for the whole party) for the expression of "tendencies . . . which considered the fight for workers' material demands as no longer relevant."[108] Then at the July Conference of the CGT Paris Regional Union Henri Raynaud, an important CGT leader, called the *libérez Duclos* strikes a sectarian error.[109] The strikes "did not take account of the diversity of the situations in the different sectors," said Raynaud, adding that the CGT was "the organization of all the workers and it cannot base its actions on an avant-garde."[110] Self-criticism was in order in the Federation of Railroad Workers, the other key CGT sector involved in the June 4 fiasco.[111]

June 1952 was the beginning of a critical turning point for the CGT, although it was far from clear at the time. Further politicization meant organizational suicide, and the CGT leadership knew it. Whatever happened in the political sphere, the CGT had to move back towards contact with the working-class rank and file. The rest of 1952 and much of the next year made such a move difficult, however. The PCF went through the painful Marty-Tillon purge in the fall of 1952, causing several months of party activity to be given over to purely internal questions, a process which limited the energy which Communist militants in the CGT were able to devote to their union activities.[112] Simultaneously, the government pursued its attempts to take legal repressive action against the PCF and CGT, causing further energy drains to deal with governmental harassment. In October 1952 Alain le Léap (co-Secretary–General of the CGT) and a number of younger party militants were arrested for alleged participation in efforts to "demoralize the army." In the next month several other CGT leaders (including André Tollet and Lucien Molino, a protégé of Benoît Frachon) were arrested, along with *L'Humanité* editor André Stil (for the second

107. *Le Monde*, 7 June 1952.
108. *L'Humanité*, 19 June 1952.
109. *L'Observateur*, 12 June 1952.
110. *Combat*, 23 July 1952; André Marty, *L'affaire Marty*, p. 160.
111. Cheminots, p. 351; *L'Humanité*, 4–5 September 1952 for Central Committee; also PCF, *Histoire du PCF*, pp. 538–539.
112. PCF, *Histoire du PCF*, p. 529; *L'année politique 1952*, pp. 61–63. See also Charles Tillon, *Un procès de Moscou à Paris* (1971); Yves le Braz, *Les rejetés: l'affaire Marty-Tillon* (1974).

time).[113] By March 1953, the campaign had led to the suspension of the parliamentary immunity of several PCF deputies. At the same moment, arrest
warrants were issued for Benoît Frachon himself, together with Marcel
Dufriche, another top CGT leader. Both went into hiding.

The spring of 1953 began to bring some clarity to the situation. Stalin's
death, the truce in Korea and the détente which seemed to be emerging
removed some of the urgency from the PCF's peace campaign. The phrase
"peaceful co-existence" began to crop up here and there in party statements. *Marty-Tillon* was finally digested by the party. Most importantly,
"Maurice" returned from the Soviet Union, to be greeted by expressions of
exaggerated adulation by his comrades (Aragon's chef d'oeuvre "Il re-
vient" appeared at this point) which may well have been disguised expressions of relief. Thorez, whose capacity for work was substantially limited
from this point on, nonetheless rapidly took the party back towards United
Frontism in recognition of the changed political situation in France and the
world. While renewed PCF United Frontism was unlikely to be greeted
with immediate success—the PCF was to navigate in a sea of anti-
Communist hostility for years to come—it did indicate that extreme PCF
sectarianism towards other forces in France might come to an end. PCF appeals to the SFIO for unity on the Left quickly followed, as did CGT appeals to non-CGT labor groups. And in May 1953, the PCF encouraged
PCF withdrawals in favor of well-placed Socialist candidates in municipal
elections. Benoît Frachon first broached the possibility of unity-in-action at
the top of the labor movement to a Conference of Paris metalworkers in
late May 1953. The June 1953 CGT Congress abounded with such
proposals.[114]

The central proposition in Thorez' first major speech after his return (to
the June 1953 PCF Central Committee meeting) was that "the decisive fact
of the hour is the progress of the idea of unity in the popular masses."
Thorez' optimism about the level of social discontent among French workers was proven correct sooner, perhaps, than even he expected. And in the
process important evidence about the progress of the CGT's self-reap-
praisal came out. By spring 1953 an atmosphere propitious for working-
class action had come to exist. Right-Center governments had blocked the
minimum-wage level for twenty months while refusing even to convene the
official commission charged with investigating the adequacy of the
minimum wage. Because of this, and because of the unanimity of perspective between governments and *patrons*, wages had begun to lag seriously behind prices, particularly in the public sector. Ebullition at the working-

113. *L'année politique 1952*, p. 150.
114. See CGT, *Congrès national*, June 1953; also Roger Pannequin, in *Cahiers du Communisme* (May 1953).

class base indicated that ordinary workers were indeed aware of this. Despite all this, August 1953 surprised everyone.

Everything began with a request from the government of Joseph Laniel to the National Assembly for special economic powers to allow the government to modify the professional status of public-sector workers by decree. To protest this the CGT routinely mobilized for a Day of Action on August 4. The CFTC supported the CGT's call, but *Force Ouvrière* did not.[115] The August 4 action proved successful, but not spectacularly so. On the next day, however, strange things began to happen. First off, it became known that the Bordeaux *Force Ouvrière* post-office workers had voted to carry on an unlimited strike against the Laniel decrees, against the desires of the FO Post Office Federation. The Bordeaux wildcat spread rapidly through provincial post-office centers to the point where the FO Federation was obliged to support and generalize it. Since FO was particularly strong among post-office workers, this meant that the CFTC Federation, and then the CGT, were obliged to follow suit.[116] The militancy of the post-office workers was all that was necessary to trigger a massive public-sector strike. By August 7, and without union prodding, the entire public sector, with the exception of the coal miners, was on strike, two million strong. By the middle of the next week, after union organizations had caught their breath and thrown their resources behind the movement, four million workers were out, including many in the private sector.[117]

Why the government had been impolitic enough to provoke such a huge strike was an interesting question. Undoubtedly Laniel and his advisers had calculated that the risks involved in solving the government's budgetary problems on the backs of public-sector workers were minimal. Civil servants were not known for their militancy and, when they did protest, were not prone to strong action. Moreover, public-sector workers were unpopular with other workers and the public. The decrees were judiciously timed to fall during the summer vacation period, when strike action in France was rare. Finally, the organized labor movement in France, on the strength of its Cold War record, would be too weak to react. In fact, the government was using the wrong arithmetic. Available evidence did indicate that the working class and its organizations were out of phase with one another, but not that the workers themselves were apathetic. Rank-and-file French workers had good reasons to be upset. Wages were down. The Laniel government was a provocation in itself, headed, as it was, by a real *patron* in power surrounded by like-minded colleagues. Moreover, the decrees were a frontal attack on the legal status of public-sector workers, one of the

115. Elgey, *Contradictions*, p. 153.

116. Elgey, *Contradictions*, p. 151; Lefranc, *1944–1968*, p. 115; Branciard, vol. II, p. 184.

117. See François Sellier, "Signification économique et sociale des grèves actuelles," *Signes du Temps*, July 1960, p. 25; Gibelin, *Socialisme ou Barbarie* (January–March 1954), p. 25.

more important working-class victories of the post-Liberation years. And to top it off, the government's attack, victimizing those it felt to be least likely to react, at a moment when any reaction would have been difficult, was transparently cynical.

The CGT's response to the exploding movement was cautious and circumspect. Only after the FO and CFTC Postal Federations had sanctioned the wildcat did the CGT do so. And only when the larger strike entered its second week did the CGT begin to take a leading role in its direction by expanding it in those areas where it had most power (the railroads, the mines, the private sector). Most important, the Confederation was scrupulously careful to avoid politicizing the strike, sticking closely to the material issues which had caused the wildcats in the first place. Clearly, the CGT had already thought a great deal about the problems which it had faced (and to a large extent created) in the 1947–1952 period. It knew that any movement which it initiated or quickly tried to dominate risked immediate isolation. Moreover, there was little need to politicize the strikes, since the strikes, opposed as they were to governmental actions, were political by their very nature. And the origin of the strikes in wildcats gave the CGT access which it had been lacking for years to masses of workers. Thus by waiting until other unions had committed themselves and until mass working-class support for the strikes was apparent, the CGT could guarantee a movement which was as extensive, successful, and united as possible. The contrast between CGT behavior in August 1953 and June 1952 could not have been more striking.

The CGT's astuteness paid off. Collaboration with the CGT so frightened FO and CFTC that they tried to work out a secret agreement with the Laniel government.[118] Alas, Laniel proved to be a true man of the Right, unwilling to give FO and the CFTC enough to allow them to settle with honor.[119] The strikes continued. PCF and Socialist deputies then petitioned for a recall of Parliament which, had it occurred, might have overthrown the government and, in turn, begun a shift to the Left involving the attenuation of Communist isolation. The recall move was defeated by a fraudulent vote-counting procedure, but the implications of the situation had become clear to an important part of the governmental majority. The MRP, under strong pressure from the CFTC, obliged Laniel to reopen negotiations with the CFTC and FO. The back of the movement was then broken, after three weeks of striking, when Laniel promised to review the decrees and offered certain concessions to the strikers. FO and the CFTC called back their strike orders and the strikers went slowly back to work.[120]

118. *Le Monde*, 9–10 August 1953.
119. *La Croix*, 17 August 1953; *Le Monde*, 15 August 1953; Elgey, *Contradictions*, p. 158.
120. The fact that non-Communist trade-union leaders were more willing to compromise the demands of strikers than to allow the continuation of a situation which might benefit the CGT and PCF was made apparent to many during the August strikes. After settlement was

The August 1953 strikes were the first movements in the CGT's new "post-sectarian" phase. The CGT's "last-in, last-out" tactics reflected the Confederation's new tactical considerations and were meant as building tools towards an end to CGT isolation.[121] The strikes themselves demonstrated conclusively how far the CGT had fallen out of touch with ordinary workers as a result of its exaggerated transmission-belt posture in the 1947–1952 period. The largest strike movement in French postwar history had occurred not because the CGT had been doing its trade-union job of protecting rank-and-file interests, but because the French working class, on its own, had decided to stand up and be counted. The CGT was astute enough at this point to know how to shape the movement to a successful conclusion. But the content of this astuteness consisted mainly in preventing the strike from being identified too closely with the CGT because the Confederation's leaders recognized that such an identification would have been disastrous for the strike. That the CGT had been able to devise such tactics provided important evidence that the Confederation had decided, after years of being a PCF political claque rather than a trade union, to get back in touch with the working-class masses. But clearly much more remained to be done before the CGT could claim again to be a genuine labor mass organization.

Nonetheless, given the context, the balance sheet of the 1953 strikes was positive for the CGT. The "last-in, last-out" tactic had obliged FO and the CFTC to settle with the government on terms that fell quite far short of what the strikers really wanted. This undoubtedly helped the CGT to reestablish itself as that branch of the labor movement which cared most about the real problems of workers. Moreover, the "sellout" of the strike by the CFTC leadership set in motion a process of internal conflict within the CFTC which was eventually to lead to a dramatic and positive reformulation of Catholic trade unionism in France. The bottom line lay elsewhere, however. Much of the boldness of the political Right in France in the early 1950s had been predicated on a dormant working class, cut off from and indifferent to its class organizations. The movements of 1953 proved quite conclusively that French workers were neither apathetic nor bought off (as some commentators had decided), and that they could not be abused beyond certain limits.

---

reached between FO, the CFTC, and the government, the CGT continued its strikes for several days in order to get whatever mileage it could from the insufficiences of the settlement. Considerable unhappiness did develop at this point among *Force Ouvrière* militants concerning the tendency of their leaders to shun conflict for fear of CGT and PCF action. Perhaps more important were the emergence of similar feelings in the CFTC, where the Confederal leadership's tactics during and at the end of the strike reinforced a militant opposition faction which was later to begin challenging the old CFTC leadership.

121. Branciard, vol. II, p. 84; Lefranc, *1944–1968*, p. 119.

Criticism and Self-Criticism

The CGT's long march away from its Cold War problems had only begun by the time of the 1953 strikes. Attempting to build a new momentum of industrial struggle in the fall of 1953 the Confederation called a series of strike actions unilaterally, almost all of which failed. The CGT was still too weak to initiate working-class movement on its own and too isolated to engage the support of other unions under its lead. Agitation in early 1954 around the minimum-wage level did achieve some unity-in-action (although not officially: the CFTC and FO promoted simultaneous demonstrations with those of the CGT, but no prior agreement was reached between the Confederations) and some success.[122] Trying to capitalize on such progress, the CGT spent two months after these January demonstrations attempting to organize a twenty-four-hour general strike on the minimum-wage issue. The problem was that no unity between unions could be negotiated, and the main reason for this was the CGT itself, which had decided on the shape and slogans of the strike which it desired to have before talking with the other unions.[123] *Force Ouvrière* wanted no part of the proposed strike (suspecting, reasonably, that the CGT might use the occasion to agitate against German rearmament).[124] The CFTC debated the proposal for weeks, finally deciding to promote an action parallel to that of the CGT. Finally, on April 28, 1954, the proposed twenty-four-hour strike took place. By this time any semblance of unity between unions had disappeared and the CGT acted virtually on its own (the CFTC held its very tepid parallel protest, while FO actively opposed the action). The CGT strike was quite apolitical, stressing the minimum-wage question, but this was not enough to save it. The Confederation cried victory, but again privately admitted defeat.[125]

The failure of the April 28 strike was important. The CGT had fully expected to move from the strikes of 1953 to a period of major industrial struggle. In the event, the CGT failed to build any mass action at all in the months following August 1953. The fiasco of April 28 was the last straw. How much trouble the CGT was in became clear at the June 1954 PCF Congress. Here, in an unprecedented tirade, none other than Jacques Duclos took the CGT to task. And none other than Benoît Frachon, long one of the most powerful figures in the PCF, was obliged to do a public self-criticism. In Frachon's words,

> We did not learn the lesson of the movements of February and June 1952. We did not pay attention to the development of the trade-union

122. J. Toulouse, "Des grèves d'août 1953 au gouvernement Mendès-France," *Informations Sociales* (1 September 1954); *Le Monde*, 30 January 1954; *Combat*, 29 January 1954; PCF, *Histoire du PCF*, p. 553; *L'année politique 1954*, p. 157.

123. Gibelin, p. 1943.

124. *Le Monde*, 29 April 1954; *L'Humanité*, 29 April 1954.

125. *Le Populaire*, 29 April 1954; *Le Monde*, 30 April 1954.

struggle and its enlargement to new strata of the working class, nor did we take any dispositions to enlarge our action. . . . Instead we acted in an unthinking way by following the movement of that part of the working class which was already prepared, with the inadmissible illusion on our part that this would be decisive in bringing along the mass of workers. . . . Another error [of the April 28 strike] was to have thought that the demand for a guaranteed minimum wage would be sufficient to lead to unity-in-action. . . . It proved to be not a slo-gan of unity, but of confusion, and we hindered the struggle which was developing at the time.[126]

Frachon was admitting that the CGT, on April 28, had called a general strike on an issue which did not touch the bulk of French workers. He was also granting that the CGT had tried to decree a basically inept strike from the top. As Duclos pointed out, all of this indicated serious neglect by the CGT of its *travail de masse*. The CGT assumed that its calls to action would in themselves be enough to create action and it therefore neglected the tasks of building action through long, hard organizing around real problems. Duclos concluded that the CGT's errors led to strikes provoked by "active minorities" among "unorganized majorities," a style of action which was bound to lead to sectarianism and reinforce isolation.[127]

The PCF leadership had decided to oblige the CGT to confront some of the organizational distortions which the Confederation's Cold War posture, dictated by the party, had created. That the party meant business was clear not only from Duclos' harsh words, but also from the elimination of several important CGTers from the PCF Central Committee (Lucien Molino, André Lunet, Olga Tournade and Roger Linet). August Lecoeur, who met his unpleasant end at the 1954 Congress, was also publicly blamed for part of the CGT's failure.[128] Rumor had it that Frachon himself had to fight for his political life at this juncture as well. The whole process was a painful one for the CGT. Nonetheless, PCF criticisms of the Confederation were correct. Excessive politicization, which had been toned down after June 1952, was only one aspect of the CGT's Cold War problem. Manipu-lative organizational habits—privately attributed to Lecoeur in his steward-ship as PCF organizational secretary—had also developed, which con-tinued to undermine CGT effectiveness even after it began to turn back to more strictly trade-unionist behavior. Beginning in 1948, the CGT had become progressively more isolated, and its contacts with the broader working class had become ever more difficult. The temptation had grown, especially given the CGT's basically political orientation through most of

---

126. See Frachon's self-criticism in *Cahiers du Communisme* (July 1954) (report of the thir-teenth PCF Congress); *L'Humanité*, 6 June 1954.

127. Jacques Duclos, *Cahiers du Communisme* (July 1954), p. 708.

128. PCF, *Histoire du PCF*, p. 555.

these years, to treat non-cooperative rank-and-file workers as lost, even as enemies. Connected to this was the development of habits of relying on those workers who were closest to the Confederation's perspectives while neglecting others. In all this, the CGT turned inward rather than outward, losing contact with the masses. The time had come for this to change.

The reorientation of the CGT was far from complete, however. To explain how the Confederation finally turned towards a more classical labor mass-organizational posture, a brief discussion of one of the stranger episodes in PCF history is necessary. Thorez' return did lead to a shift in the PCF's general strategy back towards United Frontism. This meant that the party's central goal was to mobilize mass support for and promote a political alliance with the Socialists. Given the bitterness of the Cold War and the fact that the PCF still insisted that the Socialists cease their devotion to American foreign-policy goals, progress along these lines was not easy. Nonetheless, a definite shift in the country at large towards the Left was clear by 1954. The first sign of this was the Mendès-France government which came to power in June 1954 bringing with it some hope for an end to war in Indochina plus new openings on the European Defense Community. The PCF supported the government in Parliament on these issues, while abstaining on, rather than opposing, Mendès' economic policies.

When Mendès replaced the European Defense Community with direct German rearmament through the London Accords, the PCF's position on him shifted abruptly. From this point onwards, the Mendès-France experiment was seen by the party as a new danger rather than a promising opening towards a new Popular Front. The revised line on Mendès was summarized by Thorez at the May 1955 Central Committee meeting. "The friends of Mendès-France attempt to mask the reactionary politics of the government under the camouflage of the 'New Left' label. . . . These politicians confess their anti-Communist purposes. They want people to believe that it is possible to change French politics without the Communists."[129] Mendès and his allies aimed "to capture the feeling in favor of the union of popular forces . . . and use it for the profit of the *grande bourgeoisie* . . . to build a political and electoral organization directed essentially against our party and the hopes which it bears."[130] Decoding this diatribe was not difficult. The PCF sensed a movement towards the Left in the French electorate. It hoped to use this movement to promote a United Front alliance. At the same time, it perceived that Pierre Mendès-France was attempting to use this same popular upsurge in support of a reformed alliance between Centrist forces around Mendès and the SFIO, to the exclusion of the PCF. Mendès therefore stood in the way of the PCF's strategic

129. *L'Humanité*, 28 May 1955.
130. Maurice Thorez, "La Paupérisation," *Cahiers du Communisme* (March 1955).

goals and had to be discredited. Mendèsism, to the PCF, was simply a more subtle reformulation of the anti-Communism (including anti-Sovietism) of the Third Force arrangements of the late 1940s. But because it was more subtle by virtue of its explicit reformism, it was more dangerous.

Discrediting Mendèsism became an important priority to the party at this time, then. The first, and most important, problem to be faced was the danger that Mendèsist reformism might mislead the working class (or, in clearer language, might appeal to parts of the PCF's own base). At this juncture, partly to deal with this problem, the party produced several of the strangest theoretical statements in all of its history (and perhaps in the history of all Third International-derived Communist parties), about the "pauperization" of the French proletariat. A great many observers, including Mendès and his "New Left" colleagues, had noted that the French economy seemed to be turning towards postwar prosperity. To the Mendèsists, this meant that important reforms were becoming possible and that the growing "pie" would henceforth allow the development of a full-blown consumer society in France. The pauperization analysis—which built on earlier PCF work about the effects of Marshallization—simply denied that such things were true, against all evidence. France was a declining imperialist capitalism, said Thorez (who, as the party's leading thinker, authored the pauperization texts) and French capitalism was incapable of improving living standards. In fact, it was actually promoting both the relative and absolute pauperization of the proletariat. Not only had the relative share of wages in total French national income gone down, Thorez claimed, but absolute real wages were declining as well. Workers had been better off in the thirties. Some zealous proponents of the Thorez analysis even claimed that workers had been better off prior to 1789! Thus the claims of the Mendèsist reformists were little more than attempts to brainwash the workers and prevent them from understanding the truth about their situation.

The pauperization analysis was very wrong, yet another indication of how far out of touch the Thorez leadership had become with French social reality. However it was primarily designed to provide the PCF with counter-arguments to Mendèsist reformism to be used with workers, and this meant that it had to be implemented by the CGT. First, however, it had to become part of the CGT's own theoretical baggage, a process which led to serious internal conflict in the CGT itself. The main problem was that there were a number of Mendès-style reformists among the non-Communists in the CGT leadership. Beyond this, the CGT itself, because of the complexity of its past, was publicly committed to a platform which was not that different from what the more radical Mendèsists were proposing.

In 1948, just after the drastic shift to Third Force politics in France, the CGT leadership had commissioned the Confederation's economic section (which was coordinated by Pierre LeBrun, a non-Communist Confederal

Secretary) to produce a CGT "Program of Economic and Social Redress-ment" which would include a series of CGT proposals for government economic policy involving industry-by-industry structural reforms, fiscal change and foreign-trade innovations.[131] The purpose of this program, at the time, was to give the Confederation a platform to show workers what would be politically possible in France should Third Force governments give way to a new Popular Front (while providing simultaneously an index for judging what the cost of actual Third Force rule was for the French working class). After 1948, the CGT Program was elaborated and expand-ed at successive CGT and Federation Congresses.[132]

From the pauperization perspective, the CGT Program was a serious lia-bility, however. Prior to 1954 French governments showed no inclination to reform anything. With Mendèsism, however, many of the measures which the CGT proposed were placed anew on the political agenda. In this context, the PCF reasoned that the CGT Program might lead workers to believe that solutions to their problems might come from bourgeois politi-cians of the Mendès stripe, rather than from the PCF and a Popular Front. Thus the Program had to go.

The Anti-Program campaign began at the November 1954 National Con-federal Committee meeting. There Léon Mauvais proposed a new CGT Program, consisting entirely of bread-and-butter union demands, to replace the old.[133] Then at the 1955 CGT Congress, all of the major PCF/CGT leaders buried the old Program under an impressive barrage of rhetoric. Benoît Frachon took the lead. It was necessary, above all, said the Secretary-General, to "make sure nothing in the general politics of the CGT or in its Program leads towards compromise, towards class collabora-tion."[134] The old Program promoted illusions that "planning," and an *économie dirigé* which would benefit workers, was possible under cap-italism. It suggested that nationalization of industry per se would bene-fit workers. In general, the Program had "disoriented our comrades in the presence of enemy campaigns." As Frachon emphasized, "There isn't a Chinese wall between the proletariat and the bourgeoisie. The latter tries to promote the penetration of its ideology among us in a thousand ways . . . the least relaxation of our vigilance can cause errors which will lead us away from the working class."[135] As Frachon pointed out in another context, French capitalists did not need the prompting of trade unions to modernize at the expense of the workers.[136]

131. CGT, *Congrès national, 1948*, pp. 32–33.

132. CGT, *Congrès national, 1951*, pp. 272 ff. See *Revue des Comités d'Entreprise*, no. 62 (May 1953), p. 8.

133. CGT, *Congrès national, 1955*, "Programme d'action," pp. 397–411.

134. Frachon at CGT, *Congrès national, 1955*, p. 46.

135. CGT, *Congrès national, 1955*, p. 44.

136. Frachon in *L'Humanité*, 3 May 1955.

Frachon's final comments to the Congress got to the heart of the matter. Referring to the original Program he urged "Reread this document. There really is everything in it necessary for a sane economy. . . . Only one thing is missing . . . in order for it not to remain a pious desire—a very small thing—state power, the socialization of industry. Without this very small thing, it is only a dangerous illusion which substitutes myth for the reality of class struggle."[137] In essence, the old Program, and the reformists within the CGT who defended it, were indicted for ignoring the whole question of working-class political power. Worse still, the Program over-looked the necessity of the Communist Party as the "party of the working class" being the motivating factor behind socialist change.

Benoît Frachon's irony in fact covered up an even more profound irony in the entire CGT Program debate. For political reasons of a short-term na-ture the PCF had enjoined a major policy change on the CGT. The direc-tion of this policy change, however political its origins, was towards a signi-ficant de-politicization of the CGT. The new Program of Action which the 1955 CGT Congress substituted for the condemned reformist document was nothing more than a long list of defensive and economistic demands to improve working-class living standards.[138] In the words of a defender of the new Program, it was "necessary in the present period to mobilize the working class for the class struggle . . . the unity of the working class must be constructed before this class can think of rebuilding the country's eco-nomy."[139] Compared to the CGT's rejected Program, the new Program was apolitical. The logic in all of this followed from the pauperization theory. If declining French imperialism implied the compression of working-class living standards, then the primary way to mobilize the French working class for change was to generate labor-market struggles to defend working-class conditions. No longer were high political struggles around foreign policy issues seen as the primary means to open the road to change in France (although such struggles, particularly around German re-armament, were to be by no means abandoned during the post-1955 period). The contradiction of French capitalism which really counted, ac-cording to the pauperization analysis, was an economic one. Economic struggle was the way to deal with it, then. The CGT was finally to be al-lowed again to be a trade union.

Paradoxes abounded at this point. As a response to Mendèsist refor-mism, pauperization involved a grotesque misunderstanding of the dynam-ics of postwar French capitalism. Based on an absurd projection from the 1949–1950 Marshallization analyses of the Cominform, it would render the PCF quite unable to decipher the facts of the extended period of economic

137. CGT, *Congrès national, 1955*, p. 44.
138. Ibid., pp. 397–411.
139. Ibid.

change and boom which was opening up. Moreover the ways in which it was enunciated and imposed further underlined the extent to which internal Stalinization continued to flourish in the party. For the CGT, however, pauperization meant a move towards a degree of mass organizational sanity after long years of very costly transmission-belt over-politicization. However wrong-headed the pauperization theory was, it relocated the primary contradiction of French capitalism in the economic realm, away from foreign policy issues. This relocation was bound to push the CGT back towards the working-class masses, since mobilizing workers in the market was what the party henceforth wanted the CGT most to do. In the longer run, the shift back to market action might even make unity-in-action with other labor organizations a possibility for the first time since the beginnings of the Cold War. Not that the pauperization perspective was ideally suited to the CGT either, since it was destined to orient the Confederation towards a very narrow economistic definition of what labor-market action ought to be. But it did allow the CGT to begin recentering its organizational calculations in accordance with its perceptions of the rhythms of the labor market. For the moment, this was a substantial step forward.

PART TWO

Relative Autonomy or "Liberté Surveillée"?

Chapter 4

A WORLD OUT OF JOINT—
THE END OF THE FOURTH REPUBLIC?

1955 initiated an important reconsideration of PCF–CGT relationships. During the deep Cold War years the CGT had become a political claque for the PCF. Exaggerated transmission-belt behavior had brought the Confederation to the very edge of a dangerous precipice, beyond which its ability to function as a labor mass organization was threatened. Because the party wanted union power in the longer run more than it needed the CGT as a para-political strike force, and because major changes in the environment around both party and union had intervened, the CGT began to alter its positions. The transmission-belt relationship between party and union was to be discarded. In its place the design of a "relative autonomy" model of PCF–CGT ties was sketched. Basic to this was CGT recognition that its mass influence depended upon success at promoting working-class interests in the labor market. To do this the primary focus for action had to be the labor market itself, not the political sphere. This did not mean, to be sure, that the CGT was about to sever its contacts with the PCF. The premise of relative autonomy was that the CGT—or any other union, for that matter—when deliberating about the raw facts of the labor market, would be able to discern from such facts a number of different, equally plausible, strategic possibilities. From this range of possibilities, any one of which might allow the Confederation to maintain or deepen its mass organizational influence, the CGT would choose the one which best promised to promote PCF mobilizational goals.

"Relative autonomy" was "relative" then, in large part because the CGT retained its commitment to promoting the political outcomes desired by the PCF, even if it was henceforth to attempt to do so *as a trade union*, and not as a directly political support force for the party. Relativity had another dimension as well. Even after its shift away from transmission-belt overpoliticization, the Confederation would continue to use PCF theory as the source of its maps of French society and of the French working class. In a *formal* sense, such use would not distinguish the CGT from other French trade unions. All had maps of the social world, explicit or implicit notions of the dynamics of French capitalism and French class structure, around which they constructed their goals and actions. The peculiarity of the CGT was, however, that *its* map of the social worlds was derived directly from that devised by the PCF. CGT autonomy was thus "relative"—i.e., limited—in two different ways: by its need to find a labor-market strategy congruent with PCF political goals, and by its use of PCF theory to understand the world. Despite relative autonomy the Confederation was vulnerable to inappropriate PCF strategy and/or inadequate PCF theorizing. The shift towards relative autonomy would not therefore leave the Confederation free of the PCF and its many problems.

In the abstract, relative autonomy seemed an important advance on transmission beltism, even if its ultimate purpose, that of creating a union which would be open and credible to French workers of any and all political persuasions, while at the same time using this union, in the last instance, to promote PCF fortunes, was a bit like squaring the circle. However, recognition of the need for change in PCF–CGT relationships did not create such change in itself. The CGT possessed certain long-standing and cherished notions about the structure of the French labor market which still stood in the way of relative autonomy. Serious labor-market activity would depend upon unity-in-action with other union organizations, and the CGT could not hope to generate it all alone. Yet the CGT's insistence, based, in part, on schematic Marxism-Leninism derived from the PCF, that it was the only legitimate mass-organizational representative of French workers—that other unions were founded on bourgeois conspiracies to mislead French workers—made serious collaboration with other unions virtually impossible. In the long run, as well, the pauperization theory which the CGT had borrowed part and parcel from the party, would also pose problems. If pauperization had the virtue of pointing the Confederation back toward events in the labor market, its wrong-headed sense of the dynamics of French capitalism might eventually become a liability. Such doctrinal questions put aside, developing relative autonomy was a delicate art for which the CGT, in 1955, was not terribly well prepared. It was not a simple matter to choose that specific labor-market strategy which simultaneously maximized the CGT's trade-union plausibility and the PCF's political goals. Old habits of reducing everything to politics were deeply ingrained in the CGT, in the leadership, but perhaps even more at middle levels of the organization where party militants predominated. In addition, even if the art of relative autonomy could be mastered, a task which clearly would demand lengthy apprenticeship, the question remained of in what circumstances it would still be appropriate to politicize the CGT.

Modern French history has been filled with crises in which the politicization of trade unions beyond simple labor-market activity has been of major importance; one has only to remember the beginnings of the Popular Front or the Resistance. Crisis politicization could not be excluded, even with relative autonomy. But how much politicization, in what circumstances, and who was to decide? Beyond all this, of course, lay the fundamental question of whether relative autonomy would turn out to be a suitable redefinition of party-union relationships even if it could be worked out properly!

By 1955 the PCF had itself shifted back toward a United Front orientation. Within this perspective, the CGT acquired important new tasks. As conceived by the PCF, this new United Frontism would combine mass action "from below" with political maneuvering "at the top." A mass popular movement from below would create the groundswell of feeling which might, in turn, prod reluctant United Front candidates for political partnership—the Socialists and Radicals—towards new willingness to cooperate with the Communists. The pauperization analysis indicated the precise path for the CGT to follow in promoting mass mobilizaton. Since the central contradictions of French capitalism were economic, defensive struggle for working-class demands was the route to take.

Futile United Frontism: 1955–1958

The CGT Tries on Its New Clothes

The working class was not reluctant to act. Another major strike wave in summer 1955 demonstrated quite well how the CGT intended to use its new relative-autonomy position—and what pitfalls even this new approach faced. The shape of postwar French economic modernization was becoming clearer, and one of its central aspects was a shift in economic activity towards more dynamic sectors of the economy away from more traditional areas. Given the geographical structures of the French economy, this also meant that certain regions would prosper, while others were destined to decline. The summer 1955 strikes were sparked by just these changes.

By the early 1950s the French shipbuilding industry, faced by newly threatening international competitors, began to take drastic steps to survive. Mergers and work rationalization, the measures decided upon, were taken with the industry's traditional disregard for the lives of its employees. Among workers whose pay was already low, changes in work norms and job classifications involving de facto wage cuts were not well received. Thus, beginning with a small group of solderers, in June and July 1955 the entire St. Nazaire metal-working complex went out on strike. Unusually solid unity between local trade-union organizations facilitated the spread of the strike throughout the city. The spectacle of the bulk of St.

Nazaire's work force standing up in protest, even in the face of the police, gave the strike national publicity.[1]

The extent of rank-and-file support for the St. Nazaire movement—which surprised even local union leaderships—forced the shipbuilders to grant a substantial wage increase.[2] The strikers' success in St. Nazaire, in turn, inspired other workers on the industrial periphery of France to move.[3] In neighboring Nantes, in early August, militant actions forced an important settlement on the *patronat*. When the bosses later reneged on the agreement (claiming that it had been signed under duress), five hours of street warfare ensued. In response to arrests made in the street action, indignant workers then tried to break into the prison to release their fellow strikers. Clashes between the prison attackers and Riot Police (CRS) led to many injuries and one death.[4] Similar, if less spectacular, confrontations occurred elsewhere. Underneath them all was a rebellion against growing disparities between "advanced" and "backward" areas of the country.[5] The relative prosperity which was emerging in 1954–1955 benefited those regions where newer forms of economic activity existed (the Paris region, first of all), while living standards in regions without such activity fell behind. Such "natural" wage differences between regions were reinforced by an administrative institution called *zones d'abattement de salaires* (differentiated wage zones within France) which slanted the country's wage structure in much the same ways as it was already exaggerated by the structure of economic development itself.[6]

Such was the context within which the CGT tried out its new trade-union posture. These regional movements presented the CGT with two possible tactical options. It might, first of all, seize upon the specific problems of workers in declining regions and use CGT organizational resources to push militant local strikes to the limit. This choice promised to maximize gains for workers on France's industrial periphery. The second option was to use the summer 1955 militancy as a launching pad for nationwide strike action to force high-level national negotiations. Both courses were plausible, although the second, because more ambitious, carried higher risks. The CGT

1. *Le Monde*, 25, 29 June 1955; *L'année politique 1955*, p. 161.

2. Branciard, vol. II, p. 209.

3. Branciard, vol. II, p. 209; *Le Monde*, 7 July 1955, 23 August 1955, 22 September 1955. From St. Nazaire the movement spread from city to city up and down the Atlantic Coast, up the Loire toward Paris, along the Mediterranean, into the eastern provinces.

4. *Le Monde*, 21 August 1955; *L'année politique 1955*, p. 163.

5. The literature on France's regional problems is enormous. See, among other works, the early classic by Jean Gravier, *Paris et le désert français* (1947); J. la Jugie, "Aménagement du territoire et développement économique régional en France," in *Revue d'Economie Politique* (January-February 1964); the regional section in Pierre Massé, *Le Plan ou l'anti-hasard* (1965).

6. François Sellier, "Signification économique et sociale des grèves actuelles," *Signes du Temps* (July 1960), p. 25.

decided what to do by reference to broader PCF political goals. A nation-wide strike movement leading to high-level negotiations demonstrating deep popular discontent might influence forces of the non-Communist Left and Center to contemplate political cooperation with the PCF. Further-more, with the national election campaign of 1956 at hand, such a move-ment might well enhance the electoral chances of the Left. Thus the CGT chose the second option. The Confederation's choice had important im-plications for the regionally peripheral workers whose discontent had sparked union action in the first place, however. The success of national strike movements depended upon support from public opinion. In order to ensure such support, the CGT had to moderate the intense local militancy which had marked the initial struggles. If the CGT's attempts at gener-alizing the movements failed, then, the moderation which it imposed in the provinces might well limit the success of local actions.[7]

Spreading the strike wave to Paris was the central goal of the CGT's generalization tactic. Thus when Parisian workers returned from summer vacations they were greeted by strong CGT insistence "to be inspired by the example of St. Nazaire." However inspiring the St. Nazaire example might have been, circumstances, alas, were very different in Paris. Parisian workers had many problems, but the Paris region had benefited from the regional maldistribution of whatever prosperity had come to exist.[8] The CGT's plans for a national movement therefore proved difficult to imple-ment. The Confederation did what it could to initiate action, particularly in those Parisian sectors where it was strongest, but to little avail.[9] Where strikes had emerged from below, as in the provinces, they were strong. Where they were promoted by union apparatus, they were weak.[10] In Paris, they were generally weak. Complicating the CGT's plans, other union or-ganizations refused to follow the CGT's lead in strike development, leading to union disunity in just those places where rank-and-file support for strikes was lowest.

At this point the CGT's efforts encountered an unexpectedly astute counter-attack from the French *patronat*. The militant provincial strikes of the summer had cost French employers a lot. To prevent the spread of such costs throughout the whole private sector of the economy, the CNPF decid-ed on an unusually subtle (for the CNPF) strategy. It proposed granting across-the-board five percent wage raises, which were substantial, of couse,

---

7. *Socialisme ou Barbarie*, no. 18 (January-March 1956) has some interesting examples, esp. p. 14; also articles by J. Simon and Daniel Mothé. The CGT's contention (important in the pauperization analysis) was that struggle, and not the largesse of employers, led to better-ment. Such negotiations ideally would also lead to recognition of the CGT as an *interlocuteur valable*, a major step toward ending the CGT's Cold War isolation and enhancing its national legitimacy. CGT-enforced local moderation was deemed justifiable on the basis of such tactics.

8. François Sellier, p. 25.

9. *L'Observateur*, 22 September 1955 (Lucien Rioux), p. 18.

10. *Le Monde*, 18 September 1955.

but much less than those which had been won in earlier provincial struggles. Moreover, in exchange for these raises, the CNPF wanted to extract agreement on more regular procedures of negotiation and mediation from the unions.[11] The CGT's plans, the CNPF's counteroffensive and trade-union disunity all came together at Renault (which, though nationalized, behaved progressively more as the industrial leader of the private sector). The Renault administration seized the initiative by negotiating an agreement with *Force Ouvrière* and the CFTC. The Renault accord, a landmark in post-war French industrial relations, was a four-year agreement in which Renault workers were to receive a four percent annual guaranteed raise, three weeks of paid vacation and the establishment of a "paritary commission" which would signal if and when annual wage raises fell behind the cost of living. In exchange for all this, Renault administrators secured a limited anti-strike agreement from the union signatories. The whole accord was prefaced by an eloquent preamble which spoke of the common interests of workers and employers in increased productivity.[12]

The accord plunged the Renault CGT into confusion. At first Renault CGTers rejected the accord as "class-collaborationist," and began a campaign to persuade Renault workers to refuse to support it. Frachon announced that the Renault CGT "ought to affirm clearly that the preamble to the Renault accord and any other clause on productivity . . . tending to impose capitalist and reactionary theories of class collaboration do not bind either trade unions or workers."[13] The Renault rank and file, however, did not agree. The CGT then had to choose between the unpleasant alternatives of signing the accord—an attitude dictated by rank-and-file feeling—or refusing it and risking isolation. Eventually the Renault CGT reversed its position on the matter and signed. This about-face, however, caused divisions within the Renault CGT apparatus—CGT opponents of signing apparently claimed that "to sign is to deny the theory of pauperization."[14] More important, by the time the CGT had sorted all of this out, the 1955 strike movement had long since expired.

At the beginning of the 1955 strike movement the CGT had been full of optimism. To Frachon "the discussion which preceded our Congress and our Congress itself contributed to the destruction of myths . . . which hid the reality of things from the working class." The "class-collaborationist"

11. Lefranc, *1944–1968*, p. 125; *L'année politique 1955*, p. 164.

12. Pierre Naville, "L'accord Renault est-il un nouveau 'contract social'?," *Esprit* (June 1956) (also in Naville, *La classe ouvrière et le régime Gaulliste* [1964]); and Benoît Frachon, "L'accord Renault et les intérêts véritables des travailleurs," in *La Vie Ouvrière*, 7 November 1955; also *L'année politique 1955*, p. 166. The Renault accord was not an entirely original invention of the Renault management, having been inspired by similar accords concluded earlier at FIAT in Italy.

13. Frachon, *La Vie Ouvrière*, 7 November 1955.

14. *L'Observateur*, 15 September 1955.

errors of the Confederation had been corrected, with the result that "the workers can see more clearly and have taken the right road."[15] By August, Etienne Fajon felt able to proclaim in *L'Humanité* that "the grand ideas developed by Maurice Thorez on pauperization have profoundly penetrated the working class. They have contributed to the dissipation of illusions about the amelioration of exploitation under capitalism."[16] Yet the strike movement which had prompted such optimism collapsed in the face of a skillful counter-offensive from the CNPF.[17] Clearly the CGT did not yet know quite how to function in its new relative-autonomy posture. Its choice of labor-market tactics between conceivable options had been wrong. In the hope of promoting a mass-strike movement which would aid PCF mobilization plans it had sacrificed a promising regional-strike outbreak.

The Perils of the PCF

The PCF was no more successful at its renewed United Frontism than the CGT had been at trying out relative autonomy. As the 1956 elections approached, the party desperately tried to convert a visible electoral shift to the Left in the country into a new Popular Front. Incessant overtures to the Socialists fell on deaf ears, however.[18] The Socialists, still obsessed with the Cold War, were much more interested in building a new Third Force coalition with Mendès-France. Undaunted, Communists went to the polls massed around the slogan "to prepare the victory of a new Popular Front, vote Communist!" Socialists and Radicals presented themselves as a Left-Center *Front Républicain*. Nonetheless, despite the divisions within the Left, the PCF held some hope that the results of the elections might change things. Were the PCF to maintain or increase its electoral strength while the Right also held its own (at this point the Poujadist movement was reaching its apogee) any *Front Républicain* government would be hard-pressed to maintain a parliamentary majority. In such circumstances Socialists and Radicals might eventually be forced to choose between opening to the Left or Right. Opening to the Left would be the only way in which the two parties could carry out their reformist goals.

The election results created the situation anticipated by the PCF. The PCF did well (twenty-six percent of the vote) while the Poujadists polled thirteen percent. In the new National Assembly the PCF and Poujadists controlled one-third of the seats, the classical Right controlled another third, leaving the *Front Républicain* with the rest. The Socialists and

15. Frachon in *L'Humanité*, 25 June 1955.
16. Etienne Fajon in *L'Humanité*, 27 August 1955.
17. Frachon, *Au rythme des jours*, vol. II, p. 92 (reprinted from *Rassegna Sindacale*, 29 February 1956).
18. *L'Humanité*, 1 December 1955; PCF, *Histoire du PCF*, pp. 591–592; *L'année politique 1955*, pp. 93–96.

Radicals were caught. Jacques Duclos was quick to announce, "today, as twenty years ago, the Communist Party is resolved to devote all its resources to the construction of a new Popular Front."[19] And, as a gesture of sincerity, the party's first act in the new legislature was to support the SFIO's candidate for President of the National Assembly. Guy Mollet was adamant about refusing Socialist-Communist cooperation, however, and the Socialists opted to form a minority government rather than opening to the Left. The PCF did not give up. As Duclos noted to the January 1956 Central Committee, "a minority government refusing to base its support on all of the Left without exception will become the hostage of the reactionaries. Our party must do everything to develop a mass movement throughout the country . . . to push for a government of the Left. . . ." The order went out to the party rank and file to leave no stone unturned in its efforts to create a mass movement demanding a new Popular Front.[20] In the meantime, the PCF decided to support the minority Mollet government in the National Assembly.

Partly because of Communist support, the Mollet government did legislate some important reforms in the first few months of its tenure. Workers acquired three weeks of paid vacation (something of a recognition of a fait accompli since the 1955 strike movements had already succeeded in winning three weeks, at least in the private sector of the economy), the *zones d'abattement* of wage levels were reduced, and new social-security arrangements for the elderly were voted. Mollet refused, however, to create a sliding scale tying wages to inflation or to raise the minimum wage, both central PCF and CGT demands. From the point of view of the PCF the fact that the government was not producing as much social reform as desired was less important, however, than the fact that Mollet seemed determined to carry on a brutal colonial war in Algeria.

It was on the Algerian issue that the PCF's renewed United Frontism met disaster. In principle, the PCF opposed the Algerian War. In practice, this opposition was muted indeed as long as the party cherished some hope that Mollet might open to the Left. Thus the PCF publicly denounced armed repression in Algeria, but not to the point of risking loss of contact with the Socialists in government. The party was caught to the point where, in March 1956, it voted for the Mollet government's proposal of "special powers" for the Minister-Resident in Algeria.[21] In Etienne Fajon's words, "the vote of the Communist group is not . . . a vote of approval of the military measures taken by Guy Mollet. It is a large political gesture which opens the road to the development of common action between Communists

---

19. *L'année politique 1955*, p. 101; *L'année politique 1956*, p. 79; PCF, *Histoire du PCF*, p. 499.

20. *Le Monde*, 19 January 1956.

21. PCF, *Histoire du PCF*, p. 602; *L'année politique 1956*, p. 41.

and Socialists."[22] Fajon had made a mistake about the road which the Communist vote opened. The special powers which the party supported were used by Minister-Resident Robert Lacoste to intensify the repression of Algerian rebels. The PCF's new United Front thrust had led it into a trap. Socialist anti-Communism was, alas, much too strong to be softened at this point by Communist gestures of good will. In addition, the commitment of the Socialists—not to speak of every other major non-Communist group in France—to repressive strategies in Algeria was considerable. As a result the PCF found itself giving de facto support to policies in Algeria which it professed to find completely abhorrent.

The PCF could not follow such a course for long without completely abandoning its integrity. In June 1956, the PCF abstained in a parliamentary vote of confidence on Algeria.[23] Then in July the party voted against the government's military budget, ending its support of Mollet.[24] Even after July the PCF's opposition to the war was halfhearted, however. The party press did turn to constant vilification of Mollet and his colleagues, but little in the way of significant mass action was promoted. The PCF opposed the initial shipment of conscripts to Algeria in speeches and in the press, but little direct action occurred.[25] Around the Algerian issue the party was unwilling to engage in anything like the activities which it had undertaken earlier in the Cold War period. One reason for this was that it continued to hold open the possibility of a new Popular Front and did not want to isolate itself by a new outpouring of militancy. Beyond this, the party could not be sure that its own rank and file would follow any militant anti-war campaigns. That considerable working-class nationalism existed, and perhaps a degree of racism, around Algeria did not escape the party's attention.[26]

Thus the PCF botched its first attempts at post–Cold War United Frontism, much as the CGT had botched its first try at new labor-market activism. The party leadership had made serious misjudgments about how far, and in what circumstances, to conciliate a Socialist government bent on colonial repression. The party was able to pull back from its exposed

22. *L'Humanité*, 12 March 1956.

23. PCF, *Histoire du PCF*, p. 604.

24. Ibid., pp. 613–621; *L'année politique 1956*, p. 79. It was not only Algeria which led the PCF to withdraw support from the government. The government had been particularly active in taking anti-Communist initiatives. In May it had seized issues of *L'Humanité* and *Humanité-Dimanche*. It had also consistently dealt with any and all labor organizations except the CGT.

25. On this question Mothé's description of the CGT's action on the call up of reservists at Renault is invaluable. See Daniel Mothé, *Journal d'un ouvrier* (1959). Edgar Morin saw the CGT and PCF moderation on the war as the decisive factor in the failure of French intellectuals to set up a strong anti-war movement (see Morin, *Autocritique* (1959), p. 192).

26. François Fejtö, *The French Communist Party and the Crisis of International Communism* (1967), p. 48; Jean Baby, *Critique de base* (1960), p. 76; Fauvet, vol. II, p. 284.

position, but only after serious compromises had been made. Such compromises were very badly received in certain social strata, intellectuals in particular, whose opposition to the Algerian War was to become a major factor in French politics. In the meantime, the party was in for even worse problems stemming from its ties to the international Communist movement.

The PCF's response to the events of the Twentieth Soviet Party Congress in 1956 involved mistakes of a different, and higher, order. Despite the fact that the PCF delegation to the Twentieth Congress had seen and perused Kruschev's secret speech about Stalin's crimes, the PCF leadership at first simply denied that any such speech had ever been made. Attempts to accuse the most august organs of the Western press of lying failed when the Italian party leadership publicly acknowledged the content of Kruschev's revelations. Still, the PCF treated the Soviet Congress as a non-event. The party did have to raise some of the questions Kruschev had opened up once the authenticity of the secret speech was recognized, but it did so mainly to sweep as much as possible of the damaging material under the rug. In June 1956, the Central Committee issued a pamphlet on "How the Cult of Stalin's Personality Was Overcome in the USSR" which minimized Kruschev's revelations (the problem was the "cult" and not Stalin's crimes) while lavishing congratulations on the Soviet Party for its unique gift for self-criticism. The PCF was quick to announce also that no such "cult of personality" existed in the French party, whatever unfortunate excesses existed in the Soviet Union. At the same moment Maurice Thorez delivered himself of the opinion that the major lesson to be learned from the Kruschev revelations was that the PCF had consistently been correct in its strategic choices.[27]

The PCF's immediate concern was to minimize the internal costs of the Soviet crisis. The Kruschev revelations shook the confidence of many stolid Communists who had long lived within a party whose strident insistence on the infallibility and unsurpassed socialist virtue of Stalin and what he had accomplished was total. Given the PCF's very recent experience with internal confusion (the years of Thorez' absence in Moscow) it was judged equally important to deny resolutely that any of the problems which existed in the Soviet party had their French counterparts. Thus the message of the June 1956 Central Committee was "unity," "unity" within the party and "unity" with non-Communists in France to build a new Popular Front.

De-Stalinization was to be the order of the day for most of the Communist movement for some time after the Kruschev speech. Not so for the PCF. Why the party insisted on swimming against the current in international Communism is still unclear. Thorez' anxiety about what might have

---

27. PCF, *Histoire du PCF*, p. 613; see Thorez in *L'Humanité*, 27 March 1956, reprinted in Thorez, *Oeuvres Choisies*, vol. III, pp. 45 ff; also Thorez' speech to the Central Committee at Arceuil, 9–10 May 1956, pp. 71 ff.

happened internally were the PCF to have moved in new directions may have been the most important factor. Creating a major inner-party crisis—one would certainly have followed if the Kruschev report had been taken seriously—at this particular juncture would effectively have been very dangerous. The party needed all of the cohesion which it could generate in the Algerian situation. And it had still not given up hope that the ultimate results of the 1956 election would be new collaboration with the Socialists. Moreover, Thorez may have had good reasons to fear for his own position in the event de-Stalinization were pursued, given the nature of his own leadership and the degree to which the PCF had been implicated in Stalinism because of it. Beyond such considerations, however, it seems that Thorez was personally, and quite actively, opposed to the new directions being taken by Kruschev. If we are to credit Philippe Robrieux, Thorez hoped that opposition to Kruschev within the Soviet leadership would prevail (which it ultimately did—in 1964). And he acted to achieve this goal by maneuvering in the international Communist movement, even approaching the Chinese at several points.[28] For whatever reasons then, an historic opportunity was passed up, at costs to French Communism which are still being paid.

In the short run the PCF's strange response to the Kruschev speech undermined its assiduous efforts to end its isolation. This was bad enough, but the Twentieth Congress was followed only a few short months later by Soviet intervention in Hungary. Predictably, the PCF saw the Hungarian uprising as a reactionary movement led by counter-revolutionaries and fascists (although it was willing to grant that the Hungarian CP had made serious errors allowing the crisis to emerge).[29] And the party gladly supported the Soviet intervention, proclaiming that, because of it "the cause of socialism triumphed in Hungary."[30] With Soviet tanks in the streets of Budapest and thousands of refugees fleeing across the Austrian border, such a position was not likely to help the PCF in France. PCF support for Moscow on the Hungarian question further undermined whatever progress the PCF might have made towards persuading non-Communists that a new Popular Front was desirable. Protests against Soviet actions abounded in France, and included all of the PCF's potential United Front allies (plus all of the CGT's colleagues in the labor movement). The extreme Right in France even felt emboldened to attack PCF headquarters and the *L'Humanité* building in Paris, leading to a long night of street warfare between party militants and the invaders.[31] PCF and CGT calls to a "day of

28. Philippe Robrieux makes a strong case for this; see Robrieux, *Maurice Thorez* (1975).
29. PCF, *Histoire du PCF*, p. 625.
30. Ibid., p. 627; *L'Humanité*, 3 November 1956.
31. PCF, *Histoire du PCF*, p. 628; *L'année politique 1956*, p. 172. The next day no newspapers appeared at all as the CGT pulled out its entire Paris press sector to protest the attack on *L'Humanité*.

anti-fascist action,'' attempts to regroup party forces in a chaotic situation, failed completely.[32]

Although the PCF's position on Hungary was ruinous, the Hungarian situation did provide a new piece of datum about changed relationships between the PCF and CGT. The Confederation knew full well that if it followed the PCF's line on Budapest it would isolate itself within the labor movement for some time to come and, quite possibly, create serious conflict within the CGT itself. Despite this, there was considerable feeling among PCF leaders of the CGT that the Confederation should take a pro-Soviet stand. In the Confederal Bureau meeting to discuss the issue, however, debate was stormy, with at least three of the Bureau's fourteen members (Alain le Léap, Pierre LeBrun and Jean Schaeffer, all non-Communists)[33] resolutely opposed to CGT alignment on the PCF's positions. In the recent past, such opposition would not have made much difference. This time, however, it counted. The CGT leadership was deeply concerned with its strength in the labor market and feared that its own rank and file would not follow if the Confederation supported the Hungarian intervention.[34] Thus the Confederal Bureau finally refused to take an offical stand on Hungary at all, but to allow a "liberty of diversity" to the CGT's constituent federations. In the words of Lucien Rioux, *France Obser-vateur*'s astute labor columnist, "for the first time the Communist Party has renounced burdening the trade union that it influences with its own positions."[35] Thus despite the PCF's own strong feelings on the Hungarian question, relative autonomy was honored.

The CGT's discretion on Hungary, important though it was, was also contradictory. Granting "liberty of diversity" to federations meant allowing numbers of federations to take offical pro-Soviet positions, despite Confederal unwillingness to take a stand. The consequences of this were predictable. Fights occurred at Renault over Hungary between CGT and FO delegates.[36] In the Paris transport system a CGT section passed a resolution which explicitly condemned any CGT work stoppages over Hungary.[37] The CGT *Fédération du Livre*, perhaps the key non-Communist CGT Federation, passed a strong resolution against the Hungarian repression.[38] A similar resolution was passed by the CGT section of the *Caisse Centrale* of social security in Paris. The CGT civil servants' federation circulated a petition demanding an extraordinary CGT Congress on Hungary. Non-Communists in the CGT signed public

32. *L'année politique 1956*, p. 102.
33. Fauvet, vol. II, p. 293; *L'année politique 1956*, p. 104.
34. See *Combat*, 14 November 1956 for some evidence on the rank and file.
35. *L'Observateur*, 29 November 1956, p. 7.
36. Mothé, *Journal*, p. 127.
37. *Combat*, 14 November 1956.
38. *Le Monde*, 2 December 1956.

statements in the press. Most important, the CGT suffered some losses in professional elections following Budapest. The average loss, ten to fifteen percent, was not immense, but chastening enough to induce a degree of caution in CGT activity well into 1957.[39]

Party and union were trapped. Neither could do much more than try to roll with the punches coming their way. Thorez used the Suez expedition, which immediately followed Budapest, to try and explain away the party's problems: "the French bourgeoisie . . . has tried to divert the profound feeling of the country about the war in Egypt. To do this they have attempted to exploit the Hungarian events, organizing a formidable enterprise of brain-washing with the aid of the press, radio, television, the clergy, etc."[40] Léon Mauvais reiterated the *diversion hongroise* theme within the CGT. The clear purpose of the *diversion* theme in both party and union was to make people forget about Budapest as rapidly as possible.

The limits of movement towards relative autonomy in the CGT were made very clear at the 1957 CGT Congress. As a result both of general political changes after 1954 and of the brutal debate over the CGT's economic program at the 1955 Congress an active opposition within the Confederation had emerged. Led by Pierre LeBrun and backed by many non-Communist CGT leaders (plus much of the CGT's non-Communist voting strength), this opposition came to the 1957 Congress with a number of proposals for change in the CGT. The most important were contained in a resolution on trade-union unity. What was needed, the resolution claimed, was fuller "trade-union democracy" within the CGT. With such democracy, the road to unity-in-action with other unions might be opened anew. The CGT should institutionalize respect for organized minorities and "tendencies." It should also outlaw the duplication of trade-union and political functions. The Confederation should, in addition, use the secret ballot in deciding important questions and not take political stands unless Confederal-level unanimity could be achieved. LeBrun, in submitting the resolution, intimated that it had been written after long discussions with "comrades who had left" (i.e., people within *Force Ouvrière*). It was also known that FEN (the National Teachers' Union) militants had played a role. The Congress was aware, then, that LeBrun was speaking for forces outside the CGT who might move towards real unity-in-action if the CGT could bring itself to take steps to allay some of their fears.

In order to present their case, LeBrun and friends had to break a major CGT taboo, that of exposing or acknowledging actual PCF power within the Confederation. To cite *Le Monde*'s summary of the opposition's position, "a trade-union organization ought not be to the 'relay' of a party in a

39. *La Croix*, 12 December 1956; *Bilans Hebdomadaires* (December 1956); *France Observateur*, 6 December 1956; *L'année politique 1956*, p. 173.
40. *L'Humanité*, 22 November 1956.

country like ours where the working class is ideologically divided. Pluralism cannot be rejected if one wants to create real and lasting trade-union unity." In the CGT context, however, claims that the CGT was not democratic enough and that the PCF dominated its decisions were dynamite.

The debate which followed buried the LeBrun resolution. The "PCF front" contention was dismissed out of hand by ritual arguments that no one but PCF unionists could possible have accepted. The CGT was a mass organization, open to all who worked, no matter what their political persuasion. To cite Frachon, "a unified trade-union organization, bringing together all workers, can only be an organization 'without party,' and cannot adopt the program of a party. Parties have their own organizations to back them and trade-union members have the right to belong and be active in any one of them. . . ." Thus the fact that Frachon and large numbers of his colleagues were Communists had nothing to do with their roles as leaders of the CGT! The CGT was an organization of workers for trade-union purposes, some of whose leaders were Communists, all of whose leaders were elected because of respect which they had won as trade unionists. The danger, to Frachon, was not in the existing apolitical CGT, but in the official recognition of "tendencies" which the LeBrun resolution proposed, a recognition which could only lead to partisan politicization. There was, of course, nothing new in this rather jesuitical way of conjuring one of the CGT's main problems out of existence. But the very fact that nothing new could be produced at this point said a great deal about the incompleteness of the CGT's post-Cold War change.

It was left to Henri Krasucki, a rising young protégé of Frachon, to put the opposition in its place. To Krasucki, the problem of "tendencies" was beside the point. The real issue was the misleadership of workers by the heads of other unions in France. In one way or another, it was the leaders of FO and the CFTC who were doing the dirty work of the French ruling class. Thus the CGT was not responsible for trade-union disunity in any way, it was all the fault of trade-union misleaders. The only serious way to overcome disunity, then, was to expose this misleadership to workers.

That the LeBrun resolution had no chance of passage was obvious. It was, in fact, withdrawn before it came to a vote. But it did serve as a catalyst for the Confederal leadership to enunciate its views of what the CGT was. And the package which emerged did not augur well for prospects of trade-union unity. Aside from the predictable reassertion of the taboo on discussion of PCF power within the organization, the core of the leadership's response was a firm denial of the existence of pluralism within the French working class. There was only *one* French working class. Its interests were clear and specifiable. The CGT was the *only* legitimate mass-organizational representative of this working class. Therefore the CGT was the *only* trade union which could define the market interests of the French working class. It followed from this that other unions were bourgeois plots. Workers who supported such unions were simply brainwashed. Relative autonomy, at this point, could only be very, very partial, then. The CGT could not seriously pursue working-class interests in the labor market without recognizing the genuine roots of trade-union pluralism in the sociological and partisan diversity of French workers. In the absence of such recognition, the trade-union unity-in-action which was the sine qua non of serious labor-market action could not be achieved. Behind all of this, of course, were profound contradictions in the PCF's own strategy. It wanted the development of mass labor-market struggle to build the social support needed to lead to a new United Front. But it did not yet understand that such struggle could not occur unless it allowed the CGT to deal realistically with the structure of the French working class, a step which would, of necessity, involve further expansion in the CGT's mass-organizational autonomy. It was not enough to prod the CGT away from exaggerated over-politicization towards market action without, at the same time, allowing the CGT to live among French workers in a less sectarian way.

The internal opposition also raised the issue of the appropriateness of the Confederation's pauperization perspectives. Exclusive stress on pauperization, claimed Pierre LeBrun, made little sense to large numbers of workers, especially those involved in, and to a degree benefiting from, technological progress. In the words of an anonymous CGT militant, writing in *France Observateur*, "we cannot understand the economic phenomena going on before our eyes if we think that monopolies are *exclusively* Malthusian." To the opposition, if the Confederation insisted on the pauperization line, its base might, in time, be progressively confined to relatively backward sectors of the economy, leaving workers in the more dynamic sectors outside the influence of the CGT and in the hands of whomever cared to address themselves to their real problems. In response to this, the leadership brought forth reams of statistical "evidence" about pauperization. The irony of the situation was inescapable. The CGT had just denied that it had any ties to the PCF. Yet when Congressists raised the issue of the utility of the Confederation's central economic perspectives, which had clearly originated in the PCF, and not in the CGT, PCF leaders in the CGT rushed to defend these views at all costs. This was less important than the issue itself, however. CGT adoption of the pauperization analysis, if it did help the Confederation recenter its focus on the labor market, was likely to lead to relative CGT neglect of certain sectors of the work force and certain forms of new labor-market action arising from these sectors.[41]

Lack of internal democracy in the CGT, Confederal positions which

41. Pierre LeBrun in *Le Peuple*, 1 October 1856, 10 June 1957, and at the 1957 Congress, p. 91. See also Frachon and Krasucki's responses at the 1957 Congress. Also Marcel Gibelin, "La division syndicale et l'unité d'action," in *Les Temps Modernes*, no. 112–113.

made unity-in-action with other unions impossible and the contradictions of the pauperization analysis all attested to the incompleteness of CGT relative autonomy at this point, in addition to pointing to serious problem areas for the future. In the immediate, however, the CGT had to confront the liabilities of its Cold War ties to the PCF in concrete ways. The Hungarian mess, despite the CGT's complicated efforts to avoid being implicated in PCF positions, was costly. It meant, to begin with, that the Confederation was unable to generate any serious mobilization around Suez. This was bad enough in itself, but it symbolized deeper problems. The nationalism which had already become evident around Algeria was further stimulated by Suez, penetrating popular social strata, up to and including the CGT rank and file. In the light of the 1958 crisis which ended the Fourth Republic the inability of the CGT to act credibly around Suez undoubtedly weakened the Fourth Republic's capacities to resist the actions of Algerian *ultras* eighteen months later.

The Fall of the Fourth Republic and the Failure of Crisis United Frontism

The May Crisis

Post-war France seems addicted to crises which occur in May. In May 1947, Communist Ministers were evicted from the government, marking the official beginning of the Cold War in French domestic politics. May 1968 we will have the occasion to examine later. May 1958 marked the end of the long-agonizing Fourth Republic.

The storm broke in the spring of 1958, when political paralysis in Paris and right-wing rebellion in Algeria called the existence of the Fourth Republic into question. In part because of the continued exclusion of the PCF from French political life, no majority for the sane liquidation of French colonialism in Algeria could be formed after the 1956 elections. The tenuous hold on power of the Mollet government meant that compromise with the Right and Right-Center on colonial policy was necessary, and this led directly to a policy of military repression of the Algerian liberation movement. This policy, in turn, encouraged the consolidation of an ultra-colonialist Algerian sub-society with deep roots among Algerian *colons* and in the French army. Carrying on the war in Algeria also magnified nationalist fever in France itself. Repressing the Algerians was not an unpopular cause to begin with. But with the full engagement of the French army, which included large numbers of conscripts, plus efforts by governments and the military to generate public support for bloody and costly action, extreme nationalism penetrated many sectors of French society, up to and including those whose traditional political allegiance was to the Left.

The crisis opened when, after a protracted ministerial crisis, Pierre

Pflimlin, an MRP leader suspected by the Right of "softness" on Algeria, was nominated to become Premier. In response to this, the Algerian sub-society rebelled. Riots, demonstrations in which the military played a prominent role, and a general strike in Algiers culminated in the establishment of an ultra-colonialist *Comité de Salut Public* in Algiers on May 13. Confusion abounded about what was going on. At the very least, the Algerian uprising was an open and illegal attempt by the *colons* and much of the officer corps in Algeria to veto political choices being made by Parliament in Paris. And there were clearly elements involved in the rebellion who sought a right-wing military *coup d'état*.[42] Important Gaullists were also in the middle of things. At the time, however, just who was involved, what connections they might have had with mainland political groups and which elements of the insurrectionary coalition would come out on top were all unclear.

The PCF did not hesitate a moment about what to do, nor did the CGT. Immediately, party and union moved into a posture of "crisis United Frontism." Democratic institutions were being threatened from the Right. Such a threat was perhaps the one thing which might overcome anti-Communism in the non-Communist Left and Center. The PCF's tactics were, in such circumstances, to do anything and everything possible to promote an alliance, even if temporary, with forces willing to come to the defense of the Republic. If successful, these tactics might well preserve the Republic, not an unimportant goal since in the event of any right-wing takeover one of the first targets would be French Communism. Beyond this, however, United Front collaboration to defend the Republic might well provide the breakthrough which the PCF had sought for some years to make United Front collaboration possible more generally. Thus the PCF bent over backwards to promote a strong Republican majority in Parliament to face the rebels. Asking nothing in exchange except resistance to threats from the Right, the PCF offered support to any political grouping which would stand up for the Fourth Republic.[43]

Crisis United Frontism involved simultaneous political action at the top by the PCF directed towards fellow Republican parties and CGT attempts to develop a mass mobilization against the Algerian rebels at the rank-and-file level of the labor movement. On May 13 the line went out within the CGT to subordinate all tasks to building a mass anti-fascist campaign. Benoît Frachon gave the word, plus the appropriate historical parallel, in *L'Hum-*

42. The list of books and pamphlets about May 1958 and related phenomena is endless. See Jean Touchard, "La fin de la IVe République," *Revue Française de Science Politique* (November 1958), for those published in 1958.

43. *L'année politique 1958*, p. 216; also see *Revue d'Action Populaire* (July-August 1958), p. 357. Among other things the PCF abstained on a key May 13 vote in Parliament which allowed the government to carry on. On May 16 the PCF voted in favor of the declaration of a "state of urgency."

anité: "the military *coup de force* in Algiers, the attempt of the *factieux* to impose an authoritarian and anti-republican government in France, constitute grave dangers. The working class will react vigorously, as it did the twelfth of February, 1934. It will unite for powerful action which will sweep away the rebels."[44] On May 14 the CGT Administrative Committee issued a "call to the working class for United Action in defense of liberties and the Republic" which signalled the beginning of all-out Confederal efforts to bring the troops together. Federations were told to pass resolutions against the "fascist *coup de force* in Algiers" and the entire CGT apparatus moved to constitute rank-and-file anti-fascist committees at plant level, open to any workers who desired to participate. A number of brief local work stoppages of protest were promoted as well, although ominously enough, none were really successful.[45] The CGT leadership also moved to promote unity at the top around the "save the Republic" line with other union leaderships.[46]

On May 14, however, the situation became even more confused, after General Salan uttered his famous *Vive de Gaulle* call from the balcony of the Algiers forum (having been prompted to do so by Léon Delbecque, a government Minister working against the government). On May 15, the General announced that he was "holding himself ready to assume the powers of the Republic."[47] De Gaulle's entry on the scene complicated the PCF's problems. The *colon* rebels in Algeria were fascists, according to the PCF. General de Gaulle was more difficult to label. The party decided that his goal was something which it called "personal power." At this point, however, what was uncertain was whether de Gaulle would simply be a front man for the fascists or whether he would use them to come to power on his own terms. The PCF and CGT wanted no part of either fascism or "personal power" and committed all of their resources to opposing both possibilities. Those forces of the non-Communist Left and Center upon whom the PCF's crisis United Frontist hopes depended were less likely to conflate these two possible outcomes. If fascism were indeed at issue, then perhaps a new United Front might be arranged. But if General de Gaulle's return proved more likely, many politicians central to the PCF's United Front plans might prefer this possibility to collaboration with the Communists.

In all of this uncertainty, the efforts of the PCF and CGT went unrewarded. PCF support for the government led to no "save the Republic" political alliance. And no trade-union organization volunteered to join in

---

44. Frachon in *L'Humanité*, 13 May 1958. Volume II of Frachon's *Au rythme des jours* contains an extremely useful review of PCF and CGT activities in the May 1958 crisis taken originally from *Le Peuple*, 1 June 1958 (see Frachon, vol. II, pp. 196–224).

45. *L'année politique 1958*, p. 211.

46. Frachon, vol. II, p. 200.

47. *L'année politique 1958*, p. 58.

Republican unity-in-action with the CGT. As long as the situation was fluid, non-Communist political and trade-union forces were keeping all options open. None wanted anything resembling a United Front until it became crystal clear that no other possibilities existed.

A Gaullist solution to the crisis gradually emerged. Guy Mollet wrote a public letter to de Gaulle on May 16 which implied that the SFIO might not object to de Gaulle coming to power if he recognized the legitimacy of the existing government, disavowed the Algerian Committees of Public Safety and agreed to follow constitutional procedures.[48] On May 19, General de Gaulle cryptically announced that he was ready to take over the task of "governing the Republic." In the following week political forces of the parliamentary Right (Antoine Pinay and his party, in particular) began publicly advocating de Gaulle's legal accession to power. And, while Guy Mollet himself did not publicly support de Gaulle, it became generally known in political circles that Mollet and de Gaulle had made private contact to discuss the possibility of a de Gaulle government.[49] When Corsica was invaded from Algeria on May 24, it became even more obvious that a solution to the crisis which mollified the Algerian *ultras* had to be found quickly or civil war was possible. Whatever game General de Gaulle was really playing, he was not directly part of the Algerian extreme Right, yet the *colons* seemed willing to support a Gaullist change in the metropole. This was good enough for the non-Communist Left and Center, for whom nothing but open fascism was less desirable than dealing with the Communists. "Personal power" became inevitable.

As the turn toward Gaullism became clear, the PCF and CGT were obliged to choose between acquiescing in the General's return or fighting on their own. They chose the latter. If potential United Front allies were unwilling to listen to calls for unity at the top, party and trade union were forced to try and mobilize people independently from below. On May 19 the CGT Seine Union called a general strike against de Gaulle and the Algerian *ultras*. It was a complete failure. FO and the CFTC refused to join, and the Paris CGT had a great deal of trouble pulling out its own supporters.[50] After the Corsican invasion, the CGT once again attempted to act on its own, calling a national general strike.[51] This movement, on May 27, failed almost totally as well.[52]

The likelihood of a Gaullist succession broke the back of PCF and CGT "crisis United Frontism." Once it became clear that General de Gaulle

48. *L'année politique 1958*, p. 88.
49. Guy Mollet, *13 mai 1958–13 mai 1962* (1962), pp. 8–10.
50. Daniel Mothé on the Renault strike, part of a series of shop-floor reports on the May crisis in *Socialisme ou Barbarie*, no. 25, p. 67.
51. PCF, *Histoire du PCF*, p. 655; Guy Mollet publicly advised Socialist workers not to join the CGT.
52. *Le Monde*, 27, 29 May 1958; Serge Mallet, *Le Gaullisme et la gauche* (1964), ch. 1.

would come to power legally, the PCF's anti-fascist calls fell on deaf ears. De Gaulle, and not the Algerian *ultras*, would profit from the May crisis. However, once party and union decided to carry on independently to try and block General de Gaulle's arrival, they had to find new rallying cries to promote mobilization. Thus de Gaulle, if not a fascist himself, was presented as possibly "opening the way for fascism." And he was portrayed as the front man for the extreme colonialist wing of the French bourgeoisie, with the implication that, were de Gaulle to come to power, the war in Algeria would be intensified to the utmost. The problem with this line was that few, besides the party faithful, found it convincing. There were other plausible interpretations of the Gaullist upsurge. Perhaps personal power was not the ultimate recourse of France's worst reactionaries. Might it not be a new strategic option for more dynamic sectors of the French capitalist class seeking a more coherent and less parliamentary political system through which to implement their plans for French modernization? Would not the charisma and nationalism of General de Gaulle buy time and a degree of labor peace for the unfolding of important economic restructuring in France? In 1958, as in the turn to the pauperization analysis of 1955, the PCF analysis lacked subtlety, and assumed that French capitalism had nowhere to go but towards labor-repressive authoritarianism. The party further assumed that the French *grande bourgeoisie* had a life and death stake in empire.

Whatever Gaullism did turn out to be, the PCF's crisis United Frontism from below was unsuccessful. Worse still, the party's insistence on carrying the CGT into a series of unilateral protests repoliticized the Confederation and ran directly counter to the logic of the CGT's new relative autonomy position. And the CGT proved no more successful at creating a mass movement against de Gaulle than did the PCF. The fact that French workers were not particularly interested in opposing the Algerian War had become abundantly clear in CGT efforts to promote anti-war feeling after 1956. Nationalism—and to a degree, racism—had found their way into the heads of many French workers. In May 1958 much of this came out. An observer at Renault reported the existence of *Algérie Française* sentiment among workers at Renault.[53] Other observers reported considerable working-class support for de Gaulle based on the General's skillful use of nationalism.[54] Most important, workers showed little desire to put themselves out to defend the Fourth Republic.[55] Cynicism about the French political situation was widespread, against which PCF and CGT mobilization plans had little effect. Party and trade union had only themselves to blame for part of this cynicism, of course, having had very little good to say to workers about the Fourth Republic throughout most of its sad history.

53. Daniel Mothé, in *Socialisme ou Barbarie*, no. 25, p. 67.
54. Ibid., p. 67.
55. Ibid., p. 73; *L'année politique 1958*, p. 211, also p. 71.

By May 28, the date of the only really successful mass demonstration of the crisis period—called by non-Communists—General de Gaulle was on his way. Pflimlin resigned as Premier and the General was designated as his successor, coming to power legally under the constitution of the Fourth Republic. How skillfully de Gaulle had exploited the chaotic situation became clear in the days which followed. The Socialists, who the Communists had hoped would oppose the change, split evenly on support for de Gaulle.[56] Guy Mollet and Max Lejeune accepted ministerial posts in the General's new government. Rumor had it also that Robert Bothereau of *Force Ouvrière* and Robert Bouladoux of the CFTC had also been offered jobs in the government, but had declined. De Gaulle had obviously bought up some opposition to his arrival by offering key non-Communist Left politicians posts in his new cabinet.

Some indication of the mentality which prevailed in the minds of those whom party and trade union had hoped might be persuaded to join United Front-type arrangements can be gleaned from the comments of Raymond le Bourre, a Gaullist-leaning leader of *Force Ouvrière* at the time. According to le Bourre, the biggest fear of the FO leaders in the crisis had not been fascism or personal power at all, but a PCF takeover. In le Bourre's words, it had been thanks to non-Communist trade unionists and workers "that the Popular Front had not been created, that France had not seen the first elements of popular democracy built on her soil." Le Bourre added that all of the crisis-unity offers of the CGT had met uniform treatment at FO.". . .The letters which come . . . from the Rue la Fayette go directly into the wastebasket. . . ."[57]

The Aftermath of May

PCF and CGT post-mortems on the May crisis took on the familiar "we were infallible" form which was so common during these beleaguered years. Georges Séguy, one of the CGT's rising young men, wrote in the June 1958 *Cahiers du Communisme*:

If the strikes, the demonstrations in Paris and the provinces have not prevented, despite their power, the arrival of personal power, they have led to great progress in the unity of republicans, of the United Front of Socialist and Communist workers. . . .What would have happened in the course of those grave days and decisive nights of May 1958 if the working class had not had a powerfully organized, lucid and militant Communist Party? The answer is easy: without the immediate and powerful answer of workers, the vigilant unity of republicans, many fearful politicians ready to capitulate would have given

---

56. In the investiture vote in Parliament forty-two Socialists voted for de Gaulle, while forty-nine voted against.

57. Raymond le Bourre, *Le syndicalisme français dans le Ve République* (1959), pp. 20, 21.

up the ghost in the first hours of the offensive, the Republic would have been brought down in the worst possible conditions.[58]

As for the arrival of personal power, the PCF blamed it on the non-Communist Left and Center. In the words of Roger Garaudy, writing in the same June 1958 issue of *Cahiers*:

> The installation of the dictatorship would have been impossible without the politics of the Socialist leadership characterized by the violation of the program ratified by universal suffrage on January 2, 1956, by the pursuit of the Algerian War, by capitulation to ultra-colonialists, by anticommunism, and their obstinate refusal to base their actions on the working class and democratic forces.

Garaudy added:

> Experience proves once more that one cannot struggle effectively against fascism without the Communists and that one cannot struggle against the Communists without playing into the hands of the fascists. . . .[59]

Benoît Frachon had similar things to say about the leaders of *Force Ouvrière* and the CFTC, the CGT's potential union allies:

> Despite the systematic, urgent and ceaselessly renewed propositions of the CGT to the FO and CFTC leadership, these leaders preferred to carry on their sordid anti-unity maneuvers hidden under the vocabulary of 'free trade unions'. . . .We saw the use of bad arguments about the Hungarian events and the alleged danger of a Communist dictatorship when military dictatorship was knocking at our doors. . . . They were discussing the sex of angels while the besiegers were tearing down the walls of Byzantium.[60]

Maurice Thorez offered the party's definite theoretical analysis of recent events at a special PCF conference in July 1958. According to Thorez, "since the first of June, France has lived under a regime of military and personal dictatorship which was imposed by threats and force. This regime supports itself on the most reactionary, most chauvinist and most colonialist sectors of the *grande bourgeoisie*. . . ."[61] Thus, to Thorez personal power was not fascism, but might well "open the road to fascism." Personal power had become possible because "for twelve years democracy had

58. Georges Séguy, "Unité ouvrière et rassemblement antifasciste," in *Cahiers du Communisme* (June 1958), p. 905.

59. Roger Garaudy, "De Gaulle et le fascisme," in *Cahiers du Communisme* (June 1958), p. 905.

60. Benoît Frachon in *Le Peuple*, 1 June 1958.

61. Maurice Thorez, "Union et action de tous les républicains pour le non," in *Cahiers du Communisme* (August 1958), p. 1109.

been declining in France due to anti-Communism." With the advancing crisis of French capitalism, the democracy of the Fourth Republic, far from perfect in the party's eyes, had become too costly for the French bourgeoisie to maintain.

Personal power was but imperfectly installed after the events of May 1958. General de Gaulle had assumed the office of Premier, under the constitution of the Fourth Republic, with the intention of transforming French institutions towards the strong Presidential regime which he desired. In order to legitimate his desires, however, the General had to submit his new constitutional plans to a referendum, which he scheduled for autumn 1958. Voters were to be asked to answer a simple "yes" or "no" concerning the proposed changes. The referendum gave the PCF one more chance to promote its crisis United Frontism. According to Thorez, democracy was at stake in the referendum, and "to save it, to re-establish it, it is necessary to overcome the division of the Left." The PCF's position was simplicity itself, then. A *no* vote on the new constitution would be a vote for democracy. On the other hand, "the yes votes of October 5 will be yes votes for fascism."[62]

To organize the *non* campaign the PCF mobilized its rank and file with an intensity that Communist militants had never before witnessed. All other business was suspended. Party members were asked to give up their summer holidays to work for the cause. The CGT did the same, in its own ways, within the union movement. The party's appeal was organized around the democracy versus fascism argument. The CGT also stressed this, but added further the anti-working class biases of the new regime, which had already manifested themselves in the austerity measures of the General's first Finance Minister, M. Pinay.[63] The Confederation also stressed the absence of constitutional guarantees for the social and economic rights of the workers in the document which General de Gaulle was presenting.[64]

Crisis United Frontism worked no better in the fall of 1958 than it had in the spring. The party began its campaign advocating a return to the 1946 constitution as a solution to the institutional dilemmas faced by France. This position had so little appeal to anyone that the party leadership was forced to modify it in mid-campaign.[65] Its new position—for a new Constituent Assembly if *non* votes prevailed—brought it closer to those few important non-Communist politicians who also advocated a *non* response, François Mitterrand, Christian Pineau and Pierre Mendès-France, among

---

62. Ibid., p. 126. See on such questions, Frédéric Bon's excellent essay, "Structure de l'idéologie Communiste," in Fondation Nationale des Sciences Politiques, *Le communisme en France* (1969), pp. 107–140.

63. *L'Humanité*, 12 July 1958.

64. *L'Humanité*, 2 August 1958.

65. J. A. Faucher, *La gauche française sous de Gaulle*, (1969), pp. 13–15.

others. However, Guy Mollet managed to get the SFIO to take a *yes* position, dashing the PCF's hopes for an electoral alliance at the top with the
Socialists. The CGT, which took an open *non* stance, ran up against the refusal of the CFTC, FEN and *Force Ouvrière* to take any position at all.
Trade-union unity-in-action on the constitutional question proved impossible as well, then. The electoral results of the efforts of party and union
were disastrous. The constitution of the Fifth Republic was ratified overwhelmingly. Worse still, much of the PCF's normal electorate voted
"yes." As Marcel Servin, organizational secretary of the party, commented, "this is the first time since Liberation that this has happened. One
voter in five did not hear us."[66] The party lost approximately 1.5 million
voters from its usual total, according to the PCF's own estimates.[67]

The first legislative elections under the new constitution, in November
1958, proved even more unpleasant for the PCF than had the referendum.
The PCF polled only 3.83 million votes (twenty percent) as opposed to 5.53
million (twenty-six percent) in 1956.[68] In terms of seats in Parliament the
party dropped from 150 in 1956 to only *ten* in 1958, in large part because of
the new Gaullist electoral laws. Candidates on the non-Communist Left
who had joined the PCF in advocating *non* in the constitutional referendum were also demolished. The message was unmistakable. The appeal of
Gaullism was very strong, even at the heart of the Communists' electoral
base.

Both party and trade union had reason to be very worried. However, the
situation was so serious that such worrying had to be carried on in private.
Public worrying came from non-official, but still very important
sources—"fellow traveller" groups and from the party rank and file. Much
was made of the strange pattern of PCF mass political socialization in the
years after 1947, for example. For the PCF to expect workers to defend a
Republic whose leading figures the party had castigated as traitors, pawns
of the American imperialists and tools of the French bourgeoisie, was
naive.[69] To the degree to which the party's earlier efforts had been successful, and there could have been little doubt that many of the party's
messages about Fourth Republic politics rang true to workers, then its
"Republican" mobilization in 1958 was bound to fail. In the words of
Serge Mallet, one of the leaders of a new school of "New Left" Marxist intellectuals beginning to challenge the PCF's ideological hegemony in
France, "the masses, and in the first place the working classes, felt no
desire at all to fight for the corrupt and garrulous *parlementaires* who had
lied to the country for years. . . . In these conditions to believe in the pos-

---

66. Ibid., p. 121; *L'Humanité*, 2 October 1958.

67. *L'Humanité*, 10 October 1958; see Maurice Thorez's speech to the October 4 Central
Committee, in *Oeuvres Choisies*, vol. III, p. 91 ff.

68. *L'année politique 1958*, pp. 141, 145.

69. Fauvet, vol. II, p. 301.

sibility of mobilizing the people for a return to the Fourth Republic is to demonstrate the most complete lack of political realism. In fact, such a belief opens all doors to Gaullist demagogy counting essentially on the desire for change."[70] Mallet continued to contend that the PCF had misunderstood Gaullism by consistently equating it with the traditional French labor-repressive extreme Right. De Gaulle was not a classic right-wing politician in several important ways. His anti-Left feelings were submerged in rhetoric which promised "participation" and "reformism," accompanied by vigorous nationalism. In the circumstances of 1958 then, de Gaulle was the only active force proposing change, since the PCF insisted on defending a bankrupt regime. Because of this de Gaulle's positions were bound to appeal to some workers.

Even deeper criticism of the party's strategic judgments came from within the PCF itself. The *Sorbonnes/Lettres* Section of the party allowed its critique to be published in *France Observateur*, an unheard-of-heresy. To the *Sorbonne/Lettres* group, the party's attempt to "give life to a dead regime which no one wanted at any price" was not "an accidental error of judgment. . . . For quite a while the party leadership has lost the habit of studying and taking account of facts. It mistakes its desires for reality." In particular, the leadership had lost touch with the meaning of the liberation struggles of colonial peoples. To the dissidents, the development of such struggles

> has continually aggravated the contradictions within the French bourgeoisie to the point of threatening parliamentary institutions. By its considerable lateness in bringing these problems to the forefront of the conciousness and struggle of the masses, by its incapacity to propose concrete solutions for decolonization based on a serious analysis, the party has found itself outflanked by the wave of nationalism which, because it was not clearly fought, finally penetrated sectors of the French working class.[71]

The price paid for all this might be great, asserted the critics. "The provisional victory which the French bourgeoisie has just won assures it a respite which it may use to its profit to reorganize and structurally modify French capitalism in the direction of a modernized and competitive capitalism, capable of spreading reformist illusions for a more or less prolonged period throughout the working class."[72] The party leadership's errors had, in other words, helped give French capitalism a new lease on life.

At the time, the significance of such criticisms was buried in the tumult of events. Moreover, the critics were soon buried in a wave of sanctions and expulsions which destroyed the *Sorbonne/Lettres* Section itself. Not

---

70. Serge Mallet, *Gaullisme*, p. 9.
71. See *France Observateur*, 16 October 1958, p. 8.
72. Ibid., p. 2.

far from the surface, however, lay a deep malaise in the PCF, accompanied by growing dissatisfaction with the Thorez leadership. In 1956, around the Twentieth Congress and Hungary, and in the 1958 crisis, the PCF had made profound strategic and tactical mistakes at great cost to its ability to promote the kinds of solutions which it desired. Covering up Kruschev's "secret speech," refusing to take any serious steps to de-Stalinize its own activities and going down the line to support Soviet intervention in Hungary all had made it impossible for the PCF to make any progress in France along the United Front path to which it was formally committed. The party's inability to generate any important anti-Algerian War movement made things worse. Then, in 1958, its inability to generate anything more than campaigns which defended a regime which no one wanted any longer and which labelled one of France's most skilled Right politicians a "fascist" led to obvious disaster.The record was clear. If one included the period of chaos and confusion which attended Maurice Thorez' convalescence in the Soviet Union earlier, the PCF's balance sheet for the 1950s showed mistake after mistake. Theoretically, from the peace movement, through pauperization, to the representation of Gaullism as the vanguard of a bourgeoisie which could not survive without colonialism, the party was far out of touch with the evolution of French capitalism. And beyond this lay organizational issues as well. Maurice Thorez and a very small, closed group of *fidèles* made *all* important decisions. The fact that the party then carried such decisions out without question, despite their questionable wisdom, was further evidence of the problem. Stalinism—the cult of "Maurice," the degeneration of democratic centralism into authoritarian commandism, and the reduction of most party members to a role of ratifiers of decisions in whose making they had had no role—was not simply a moral problem for the PCF. It had serious practical consequences as well.

In the long run the PCF would have to change, if only to bring itself back into touch with French reality enough to influence French events. However, the party had missed its most important opportunity to begin changing with its odd response to the Twentieth Soviet Congress. Problems not recognized are problems not solved. However, if the Thorez leadership seemed unaware of the party's difficulties, the same could not be said for others. The *Sorbonnes/Lettres* affair was a harbinger of bad times ahead. The party's mistakes had caused its hegemony over theoretical and strategic thinking on the Left to begin to crack. Intellectuals could no longer make sense of what the party was doing. Moreover, the whole world of French intellectuals—schools, universities, occupations—was changing rapidly with changes in the structure of French capitalism. Either the party would change to deal with the growing gap between it and the French intelligentsia or it would be in trouble. It was no accident then, that divisions within the PCF—stretching up to the *Bureau Politique* at their most profound point—began to grow between Thorez (and coterie) and party militants in the intellectual world. And the fact that students were about to become a major thorn in the party's side was also predictable.

Whatever the future was to bring, the short-run lessons for both the PCF and CGT from the 1958 crisis were clear. Because of the departure of a significant part of both party and union rank and file to support de Gaulle in the crisis, neither the PCF nor the CGT could predict what the response might be to any new calls which they might make. Thus it was quite risky to promote any action which by its militancy or boldness might leave party and union without mass support. Caution had to be the rule until more certain links with the rank and file had been reconstructed. Beyond this, the PCF, which maintained its general United Front goals, was hard-pressed to do much of anything at all, given the losses which it had suffered in the 1958 elections. Thus the CGT's actions became doubly important. The labor market had rhythms of its own. Even if Left political action on the parliamentary level was impossible in the new situation, developing social protest in the labor market was still an option, especially if the Gaullist regime did turn out to be as anti-labor as the CGT expected it to be. Even here, however, circumstances dictated CGT prudence. The Confederation could not count on massive and immediate working-class rebellion against Gaullism. Moreover, the recession and slack labor market of late 1958 and early 1959 made conflict promotion even more difficult. Initial forays (a failed railroad strike in the autumn of 1958; the renegotiation of the Renault accord in December of the same year) indicated that, at least in the public sector, unions were on the defensive.[73]

The new regime's first significant labor conflict revealed a great deal. After some low-level action in the public sector, all of the major unions decided to build towards extended actions on the railroads for June 1959, for an eight-hour general strike to be followed by a number of short "harassing" strikes, until the government granted concessions.[74] The government, whose main lever for controlling the economy was its ability to determine public-sector wages, was faced with a challenge. It began to respond by attempting to divide the united rail unions by minor concessions and special meetings with non-Communist union leaders. These tactics failed, and the government then threatened to requisition the railroad workers if the strike orders were maintained. The CGT proposed to confront the government nonetheless, but the government's threats frightened *Force Ouvrière* and the CFTC. At this point, the Minister of Transport stepped in to offer the FO and CFTC rail unions some new concessions. The withdrawal of the FO and CFTC strike orders left only the CGT still com-

73. Lucien Rioux in *France Observateur*, 16 October 1958, p. 8, *France Observateur*, 11, 18 December 1958; also Lefranc, *1944–1968*, p. 155.
74. See François Gault in *Témoignage Chrétien*, 19 June 1959, p. 4; *L'année politique 1959*, p. 66.

mitted to act. Given the unpredictability of rank-and-file response, the CGT withdrew its strike order as well.[75]

Thus the railroad workers were forced to back down in the face of the government's requisition threat, ending the first major test of the Gaullist government's will to carry out economic austerity. Yet a precedent had been set. The regime had presented itself to French workers as a progressive and "social" alternative to the Fourth Republic. In the heat of crisis, many workers had believed it. In the longer run, however, these claims would have to be backed up by action. The continuation of a degree of working-class Gaullism would be contingent on the betterment of working-class conditions under the Fifth Republic. If the regime did not pay off for workers, the Left and the unions would find their traditional bases once again.

75. Gault, p. 4.; *Le Monde*, 12 June 1959; *L'Humanité*, 12 June 1959.

Chapter 5

AN INTRODUCTION TO THE FIFTH REPUBLIC: THE ALGERIAN INTERLUDE AND BEYOND

At the time of the change in Republics the PCF and CGT had reevaluated long-standing issues about the appropriate relationship between political party and labor mass organization. During the postwar period, and particularly during the worst days of the Cold War, the PCF had tried to make the CGT, a trade-union body, march to strictly political drums. This experience had turned out badly for the CGT. By the mid-1950s changes in party-union relations were underway from the earlier "transmission belt" model towards what we have called the "relative autonomy" of the CGT. Henceforth the actions of the CGT would have, as their primary frame of reference, the specific rhythms of the work worlds of its supporters and the labor market. In this way the "mass integrity" of the CGT, which had been jeopardized in the post-war period, could be respected anew. Relative autonomy did not mean, of course, that party and union were to be *independent* from one another. It meant, simply, that a more suitable division of labor between them would come to exist, with the party doing politics, the union doing unionism, each operating within separate spheres with their own specific dynamics. The CGT would thus face a labor market whose movement would, at any given time, allow a range of options for trade-unionist strategic choice. The Confederation's task, in its new uniform, would be to decide upon the specific strategy which would be most likely to complement, in its mobilizing effects, the political goals of the PCF.

There were, to be sure, a great many practical problems for the PCF and CGT to face in adjusting to this new division of labor. It was therefore not astonishing to find the CGT behaving with a certain amount of uncertainty and confusion as it began to take its new posture seriously. Within the broad definition of relative autonomy, there were certain inevitable ambiguities. Developing trade-union strategy which respected the realities of the labor market but which was also complementary to broad PCF political goals was complicated. With the best intentions in the world it would still be easy for the CGT to *force* complementarity with the PCF, to err on the side of too much politicization, especially given the experiences of the organization in earlier years. Error in the other direction, towards too much CGT independence from PCF goals, was also possible, although, given Communist control in the CGT, less likely except through inadvertance. Then what should the CGT do in moments of political crisis—without falling back into the old problems of the transmission-belt period? Moreover, important issues of the CGT's self-understanding, strong legacies of the transmission-belt years and of the Stalinist political reflexes which had underlaid them, remained to be resolved. The problem of internal CGT democracy remained unacknowledged, for example. And the Confederation's insistence that other trade-union organizations were simply the labor arms of an imperialist conspiracy—and the denial of the structural complexities of the French working class which justified such insistence—still presented an insuperable barrier to the trade-union unity-in-action to which the CGT itself claimed to be committed.

Such problems were real, and difficult to resolve. Nonetheless, the CGT's shift to relative autonomy was clear. By the late 1950s the CGT was ready to act in its new role to complement PCF political strategy. The problem was that the PCF had no coherent strategic position for the CGT to complement.

The PCF was in trouble. Indices of this abounded. It remained isolated in French politics. It had lost a considerable amount of electoral support in 1958. It was quite uncertain about its mobilizational capacities in general. It had responded to the Twentieth Soviet party Congress by burying its head in the sand. It had supported, at great cost, the brutal Soviet intervention in Hungary. It clung to a theory of capitalist development, embodied in the pauperization theses, which was so far off the mark that even numbers of important Communists had come to doubt its utility. It had begun to alienate itself from France's intellectuals. It continued to regulate its internal affairs as if Stalinism were still a model for "proletarian democracy." And the list went on.

The party's real problems were much more profound, however. Its entire strategic vision had been a muddle of contradictions when first elaborated in the Popular Front and Liberation years. Subsequent events made it even more implausible. At the core of PCF United Front reformism was a policy of alliance between Communists and other forces of the Left and Left-Center. The party's goal for the first phase of change in France was to construct and consolidate a working United Front, endow it with a program of structural reforms and bring it to power electorally. In subsequent phases, all contingent on the success of the first, the party desired to implement these reforms in ways which would vastly increase its own strength within the United Front while simultaneously increasing the Front's political clout within France itself. At some point—here we must be vague because the party itself was vague—the United Front would be strong enough, and the PCF in a sufficiently powerful position within it, to move towards a French-style "Popular Democracy." From this juncture, presumably, France would move, in its particularly French ways, towards the basic institutional structures of the other Popular Democracies—centralized economic planning based on public ownership, a one-party "dictatorship of the proletariat," and so on.

In practical terms, at least in the shorter run, French Communist strategy was genuinely reformist, with the proviso, of course, that the goal of such reformism was the transcendence, and not the patching up, of French capitalism. The party lived in France to the extent that it had discarded the likelihood of revolutionary change via a *"grand soir."* Here the PCF's strategic realism stopped, however. United Front reformism could get nowhere without pliable allies. Yet potential allies knew full well that the ultimate logic of PCF strategy was to use a United Front to manipulate, emasculate, and, in the last analysis, swallow up, its alliance partners. The experience of the Eastern European Popular Democracies was clear enough to alert likely United Front allies of the fate which would await them should the PCF's strategic logic continue through to its end.

The party's staunch devotion to things Soviet made its strategy even more implausible. To the PCF the Soviet Union remained a genuine workers' paradise, within which exploitation had been abolished, socialist economic rationality established and proletarian democracy installed. Emulation of the Soviet Union was the party's ultimate goal. Alas, as of the later 1950s, few French people outside the party could share this warmth of attachment to the Soviet model. The fact that exploitation per se, even if not of a capitalist variety, persisted in the USSR was evident for all to see. The myth of Soviet economic efficiency was beginning to crack as well, Sputnik notwithstanding. And, as for proletarian democracy, it was a strange democracy indeed which erected a bureaucratic party to power acting as a substitute for the working class in the absence of elementary civil and political liberties. That the PCF should pride itself for the creation of proletarian democracy within its own ranks doubtless deepened the scepticism of potential United Front allies. Last, but not least, the PCF had compiled a rather unenviable record of subordinating its own domestic goals to the service of Soviet diplomacy.

Neither the PCF nor the CGT knew it, of course, but the change in Republics, plus changes in the international Communist movement, were about to present the PCF with new opportunities to resolve many of the contradictions which plagued its strategic vision. In France, triumphant Gaullism, by providing a pole around which a coherent Center-Right majority could organize itself, would polarize French politics between Left and Right. In time, Socialists and the Center-Left would have to face the reality that the most plausible path back to power for them lay in building a Left oppositional coalition which would include the Communists. Internationally, the Soviet shift towards peaceful coexistence would eventually provide the PCF with much greater freedom from the dictates of Soviet foreign policy, freedom which would be further enhanced by the relative disaggregation of the world Communist movement in the 1960s. In short, although the PCF did not know it yet, Eurocommunization was on the horizon. If the party could jettison the theoretical and ideological baggage which made its United Frontism unworkable, then it might be able to construct a viable strategy for change. And with a plausible PCF strategy the CGT might then be able to maximize the new possibilities, both for itself and for the PCF, of its relative autonomy posture. Before all of this became clearer, however, considerable pain and confusion had to be experienced.

PCF and CGT and the End of the Algerian War

Both the PCF and CGT bumbled through the first months of the new regime, sure neither of what was happening around them nor of their popular support. As we have remarked, the party shifted away from its crisis analysis of de Gaulle as the harbinger of French fascism towards a slightly less embarrassing misunderstanding of the situation in which personal power was a new form of front for the rule of reactionary bourgeois forces. Personal power was not fascism, but by undermining parliamentary democracy in France to the degree it did, it made slippage towards fascism more possible. Behind personal power, in keeping with the broad theoretical lines of the pauperization analysis, lay a bourgeoisie which could no longer afford the relatively free and open ways of parliamentary democracy and needed, for its very survival, to maintain colonialism. That the situation was much more complex than this, that the change in regimes might have had, in part, to do with the needs of an expanionist, modernizing fraction of the French bourgeoisie quite anxious to rid itself both of the encumbrances of a dying colonialism and of an inefficient and unstable Republic, was unthinkable from within the pauperization paradigm. Yet by 1959 there existed important oppositional currents within the PCF, by now even stretching up to the *Bureau Politique*, who found the pauperization analysis inadequate. The CGT's problems were much simpler. Because of the Confederation's failure to carry its base with it in the 1958 crisis and because of the slackening effects on the labor market of austerity measures imposed by the new regime late in 1958, it had to be very wary not to promote actions beyond its capacity to mobilize, lest it suffer further defeats.

The pauperization logic of the PCF's analysis of the new regime almost led to disaster on the Algerian issue. After the dust of the 1958 crisis had cleared, General de Gaulle, a political strategist of considerable skill, moved to take his distance from the Algerian *ultras* who had brought him to power. On September 16, 1959, the General made his first major speech on Algeria, proposing that the Algerian people would be given a choice from three options—continuing integration with France, "association" (some sort of federation arrangement), or secession. For the first time the General used the term "self-determination." In response to the *autodéter-mination* speech, the PCF, first Jacques Duclos (Thorez then being in Russia) and then the *Bureau Politique*, denounced the General for perpetrating a hoax and deliberately misleading the nation about Algeria. It did not take Thorez himself long to figure out that this position was dangerous. The General was moving towards ending the Algerian imbroglio, however tentatively. If the party opposed his regime, it would nonetheless be imprudent for the party to work against his effort to disengage France from the war. For one thing the absence of the PCF from the ranks of forces promoting self-determination, even if de Gaulle had now appropriated the phrase, might seriously compromise the aggregate strength of these forces, thereby making the quest for self-determination more difficult and playing into the hands of the forces of *Algérie Française*. For another, a de facto front of pro-self–determination progressive forces was forming. For the PCF not to have been part of it would have meant losing all possibility of influencing this front (what self-determination actually meant in practice had yet to be clarified), and more importantly, missing the first opportunity for genuine unity-in-action with such forces to present itself since 1947. Thus, pauperization theory or not, the PCF, in November 1959, shifted its position on the regime's Algerian politics.

The party's initial "peace" line was complicated. At the November 1959 Central Committee meeting the party noted that the *grande bourgeoisie* had begun to change its mind on the war because "pacification" in Algeria had failed, because a strong domestic peace movement was emerging, and because international opposition to the war was isolating France. In other words, the bourgeoisie was being dragged, kicking and screaming, away from a war which it really wanted to win. For this reason, the Gaullist regime could not be relied upon, according to the Central Committee:

> The fact that the regime of personal power was only able to come to power with the aid of the 13th of May conspirators, the *ultras* in Algeria and the military chief allied to them, renders it singularly hesitant and weak in the face of them. It is this which explains the tolerance of the government towards the *ultras* and fascists. . . .[1]

The January 1960 attempt to mount another insurrectionary movement by

1. Fauvet, vol. II, p. 309.

these very same *"ultras* and fascists" (the famous Barricades Days) indicated that the regime was no longer in the good graces of the *Algérie Française* forces.[2] From this point, and each after its own fashion, both PCF and CGT were to place anti-war action high on their agenda.[3]

With the political Left, including the PCF, virtually eclipsed as a viable source of mass political action as a result of the 1958 crisis and elections, the burden of anti-war activities fell to a peace movement in which trade unions were key elements.[4] Once again, then, the task of producing a mass movement of social protest which might lead to later political payoffs—by generating habits of unified action on the Left—was assigned by the PCF to the CGT. This time, however, the CGT was not about to mix up its anti-war politics and its trade-union activity in the labor market. Moreover it was not going to stand politicized alone.

The first major peace action following the PCF's shift away from its Leftist position occurred in response to the "Barricades" in January 1960. The uprising in Algeria prompted a hurried series of meetings between trade-union and student leaders which resulted in a one-hour national general strike. Difficulty in reaching a unified agreement followed when *Force Ouvrière* refused to meet with the CGT, but the problem was resolved when each of the groups involved (the CGT, CFTC, *Force Ouvrière*, FEN and UNEF—the student's union) agreed to call out their own following separately, but around the same issues, to affirm "attachment to republican legality and to a policy of self determination."[5] As an important exercise in mass mobilization, the strike was a success. It alerted the Algerian *ultras* and the general public in France to the fact that the totality of French organized labor was strongly in favor of a negotiated settlement for self-determination in Algeria and that it would take to the streets to oppose fascist illegality.

The mass anti-war movement centered on labor and desired by the CGT was not without its ambiguities, as the Barricades and subsequent general actions made clear. The Barricades action was not officially in favor of General de Gaulle's policies, but its slogans were, in fact, difficult to distinguish from the General's positions. In effect, the CGT's choice of peace tactics could not help but bring de facto support to the regime. It was the regime which was threatened by the Algerian *ultras* at this point, and it was the regime which had pledged to implement self-determination. Mass ac-

---

2. See R. Macridis and G. Brown, *Supplement to the De Gaulle Republic* (1963), pp. 9–10.

3. On this whole question see the excellent review by Hélène Carrère d'Encausse, "Le Parti Communiste Français et le mouvement de libération nationale Algérien" in *La politique des puissances devant la décolonisation*, an unpublished colloquium of the Fondation Nationale des Sciences Politiques (1962).

4. Branciard, vol. II, p. 229; Pierre Belleville, "Les syndicats sous la Vᵉ République," *Esprit* (March 1962), p. 384.

5. *Le Monde*, 3 February 1960; *Combat*, 3 February 1960; *France Observateur*, 4 February 1960; Georges Lefranc, *1944–1968*, p. 183.

tions to protest the outrages of the *ultras* and to demand self-determination did reinforce de Gaulle's position. Support for such mass actions could conceivably have followed as much from working-class support for de Gaulle as from working-class opposition to the war.[6] And the result of such actions could conceivably have deepened working class political support for de Gaulle. The only way in which PCF and CGT might have avoided such ambiguities would have been to have opposed both the regime and the war. However, as party and union realized, this would have had the dual disadvantages of strengthening the hands of the *ultras* and frittering away the obvious opportunity of acting in concert with other Left and Center forces. By this point as well the PCF may have begun to sense that aspects of Gaullist foreign policy, in particular the General's desire to resist American hegemony, were quite positive.

Thus, as the Socialist paper, *Le Populaire*, commented, "the CGT is offering its good and loyal services to lead to the triumph of General de Gaulle's policies."[7] CGT and Communist moderation, however, opened space on the extreme Left for forces willing to oppose both the war *and* the regime. French intellectuals and students, freer than the PCF and CGT from the need to make complicated calculations to conciliate the interest of different social and political forces, were eager to engage in ever more dramatic anti-war actions, draft resistance and open aid to the FLN, for example. Party and union firmly opposed such actions, using considerable vehemence in the process. PCF and CGT were caught in the logic of their mass anti-war movement perspective. Had they sided with the energy and extremism of the students they would have rendered themselves ineligible for participation in the de facto anti-war front of political and union forces to their Right. By opting for such participation, however, they further opened the breach between the party and the intellectual world, which was to prove very costly in the near future.[8] Problems of communication between students and the PCF and CGT grew deeper and deeper, as illustrated by the baroque confusion surrounding the events of October 27, 1960.

By the beginning of the 1960 academic year the entire student world was in ebullition about war, enamored of the idea of hyper-militant anti-war tactics and well-mobilized by UNEF (the *Union Nationale des Etudiants Français*—the French students' union). When UNEF proposed the calling of a mass anti-war action for October 27, to include unions, the CGT refused, asserting that it could not associate itself with a demonstration "of which it had discussed neither the objectives nor the means."[9] Neither the

6. Serge Mallet, *France Observateur*, 4 February 1960, p. 8.

7. *Le Populaire*, 22 January 1960.

8. On this general question, see Philippe Robrieux's marvellous autobiography, *Notre génération communiste* (1977).

9. Commentary by Léon Mauvais in his report to the 1961 CGT National Congress, CGT, *Congrès national, 1961*, 28 May–2 June 1961, p. 36.

CGT, nor the PCF, which acted similarly, were willing to risk being *forces d'appoint* (support troops) for student activists whose politics were suspect. To circumvent UNEF's appeal, the CGT Confederal Bureau proposed that all interested organizations meet together to plan a unified October 27 demonstration, a "National Day of Action for Peace in Algeria, for Negotiations." This plan went awry when the government banned the proposed demonstration. The CGT, faced with the prospect of sanctioning an illegal demonstration and thus directly confronting the government, withdrew its support (as did the PCF). UNEF and other groups went ahead, however, and parts of Paris became civil war-like, with anti-war demonstrators separated from the advocates of *Algérie Française* by walls of police. The CGT, meanwhile (supported by the PCF), called a series of dispersed, legal and very tame demonstrations of its own for the same day, attempting to keep its own supporters away from the Latin Quarter.[10] The result was increased bad blood between the CGT and students. For the PCF things were worse, however. The mass base of the student movement, following UNEF, fell progressively away from any Communist influence, with Communist student groups suffering the consequences.

As it turned out, PCF and CGT policies during this period were even more complicated than they seemed at first sight. Moderation to promote a large anti-war front, even at the cost of alienating intellectual sectors of the population, was not all there was. Another subtle, and somewhat less comprehensible, nuance was displayed in later 1960 and early 1961 in the face of General de Gaulle's referendum on Algerian self-determination. Party and CGT both came out for a strong *non* vote. Apparently the PCF and CGT perceived the 1961 referendum situation as one which provided a safe forum from which to attack the regime without undermining its stability. It is clear that they analyzed the referendum as primarily a plebiscite for de Gaulle rather than as a critical step towards peace in Algeria.[11] Moreover, it provided them with a convenient way of answering

10. Ibid., p. 36. The controversy around October 27 caused some trouble at the trade-union base. At the Bagneux plant of Thompson-Houston electronics, for example, disagreement over participation in the illegal UNEF demonstration split up a functioning unity-in-action agreement between the CFTC and CGT (see Serge Mallet, *La nouvelle classe ouvrière* pp. 226–227). And at the level of upper-echelon leadership the atmosphere around October 27 was poisonous. When the Seine Departmental CGT leadership was excluded from a mass meeting at the *Mutualité* in Paris on the evening of October 27, Léon Mauvais labelled the meeting "the conclusion of personal manipulations of the leaders of FEN and SNI [the independent teachers' union] in particular with Guy Mollet, as well as with the Minister of the Interior and the Prefect of Police" (Mauvais, CGT, *Congrès national, 1961*, p. 36). Mauvais claimed to the 1961 CGT Congress that the maneuvering in question was an attempt by the FEN to substitute a "round-table" position on ending the war for the PCF-supported position of direct negotiations with the Algerian Provisional Government. Mauvais further accused the "maneuverers" of attempting to use the CGT as a *force d'appoint* for this modified and edulcorated anti-war stance.

11. One wonders, in retrospect, how party *militants* were able to follow such tortured logic. Judging from the party crisis which followed, numbers of them were not.

their critics who accused them of supporting the regime. However, if the PCF and CGT thought that the referendum might be the starting point of United Front-style opposition to de Gaulle, they were sadly mistaken.[12] At the polls party and union found that their only companions in the *non* camp were *Algérie Française* supporters. Indeed, there was even some internal opposition within the CGT Confederal Bureau to the CGT's stance (Pierre LeBrun, fast becoming a staunch Gaullist, opposed the leadership). And there was no groundswell of popular support for the *non* position, which met overwhelming defeat at the polls.

For the PCF, the vagaries of its peace tactics and the inappropriateness of its general analysis of the new regime had their costs. A current of opposition to the Thorez leadership, or at least to its understanding of the situation which the party faced, had emerged in the 1958 crisis, and had grown as the peace movement had developed. The notion that Gaullism was not simply the last, illiberal gasp of a declining bourgeoisie, but instead the vanguard of a more dynamic, modernizing fraction of the bourgeois class had made its way up to the highest levels of the party—the pauperization perspective, in other words, was losing its credibility. On top of this, the inability of the party to develop peace tactics which could mobilize the student and intellectual world became another source of inner-party discontent. In essence, both the theoretical and tactical judgment of the Thorez leadership was being called into question. Thorez, deploying all of his considerable organizational skills and power, moved to counter the threat, and in early 1961 the PCF proceeded to one of the more serious purges of upper-level Communist ranks since the early 1950s. Marcel Servin, the PCF's organizational secretary, and Laurent Casanova, the party's coordinator of intellectuals, were demoted, while a larger group of "Young Turks" of lesser importance (J.P. Vigier, Jean Pronteau, M. Kriegel-Valrimont, P. Souquières) were severely disciplined. At the same time the PCF student group, plus its newspaper *Clarté*, were "taken in hand."[13] The accusations against Servin and Casanova were specifically directed to peace issues.[14] Casanova, who had been the chief PCF representative to the official *Mouvement de la Paix* (a mass organization of anti-war forces) was accused of "opportunism," and of sharing the perspectives of *France Observateur*. In more ordinary language, Casanova had been reluctant to

12. See, in particular, Gérard Adam, "L'unité d'action CGT-CFDT," *Revue Française de Science Politique* (June 1967), p. 578; Lucien Rioux in *France Observateur*, 25 May 1963.

13. François Fejtö claims that the purge occurred in response to a developing plot, perhaps with connections in Moscow itself, to overthrow the Thorez leadership. The plot's base was in the Politburo and the Central Committee of the PCF. See Fejtö; also Jean-André Faucher, *La gauche française sous de Gaulle* (1969), pp. 64–66. See also Philippe Robrieux, *Maurice Thorez* (1975), and *Notre génération communiste*, in which the Fejtö analysis is largely confirmed.

14. These accusations were a cover for quasi-fractional activity in the *Bureau Politique* by Servin and Casanova and Thorez's unwillingness to allow any serious opposition. See Fejtö; Robrieux, *Thorez*.

promote the PCF's line in the Peace Movement around the October 27 demonstration and on the January 1961 referendum, undoubtedly because much of the Peace Movement had little sympathy with the PCF's position on either action.[15] Marcel Servin was accused, among other things, of neglecting to promote Committees for Peace in Algeria at the rank-and-file level.[16]

The Servin-Casanova "affair" was, in fact, to be the Thorez leadership's last gasp of intolerance. Thorez himself was soon to depart the scene (by 1963 his control over the party had loosened; in 1964 he died) and the party was about to begin its long turn towards Eurocommunism, a shift which the Servin-Casanova "fraction" had, in effect, been advocating before its time had come. The 1961 purge promoted a number of younger party figures to places of responsibility for the first time. Servin was replaced by Georges Marchais, Casanova by Roland Leroy. At this point both were seen, and behaved, as the *hommes de main* of Maurice Thorez. Later, after the incomplete *aggiornamento* of Waldeck Rochet, both were for a time to be leading figures in PCF Eurocommunization, such as it was. Unfortunately, Communists in 1961 were unable to predict the future. The Servin-Casanova affair left the party confused and isolated.

Fortunately for the PCF and the CGT, given their confused state, the war went on, presenting them with clear actions to take. In late April 1961, the army in Algeria attempted a military coup in response to the regime's move to negotiate with the FLN. The CGT, CFTC, FEN and UNEF unified to call a one-hour general strike (FO ran a parallel action) which was massively followed. In the heat of panic, the PCF and CGT even asked the government to arm a workers' militia. The government, however, thought better of doing this.[17] At Renault in Paris, however, the CGT and CFTC, on the suggestion of Renault management, did occupy and prepare to defend the plants.

As negotiations came nearer, the Algerian *ultras* became more desperate, finally forming the terrorist *Organisation de l'Armée Secrète* (OAS) to do violence against anti-war forces and the regime. Leaving earlier disagreements behind, all anti-war forces mobilized against the OAS. The CGT in particular generated an impressive mass movement in the anti-OAS struggle. And, paradoxically, the anti-OAS campaign allowed both PCF and CGT to begin separating their anti-war actions from de facto support for the regime. On February 8, 1962, the CGT, CFTC, UNEF, *Parti Socialiste Unifié* (PSU) and PCF called a mass anti-OAS demonstration in Paris, under the banner of "le fascisme ne passera pas." The government banned the demonstration, but this time the groups concerned decided to go ahead

15. Fauvet, vol. II, p. 312.
16. Ibid., p. 312, 313–315.
17. *Combat*, 2 May 1961.

anyway. The regime's response was its usual one, droves of police, who took after the demonstrators with unusual savagery, even for French police. After chases up and down streets, the eventual result was the massacre of eight demonstrators, all CGT members, at the entrance to the Charron metro station. The Metro-Charron incident allowed PCF and CGT to make some new points. The original demonstration had been against the OAS. The massive protest march after Charron was against the regime.

The political results of PCF and CGT activities in the last years of the Algerian War were difficult to evaluate. Both had joined in general anti-war activity after initial mis-steps in 1959. For the PCF, however, any benefits of this in terms of increased contact with other political forces were limited by the party's strange journeys into sectarianism in 1961 around the referendum and the Servin-Casanova *affaire*—events which were undoubtedly connected. Moreover, a number of things which the party tried out during these years, such as its call for the creation of local and shop-level Committees for Peace in Algeria, simply failed.[18] As for the CGT, it did become politicized, to a degree, in these years, around war issues. In form, however, it did not behave differently in this respect from other French unions. In content, its occasional support for PCF sectarianism caused problems. Most important, however, the CGT did not cease existence as a trade union throughout this period, as it had during the deep Cold War years.

Relative Autonomy in a Wartime Labor Market

While the CGT was deeply involved in the anti-war movement it was also leading a parallel, and quite distinct, existence as a trade union. The first months of the new regime were fallow ones for the CGT, as for other French unions. The political defeats of the 1958 crisis, plus the industrial defeat suffered by the CGT in its attempt to promote a railroad strike in June 1959 made the Confederation quite uncertain about its support at rank-and-file level, an uncertainty compounded, as we have mentioned, by the effects of the Pinay/Rueff austerity measures and the consequent recession of 1959.[19] Patience was the order of the day for unions. Although nothing much was possible for the moment, the fact that wages were being held back, and had been held back since the change in regimes, was certain to create a backlog of grievances in the near future.

By early 1960 the atmosphere began to change. The general setting had

---

18. See Serge Mallet in *France Observateur*, 4 February 1960, for a description of one such committee at Nord Aviation.

19. *Le Monde*, 8 December 1969.

not been altered. The Government was deploying rhetoric and persuasion to prevent any wage increases of more than four percent per year—the rude beginnings of a Gaullist incomes policy—and private-sector employers, finding the new regime a cooperative ally, continued their open hostility to unions. Underneath the surface, however, the pot was beginning to heat up, especially in the private sector. Numbers of *grèves tournantes* (rotating strikes) occurred, dispersed throughout the country, promoted, more often than not, by the CGT, which was acting, at this point, on a "United-Front-from below" industrial tactic, going ahead on its own without agreement from other unions. The actions were modest in scope, locally focused on limited material demands, quite unconnected with one another, with the CGT making no attempt to build them into broader national movements.[20] The remarkable thing about these actions was that, because they took place in a tightening private-sector labor market (the Gaullist austerity plan had succeeded, to a degree, and French economic activity was starting up again), they worked. Often they managed to extract raises in excess of Pinay's four percent from employers more concerned with expansion than inflation. Results were uneven. According to François Sellier, "expanding firms in need of labor power went beyond official recommendations. Those crafts and qualifications most in demand were favored. For the rest, the action of the Government allowed employers to temporize and respond negatively. . . ."[21] Certain sectors and certain regions shot ahead. Others fell behind. The important thing to the CGT was that breakthroughs were possible. Working-class combativeness seemed to be re-emerging.

The story in the public sector, where the Government could enforce its wage-control goals, was different. The CGT actively promoted a number of public sector movements in 1960, to little avail. A general strike of railroad workers in May got nowhere. Civil servants on strike in June got nowhere.[22] And when the Government found that verbal intransigence was

---

20. Lucien Rioux in *Tribune Socialiste*, 4 August 1960.

21. Serge Mallet, *France Observateur*, 9 June 1960, claimed that the strikes were ninety percent victorious.

22. See Léon Mauvais, "Un nouvel essor des luttes revendicatives de la classe ouvrière," in *Cahiers du Communisme* (June 1960), on *unité d'action à la base*. See also Georges Séguy on this question for the railroad workers in "Origine, signification et enseignements d'une grève," *Cahiers du Communisme* (July-August 1960). After the defeat and humiliation of railroad workers in June 1959 (which the CGT railroad workers' Federation blamed on the CFTC), the CGT Federation convened a special "criticism and self-criticism" conference which decided on an intensive campaign to build towards a new confrontation with the government (Cheminots, p. 289; Séguy, *Cahiers du Communisme* [July-August 1960], p. 31.) The approach was to be one of "unity in action from below." The CGT promoted the movement, a general strike on 30 May 1960, on its own, without prior consultation with other unions. The action (which was eventually supported by *Force Ouvrière* and autonomous railroad unions) was successful in stopping trains for twenty-four hours (*Le Monde*, 1 June 1960).

not, in itself, enough to intimidate public-sector workers from striking, it sent in the police.[23]

1961 brought more of the same.[24] The success of local union actions in the private sector so alarmed the Government that Prime Minister Debré felt obliged to send a public letter to the *patronat* urging the CNPF to co-operate more fully in keeping to the four percent guideline.[25] And the Government maintained its public-sector intransigence, despite continuing CGT agitation.[26] Public-sector wages began to lag rather obviously behind those of the private sector.[27] A clear pattern of industrial conflict was emerging, one which was to be of considerable importance later. As Michel Bosquet (André Gorz) wrote at the time, private-sector workers were winning eight percent increases by striking, while "the state imperturbably applied its golden rule. Refusing to talk with public-sector workers, the state 'informs' them that their wages will be raised this year by 4.5 percent (and by this much next year). And because of the ways in which these raises were to be stretched out in several slices, they really represented only 2.8 percent in a full year." Bosquet concluded, "the direct and indirect employees of the manager state are paying almost by themselves the costs of a wage policy which, in itself, is hardly equitable and which, moreover, the state is demonstrably unable to impose. . . ."[28]

Thus despite its anti-war politicization, the CGT plugged doggedly away at developing action in the labor market in ways which were quite separate from its political goals. The CGT was concerned not to create any major industrial crisis which might cause trouble for the Gaullist regime in the delicate last period of the Algerian War, one reason why the Confederation

23. After June 1960 movements among Paris transport workers, twenty-nine RATP workers were severely reprimanded for participating. *Le Populaire*, 8 June 1960; *Le Monde*, 19 June 1960.

24. Strike figures 1957–1961, from *Le Monde*, 22 August 1959, 9 August 1961, 2–3 July 1962.

Year	Number of Conflicts	Number of Workers Stopping Work	Days Lost
1957	2623	2,161,000	4,121,317
1958	954	858,000	1,137,741
1959	1512	581,000	1,938,427
1960	1494	838,562	1,069,958
1961	1963	1,269,504	2,600,570

25. *France Observateur*, 24 March 1961; *Le Monde*, 19 March 1961. This letter, it is worth noting, marks the first attempt at an incomes policy in the Fifth Republic.

26. For examples of this on the railroads see *Libération*, 24 October 1961; *Le Monde*, 19, 26 October 1961; *France Observateur*, 26 October 1961.

27. *Le Monde*, 18 May 1961.

28. Bosquet in *L'Express*, 26 October 1961, p. 15.

was not eager to generalize the many local private-sector movements which it did promote. But there were other, more industrial, reasons for its decision to hold such conflict below a certain level of intensity and breadth. Rank-and-file militancy existed, but it was dispersed. Moreover, the 1958 crisis and its aftermath had blurred communications between trade-union organizations and their base. Thus rank-and-file responses to any attempt at generalized action were unpredictable. Slow, painstaking building activity, reconstituting the links between the CGT and its supporters, might pay off in the near future at a time when both political and trade-union risks had been minimized. In the short run, CGT tactics were aimed at rekindling labor militancy without diverting energy from the need to win peace in Algeria. In the longer run they were meant to lay the foundations for broader struggle in the years following the War's end.

The Payoffs of Peace

The Algerian War came to an end in June 1962, and with this came the end of the long agony of Fench decolonialization. The Fifth Republic, which had come into being as a result of the Algerian conflict, thus had to face normal conditions for the first time. The postwar period would also provide new circumstances for the PCF to implement its United Front goals, and a new setting for the CGT to act industrially.

It did not take long for events to reveal that the political environment faced by the PCF was indeed changing. The first major post-Algerian political event, a referendum proposed by the Government for fall 1962 to allow the direct election of the President of the Republic, revealed the existence of a broad and potentially united opposition to the Gaullist regime. Almost all non-Gaullist forces opposed the referendum proposition. On the Right, the General's abandonment of the Algerian *ultras* was the obvious motivating factor. On the Left, opposition followed from more complex reasoning. Direct election of the President was a giant step further towards a presidential regime, giving the President of the Republic a national electoral base independent of Parliament. Much of the Left felt that presidentialism was undemocratic. The referendum device itself, which allowed General de Gaulle to bypass political bodies through direct personal plebiscite, was also seen as undemocratic.[29] The proximity of this particular referendum to the legislative elections scheduled for later in the fall of 1962 was not overlooked. A successful personal plebiscite by de Gaulle would greatly enhance the chances of Gaullist candidates in the subsequent elections. A *cartel des nons* opposing the referendum proposition thus formed, including the PCF, SFIO, Radicals, MRP and assorted Right groups.

29. Macridis and Brown, p. 66.

Trade unions as well (and for once, not only the CGT—certain CFTC Federations organized for the *non* side) participated.

For the first time in many years the PCF and CGT took a major political stand in company with other forces without precipitating a rash of anti-Communism. The General himself was forced to acknowledge the *cartel*, and threatened to resign if the electorate rejected his proposal. There was little danger, it turned out, since sixty-two percent of those voting voted *oui*. But the thirty-two percent *non* was the highest negative response to the General thusfar. And, when abstentions were counted, less than a majority of eligible voters had supported de Gaulle. The General's position was still strong. But he was not invulnerable. More important, the PCF no longer stood alone in opposing him.

Further small progress for the PCF occurred at the ensuing legislative elections. According to the new Constitution, they were to be held in two "rounds." Any candidate winning an absolute majority in the constituency on the first round, was elected. Otherwise, a runoff was held the following week between the top vote-getters of the first round. On Round One of the 1962 elections nothing extraordinary happened, excepting the fact that the PCF regained many of the seats which it had lost in 1958. On the second round, however, an important United Front breakthrough occurred for the PCF. On the urging of Guy Mollet of the SFIO and the PCF leadership, Socialist and Communist candidates in many constituencies concluded agreements to throw their electoral support to the candidate best placed between them to defeat the Gaullist candidate. For Mollet and the Socialists, this was a major opening to the Left, the first time anything like it had happened since the beginnings of the Cold War. PCF–SFIO collaboration was limited, to be sure. There was no Popular Front, action agreement or common program at the top between the two parties. Electoral exchanges were worked out ad hoc on a constituency level. Despite the modesty of the arrangement, however, Communists bent over backwards to make it work, sometimes even to the point where Communist candidates withdrew in favor of Socialists who had done less well in the first round (this was the case in PCF support for its erstwhile arch enemy Jules Moch in the Hérault). By and large, the agreements were successful. In the fifty or so departments where they were concluded, thirty candidates of the Left were elected.[30]

The Gaullists were even more successful, however, obtaining nearly an absolute majority in Parliament—a majority if close allies were counted. Paradoxically, this was also encouraging for the PCF. The consecration of Gaullists as the majority hastened the collapse of the Right and Right-Center towards Gaullism, a fact which narrowed the political space at the Center of the French political spectrum. This, in turn, meant that Center-

---

30. Ibid., p. 106.

Social Democratic coalitions were less and less viable. The SFIO and the Center-Left had therefore to begin taking the possibility of a unified Left opposition to the Gaullist majority seriously. And no unified Left opposition without the Communists would be politically plausible, a fact which relative Communist success in the elections underlined (the party quadrupled its parliamentary strength, going from eleven to forty seats). United Frontism looked like an ever more promising strategy. As of 1962 the distance between promise and reality was still great, however. The Socialists and the Center-Left had a long way to go before they could overcome their Cold War prejudices and their proclivities for unprincipled coalition-mongering. Moreover, unless the PCF made a United Front happen, in part by resolving some of its own strategic contradictions, unity on the Left was unlikely.

The PCF's Fifth Republic trajectory was, then, likely to be a long and complicated one. The CGT's goals, although ultimately complementary to those of the PCF, had a shorter-run focus. The Gaullist regime had to be de-legitimated. Popular forces had to be mobilized against it. In the longer run such popular mobilization, primarily that of workers in the labor market, might contribute to the political success of the PCF's United Front plans. More immediately, however, the generation of such mobilization in itself was important. French trade unionism, including the CGT, had fallen into a period of decline and demoralization beginning with the Cold War. The only way to reverse such trends was to prove that the union movement could fight its membership's battles in the labor market. As of 1962 the question was quite simply to demonstrate that unions and workers could *act* in the new political context. Once this demonstration had been made, then other, more complicated issues such as reestablishing a degree of trade-union unity-in-action could be addressed. The first months of "normal" Gaullist rule were therefore critical for the CGT.

The CGT greeted the end of the war with a public flourish which intimated that the trade-union restraint of the war period was over.[31] Nothing spectacular followed immediately, however. Instead, action continued along much the same lines as during the war. *Grèves tournantes* in the private sector continued, and were often successful.[32] Agitation was almost constant in the public sector, but the government refused to budge.[33] Other union Confederations and Federations began to urge the promotion of more generalized forms of action (at *Electricité et Gaz de France* and on the railroads, for example), but the CGT was not interested.[34] The Confederation was still cautious about rank-and-file sup-

31. *L'Humanité*, 7 April 1962; *France Observateur*, 26 April 1962; *Combat*, 14 June 1962; *Le Monde*, 28 April 1962.
32. Lucien Rioux, *France Observateur*, 31 May 1962.
33. See, for example, reports on the wildcats on the railroads, *Le Monde*, 26, 29 April 1962; *Combat*, 18 April 1962.
34. See Georges Séguy's statements on strike generalization, in *L'Humanité*, 5 June 1962.

port for more general movements and, furthermore, was concerned lest industrial action disrupt the pre-electoral climate.[35] Nonetheless, and almost despite trade-union leaderships, an industrial time bomb was ticking away under the Fifth Republic. Disparity between the wages and conditions of private- and public-sector workers continued to grow. In later 1962, for example, a new contract at Renault (nationalized, but autonomous) granted workers a fourth week of paid vacation, to be emulated by a rash of similar accords throughout the private sector. Yet the government grimly refused to unfreeze public-sector wages, going to great lengths, when necessary, to refuse to do so. In December 1962 police were sent in to break up a strike of Paris transport workers, followed by army engineers to get the RATP, Metro and buses rolling again.[36]

The government's wage-control policy in the public sector probably hurt coal miners worst. According to the miners' unions, miners' wages had fallen further behind the private-sector average (eleven percent by 1963) than in any other branch of the public sector.[37] Beyond this, the miners' jobs were threatened. The Gaullist regime, in its pursuit of modernization in France, had adopted a cheap-energy policy, using Middle Eastern oil as the energy basis of its industrial plans. This policy had made coal a problem product in the energy market, and the future of the mines was clearly in question. By 1962–1963 the handwriting was on the wall. A substantial reduction in the numbers of miners plus the closure of uneconomic operations were impending. Despite this, governments displayed little aptitude, for, and less interest in, devising serious policies for converting mining areas to more promising activities. Such negligence (which, recurring often, was to prove an Achilles' heel of Gaullist economic-modernization strategy) was dangerous. Mining communities in France were bastions of intense working-class culture and solidarity.[38] As sociologist Pierre

35. *L'Express*, 21 June 1962, p. 19; *Témoignage Chrétien*, 22 June 1962; *Tribune Socialiste*, 23 June 1962; *France Observateur*, 31 May 1962.

36. *L'Humanité*, 12 December 1962; *L'Express*, 13 December 1962.

37. Governments had felt over the years that they had the miners in a vise. "Rocking the boat" by industrial militancy might well precipitate rationalization operations which might, in turn, threaten miners' jobs. The judgment that miners would be unlikely to protest a wage freeze made all the more sense given the extreme division among miners' trade unions. The bitterness caused by the strikes of 1947–1948, particularly between the CGT and CFTC, remained strong and was reinforced periodically by new sources of disagreement (over the European Coal and Steel Community, for example). See Pierre Belleville, *Une nouvelle classe ouvrière* (1963), p. 245.

38. The first signs of profound unrest among miners came not from the North of France, but from the Aveyron, whose mines were the most economically marginal. Décazeville and the Aveyron district, where trouble first occurred were, ironically enough, the places where Emile Zola's *Germinal* had been set, where the seeds of socialism had supposedly been planted beneath the ground when the miners took up the class struggle against their employers. In December 1961 the struggle of the Décazeville miners was one of desperation, since most of the Aveyron mines were scheduled to be closed, leaving the region economically desolate. The Décazeville miners struck against the proposed closure by occupying their pits in the dead of

Belleville wrote, "Our avant-garde sociologists don't come to Liévin to document the end of the working class. Nowhere else does a group remain as closed in on itself."[39]

Discontent among miners had been clear before the end of the Algerian War. It was only in autumn 1962, that preparation for action began, however, replete with disunity between miners' unions and much confusion. All of the miners' organizations were wary about tactics, both because of the relatively untested trade-union climate at the base and because miners had had great difficulty in acting at all since the crippling strikes of 1948. Thus the first, and perhaps most important, major strike of the Fifth Republic staggered its way into being. The CGT, most cautious of all the unions, called for a "productivity strike" (*grève de rendement*) in January 1963, which failed because the other unions refused it support.[40] Next *Force Ouvrière* and the CFTC (which was quite strong in the mines) called for an unlimited strike beginning on February 1.[41] The CGT, labelling this call "irresponsible," refused its support, which caused the CFTC to withdraw its call. FO went ahead alone and its action failed miserably.[42] The government's complete unwillingness to take the miners' problems seriously in mid-February discussions (it proposed derisory concessions in-exchange for binding limitations on the right to strike) galvanized the unions anew, however, leading them all to call for action on March 1 (although the CGT called only for a forty-eight hour strike, FO and the CFTC called for unlimited action).[43]

The March 1 strike calls began the drama. The Pompidou government reacted in a way which was to become typical for Gaullist cabinets in such circumstances, attempting to beat down the miners' movement by invoking the authority of the regime. It decided to requisition the miners. It had all kinds of evidence in hand to support such an authoritarian tactic. The winter had been cold, the government, in anticipation of a possible strike,

---

winter. Their fight, which lasted sixty-six days and gathered support from the entire population of the region, attracted a great deal of national attention. See André Quintard, "Les mineurs de Décazeville entre l'Europe des monopoles et le pouvoir personnel," in *Cahiers du Communisme* (May 1962). See also Philippe Bauchard and Maurice Bruzek, *Le syndicalisme à l'épreuve* (1968).

39. Pierre Belleville, "La grève des mineurs," *Perspectives Socialistes* (April 1963), p. 5.

40. *Libération*, 11 January 1963; Belleville, *Nouvelle classe*, p. 245.

41. Frachon, vol. II, p. 342; Lefranc, *1944–1968*, p. 174. Benoît Frachon later wrote "at the moments when conditions were such that the miners were ready to strike, the conditions for popular support of their movement were bad. Intense and prolonged cold weather had settled on the country. The government had arranged things so that, here and there, coal was lacking for domestic heating. Each day the press talked of old people or children dying from the cold. . . . Our comrades of the Miners' Federation understood the situation well and carefully weighed its consequences. In contrast, the FO and CFTC federations hardly cared and pushed for the outbreak of the strike at the beginning of February, in the middle of the domestic heating crisis."

42. *Le Monde*, 17 February 1963.

43. *Le Monde*, 14, 20 February 1963; *L'Humanité*, 26 February 1963.

had allowed coal stocks to run down, so that a strike-induced energy crisis would, in all likelihood, turn public opinion strongly against the miners.[44] Moreover, the miners' unions, as we have seen, were divided.[45] The government's requisition order (which was set to come into effect only after the CGT's forty-eight-hour movement had ended) was designed to play on this division.[46] It also was targeted to exploit divisions between the miners—the first day of its legal effect was a day when the miners of the North region, most militant in support of strike action, were off, while the miners of Lorraine, much less set on striking, would face the requisition order alone, hopefully to be intimidated.[47] The government's choice of the requisition tactic was not without subtlety, then. Still, the government's intention could not have been clearer. Strike action in the mines would be the first serious labor conflict of the Fifth Republic. The government was determined to break the miners' movement decisively because of this. It hoped, by doing so, to end public-sector agitation for some time to come. A great deal was at stake therefore.[48] The one variable which neither the government nor the unions could predict was the actual depth of discontent among the miners themselves.

As it turned out, the monarchical dignity with which General de Gaulle issued the order requisitioning the miners from Colombey-les-Deux-Eglises was matched by the militancy with which the miners struck. Rank-and-file ardor was so strong that the CGT—fearing for its own position if it stuck to its forty-eight-hour strike call—joined FO and the CFTC in pushing for an unlimited movement. In Lorraine, allegedly the "weak" miners' area, miners disregarded the government's order altogether. The next day Northern miners followed the lead of their Lorraine comrades, refusing to abide by the requisition order.[49] The overwhelming power of the movement at the rank-and-file level forced a united miners' union front for the first time in fifteen years.[50] The entire population of the mining regions expressed its

44. Lucien Rioux, *France Observateur*, 7 February 1963.

45. Bauchard and Bruzek, p. 18.

46. *Le Monde*, 28 February 1963.

47. On the government's tactics see Serge Mallet, in *France Observateur*, 28 March 1963. Lorraine as a region was much less monoindustrial, less centered on coal than the north, with a much higher incidence of practising Catholicism than the north as well. The region also had a fundamentally different political history and outlook than the north—in Lorraine the Gaullists had a base while the north was almost monolithically Leftist. See Pierre Belleville, *Nouvelle classe*, and especially the same author's *Laminage continu* (1969).

48. *Bulletin du Club Jean Moulin* (March 1963).

49. On the strike see Pierre Belleville, *Nouvelle classe*, ch. VII; the same author's articles in *Les Temps Modernes* (June 1963)("Après la grève des mineurs. . . .") and *Perspectives Socialistes* (April 1963)("Les enseignements de la grève des mineurs"); Lefranc, *1944–1968*, pp. 174–176; André Gorz, "La grève des mineurs" in *Temps Modernes* (April 1963); Bauchard and Bruzek, ch. I; George Ross, "Anatomy of a Strike in the Manager State," *New Politics* (Spring-Summer 1963).

50. At a later point a close collaborator of Prime Minister Pompidou commented, when asked to explain the failure of requisition, "ne cherchez pas, nous avons fait une gaffe de première grandeur"; see also Belleville, *Nouvelle classe*, p. 174–175.

solidarity with the strike—from women and merchants to the Church.[51] Moreover, public support for the miners was strong throughout France. The miners captured public attention as no social cause had yet done in the Fifth Republic, in part, perhaps, because the miners had dared to defy General de Gaulle. The miners' action demonstrated that the government had misunderstood both the miners and the nature of its own power. It had attempted to break a strike by invoking the authority of the regime. Instead it had ensured the success of the strike. And in the process it had shown that the magisterial authority of the new Republic did not stand above the mêlée of class conflict, despite the beliefs of the General and the hopes of the social forces behind his regime.

The movement didn't stop there, either. Other public-sector groups besides the miners had long-standing grievances. In the circumstances, striking on the miners' coattails seemed a good idea. On the broader tactics to follow in the public sector, unions were again divided. The CGT was cautious, against any general strike and for restricting the movement to miners, if possible, with the exception of short, symbolic solidarity actions in their support. The Confederation was afraid of drowning the miners' action, and its massive public support, in a larger public-sector movement which, by threatening important services, might give the regime an opportunity to recoup its losses. The CFTC, in particular, wanted broader action proposing general strikes in the Lorraine region[52] and in the metalworking trades[53] but the CGT was able to prevail.[54] Expansion of the strike in minor ways could not be prevented, however, since rank-and-file pressure for action in certain other sectors of the work force was strong. In Lorraine, iron workers went out.[55] In southwest France the Lacq natural gas workers went on strike.[56] And during the entire public-sector strike period, there was a great deal of agitation in the private sector, particularly around the demand for a fourth week of paid vacation.

The government wisely forsook the course of attempting to enforce its requisition order in the face of the miners' action (thus avoiding a larger explosion with strong political overtones). Instead it resorted to the tactics of attrition, announcing that no negotiations were possible until the strike had been ended and then retreating into ten days of silence in the hope that time would undermine the strike's momentum and support. Then, in the middle of the strike's second week Prime Minister Pompidou surfaced long enough to tell television spectators that inflation would follow were the

51. Ibid., p. 259; Lefranc, *1944-1968*, pp. 174-175.
52. *Le Monde*, 3-4 March 1963.
53. Belleville, *Temps Modernes*.
54. Ibid., p. 2388.
55. Ibid.; also Belleville, *Perspectives Socialistes*, p. 17.
56. Branciard, vol. II, p. 266.

government to relax its vigilance on public-sector wages.[57] At about the same time Gaullist circles in Parliament and press spread dark charges that the strike was "political," i.e., that the Communists were behind it. Despite all this, and despite the fact that the iron and gas workers settled after two weeks, the miners' strike continued unabated. It was finally ended, after thirty-five days, in a rather striking tactical coup by the Pompidou cabinet.

In the third week of the strike the government (taking up a *Force Ouvrière* suggestion that it had earlier dismissed) announced that it would set up a panel of "three wise men" to do a crash examination of the wage situation in the public sector. The *sages*, as they were called, reported finally that miners' wages were indeed far behind those in the private sector of the economy, and even behind those in the rest of the public sector (although not as far behind as the miners' unions had claimed). The government then made an offer to the miners' unions based on the *sages'* report. After a round of union rejection and governmental modifications, the miners accepted and went back to work with a 12.5 percent wage raise, a fourth week of paid vacation and the vaguest of promises that the future of the mines would be seriously examined. Thus ended the first major working-class struggle against the new regime.

The government had been defeated by a massive strike. Still, it had demonstrated a degree of tactical flexibility after its initial, and serious, authoritarian gaffe. It had been clear to the government for some time that simple wage freezing and exhortation in the public sector did not work to promote the kind of labor discipline and economic stability needed by the Gaullists, whose determination to promote French economic modernization by a strategy of government-induced structural reorganization of French capitalism was now clear. Trying to beat back the miners' strike by authoritarianism demonstrated what the government's first line of defense against labor struggle was. In essence, General de Gaulle believed that industrial conflict promoted in disagreement with his government's judgment of what was best, economically, for France was a form of lese majesty. Requisitioning the miners seemed an appropriate way to deal with such a transgression. It didn't work. That the regime was then able to turn to more modern means to the same ends was indicative of its resourcefulness and its complexity. The government needed institutional and ideological devices to separate its role as economic policy maker from its role as public-sector manager. Without such devices every important movement in the public sector became a political and economic threat and, in addition, provided grist for the mills of the opposition. The events of 1963 settled the

---

57. Georges Frischmann, "Où en est la conscience de classe," *Cahiers du Communisme* (April 1963).

government on the new tactic of a formal incomes policy, to be associated with the Economic Planning Commission.[58] The *sages* were meant as the opening wedge of this policy, a precedent for the "neutral" adjudication of public-sector wage problems. If thunder from the Elysée Palace was not enough to keep workers from rocking the Gaullist economic boat, then, perhaps, the mystifying ponderation of technocrats might be.

For the CGT, the miners' strike was a critical turning point. Although the Confederation, even more than the other unions involved, had been uncertain of the depth of rank-and-file discontent among miners (and had acted cautiously as a result), it had every reason to rejoice at the results. The strike had been a huge success, fueled, as every large successful strike was in France, by rank-and-file militancy which union organizations had not foreseen. The government had been humiliated, for the first time since the change in regimes. The strike answered a number of outstanding, and frightening, questions for the CGT. French workers had not been taken in by the "above class conflict" posture of the Gaullist regime. They were willing to fight, and fight hard, in the labor market when they felt their cause to be just. Moreover, they had demonstrated their ability to understand the economic development strategy of the new regime, one which promised economic growth, but at considerable costs to French workers. A degree of trade-union unity had been achieved during the strike as well, a development which promised much for the future. The CGT was concerned with building trade-union action in ways which, ultimately, and with due respect for the dynamics of the labor market, would complement the PCF's political goal of promoting United Front unity on the Left in opposition to Gaullism. The miners' strike, demonstrated that mass mobilization in the labor market was possible. Not only was mass mobilization possible, it also had a politicizing effect of its own, without any overt politicization by the CGT. The Gaullist government had taken coordinating responsibility for French economic development, including the regulation of the labor market. This meant that every important trade-union action in the labor market, by opposing the regime's logic for development, was by definition political, and contributed to the demasking of this logic. The more this happened, the more likely it became that working-class mobilization in the labor market would contribute to momentum towards Left political opposition. To the degree that workers and others rejected the regime's strategies economically, the political prospects for opposition to the regime were enhanced. Eventually, in all this, and with skillful Communist political work, a new United Front might be possible.

58. *Le Monde*, 19 March 1963.

Chapter 6

STRATEGIES AND COUNTER-STRATEGIES UNDER GAULLISM: RELATIVE AUTONOMY AND THE BEGINNINGS OF FRENCH EUROCOMMUNISM

The crisis of the last months of the Algerian War had brought the Gaullist regime a large amount of public support, including de facto support from the PCF and CGT. The exceptional circumstances of wartime were bound to disappear, however, and the regime inevitably faced the problem of reconstituting its hegemony in more normal conditions of peacetime. The General's favorite recourse, his mystical communion with the French nation, remained a useful stock in trade. But de Gaulle's self-presentation as removed from the petty conflicts of class, parties and politicians could not ensure the regime's success in the abstract. It had to be tied to the pursuit of specific goals. Here the General's astuteness shone through. Obstinate insistence on French independence in international politics and economic affairs was not the simple backward looking nationalism of a nineteenth-century man portrayed by de Gaulle's many opponents. Rather it was the product of deep insight on the part of the General, his advisors and the bureaucratic and economic elites who backed him. The American hegemony over international economic processes and the politics of Western capitalist states which had shaped events since World War II was weakening. Basic to this, the immense economic advantage of the United States in the post-1945 period was fast diminishing. Specific capitalist states such as France, by intelligent growth and investment strategies, might well be able to carve out new places for themselves in the highly competitive international capitalist market which was visible on the horizon. Foreign policy initiatives to roll back dependence on the U.S.A. internationally were a necessary complement to this. Gaullism's two central ideological pivots, economic "modernism" and nationalism in international politics, followed from these realizations. The regime wished to begin constructing a competitive, advanced capitalist France out of the protected, rather backwards and colonially oriented economy which it inherited. Refusal to rubber stamp American goals, taking French distance from NATO (including building the *force de frappe*), and working towards a French-centered European Common Market which might become an independent pole of economic and political development itself were all aspects of this grand strategy.

For the PCF and CGT Gaullism was an opponent *de taille*, one which, moreover, changed the shape of the battlefield in important ways. Its foreign policy was more than welcome, a fact which rendered the new regime preferable to any other alternatives except a PCF-dominated United Front. (Indeed, for the Soviet Union Gaullism was preferable to *any* other alternatives, period, a fact which was bound eventually to sharpen contradictions between the PCF and the USSR.) The new regime's economic modernism, its goals of restructuring French capitalism, creating an internationally competitive productive base, and opening up markets, would inevitably involve great sacrifice and dislocation for subordinate social groups. The regime's tendency, seen in the 1963 Miners' Strike, to react to social discontent as if it were a form of disloyalty promised much for the development of extensive social protest. And the Right and Right-Center partisan base of the regime's power clearly created a newly promising environment for both the PCF and the CGT. The PCF could only maximize the prospects presented by this new environment if it proved capable of resolving the profound contradictions in its own strategy. And, if the CGT was well engaged in processes of readjusting the relationship between the PCF and itself, the success of a relatively autonomous CGT depended ultimately on the party's ability to resolve these contradictions. The new setting provided new incentives to change for party and union. Their response to these incentives emerged in the years from 1963 to 1968.

Unravelling Contradictions? towards a New Popular Front

PCF theory did not gain much in terms of sophistication in the early years of Gaullism—the pauperization papers were re-issued, incredible as it may seem, in 1961.[1] But, by force of events and with the help of an international Conference of Communist Parties in Moscow in 1960 where discussion centered on "state monopoly capitalism," the party's positions became a bit more realistic. It became clear that General de Gaulle was not the front man for colonialist and fascistic fractions of the *grande bourgeoisie*. In-

1. See Maurice Thorez, *La paupérisation des travailleurs français* (1961).

stead, he was the representative of the "monopoly caste."[2] The regime of personal power which the General headed came from the need of this caste to limit democracy in order to promote economic goals. To cite the 1961 PCF Congress:

> French imperialism, weakened by the crisis which caused it to lose the near-totality of its colonial empire in a decade, is developing less rapidly than its rival imperialists. It forces itself, then, to tighten its grip on the nation at the expense of the working class, of the working peasantry and, in general, at the expense of all non-monopolist social groups.[3]

This same Congress's call for the construction of a *Front Unique* of the Left indicated the basic object of PCF strategy. Social support for such a *Front Unique* would come from those social groups hurt by the regime's attempts to fend off the decline of French imperialism. The object of the new *Front* would be to end personal power and establish "true democracy."[4] What was true democracy? First, negatively: true democracy was not socialism, or even the transition to socialism, but a halfway house between personal power and such a transition. Politically, true democracy was a situation which recognized "the national and democratic role of the working class, giving to the Communists, alongside other parties, the place belonging to them in Parliament and in the government. . . ."[5] True democracy was also economic democracy, involving the dispossession of the monopoly caste from its stranglehold over key positions of economic power and the transference of such positions to the people.[6]

The struggle for true democracy was something which a broad spectrum of oppositional forces could agree upon, thought the party. The ideal way to consecrate a Front of such forces, and one of the immediate goals of the party, would be the negotiation of a common program of reforms to create true democracy by such a Front. As early as the 1959 PCF Congress the party began to set out a model for such a program, involving the heady mixture of measures which follows:

> The Government emanates from a unique National Assembly, to which it is responsible. The liberties and rights of men are guaranteed by the law. Elections take place with a system of proportional representation and those elected are responsible to their electors. "Factious" organizations are dissolved, the professional army abolished,

---

2. PCF, *Histoire du PCF*, p. 666; see Frédéric Bon, "La structure de l'idéologie communiste" in F. N. S. P., *Le Communisme en France*.
3. PCF, *Histoire du PCF*, p. 691.
4. Ibid., p. 692.   5. Ibid., p. 658.   6. Ibid., p. 667.

the police purged and democratized, communal liberties respected and extended, prefects suppressed and their powers transmitted to the *Conseils Généreaux*, judges elected, the rights of agents of the state guaranteed by a democratic statute of the *Fonction Publique*, Church rigorously separated from school and state, press and cinema extracted from control by financial oligarchies, radio and television submitted to a democratic control.

The atomic industry, the oil and natural gas industry, the big navigation companies, the large iron and steel and chemical firms, business banks and insurance companies, that is to say, the established monopolies, are nationalized. Already nationalized enterprises are democratized. At all levels of economic life the initiative and control of workers and of their organizations are established and strengthened, the privileged prices accorded to private trusts at the expense of nationalized enterprises suppressed.

The democratic regime struggles effectively for the expansion of the national economy and applies policies in conformity with the interests of workers and the nation. The standard of living of the working class is raised up, agricultural cooperation encouraged in all of its forms, a statute for the *artisanat* elaborated. The energy resources of France and key sectors of industry are developed. Military expenditures undergo a massive reduction and the fiscal system is modified to strike at large incomes.

And so it went, through health-service reform, democratized education, science and culture, to peaceful coexistence.[7]

There was really very little new here from the PCF's post-1944 United Frontism. The party wanted to forge an alliance between itself and the non-Communist Left around a "Common Program" which, when implemented, would establish true democracy. Somehow or other, in ways of which the party was either unaware, or was keeping to itself, true democracy was a step towards socialism, not yet the official "transition to socialism," but a transition to the transition.[8] True, the "state-monopoly capitalism" notions, which would gradually come to displace pauperization, promised a way out of the Manichaean narrowness of the party's theoretical impasse, but this was a process which would take years to conclude. In any case, as per usual for the PCF, immediate politics were more important than theory (which tended to follow rather than shape political tactics). What was new, really new, in the party's approach to its new setting was its willingness to begin bargaining away certain important older doctrines in order to make its new United Front appeal more plausible to other forces. The party, in which leadership was passing from Maurice

7. Ibid., p. 668.   8. Ibid., p. 669.

Thorez to Waldeck Rochet, who was committed to a cautious process of *aggiornamento*, was well aware that its past attachment to Soviet dogma and Cold War positions were barriers to United Front success. Thus began PCF de-Stalinization less, initially, out of deep conviction, than from expediency. That the party chose an indirect, piecemeal approach to confront the major contradictions which blocked its progress was undoubtedly dictated by the legacies of Stalinism which persisted. Facing the full implications of the party's past at a point when this past still formed the party's way of life might have caused an internal crisis which would have rendered the party more ineffective in the present. Yet refusing to face this past head on would almost certainly place a heavy mortgage on the party's future. Nonetheless, the fact of de-Stalinization, even if it followed more from the demands of the outside world than from the logic of the party's internal life, was long overdue and welcome.

First of all, the party began to announce repeatedly that a "peaceful transition to socialism" was likely in France. Maurice Thorez' interview with the *London Times* in 1946 was dredged up to prove to everyone that the PCF had not changed its views, but there was no doubt that the party had changed its analysis of the balance of forces in France and the world.[9] To cite the May 1963 Central Committee report on "the PCF's policy of a large antimonopolist alliance": "the possibility of a peaceful transition to socialism appears when there exists such a superiority of strength on the side of the working class and its allies that the *grande bourgeoisie* is not in a position to have recourse to civil war. . . ."[10] The breadth of domestic opposition to the monopoly caste plus the international power of the Socialist camp made peaceful transition likely. The party also noted, again citing Thorez in 1946, that the path to socialism in France would be *French*, and not the same as "the one taken by the Russian Communists." By 1963 Maurice Thorez was also ready to admit that the dogma that one-party dictatorship of the proletariat was necessary for the passage to socialism was a Stalinist error, an "abusive generalization from the particular circumstances of the October revolution."[11] In France a multiparty transition was possible.[12] More specifically, "the entente between Socialists and Communists is possible and necessary not only now, but tomorrow in the struggle for the edification of socialism. . . . For us there is no Communist thesis of 'one party.' "[13] The speaker now was Waldeck Rochet, the new Secretary General, to the May 1964 Central Committee.

9. *The Times* (London), 18 November 1946.
10. *L'Humanité*, 11 May 1963; PCF, *Histoire du PCF*, p. 702; see also the *compte-rendu* of the Seventeenth PCF Congress in *Cahiers du Communisme* (June-July 1964), p. 64; and Maurice Thorez' closing speech, reprinted in Thorez, *Oeuvres Choisies*, vol. III, p. 316 ff.
11. PCF Seventeenth Congress, in *Cahiers du Communisme* (June-July 1964).
12. PCF, *Histoire du PCF*, p. 675.   13. *L'Humanité*, 9 May 1963.

Such changes were important, as everyone recognized, less for what they meant explicitly, than for the demonstration of a new Communist willingness to move to meet other political forces. In terms of their meaning, however, the changes were less than clear. A peaceful transition to socialism was still a transition to socialism, even if it were a "multiparty" transition. The Soviet experience of transition had not been disavowed in all this, except to allow that several parties might exist in a "dictatorship of the proletariat" (with the role of parties other than the Communists not spelled out). Presumably, then, the PCF still believed that, with certain modifications, the Soviet model was still to be the guide, and Soviet socialism still the model to emulate. To non-Communists in France concerned with civil liberties, parliamentary democracy and democratic procedures, the PCF's changes were not yet sufficient to allay anxiety.[14]

The path to United Front success was no clearer than the meaning of the PCF's doctrinal changes. United Frontism was not the only, or even the most likely, outcome of growing opposition to Gaullism. After the 1963 Miners' Strike the PCF was able to promote a number of United Front successes. Guy Mollet, the Socialist leader, seemed cautiously open to collaboration between the Socialists and Communists, and electoral cooperation between PCF and SFIO candidates in local elections was extensive in 1964 and 1965.[15] But local elections were small beer when compared to the first campaign for the Presidency of the Fifth Republic. As a result of the constitutional change of 1962, the President was to be elected by universal suffrage in two rounds of voting. In the first round a large number of candidates were likely to be present. If no single candidate won an absolute majority of votes in the first round a second round between the two highest vote-getters of the first round would follow. Given the fact that General de Gaulle was certain to emerge as one leading candidate, the system might very well serve the PCF's United Front ends. The loyalty of the PCF's electorate meant that the party would probably be in a position to withhold support for any anti-de Gaulle candidate of which it did not approve, ensuring his defeat in advance. Conversely, the party's support of any candidate, necessary for a plausible campaign, might be bargained in exchange for new steps towards Left unity.

A mysterious Monsieur X was the first entrant in the Presidential lists. Accordingly to the *Club Jean Moulin* and *L'Express*, both of which mounted a substantial publicity campaign, M. X was the ideal candidate. By early 1964 the man behind the qualifications was announced: Gaston Defferre. Defferre, in addition to being an SFIO deputy, Mayor of Marseilles and the center of a powerful Socialist political machine in the

14. *L'année politique 1964*, p. 29; Jean-André Faucher, *La gauche française sous de Gaulle*, pp. 141–142; Harvey Simmons, *French Socialists in Search of a Role* (1970), pp. 129–131; *L'année politique 1965*, pp. 3–7, 17–27.

15. Simmons, ch. 10; Faucher, *passim*.

Bouches-du-Rhône, was an anti-Communist and pro-American of long standing. Worse still, from the PCF's point of view, he and his advisors had well-worked-out Third Force goals. Defferre wanted to run for President as candidate of the non-Communist Left, having nothing to do with the PCF and its United Front plans except, perhaps, to trap Communists into voting for him. Beyond this he had longer-term ambitions to use the presidential elections to remodel the French non-Communist Left, making the SFIO at its core into a French Labor Party, modelled on the British and West German examples. He believed that the Federation which he envisaged, once established, would be able to recruit from its electoral Right and Left, from Centrists and from the PCF's own base, thereby precipitating the decline of French Communism. Later, as a result of complicated political tractations in 1965, he expanded his ambitions to project a large Federation which would amalgamate SFIO, Radical and MRP forces.[16]

The Defferre initiative was a serious threat to the PCF's *Front Unique* goals, and the party therefore did what it could to block Defferre's success. Maurice Thorez, just before his death in 1964, attacked the Mayor of Marseilles for wanting to patch up French capitalism. In the municipal elections of 1965 local Communists in Marseilles allied with dissident Socialists to attempt to unseat Defferre, to no avail (while elsewhere in the country Communists were loyally collaborating with other Socialists). The party also let it be known that if Defferre's offensive were successful, it would run its own candidate (Benoît Frachon, CGT Secretary-General, was the name bruited about). At the same time the party offered to negotiate a common electoral program with backers of a true United Left candidate—who would not be Defferre, of course. The juncture was a critical one for the party. Were Defferre to succeed, both in making himself Presidential candidate and in creating the large Federation, the PCF would find itself isolated again before its new United Front tactics had had the opportunity to work. As it happened, however, resistance from key non-Communists, and not the PCF, did in Defferre. Guy Mollet, leader of the SFIO, had never been an ally of M. X, and played a cagy game during the period of Defferre's initiative, consistently denying that the SFIO wanted a Popular Front while, at the same time, asserting that some form of electoral cooperation with the PCF was the best way to unseat de Gaulle. This, plus the unwillingness of the MRP leadership to buy the proposed large Federation in 1965, ended Defferre's initiative.

Waiting in the wings was a man who had been carefully organizing his own candidacy for the Presidency, François Mitterrand. Mitterrand, who had been one of the few prominent politicians of the non-Communist Left and Left-Center to oppose de Gaulle's ascension in 1958, had been very

16. Barjonet, *Le Parti communiste français* (1969); and Georges Suffert, *De Defferre à Mitterrand* (1966).

careful to be friendly towards the PCF in 1963 and 1964 when his name was first mentioned. "My attitude towards the Communists is simple. Everything which contributes to struggle and victory against a regime which leans towards the dictatorship of one man and the establishment of one party is good."[17] He had no overt intentions of using the PCF as a *force d'appoint* for Third Force politics, nor did he seem unduly afraid of some forms of cooperation with the PCF. When, in September 1965, a small Federation of the SFIO, Radicals and Mitterrand's own *Convention* (a political club of sorts) was formed, it became clear that Mitterrand had obtained the support of the non-Communist Left and Left-Center. The PCF, which had won a victory with the failure of Defferre's campaign, waited no longer. François Mitterrand became the Presidential candidate of the entire Left. The results were important. In the first round of the election de Gaulle was denied an absolute majority (mainly because of the Centrist candidacy of Jean Lecanuet) thereby forcing a runoff. In the runoff de Gaulle won, with fifty-five percent of the votes cast, but Mitterrand won forty-five percent.[18] The political strength of Gaullism, and in particular, the electoral magic of the General himself, was vulnerable. And, when steps toward cooperation with the Socialists in the 1962 and 1965 elections were considered together, it was clear that unity on the Left was politically viable.

PCF support for Mitterrand was Waldeck Rochet's first major gamble as the PCF's new Secretary-General. Waldeck was in a particularly good position to be able to take such a step. Projecting the public image of a plodding Burgundian peasant (he had, in fact, long been responsible for the PCF's work with peasants), Waldeck, inside the party, was a cautious believer in change who knew that the PCF had to move away from the patterns of the Thorez years but who understood full well the complex problems created by the legacy of those years. He was a firm believer in United Frontism, however, and, because of his credibility as a long-term colleague in the Thorez leadership, was able to bring the *Bureau Politique* and *Secretariat* along in his option for Mitterrand (although not without some difficulty—Jacques Duclos and Jeannette Vermeersch, two very powerful figures, had their reservations). Mitterrand was, in fact, far from an ideal candidate. He had a long, and unglorious, history of intrigue in Fourth Republic politics, he had only the vaguest of views about program plus quite unsatisfactory ideas, from the party's angle, on foreign policy.

What were Mitterrand's longer-term goals and where did the PCF fit into them? No one knew. Still, he was one of the very few non-Communist Left politicians able to impose his personality on the French public. And he

17. Faucher, p. 122.
18. F. N. S. P., *Les élections présidentielles de 1965*; see also Jacques Duclos, "Le grand succès de la gauche unie et les leçons qui s'en dégagent," in *Cahiers du Communisme* (January 1966).

did recognize that no non-Communist candidate for the presidency could hope for success without PCF support. The Mitterrand candidacy thus had its positive sides. Nonetheless Waldeck's gamble had certain side effects. The PCF student group, the *Union des Etudiants Communistes*, split over supporting Mitterrand, and a number of its leading militants left (including Alain Krivine, who quite quickly became a major figure in French Trotskyism).[19] United Front moderation here, as in the Algerian War, did not sit well with intellectuals and students, impatient for more drastic approaches and, as was becoming ever more clear, suffering, in their own ways, from the social distortions created by economic modernization.

Hardly had the Presidential campaign ended when preparations began for the 1967 legislative elections. Here the PCF hoped to build on 1965, adding a common program of the Left to what had been simply electoral agreements. Its eagerness was not matched by Mitterrand, Guy Mollet and the FGDS (the "small" *Fédération de la Gauche Démocrate et Socialiste* which emerged from the Mitterrand campaign). The PCF was concerned to destroy anti-Communist propensities once and for all by such a common program and since such propensities were held with varying degrees of intensity throughout much of the non-Communist Left and Left-Center, agreement proved difficult. At times sharp words were exchanged between the sides. As the elections of March 1967 came closer, however, some progress was made. In October 1966 the FGDS proposed an electoral accord of the Left accompanied by a declaration of principles. The proposal, full of ambiguities about FGDS support for Centrist candidates, was modified in some of the ways desired by the PCF at the SFIO Congress in November, to finish as an agreement between the FGDS and PCF on December 20. The accord was not a common program, much less *the* Common Program long desired by the PCF. Nonetheless it was the first national electoral agreement between the PCF and the non-Communist Left since the Popular Front.[20] How important this was became clear in the elections themselves. The PCF and FGDS won fifty-seven new seats while the Gaullists lost forty (coming within one vote of losing a parliamentary majority).[21] And these gains did not follow from any appreciable growth in absolute electoral support for the Left. They came from the workings of the electoral agreement between forces of the Left in which the FGDS and Communists threw their electoral support for the second round of the elections to whichever candidate between them had placed best in the first round.

19. Barjonet, *Pcf*, p. 201. See also Thierry Pfister and André Laurens, *Les nouveaux communistes aux portes du pouvoir* (1977).

20. *L'Humanité*, 21 December 1966; also "Un evènement de grande portée," in *Cahiers du Communisme* (January 1967), pp. 7–23, which includes the text of the accord.

21. F. N. S. P., *Les élections législatives de 1967*, part I, pp. 11–19, 87–116, also "Les élections législatives de 1967 et leurs enseignements," in *Cahiers du Communisme* (Special number, 1967).

Towards Unity-in-Action: the CGT

The CGT had parallel concerns to those of the PCF during these years, but in its own sphere of activity, the labor market. It hoped to regenerate trade-union activity in anticipation of the development of mass working-class opposition to Gaullist economic strategies. It saw such union activity not only as good in itself, but also as the foundation of broad mass mobilization against the new regime, mobilization which would ultimately become a politically useful commodity. To cite Benoît Frachon in 1963:

> In the country there are actually numerous social strata, victimized by rapacious monopolies, who realize the malfeasance of Gaullist power and who are looking for a way out . . . social strata which cannot, and do not want to, become part of trade-union organizations, but who are influenced by parties, political and economic organizations, representing their interests. It is toward the unity of these forces that we must work.[22]

First of all, however, trade-union activity had to be promoted. And, despite the success of the Miners' Strike of 1963, trade-union activity was not easy to generate. The government adopted a deflationary Stabilization Plan soon after the miners' victory which loosened the labor market considerably, making union action difficult. Moreover, trade-union differences in tactics prevented effective union campaigns.

In effect, the CGT faced a "unity" problem in the trade-union sphere which was far more urgent than that of the PCF in politics. Without trade-union unity-in-action very little could happen in the labor market. And without successful action in the labor market, mass social mobilization against the regime would not exist. And the CGT knew full well that unless such mobilization could be developed, the mass background for United Front political success would not be present. In the shorter run, however, trade-union action was even more critical. The regime was, as we shall soon see, about to deploy an ideological offensive designed to undercut the development of mass protest, particularly from the unions. Unless united union action could be mounted to counteract this offensive, the regime might succeed.

Disunity was the historic cross which the French labor movement had had to bear. It had paralyzed working-class action in the labor market throughout most of France's industrial history. In its modern form, the trade-union pluralism which followed the CGT split of 1947, it had been disastrous. In 1945 French unions had more members and more power than ever before, while the French *patronat* was on the defensive. By the early 1950s the Cold War union disunity had reversed the situation, as we have

---

22. See Gérard Adam, "L'unité d'action CGT-CFDT" in *Revue Française de Science Politique* (June 1967), p. 578; citation from Benoît Frachon, CGT, *Congrès national, 1963*, p. 35.

seen. The *patronat* had taken the offensive, union membership and support had drastically declined and the different segments of organized labor in France were quite unable to talk to one another, let alone promote union action. Politics was the key to this sudden reverse. Cold War allegiances split the labor movement down the middle, between the CGT and everyone else. When the CGT promoted action, the others refused to cooperate. When rank-and-file distress overrode the paralysis of organizations and created strikes, other organizations settled with employers as quickly as possible in order to deny the CGT any possibilities for success. Trade-union unity-in-action may well have been unreachable in any circumstances in this period, since political differences cut so deep. The positions of key union groups on unity, and in particular those of the CGT, only made things worse, however. The CGT considered *Force Ouvrière*, the logical target for unity efforts, as illegitimate. And it insisted upon a priori agreement from *Force Ouvrière* on all questions ranging from politics through general union strategy in the labor market to day-to-day tactics before unity at the top between the two organizations was possible. *Force Ouvrière*, for its part, simply refused to talk to the CGT about anything. As for the CFTC, which traditionally had lukewarm feelings about serious action in the labor market in any case (due to its devotion to Catholic doctrines of social harmony), it could only have been brought to unified action by a CGT and FO willing to act in concert in such a context. FEN, the teachers' union, quite naturally gravitated towards corporatist arrangements on its own with governments of the time.

And, since the CGT's "unity on everything, especially politics, before unity on specific union issues" position ruled out unity on anything, its major approach to FO and the CFTC consisted in denouncing FO and CFTC leaders as "misleaders," agents of the bourgeoisie in the working class, trying, where possible, to undermine them by organizing their memberships out from underneath them ("unity in action from below," the classic strategic response of both PCF and CGT in periods of isolation).

The logic of both the CGT's relative autonomy position vis-à-vis the PCF and the PCF's blossoming new United Front thrust meant that something basic had to change in the CGT's attitudes towards trade-union pluralism before mass success in the labor market was possible. And it did, beginning with the 1963 CGT Congress. "Unity in action from below," which had been the rule through the first years of the Fifth Republic, gave way to "unity in action at the top."[23] In Benoît Frachon's words, "Now the idea of unity has imposed itself . . . there are actually enough points in common in the diverse demands formulated by the various centrals and their federations to justify and realize unity in action not only on the shop level, but between the centrals themselves, in order to sustain, coordinate

23. *L'Humanité*, 21 May 1965.

and make more effective the struggles which cannot help developing."[24] From this point onwards, there were to be no more extravagant attacks on the leaderships of the other unions by the CGT. Public tirades between the CGT and the other unions became muted. Unions should agree on what they had in common. Only later on, when they had developed workable patterns of united action on such common matters should broader issues such as great issues of union strategy and politics be posed.

The CGT's new intentions mothered no immediate acts. The government's 1963 Stabilization Plan (Valéry Giscard d'Estaing's entrée onto the larger stage of French politics) made action very difficult in the private sector, while staunch governmental determination to hold down public-sector wages made action there difficult as well. *Force Ouvrière*, not surprisingly, still refused to talk with the CGT. And the CGT differed strongly about union tactics in the Stabilization Plan period with the CFTC. The CGT was cautious in the extreme. It was in favor of low-level building actions in the private sector, where possible, with more general and/or spectacular actions to be avoided.[25] In the public sector the CGT favored short, "guerrilla" type actions, movements of a protest kind which did not cause undue inconvenience to the users of public services. The CGT's positions rested on the Confederation's general analysis of the Stabilization Plan period. In the private sector the unfavorable labor market meant that strike actions could only be local when they occurred due to local circumstances. Generalization was not possible. Thus any action which became too spectacular and too public could be isolated, labelled extremist and inflationary by the *patronat* and press, possibly repressed and would almost certainly fail. And in failing it would provide anti-union grist for the government's mill, demoralize the labor movement in general and undermine the emergence

---

24. CGT Commission Administrative, 15 October 1965, in Frachon, vol. II, p. 486. At around this time the CGT went through another minor internal crisis. Pierre LeBrun refused to go along with the CGT decision to support Mitterrand, hardly bothering to conceal his Gaullist sympathies. In January 1966, *L'Humanité* attacked LeBrun for this and other things, stating that he had been "in the arms of the worst enemies of the working class." LeBrun waited a few days to see if the CGT Confederal Bureau (of which he was a part) would protest the *L'Humanité* article, which it did not, and then resigned. Jacques Marion, a member of the CGT Administrative Commission, resigned in sympathy with LeBrun. LeBrun had been a major thorn in the side of PCF leaders of the CGT for some time, leading the CGT "opposition" on the issues of the CGT "economic plans" (1954–1955), trade-union unity (1956–1959), "democratic planning" (1960s), among others. LeBrun probably never agreed with the PCF-CGT leadership's central concepts of political strategy and tactics. For a long time LeBrun held a "radical reformist" (vs. Frontist) view of things, a position which neglected to give enough recognition to the key role of the PCF in the Frontist strategy while making the trade union into a primary political actor rather than a mass organization. After his resignation in 1966, for example, the government reappointed him almost immediately to the *Conseil Economique et Social* as an "expert" whereas before his resignation he had led the CGT delegation.

25. See on this Benoît Frachon's remarks on the strategy of *grèves perlées* in CGT, *Congrès national, 1963*, p. 12.

of mass opposition to the regime. The same reasoning, only more pronounced, prevailed for public-sector movements. The government was bent on imposing a public-sector incomes policy. The CGT wanted to block this, but in order to do so a substantial, broad union movement was needed. And no such movement was possible unless the public, which consumed public-sector services, understood the issues involved and sided with the justice of the unions' cause. This meant that protest actions, which raised issues without causing inconvenience, were necessary to build any larger confrontation in which unions and public opposed the government. In short, the CGT's tactical logic looked not only at the narrow issues in any given struggle situation, but also at the broader implications of any struggle for longer-term mobilization of the working class in the labor market and for the development of mass opposition to the regime.

The CFTC did not feel responsible for such broader implications of trade-union action, at least as they were conceived by the CGT. By the early 1960s the CFTC was engaged in the profound transformations which would make it the *Confédération Française Démocratique du Travail* (CFDT) (see below) and had found a new interest in labor-market militancy of all kinds. At this point, it opted for private-sector movements which were fought through to their conclusion in successful negotiations, whatever their cost to mobilizational prospects in the private sector as a whole. And it wanted public-sector actions with "teeth," i.e., movements whose object was concessions rather than symbolic protest. The CFTC, unlike the CGT, was not bound to larger projects for social mobilization beyond the market. Indeed, because the CGT *was* bound to such projects and because this led the CGT to moderation in its day-to-day behavior, the CFTC may well have seen its freedom to be more militant as an important way to increase its own strength relative to the CGT's. In any case, it was at this point in the early 1960s, that profound strategic and tactical differences between the CGT and the CFTC–CFDT first became visible. Such differences were to mark labor action in France for a long time to come. More important, at the time, such tactical disagreement made union action quite difficult, at a moment when mobilization of any kind was a priori difficult. In the late fall of 1963 the CGT vetoed a CFTC National Day of Action as "neither thought through nor realistic." And on at least two occasions in 1964 CGT Federations called independent actions of a protest sort in the public sector to head off movements proposed by other unions which, the CGT feared, would alienate the public. In March 1964 for example, CGT railroad workers called a short action to drown CFTC mobilization for another action during the Easter vacation *départ*, a moment when the public would have been maximally inconvenienced. The same sequence of events recurred in December to drown a proposed Christmas vacation action.[26] In turn, when the CGT proposed short, symbolic protest strikes in the public sector, the other Confederations held back.

26. *Tribune Socialiste*, 2 January 1965.

The CGT's "guerilla-warfare" formula was more extensively honored in the private sector, where the CGT was relatively more powerful. Here the difficulties were less those of tactical differences between unions than the unfavorable situation which any union action faced. The government had decreed a wage freeze in the public sector as part of the Stabilization Plan and had urged private-sector employers to follow its lead. Because of the slack labor market the *patronat* had every reason to be intransigent, thus an effective entente between government and *patronat* to keep wages down throughout the economy came to exist. For the unions, conditions in the labor market made movements difficult to promote to begin with, even lower-level actions of the kind desired by the CGT. Worse still, when any action of substance did occur in the private sector, the entente between government and employers ensured that it would be rudely dealt with. In Spring 1965, for example, a strong local movement at Berliet in Lyon led to a lockout which broke the strike with no concessions. At Peugeot in Sochaux, rotating strikes, called on the eve of the introduction of a new car model, led to the firing of a large number of Peugeot trade-union delegates.[27] In response, the unions called a total strike which, after seven weeks, led to another lockout.[28] Eventually the police were called in and the movement broken by force. All of the strikers were severely disciplined, while Peugeot refused to give in on anything. After the Peugeot failure, moreover, 1965 proved to be a year almost devoid of serious trade union-action, in part also because of the Presidential election.

It was this atmosphere of trade-union failure which led to the major breakthrough creating unity-in-action. And the initiative came from an unexpected source. The CGT had always targeted *Force Ouvrière* as its most likely union ally. Instead, unity was to come from the *Confédération Française Démocratique du Travail*, the ex-CFTC. What had happened to the CFTC was truly extraordinary, a story which confounded all of the predictions of the "end-of-ideology" sociologists of the time. A decade of internal struggle in the CFTC, which had begun after the CFTC sellout of the summer 1953 strike movement, had led, in 1964–1965, to the final deconfessionalization of the Confederation. The causes of this were complex. It had taken some time, for example, for Left Catholics from the Resistance to rise to positions of CFTC power. An influx of ex-"jocistes" —*Jeunesse Ouvrière Chrétienne*—was also important. Changes in the Church's attitude towards class issues were vital. The French Church's experiences in campaigns of outreach towards industrial workers in the forties and fifties, of which the "worker-priest" episode was only the most publicized, had sensitized numbers of French Catholics to new ways of understanding society. Vatican II, of course, was not far off. Catholic

27. *Le Monde*, 15 May 1965; Lefranc, *1944–1968*, p. 189.
28. *L'Humanité*, 17 May 1965.

militants had also learned a great deal from struggle against the Algerian War. The indirect, but fundamental, role of the CGT in all this must also be mentioned. For all its faults and mistakes, the CGT had maintained its position as the major French labor organization. Because of this, notions of class and class struggle had been perpetuated and reinforced among French workers through a period—the 1950s—when such notions were being abandoned or edulcorated in many other advanced capitalist labor movements. It was the CGT, then, which had set the tone of the union environment within which the new leaders and militants of the CFTC had emerged.[29] The end result of all this was that the new majority in the CFTC which took control of the Confederation formally at its 1964 Congress, believed profoundly in militant trade-union action and was willing to act on such beliefs.[30] Beside the energetic, rejuvenated CFDT (the name changed at the 1964 Congress), *Force Ouvrière* appeared weak indeed.[31] The CFDT was destined not only to be a union partner—and rival—of the CGT, it was also already moving to the Left doctrinally and politically.

The immediate problem faced by the CGT in contemplating the CFDT was that the CFDT was committed to union strategies and tactics of which the CGT did not approve. As we have remarked, the CFTC–CFDT was interested in strike and other actions carried through to their conclusion, however localized and however difficult for other workers and the public to understand. To the CGT, extreme local militancy, which other workers and social groups who might potentially support and ally with the working class could not understand, was likely to compromise both union action and longer term prospects for mass political mobilization. The CGT had a long-standing notion of *the* working class, how its different segments fit together, plus a broader map of French society which located non-working–class groups who might sympathize with workers if union action were conceived in astute ways. In part, but only in part, such perspectives followed from the relatively autonomous CGT's responsibilities for political mobilization. The CFDT had, of course, no such political responsibilities. It also had, in practice, a relatively undeveloped notion of the relationship between specific union action and its broader class consequences. In part this was a result of the ways in which the CFTC had changed into the CFDT—new militancy emerged into certain CFTC–CFDT

29. See Gérard Adam, *La CFTC* (1964); M. Maurice, "L'évolution de la CFTC" in *Sociologie du Travail* (January-March 1965); J. C. Poulain, "La transformation de la CFTC en CFDT" in *Economie et Politique* (March 1965); G. Levard, "CFTC-CFDT," *Formation* (September-October 1965); also Stephen Bornstein, "From Social Christianity to Left Socialism: The Itinerary of the Catholic Labor Movement in France" (1979).

30. See Bornstein, ch. IV. It should be noted that a rump of the old CFTC refused to go along with the change (mainly miners) and remained as the *CFTC maintenue*, litigating endlessly with the CFDT over rights to CFTC property.

31. See J. M. Lecler, *La position*.

federations and regions while old CFTC practices of labor-market moderation (even corporativism) continued in others. In such a context, manifestations of the new militancy tended to be decentralized and somewhat devoid
of reference to broader collectivities. All of this was to change in time as
the CFDT matured, even if the changes were to prove little more to the
CGT's liking. In 1964–1965, however, the CGT was painfully aware of differences between it and the CFDT, all the more so because it understood
that the CFDT's strategic and tactical innovations were, in part, also a
recruitment gambit designed to build up the CFDT relative to the CGT.
Throughout the hard months of 1964–1965, then, relations between the two
Confederations were far from *unitaire*. Frachon and other CGT leaders
were quick to denounce the CFTC–CFDT as "anti-Communist." Eugene
Descamps, CFDT Secretary-General, in turn labelled the CGT as *Gaulliste-
de-fait*—de facto Gaullist—because of CGT moderation in labor conflict.

In fact, however, unity-in-action was needed by both Confederations.
The CGT knew that the CFDT had found new vitality and militancy. Without collaborative arrangements with other organizations, however, the
CFDT's new energy would only lead to discouragement. The CGT feared,
however, that, if left alone, the CFDT might work out a Third Force unity
arrangement with *Force Ouvrière*, an eventuality which would have had
disastrous results for the CGT's mobilizing goals.[32] The CFDT leadership
wanted union action. Only through the development of such action could
the promises of the Confederation and its new majority be fulfilled. The
CFDT was probably inclined towards collaboration with FO from a political and philosophical point of view. Yet it also knew well that FO was
something of a rump organization whose visceral anti-Communism had affected its militancy and its understanding of what trade-union action was
all about. Still, CGT and CFDT disagreed profoundly about what unions
should be doing.

It took the evident stagnation of labor action in 1965 to create unity. In
September 1965 Descamps publicly suggested that union Confederations
should meet together to define common concerns in order to get labor
struggle off the mark. Informal contacts were made on all sides. Then, in
November, at the CFDT Congress, Descamps made his suggestion more
precise. Agreement between the CFDT and the CGT was desirable.[33] The
CGT responded immediately by proposing the negotiation of a common
platform of trade-union objectives and demands. Talks began in earnest, to
be concluded on January 10, 1966, with the first major breakthrough in
trade-union unity since 1947. The CGT–CFDT unity-in-action agreement
was restricted to professional and economic matters. It set out a long list of
specific trade-union objectives under the general rubrics of improving

32. Branciard, vol. II, p. 202.
33. *Tribune Socialiste*, 26 January 1967; Branciard, vol. II, p. 262.

working-class purchasing power, living and working standards, defending and extending trade-union legal rights at the firm level, the reduction of non-productive spending in the economy, guaranteed right of employment and the reconstruction of the French fiscal system in ways less unjust for workers.[34]

The CGT–CFDT accord of January 1966 was quite as important in the trade-union realm as PCF successes in generating collaboration with the non-Communist Left were in the political sphere, if not more so. The accord meant that the two largest French trade-union organizations would begin issuing united calls to action and then using their combined resources to ensure that such calls were followed. This could not help but multiply working-class action in the labor market and lead to a greater mobilization of the working-class rank and file against the regime and the *patronat*. The accord also demonstrated decisively how differently the relative-autonomy CGT perceived the unity question. In its earlier guises, the CGT had refused to contemplate official unity-in-action unless all outstanding differences between the CGT and potential allies had been settled in the ways desired by the CGT, up to and including political differences. The 1966 CGT–CFDT accord settled *no* major differences between the Confederations. The CGT had decided to promote unity on the basis of what could unite it with the CFDT, however narrow the range of possible agreement was. In 1966 the Confederations agreed only on trade-union objectives in the labor market, bread-and-butter goals. Not only did the two organizations totally disagree on political questions, more importantly, they drastically disagreed on trade-union tactics to be pursued to achieve the labor-market objectives upon which they agreed. Of course the CGT hoped that initial collaboration on limited issues would lay the groundwork for persuasion and subsequent agreement on a larger range of questions, from trade-union strategy and tactics through politics. And the CGT knew that its own superior strength and organizational power would be significant resources to promote new agreement. Ultimately, the CGT wanted to use trade-union unity-in-action as the major tool for building mass social opposition to Gaullism, opposition which could be translated into positive support for the new United Front which the PCF hoped to build. As of 1966, however, as the French say, "this was not for tomorrow." It was very far, indeed, from what the CFDT had in mind.

Neither the CGT nor the CFDT had made *any* concessions about their differences in trade-union tactics and strategy in signing the 1966 agreement. The CGT held to its "mass" perspective, in which any and all union activity, at whatever level and of whatever intensity, was to be evaluated for its contributions to general working-class and mass mobilization. The

---

34. The accord is summarized briefly in *Le Peuple*, 15 May–30 June 1968, p. 47. Also Branciard, vol. II, p. 262; Bauchard and Bruzek, p. 282; Frachon, vol. II, p. 498.

CFDT, in contrast, preferred decisive industrial struggles, wherever and whenever they seemed possible, whatever the broader consequences. Looking to the immediate future such differences could be resolved in favor of one or the other perspective, most likely that of the CGT, which was by far the most powerful organization. Or they could not be resolved, lead to conflict and eventually cause the end of unity-in-action. Yet again they might not be resolved, cause conflict between the Confederations, while at the same time creating, in a dialectical manner, a climate of industrial mobilization with both mass and local-extreme components. This last was to be the case, leading, of course to the tremendous industrial explosion of May-June 1968. May-June 1968 was not only a trade-union triumph, however. It was also a massive strategic failure for the Gaullist regime. To understand this we must briefly turn to the strategic considerations of the regime.

Gaullist Modernism: the Regime's Strategies

If the PCF and CGT, each in their own respective spheres of practice, were determined to demystify the Fifth Republic and prepare social change thereby, the regime's task was the opposite, to legitimate its position. Its resources for this were not negligible. The fact that the regime had brought stability, political predictability and some sense of renewed pride to France at a moment when the confidence of French society was at a very low point was a distinct political asset. The carefully constructed *personnage* of General de Gaulle, who presented himself as something of a Rousseauian law-maker, was effective as well. The General had also devised a number of techniques to deepen the mysterious communications which he carried on with the French nation—carefully staged press conferences, plebiscitory referenda, Olympian addresses on important public occasions and extremely ly skillful manipulation of the media, especially television. The regime's fundamental mission, economic change, was, however, a dynamic one, and neither the gratitude of the French for 1958 nor the dramaturgy of the General were enough to ensure that this mission would achieve the consensus needed to make it successful. Here, as we have noted, Gaullist modernism entered.

La Mystique du Plan became the core of the regime's modernist thrust. Economic planning was, of course *vieux jeu* by the 1960s in France. Invented in the post-Liberation years (partly by the PCF), and carried on in the shadows of Fourth Republic instability by technocrats, the Plan was something of a dormant institution by 1958. The Gaullists felt that it was well worth reinvigorating, however. The Plan was a public document, which set out a global picture of economic goals for France to achieve over a five-year period. It was made up by a high-powered *Commissariat* of France's most prestigious economic specialists, officially after consultation of all available data, the latest in planning theory and techniques and all significant interests in French society. No matter if the Plan were really drawn up by collusion between high civil servants and the more dynamic leaders of French business, it could be presented to the public as above sordid social conflicts, legitimated by the "neutrality" of high civil servants and the high mysteries of economic science.[35] For a regime with very specific economic goals which would almost certainly involve sacrifice and dislocation for large parts of French society, the Plan seemed to provide a very good means to carry on.

The regime wanted the Plan to become the ideological axis of the nation's economic life, a strategy and tactics for national success. As the General intoned in his 1964 New Year's address, the Plan was *l'affaire de tous*. Fundamental economic choices would be more easily accepted by the French if such choices had legitimation above and beyond simple market criteria. The planning apparatus was designed, therefore, to convince people that basic choices were being made in a disinterested way with the national welfare at heart. The regime's dream was to sanctify the Plan by submitting it for approval to various deliberative bodies (the Parliament, the *Conseil Economique et Social*) and have it become a blueprint for five years of economic development. The regime was not naive, however. It realized that, if French business would have relatively little trouble digesting a plan which had been designed for (most of) it, the same could not be predicted for the French Left and French workers. Here, the regime hoped, the Plan might work its ideological effects. Were large numbers of French people to accept the Plan as a final national reference point in matters economic, the situation of unions (at least of those unions which could not be brought themselves to accept the logic of the Plan) and the Left, upon whom the regime knew better than to count, would be made very difficult. For example, if government and *patronat* could invoke the Plan as a higher good than unions' "sectional" interests when unions attempted to mount a campaign to win concessions for their supporters, then union freedom to act would be seriously limited.

There was a peculiar Gaullist, and perhaps fatal, twist in all this. In almost all other advanced capitalist societies where demands of economic development in a stable context had necessitated trade-union cooperation, institutional attempts had been made to integrate the unions—if only in a limited way—into processes for determining the constraints within which they would have to operate. With the departure of the PCF from government in 1947 and the coming of the Cold War, attempts to formulate such "corporatist" arrangements in France had come to an end, and postwar French economic development had henceforth proceeded with unions and workers excluded from decision-making. The Gaullists' *Opération Plan*

35. The best work on the plan is Cohen, *Modern Capitalist Planning: The French Model* (1969), especially the chapters on trade unions and the plan.

was a new variant on this post-1947 French path. Unions had been invited to meetings to prepare the Plan over the years, but they had soon realized that they were present only as spectators, not as legitimate and valued partners. Gaullist attempts to sanctify economic planning involved placing French unions in an economic box entirely constructed by their class adversaries. The clear hope of Gaullism in *Opération Plan* was to persuade whatever unions were persuadable that the Plan was indeed "their" affair and to place the unions who were not persuadable at a new disadvantage. The most important point was that *Opération Plan* opened no new doors to corporatist arrangements for unions. Perhaps this was because of the combative nature of French unions, at least in part. More importantly, it followed from Gaullism's own disdain for intermediary social forces, and especially trade unions. The regime apparently felt, quite predictably, that its repeated intonation of the "national interest" should be enough to secure compliance. This was a major mistake, it turned out.

Opération Plan was, then, almost a mirror image of the PCF's unity strategy. The PCF (and the CGT in the labor market) hoped to promote mass mobilization and a new United Front by capitalizing on the social discontent created by the regime's economic development policies. The regime, in contrast, wanted to use the plan to convince a critical mass of Frenchmen that its economic policies were in the national interest. Of course, the regime could only begin succeeding if French capitalism were able to "deliver the goods" in the form of important advances in living standards and personal dignity. In any case, the CGT, which was to be a critical opponent of *Opération Plan*, had seized the regime's logic without much trouble. Benoît Frachon, at the 1963 Confederal Congress, stated that "since the working class is showing that it is unwilling to be happy with vain words, the regime, in full collaboration with the men of the banks and monopolies, has invented a new illusion machine . . . the Plan."[36]

La mystique du Plan was promoted in several installments, some more complete than others. The first concrete inkling of what the regime had in mind was Giscard d'Estaing's Stabilization Plan of 1963, to which we have already referred. Governmentally-induced economic slowdowns had an honorable history in postwar France, so that Giscard's effort, amid a flood of communitarian rhetoric, to hold down wages and prices and deflate the economy to halt inflation, was not a shocking innovation. Yet the goal, that of creating a climate within which workers would be unable to struggle for wage raises, was in the line of *Opération Plan*. The government's message was that rising wages caused inflation, and that trade unions were the most important selfish interest in undermining stability. As we have seen, despite opposition by the unions, the Stabilization Plan worked.[37]

36. CGT, *Congrès national, 1963*, p. 4.
37. Ibid., p. 4.

The government's sanction and the state of the labor market led the *patronat* to cooperate against the unions, strikes were difficult to mount, and when they occurred, they usually failed.[38] The public, severely hit by inflation, was willing to buy the government's "wage-price spiral" theory of rising prices sufficiently to intimidate trade-union organizations. The success of the Stabilization Plan could only be temporary, however, lasting only so long as the public felt strongly enough threatened by inflation to endure the hardships of deflation which the plan brought in its wake. What the regime needed was a Plan perspective which was more general, and less tied to the movement of economic indicators. The Fifth Plan was the result.

Preparation of the Fifth Plan began in 1963, and its elaborate public *vernissage* lasted through much of 1964. First the planners themselves introduced their work to the public. Then it was given to Parliament, where it became the first Plan in the history of the planning operation to be deliberated upon by deputies *before* going into effect. To magnify the effect of this, the planners gave Parliament several different economic trajectories from which to choose, although only one of these *grandes options*, the one preferred by the planners, was actually spelled out in sufficient detail to allow serious consideration. After a long discussion by Parliament, the document went back to the planners again to be finalized, before it was resubmitted for a definitive vote at the end of 1964. Since the regime controlled Parliament, the outcome of such discussion was never in doubt. The degree to which all of this hoopla succeeded in legitimizing the Plan depended, of course, on the Plan's content. The Fifth Plan was designed to prepare the French economy to face the international market, in particular the growing competition of other Common Market economies. Priority was given to developing efficient export industries by creating firms of sufficiently large size (through concentration and amalgamation) to stand up to non-French multinationals. Provided economic stability could be maintained, the planners foresaw the French economy growing at a relatively high rate—five percent annually. Growth was to be facilitated by setting up new and favorable conditions for profit retention by dynamic firms. Stability was to be facilitated by an incomes policy, holding annual wage growth to three percent a year which, in turn, would hold consumption growth to 3.5 percent.

The government was optimistic indeed to believe that the Fifth Plan might be accepted as *l'affaire de tous*. The Plan clearly proposed that increased corporate profit in key sectors was the way to enhance French competitiveness. On the other hand, in the interests of stability, it asked

38. First Antoine Pinay, then Michel Debré had announced the Gaullist government's desire to limit wage raises to a given level each year, and in the early 1960s Debré had written a famous public letter to the *Conseil National du Patronat Français* to enlist its cooperation in holding wages down.

French workers to make sacrifices through its incomes policy provisions. Businessmen were being asked to make the Plan their affair, to discipline themselves so that, in the longer run, they would become more prosperous. Workers, on the other hand, were being offered an affair in which their only real control over the course of events—recourse to conflict in the labor market—would be limited, through the incomes policy provisions, in order to promote longer-run business prosperity. The incomes policy provisions were the critical innovation in the Fifth Plan, then. The Plan projected income and consumption expansion over five years, designed to allow the general growth and structural change aspects of the Plan to be achieved in stability.[39] Within this broad framework each year's national budget was to recommend a yearly growth figure for various income categories. Finally, an organization composed of "independent personalities" called the College for the Study and Consideration of Incomes would be set up to monitor the development of wages and the application of the incomes policy.[40]

General de Gaulle expressed his fervent wishes for the success of the incomes policy aspect of the Plan at his February 1965 Press Conference, declaring that "an incomes policy is too profoundly in conformity with the general trends of our time not to become everyone's concern."[41] Making it everyone's concern in fact was to involve more than simple exhortation, however. In the private sector of the economy the incomes policy was to be indicative and not imperative.[42] This did not mean that the government was completely without tools to get private-sector employers to keep wages down, but, to a large degree, incomes policy success in the private sector would depend on the voluntary cooperation of employers and unions.[43] The teeth of the incomes policy project were found primarily in the public sector, of course, where the government had direct control over wage evolution. Here, as a result of the Miners' Strike of 1963, steps had been taken to institutionalize incomes controls in rigorous ways. The *Toutée-Grégoire* procedures (named after the technocrats who had devised them) were an attempt to take the heat off governments in their management

---

39. The incomes policy section of the Fifth Plan was originally the brain-child of Pierre Massé, Commissioner of the Plan, who worked up a massive report on incomes policy after the miners' stance in 1963 and 1964.

40. Branciard, vol. II, p. 264; Bauchard and Bruzek, pp. 216–223; *Le Monde*, 15, 19–20 January, 12, 28 February 1964; Jean Magniadas, "La politique des revenus," in *Economie et Politique* (July 1965).

41. *Le Monde*, 6 February 1965.

42. Of the original Massé proposals only the general five-year projections of income growth and a series of warning indexes to signal inflationary pressures were included in the final Fifth Plan.

43. Considerable resistance to the incomes policy came also from the business community, which felt quite uneasy about giving up any of its own wage-setting prerogatives. See Bauchard and Bruzek, p. 221.

roles by delegating the setting of public-sector wage guidelines to the Plan and a series of independent intermediaries (an extension of the *sages* strategy which the Pompidou government invented to get itself out of the mess of the Miners' Strike).[44] The procedures had three phases. In the first, a "parity commission"—composed of public-sector administrators, trade-union delegates and "independent specialists"—was to meet annually to examine the evolution of wages and buying power of workers within a given public-sector area. In the second phase, the government took the figures thereby produced and considered them in reference to the Plan, its own economic goals and anything else which it deemed relevant, preparatory to deciding what the global percentage wage raise for the year to come ought to be. In the third phase, trade unions and public-sector administrators would meet to discuss precise ways of parcelling out this general percentage to specific occupational categories.

The regime's strategy was clear. Through *Toutée-Grégoire* in the public sector it would bring the problem of public-sector wage lag under control while at the same time enforcing its incomes policy goals. In turn, its public-sector efforts would stand as an example to private-sector employers, who could invoke the Plan and developments in the public sector to control the evolution of private-sector wages at the level desired. The whole apparatus was designed to place unions in a box in which they faced an entente between the government and *patronat* to enforce an incomes policy, and the likelihood of public opprobrium should they want more than they were allowed. And while the whole operation represented a considerable innovation in French wage-setting, a number of obvious problems were foreseeable. The *Toutée-Grégoire* procedures, the core of the whole incomes policy approach, were really an elaborate attempt on the part of the regime, via the planners, to have its economic cake and eat it, too. The first phase of the procedures allowed for some autonomy for the unions, but in what was essentially an accounting procedure whose limits were already circumscribed by the Plan. In the second phase the government decided public-sector wage levels, according to criteria which it alone set out. In the third stage the unions were invited back in to administer the government's decision. Essentially, the government reserved final decision-making power in public-sector wage questions exclusively for itself. The rest of *Toutée-Grégoire* was designed to get unions to implement the government's decision. The bottom line was evident: the regime wanted to get labor cooperation in an incomes policy without giving labor anything much in exchange. As in the Plan, so in the incomes policy, unions were to be spectators, invited to participate in rituals without getting a piece of the decision-making

44. On the *Toutée-Grégoire* procedures, see Bauchard and Bruzek, pp. 222–224; Gérard Adam, *Revue Française de Science Politique*, October 1966, p. 975; Jean-Maurice Verdier, "Les relations du travail dans le secteur public en France," *Revue Internationale du Travail* (February 1974); Pierre Dubois, *Mort de l'état patron* (1975).

action, and then adjured to go out and observe guidelines in whose making they had played no real role.

The structure of the regime's approach was significant. Faced with a problem which had its roots in the highly conflictual nature of French labor-management relations, it moved towards innovation. Yet it did not innovate to set up institutionalized collective bargaining and high-level corporatist collaboration between labor-market opponents. For one reason or another it was unwilling to go this far. Perhaps it did not believe that either French unions or employers wanted corporatist arrangements resembling those of other advanced capitalist societies. More likely, however, the regime itself did not want corporatist innovation. Instead it believed that its own mystique, plus the mystification of economic decision-making by Plans, procedures and technocrats would be enough. Labor, although excluded from such decision-making, would either want to cooperate nonetheless (the CFDT and FO), or would be obliged to conform (the CGT, because of the cooperation of the CFDT and FO). Here, as in many other aspects of Gaullist politics, the regime's confidence in its ability to persuade the French that it stood outside and above the mêlée of day-to-day social conflict seemed boundless. Or at least it was confident enough to run the risks involved in *not* promoting more corporatist structures.

Needless to say the regime's logic, flawed or not, was neither the PCF's nor the CGT's. Waldeck Rochet's comments on the Fifth Plan as a whole were predictable: "the government wants to make us admit that pumping up the profits of the monopolies will be, all in all, profitable for all the French."[45] Léon Mauvais, CGT Secretary, agreed, and summarized the Plan to the 1965 CGT Congress as follows: "limitation of wages and social benefits, implicit recognition of a degree of unemployment, explicit recognition of the need to expand capitalist profits and retained profits for internal reinvestment."[46] Other parts of the Left and union movement were not so harsh, at least initially. No one openly approved the Plan, but certain groups, the CFDT and the small *Parti Socialiste Unifié* (PSU) in particular, argued that the best way to oppose the government's planning strategy was not simple refusal to participate, but to become involved in the planning process in a conflictual way, not only to expose the regime's priorities, but also to suggest viable progressive alternatives.[47] This position of "contestative participation" was promoted during the consideration of the Fifth Plan, when the CFDT introduced a "Counter Plan" in the *Conseil Economique et Social*.[48] Strong CGT opposition to the Counter Plan ended

---

45. *Le Monde*, 27 November 1964.

46. Léon Mauvais, CGT, *Congrès national, 1965*, p. 14.

47. For an exposition of the "contestative participationist" approach to the plan, see Roger Jacques, "Pour une approche syndicale du Plan," *Esprit* (July-August 1961). See also Pierre LeBrun, *Questions actuelles du syndicalisme* (1964); and CFTC (Gilbert Declerq) "Pour une planification démocratique," 1959 CFTC National Congress.

48. Pierre LeBrun, CGT delegate to the *Conseil Economique et Social*, was also involved in

discussion of it very quickly, however. And since the regime had no interest in anyone's alternative plan, the Counter Plan disappeared rapidly from sight.

The regime had no reason to worry about whether the Left and the union movement approved the Fifth Plan as a whole. It was the incomes policy part of the total picture which was really important. Here there was much less disagreement on the Left and in the unions about how to react. The CGT's answer was a flat "no cooperation." It intended to carry on struggle in the labor market as if no incomes policy existed at all. Pierre LeBrun, CGT Secretary (and also a Gaullist, the Confederation choosing its spokesman for the maximum possible effect), labelled the incomes policy effort as an attempt to create a "wages police" and commented further that it called "the freedom of discussion and contractual determination of wages into question and consequently, the internal democracy and independence of the labor movement."[49] The CFDT was less intransigent, in principle, than the CGT, holding that union cooperation might be possible if structural reforms occurred and the planning process were democratized (here one finds the most convincing evidence that some genuine opening by the regime towards union participation in economic decision-making might have split the union movement). In practice, however, the realities of the Fifth Plan's incomes policy led to trade-union unity. Indeed, the government's decision to go ahead with *Toutée-Grégoire* precipitated a rare display of unity-in-action in 1964 as the CGT and CFDT met together to declare the procedures null and void. In early 1965, Georges Séguy summarized the CGT's position:

Despite opposition to the *Toutée-Grégoire* procedures reaffirmed by trade-union organizations, the government has just announced that it is going to go ahead. . . . It is trying to dupe public opinion by leading it to believe that the government is opening up to the negotiations demanded by the union. . . .

In fact, the procedure in question consists of the government figuring everything up, according to its own whim, communicating its unilateral decisions to the representatives of the workers, listening to nothing that the latter might have to say, deciding on its own to announce, in conclusion, "Here is your wage raise. Now you are free to decide with the administration of your enterprise how to share it out."

This is . . . liberty in a cage.[50]

---

the "counter Plan" episode, although he was quickly disavowed by the CGT *Bureau Confédéral*.

49. Pierre LeBrun in *France Observateur*, 4 April 1964; *Le Monde*, 13 March 1970.

50. Séguy in *L'Humanité*, 11 January 1965; see also *L'Express*, 4–10 January 1965; *Les Echos*, 7 June 1965.

General trade-union feeling, then, boded ill for the success of the regime's *Opération Plan*. Declarations were not the real test, however. Action was. Whether the regime was correct in believing that the French would be willing to follow the Plan's directions as the national interest would be known only in practice. A great deal, including the CGT's mass mobilization goals and the PCF's United Front thrust, was at stake.[51] The answers were not long in coming.

Conclusions: the Roots of May-June 1968

The regime's strategy for building its legitimacy had one decisive flaw. Despite a national-interest, above-class rhetoric, the regime consistently asked the working class to bear the lion's share of the burden of economic change. The message that workers ought to accept austerity and sacrifice with stoic discipline in order to prepare a more prosperous tomorrow was not one which French workers were likely to accept easily. If things went well for the regime in the three years after the Miners' Strike, if unions found it extremely difficult to mount serious actions, it was not because workers had been persuaded of the need for a national crusade for economic change. Rather the effects of the Giscard Stabilization Plan (slack labor market and other manifestations of recession) plus an effective government-*patronat* entente against unions, when coupled with union disunity, gave the regime a period of grace, one which could not last once the CGT/CFDT unity-in-action agreement began bearing fruit.

The initial thrust of CGT-CFDT action reflected the tactical biases of the CGT. The goal of breaking through government-*patronat* collaboration and achieving serious negotiations was to be reached by the promotion of a series of large strike actions, limited in duration, which would mobilize militants and the union rank and file, while at the same time communicating lessons about the situation to the general public. Days of Action, which the movements were called, occurred first of all in the public sector, thus against the government, and above all, against *Toutée-Grégoire*.[52] Such Days of Action were one-day, or shorter, general work stoppages, often accompanied by large public demonstrations. The first such "Day" in 1966 (whose demand was for "real negotiations") was the most powerful single strike movement, in terms of sheer numbers of strikers, to occur to that point in the history of the Fifth Republic. Even hostile crowd counters were willing to admit three million strikers (*Les Echos*), while more friendly sources (*Combat, L'Humanité*) claimed five million.[53] Benoît Frachon was so moved by the new possibilities revealed by

---

51. Frachon, vol. II, p. 495.
52. *Le Monde*, 3 June 1966.
53. *Les Echos*, 18 May 1966; *Combat*, 18 May 1966; *L'Humanité*, 18 May 1966.

united action in 1966 that he was led to reminisce about 1936 in a speech to a private-sector demonstration in front of CNPF headquarters. "We will do something else than what we did in 1936, and something better," said the CGT Secretary-General. To the *patronat*, he added, "until next time."[54]

Days of Action continued into 1967. And in May 1967 the government provided the unions with a solid new issue around which to mobilize their followers. Prompted by economic and budgetary problems, the government asked the new legislature for "special powers" to reorganize the social-security system by decree, in order to cover social-security costs by changing the structure of benefits. To facilitate a transfer of costs from employers to workers, the government proposed eliminating unions from many of the administrative posts which they had held since the immediate post-Liberation period by abolishing the electoral procedures of the original social-security system. The CGT and CFDT immediately responded to this by calling a twenty-four-hour general strike for May 27, 1967, "for our demands, against full powers" (full powers assumed by the government to change social security). As Pierre Viansson-Ponté of *Le Monde* noted of this strike, "This is the first time since before the war that a general strike order has thus been issued around a political call to action . . . by all of the large union organizations of workers and teachers."[55] The mobilization of 1966–1967 was therefore not only for strictly trade-union demands ("negotiations") it was also political, directed against the regime, as the CGT desired and had predicted. In general, the effects of the CGT/CFDT alliance were clear and immediate. There were more strike movements and there were larger actions. The labor movement took an ever larger place in the public's eye as a consistent and energetic protestor against the *patronat* and against the regime's economic strategy. The importance of all this was undeniable. The CGT/CFDT accord, plus the government's policies, had brought the labor movement back to life.

The basic problem with the CGT-CFDT campaigns of 1966–1967, however, was that, *as strikes*, they were total failures. The government did not budge an inch. The *Toutée-Grégoire* procedures were implemented in 1966 and 1967 despite union opposition—no real public-sector negotiations between unions and administration occurred. In the private sector, despite some minor victories, the national negotiations desired by the CGT and CFDT came no closer. The government carried out the 1967 social-security decrees and did not retract them. Massive rank-and-file mobilization, occurring for the first time in many years in France, seemed to have no immediate payoffs.

In fact, however, this peculiar combination of greatly increased official

54. Benoît Frachon, in *Tribune Socialiste*, 18 May 1966.
55. *Le Monde*, 5 May 1967.

union activity and an intransigent response to it from bosses and government was creating a highly volatile industrial situation. Mass mobilization,
if it led to no immediate results, was raising the combativity of French
workers. And where such combativity led to local strikes, even when such
strikes did not pay off, a degree of rank-and-file militancy not seen in years
was manifested. In December 1966, for example, research workers at Dassault Aviation in Bordeaux struck on an issue of regional wage discrimination, sat down and occupied the plant. Dassault answered with a
brutal lockout. In early 1967 Berliet-Lyon flared again (after the 1965
failure) with a sit-down strike, again to be met with a lockout.[56] Berliet proceeded to call in the police to evict strikers, causing an unusually violent
confrontation.[57] Similar abrupt, hyper-militant movements occurred in
early 1967 at various points in the *Sud Aviation* complex (St. Nazaire,
Marignane, Toulouse), among metalworkers in Mulhouse and at Renault-
Cléon and Renault-le Mans (where the action of autoworkers triggered a
larger movement in the city as a whole.)[58] A strike of monthly salaried
workers in the St. Nazaire shipyard beginning in February 1967 caused a
lockout which, in turn, led to a strike by hourly workers.[59] The monthly
workers, backed by a great out-pouring of local solidarity, managed to
keep their action going for three months (making it the longest strike by
monthly salaried workers in post-World War II French labor history).[60] At
about the same time a strike at the Rhodiacéta plant in Besançon led to a
sit-down which spread rapidly throughout the entire Rhône-Poulenc
chemical group.[61] This strike was finally settled by national negotiations,
rare for the period, after a long struggle.[62]

The January 1968 strike at the Caen Saviem factory showed how far the
industrial climate had deteriorated. The movement began as a local adapta-

---

56. *Le Monde*, 18 March 1967.

57. *Le Monde*, 22 March 1967; *Témoignage Chrétien*, 13 April 1967. Another interesting
sidelight to the Berliet movement was that the local CGT proved considerably less militant
than its CFDT counterpart.

58. The reader will do well to note that these movements occurred in exactly those
areas—Loire-Atlantique, Southwest, Besançon and the East, Normandy—and in those industries—aviation, motor vehicles, shipyards, metal finishing, synthetic textiles—which
emerged in the forefront of the massive May 1968 strike movement.

59. *L'Express*, 27 March 1967.

60. *Le Monde*, 30 March 1967.

61. *Nouvel Observateur*, 29 March 1967.

62. *Le Monde*, 24 March 1967; *Témoignage Chrétien*, 13 April 1967. The Rhodiacéta strike
was interesting because of conflicts between the CFDT and the CGT regarding its conduct.
The CFDT in Besançon originally sparked the strike over working conditions (having to do
with the work schedules of swing shift workers). When the strike spread through the Rhône-
Poulenc complex the CGT took over its guidance, leading to a wages/hours national settlement, according to its own tactical goals. The Besançon/Rhodiacéta CFDT was unhappy at
this settlement and continued to agitate around the issues of working conditions, an agitation
which bore fruit in May 1968.

tion of a national CGT/CFDT strike call.[63] The strikers then devised the tactic of a "March on Caen" to drum up local support, an act which was met with a powerful response from the *Gardes Mobiles*. Ten strikers were hurt and two hospitalized. The workers then called a city-wide demonstration of protest for the next day, which was, in its turn, charged by fully-armed riot police (CRS). Caen was transformed into a battlefield between CRS and strikers, with street warfare lasting far into the night. Eighteen people were hurt and forty arrested.[64] The vigorous presence and urgent fervor of young workers and students had been remarked on in earlier movements of this sort in 1966–1967, but in Caen their importance drew special attention. As *Le Monde* put it, "these young workers are easily the most dynamic, not to say the most impatient. At Caen they were joined by students and, it is said, by uncontrollable elements."[65]

In important ways, the new dimension of conflict which these private-sector movements increasingly displayed was due to the general effects of the CGT-CFDT accord. In the words of one labor journalist:

> These decentralized and diversified actions were made possible by the CGT/CFDT accord which is today bearing long nourished fruits. This accord . . . finally dissipated the mutual distaste and competition between trade-union militants at the rank-and-file level. As a result, rank-and-file initiatives, for a long time paralyzed by division in the labor movement, have been able to develop. CGT and CFDT militants have formed habits of reflecting upon and elaborating together their local demands, becoming less dependent upon the central decisions of their Confederations.[66]

---

63. *Le Monde*, 24 January 1968; *L'Humanité*, 24 January 1968.

64. *Le Monde*, 29 January 1968; *L'Humanité*, 27 January 1968.

65. *Le Monde*, 30 January 1968. The CGT was not unaware of the problem posed by supermilitant young workers (although, in the words of one analyst, the unions, in general "did not perceive to what extent . . . in the young, the sentiment of revolt is profound and universal"). From 1965 on a great deal of CGT discussion was devoted to their plight. The CGT's main solution to the problem was to intensify efforts to organize young workers into the CGT. On the one hand, all CGT organizations were to make special efforts to fight the battles of young workers and connect them with the struggle against Gaullism. On the other hand, the CGT organization itself was to be rejuvenated (it was at least partly in the name of rejuvenation that Benoît Frachon turned over his post of Secretary-General to Georges Séguy in 1967). Séguy, the new Secretary-General, made the youth question his special concern and spent a great deal of time developing plans for a "national festival of young workers" to be held in Paris in mid-May 1968. The young militants were impatient, however, and the CGT felt it necessary also to send out a strong anti-*gauchiste* alert. "Leftists" and "adventurists" were tempting the young to act in ways which did not fit the CGT's strategy. The CGT intended to isolate them. See *Témoignage Chrétien*, 1 February 1968; *L'Express*, 15 January 1968. See also Frachon's remarks in *L'Humanité*, 3 April 1968, 18 April 1968; Barjonet, *La CGT*, p. 198.

66. Rioux, *Nouvel Observateur*, 22 March 1967.

The fact that the regime's credibility had been tarnished by the results of the 1967 elections may also have contributed to the situation. Far more important, however, were general economic circumstances. A combination of cyclical downturn, growing European competition and the social costs of Gaullist economic strategy wreaked a great deal of havoc for French workers. CGT-CFDT unity-in-action gave them a vehicle with which to respond.

By late 1967 a combination of factors had created a situation where important segments of the French working class faced unprecedented insecurity. Industries which had not been farsighted enough to reorganize themselves to face growing international pressure (some because they had not paid attention to the Plan and others who, by astute but self-defeating political in-fighting, had used the Plan to stave off reorganization) found themselves in direct trouble, forced to increase working hours, hold down wages and even to lay off workers. Excess capacity in other areas led to similar results. Certain industries were both overdeveloped for new internationalized market conditions and struck by a short-run downturn in consumption. Motor-vehicles manufacturing was in such a dilemma, and here a great deal of the new militancy took place. On top of this Gaullist economic strategy had few effective regional policies, such that when economic activity shifted towards newer, more internationally competitive sectors, entire regions, where industry was uncompetitive to begin with, fell further and further behind. Everywhere it was young workers who felt the crunch first. Having had their expectations raised by new educational credentialing created by the regime in order to modernize the production of labor power, they found their new professional titles meant little. Rather than secure positions with dignity, they faced declassification (employment below the level of their training), short-term contracts and substantial unemployment.[67] It was not surprising, then, to find them often taking the lead in prodding their co-workers and unions to action. The latter, in the proper circumstances, were willing to move. And when workers and unions acted, they were greeted by an equally militant *patronat*, certain of government help, and ready to resort quickly to lockouts and repression.[68] Government and *patronat* both believed that intransigence would eventually break the back of working-class resistance. Evidence from the struggles of 1967 and early 1968 indicated, however, that such intransigence contributed rather to a deepening of working-class militancy and a willingness on the part of strikers to resort to more extreme tactics.

As of early 1968, the industrial situation in France was volatile in the extreme. For the CGT the situation was not without its problems. Rank-and-file mobilization, the object of the CGT's strategy, was real. However, im-

---

67. *Le Monde*, 29 January 1968.
68. Lucien Rioux in *Nouvel Observateur*, 5 April 1967; *Témoignage Chrétien*, 23 March 1967; and Michel Bosquet in *Nouvel Observateur*, 12 May 1967.

patience at the base also provided fertile ground for *gauchisme*. Extremist local tactics, which were pursued with little or no regard for the broader mobilizational prospects of the working class as a whole, had come to characterize a number of struggles in the period. More often than not, CFDT locals, with the active or tacit blessing of their Federations, were involved in the pursuit of such tactics. The effects of the CGT-CFDT accord were thus a good deal more complex than the CGT itself would have liked. Serious mass mobilization for national objectives with anti-regime political overtones had been one result of the accord, the result which the CGT had desired. But such mass mobilization had itself not led to any breakthrough towards high level negotiations. In such an environment, frustration at the base grew, and was translated into extreme local militancy which, when extended to its logical conclusion, led to hyper-militant local struggles which, the CGT feared, might undermine the general mass mobilization which it hoped to expand. The CGT also was worried about losing control over its own rank and file.

In effect, old tactical differences with the CFDT had reappeared, differences which had been temporarily put aside after January 1966. The CGT had promoted the Days of Action approach for implementing the new accord. The CFDT had reservations about such an approach, but its eagerness to create labor action of any sort overrode such reservations for a time. However, as the Days demonstrated little capacity for producing tangible union gains, the CFDT grew increasingly critical of the tactic, especially on the all-important Federation level. Indeed, in the public sector CFDT Federations began to withhold support for Days of Action, and they were later followed by some of their private-sector comrades, leaving CGT Federations to act on their own.[69] At the same time, CFDT militants began looking towards the firm-level militant actions made possible by the general mobilization following the CGT/CFDT accord, for the primary locus of their action.

On the eve of May-June 1968, then, the CGT and CFDT had begun, de facto, to go their separate ways. The CGT wanted mass demonstrations which would mobilize the working class as a whole, or in major parts, towards high-level negotiations which would humiliate the *patronat* and government and, in the process, create the social foundations for a United Front political solution. In a firm-level trade-union fight the CGT's aim was always to broaden the struggle and shift its focus upwards, to the national level, for the negotiations in the public eye which the CGT desired. The CFDT did not share these broad goals, and began to gravitate towards a strategy which focused on local-level action and gains within the firm. *Autogestion* began to emerge, here and there, as the high theoretical justification for this focus, even if the CFDT had not yet consecrated the notion officially. In the words of a *Témoignage Chrétien* journalist, the CFDT,

69. *Le Monde*, 17 November 1967.

"by posing the problem of management, by underlining the incoherence of investments, by stressing employment security, by renouncing the defense of marginal firms . . . by the conclusion of long-term accords, defining a true personnel policy, setting up within the firm a system of information and projection of information, cutting down the length of the work week without cutting down income, transforming most hourly-paid workers into monthlies, seeks, in reality, to extract personal power from the employer."[70] In contrast to the CGT, then, the CFDT's tendency was to orient struggle on the firm level towards concessions on all sorts of "qualitative" demands. The CFDT was vague in the extreme about what these demands meant. Nonetheless, the CGT thought ill of the CFDT's newly-found tactical wisdom. It smelled like "neo-syndicalism" in its refusal to contemplate the effects of local action on the prospects for the broader mobilization of workers in general. Beyond this the CFDT's vague "revolutionary reformism" centered around the firm, neglecting the need for change in the political sphere altogether.

Conflicts between the two Confederations had burst into the open over strategies to pursue in the Rhodiacéta strike of 1967 and in early 1968 negotiations with the CNPF on unemployment compensation (the CGT seeing the result of these negotiations as a great success, and the CFDT refusing to sign). They had also emerged around political issues. By 1967 the CGT had decided that the moment was propitious to begin wholesale agitation for the conclusion of a Common Program of the Left, including agitation in the direction of the CFDT. The CFDT did not respond with great eagerness, insisting that unity-in-action was workable on strictly trade-union terms alone.[71] Likewise, the CGT attempted to broaden the struggle for the suspension of the government's social-security decrees beyond unions to include political parties (in particular the PCF) on both local and national levels. The culmination of this was the December 1967 Day of Action against the decrees called by the CGT and CFDT. By something more than simple coincidence, leading PCF political figures, including Waldeck Rochet and Jacques Duclos, were in attendance at a Parisian mass demonstration. Again, by something more than chance, they were invited to take places on the podium beside CGT and CFDT leaders—thereby consecrating the Day as a United Front action. CFDT leaders present were incensed, refused to allow the PCF figures on the podium and threatened to leave themselves if the Communists insisted.[72]

Strangely enough, all of this set the stage for the events of May-June 1968. The CGT-CFDT accord had worked dialectically, primarily because of the tactical differences between the two Confederations, to mobilize

70. Raymond Butheau, in *Témoignage Chrétien*, 13 April 1967.

71. Xavier Gaullier, "Syndicats et partis politiques" in *Projets* (March 1968). See also the text of Henri Krasucki's remarks on a common program in *Le Monde*, 8 June 1967.

72. *Le Monde*, 15 December 1967.

large numbers of workers around high-level sets of trade-union demands while, at the same time, creating the conditions for highly militant local struggles.

The agreement between the two organizations had worked to promote the success of *both* Confederation's tactics. Without such contradictory developments, the great general strike of May-June 1968 might never have occurred. The contradictory nature of such developments, however, ensured that conflict between the two Confederations was likely to occur at the very same moment when serious conflict in the labor market emerged. The CGT wanted mass action leading both to high level negotiations and the creation of a political United Front. The CFDT wanted powerful local actions which won local victories, wanted no part of the CGT's political goals and, when politics was in question, leaned towards options which would exclude the PCF (dealing with the FGDS and PSU rather than with these groups plus the PCF and CGT).[73] Thus by the spring of 1968, with the labor market at the point of explosion, relations between the CGT and CFDT were at the point of disintegration.

73. See *Revue Politique et Parlementaire* (March 1968).

Chapter 7

THE EVENTS OF MAY-JUNE 1968

By early 1968 both the PCF and the CGT, each in its own way, had made some progress towards implementing their strategies. But in neither case was success at hand. The PCF, after many painstaking steps, had developed a degree of regular cooperation with forces of the non-Communist Left and Left-Center. Such cooperation occurred mainly around electoral occasions—agreements for mutual support between Left groups—accompanied by very vague declarations of principle. No Common Program for a United Left was yet in sight, although this was what the PCF desired most of all. The non-Communist Left and Left-Center was not yet sufficiently convinced of the desirability of a serious, longer-term alliance with the Communists to go this far. Moreover, the non-Communist Left itself had a great deal of rethinking and reorganization to do before it could become strong and coherent enough to be anything more than a junior partner in any formal United Front coalition with the PCF. Unity on the political Left was clearly a possibility in 1968, then, but it was far from a reality.

The CGT, as we have noted, had its own "relative-autonomy" road to follow. The Confederation's relative autonomy stance fit well within the general theoretical understanding of the dynamics of French capitalism which both the PCF and CGT shared. In this understanding the Fifth Republic was a regime in which monopolies controlled social development and used the Gaullist state to further their goals. As workers and others experienced the costs of monopoly rule in their productive lives they would be moved towards protest in the labor market. Given the tight connection between monopolies and the state, however, such protest, as it developed, would turn of its own accord towards broadly political themes. The CGT did not need to politicize the labor market unduly. The regime had already done this. What mattered for the CGT, then, was simply to promote the broadest possible mass mobilization out of labor-market protest. Working-class anti-monopoly protest in the form of defensive, bread-and-butter unionism would, if properly nurtured by trade-union organizations, become the core of a larger social mobilization against the regime. This mobilization, in turn, with skillful political work by the PCF, might become the core of social support for a new United Front.

By 1968 the CGT had advanced somewhat further down its own strategic road than had the PCF. Unity in the trade-union sphere was a necessary premise for the kind of mass labor mobilization which the CGT desired. And, with the implementation of the 1966 CGT-CFDT accord, such unity had been practically established. The reasons for this were obvious. No union organization could have hoped to achieve its goals without some kind of unity with other such organizations, a fact which the CFDT had realized in the fallow union years of the mid-1960s. Yet, as we have seen, unity-in-action between the CGT and CFDT was not without its problems. As labor mass organizations, both the CGT and CFDT looked to the dynamics of the labor market for their strategic options. The labor market, however, could only provide a range of options from which to choose. It did not dictate a single choice. Thus the CGT and the CFDT, facing the same labor market, chose different options. The CFDT felt no responsibility to shape its actions to build the working-class core of an anti-monopoly social alliance. Rather it tended to a localized focus, seizing upon local struggles and mobilizing to fight them to their conclusions, more and more often picking up new "qualitative" demands. However ill-focused the CFDT's understanding of such new issues was at this time, the existence of serious local struggles concerned with broader issues than simple bread-and-butter union demands was real. Despite relative autonomy the CGT was locked into a theoretical perspective, common to it and the PCF, which blinded it to the emergence of certain new concerns at the base. Contradictions between the CGT and CFDT over such new concerns could only grow, then.

The CFDT's strategic reading of the labor market was, of course, motivated by more than a simple observation of the working-class world. The CFDT was a dynamic and ambitious organization which was, as of 1968, well behind the CGT on almost all dimensions of trade-union strength, membership, support from non-members, mobilizing power, effectiveness and devotion of rank-and-file militants, and depth of support in central areas of the economy. One of its primary goals was, then, to develop its organizational effectiveness vis-à-vis the CGT. The CFDT desired to challenge the CGT's centrality. One obvious way to do so, given the circumstances of 1968, was to choose a strategic course which would capitalize on the weaknesses of the CGT's own strategic commitments. To the CGT, industrial conflict, when and as it occurred, was to be made comprehensible to, and supportable by, the working class as a whole. This meant by definition, moderating powerful local actions, which had little mass promise. Yet powerful local actions, for a variety of reasons, were prominent after 1966. Thus the CFDT, knowing that the CGT's hands were tied by its "mass" strategy, decided to build its own power and reputation by riding with and promoting such local actions. It hoped, thereby, to gain a reputation for militancy (and to underline the CGT's relative moderation) which would build its own organization at the expense of the CGT's. This option was enhanced by a relative openness of the CFDT at the base during this period which made it difficult for the Confederation to control militant actions run by its locals in any case. On top of all of this, of course, was the question of politics. The CFDT understood full well the essential complementarity between the CGT's mass union perspective and the PCF's United Frontism. Politically, the CFDT's biases at this point were decidedly centrist. No one in the CFDT leadership wanted to contribute to the PCF's political success.

The unprecedented crisis of May-June 1968 was to provide a series of tests for PCF and CGT strategies, for party-union relationships, and for unity-in-action between the CGT and CFDT. The student explosion which began the May events escaped PCF control and, in many ways, threatened PCF strategy. The party responded first by trying to push the student movement in directions which it found more congenial. When this failed and the crisis broadened to threaten the regime, the party tried, again unsuccessfully, to negotiate, amid social and political confusion, the kind of Left political unity which it saw as the only palatable alternative to the continuation of the regime. The CGT, pursuing its relative-autonomy strategy, suddenly found itself confronted with, then largely in control of, the largest strike in French history, which it proceeded to shape in accordance with the action criteria which it had developed earlier in the 1960s. However, since this immense strike also coincided with a moment of great political uncertainty, what the CGT did with labor-market protest was of substantial political significance. Simply coordinating the strike in accordance with the mass, defensive unionist criteria of the CGT's existing strategy had great political importance indirectly, since it meant placing strict limits on the politicization of strike action. As the crisis developed, however, there were critical points at which the CGT, in response to immediate political dilemmas confronted by the PCF, felt obliged to abrogate relative autonomy and come directly to the aid of the party. Moreover there were more than a few points during the crisis at which the party and the CGT were at odds, in particular about whether there should have been a strike at all. Finally, the openness of the CFDT to new rank-and-file demands and its political centrism created great new strains on trade-union unity-in-action, given the CGT's own commitment to mass defensive labor-market action and to the creation of a new Left United Front. Most of all, the crisis was an opportunity for the PCF and CGT to reflect upon their separate and mutual strategic undertakings and upon their relationships. Party and union directions might have been changed as a result of May-June. In fact, May-June was seen by both as confirmation of the correctness of earlier trajectories.

Students and Communists

May-June 1968 began with students. The French university, like a good many other French institutions, was out of date. Well-suited to the production of a nineteenth-century humanist elite, it grew increasingly out of phase with the needs of the advanced capitalist economy resulting from post war modernization. Students matriculating in the mid-1960s brought expectations to the university which the institution could not meet. And, to the extent that the university had begun to change to adapt to new circumstances, matters were made worse still. The traditional *licence* no longer guaranteed elite status, especially in the liberal arts and social sciences. Bourgeois cultivation, which had once sufficed to inculcate feelings of superiority, was no longer enough. Students acting out time-honored patterns of aspiration suddenly faced problematic career prospects. Demographic pressure from the post–World War II baby boom made things difficult. Educated underemployment, even unemployment, emerged.[1]

The Gaullist regime, together with high university authorities, were aware that something had to be done in higher education. Facilities had to be expanded (more educated labor was needed) and they had to be retooled to produce the variety of technically skilled personnel needed to fill critical stations in the new political economy. However, in true Gaullist fashion, changes were decreed and implemented in top-down ways with little regard for the institutional fabric which they were meant to modify. Moreover, such changes were resisted and subverted from within the conservative structures of the university itself. And, once again in true Gaullist fashion, proposed changes were backed by woefully inadequate funding.

Those who bore the brunt of dealing with an out-of-date institution in the throes of inept and chaotic changes were the students, who faced problems ranging from total confusion about what courses were to be given and how exams were to be organized to whether their education would have any relevance to the rest of their lives. The drama of such institutional problems was heightened by France's version of "youth culture" and the "generation gap" (dramatic, if as yet unexamined, changes were going on in the French middle-class family, for example). Beyond this, outside France, an international politicization of students was visible—in Germany, Holland, England, Italy, the U.S.A. and Japan, students had found radical politics and taken to the streets for one cause or another.

1. There is an infinitely large literature on the May-June student movement, from all political and intellectual points of view. That which probably comes closest in sympathy to the students themselves is the "new working class" interpretation. Here, for two good examples, see Alain Touraine, *The May Movement* (1971) and the introduction, by Charles Posner, to Posner ed., *Reflections on the Revolution in France* (1969). The origins of this school of analysis may be found in Alain Touraine, *La conscience ouvrière* (1966) and Serge Mallet, *La nouvelle classe ouvrière*. See also Touraine's more recent book, *Le mouvement étudiant* (1979). We will have occasion, in the notes for the rest of this chapter, to cite other general works on the student movement.

In 1967–1968, French students were a "lonely crowd," to use Raymond Aron's borrowed label.[2] French student life was anomic and individualized in the extreme, creating a milieu in which discontent, when it existed, was difficult to detect. Rapid expansion of the university in the 1960s meant that by May 1968 Paris held 200,000 or more students, plus large numbers of intellectuals (researchers, teachers) whose destinies were closely bound to those of students. If, and when, such large numbers mobilized in France's capital, a great deal of social disruption was possible.[3] Moreover, the political bonds tying students to the rest of French society had become particularly weak by the mid-1960s. The Fourth Republic had provided students with a legacy of cynicism. On top of this, the distance and authoritarianism of the Gaullist regime—whose ideological appeals were directed to older generations—had acted to discourage grass-roots political activity "within the system." Student years had traditionally been a time for "trying on" Leftism in France. Yet traditional forms of Leftism, in particular French Communism, had lost much of their attractiveness. For generations of Leftist students—from the thirties to the early sixties, the PCF's student organizations had provided a home, one which linked them to broader French political life through the PCF's political goals. Beginning with the Algerian War, this changed. As we have noted, the PCF's moderate antiwar stance lacked appeal for more militant students, who joined the UNEF instead. Then the PCF's turn towards a new United Front drive after the War seemed tame indeed to students whose impatience was whetted by the successes of Third World struggles in Cuba, China and Vietnam. Communist youth organizations themselves were not immune from such currents, and the party's unnecessarily brutal ways of "taking in hand" its student groups (in the "Italian" crisis of 1963–1964, and in the Leftist rebellion against PCF support of François Mitterrand in 1965) made such groups even less appetizing for potential recruits.[4] Moreover, by the mid-1960s, important groups of activists had either been expelled from, or had abandoned, the PCF's student fronts.[5] Talented student militants, who earlier would have begun political careers in the PCF, had moved on to a universe of New Left groups, mainly "Third Worldist" in inspiration (Maoists, Trotskyists, and so on). The PCF thus lost contact with student events.[6] And these Leftist groups could agree among themselves about very little except for one thing, that the PCF had "sold out" to "revisionism."

2. See Raymond Aron, *La révolution introuvable* (1968), a collection of Aron's articles in *Le Figaro* for the May period which takes the student movement much less seriously as a social movement than the above.

3. Aron, in *Le Figaro*, 15 June 1968, discusses this more thoroughly.

4. Thierry Pfister and André Laurens, *Les nouveaux communistes aux portes du pouvoir.*

5. The best account of all of these intricate goings and comings in the PCF's youth groups is Henri Weber and Daniel Bensaid, *Mai 1968, répétition générale* (1968). The authors were both ex-PCF youth group members, actors in May-June themselves who became Trotskyites.

6. André Barjonet, *Le PCF*, pp. 105 ff.

The PCF's new impotence in the student world was to be a very important factor in the events of May-June 1968.

The drama of student discontent emerged in the 1967–1968 school year. The campus of the Université de Paris at Nanterre, an architecturally and socially bleak suburb of Paris, produced the spark. Nanterre was a new facility whose faculty, pedagogy and procedures were still in a trial-and-error stage in the autumn of 1967. Physical and organizational problems at Nanterre were compounded by the nature of the campus population—"second-level" liberal arts and social science students—people who were unable to enter elite faculties and therefore those most sensitive to the intellectual and labor-market problems of the French university. Students at Nanterre were unsettled and unhappy, demonstrating both by a series of protests around governmental plans for university reform and university rules and regulations, particularly those governing dormitory hours and life, beginning in the fall of 1967. Other issues quickly emerged—the new system of courses and exams (the Nanterre administrators understood only slightly more of what was going on than bewildered students themselves), the presence of plainclothes police mingling with students on campus, and the alleged existence of a "black list" of troublesome students.[7] Daniel Cohn-Bendit first established his notoriety and leadership in the autumn of 1967 by agitation around such issues, notably in a pugnacious confrontation with Gaullist Minister François Missoffe over sexual repression and campus rules at the opening of the campus swimming pool. Later in the fall a major confrontation occurred when women students occupied a men's dormitory. The police arrived, a riot and a student strike followed. By January 1968, Nanterre had become a completely mobilized campus in which suspicion on all sides, anti-police paranoia and constant agitation permeated student life.

Leftist activities around the Vietnam war flourished throughout the University of Paris during the early months of 1968 and further heightened tension at Nanterre. The arrest of a Nanterre militant for participation in a demonstration at the American Express office in Paris, and the Nanterre administration's subsequent handling of his case, led to the calling of a mass meeting on campus on March 22, the date which gave *le mouvement du 22 mars* its name. The *22 mars* movement, an ad hoc organization led by Cohn-Bendit,was blessed with a touch of political genius. Ecumenical in principle, it avoided the endless bickering over principles, strategies, and tactics which traditionally accompanied French Left student politics.[8] It attempted none of the long, painstaking ideological indoctrination which tra-

---

7. André Gorz, in Posner, ed., p. 260; also Claude Lefort in Lefort, Morin and Coudray, *Mai 1968, la brèche* (1968), p. 44; Philippe Labro, *Ce n'est qu'un début* (1968), p. 4.

8. There were established Left groups on the Nanterre campus, but with little appeal. Moreover, once *22 mars* developed a successful formula for mobilization, they were obliged to follow Cohn-Bendit et al. or play no role at all. Gorz in Posner, ed., p. 260; Labro, p. 66.

ditional student Leftist groups felt necessary. Instead it proceeded directly to action, provocative action which provided university officials (and later the government of France) with an immediate choice between repression or concession. In ordinary circumstances such direct-action tactics would have been a gamble, at best. But the circumstances prevailing at Nanterre, where an already mobilized and deeply unhappy student body faced a bewildered administration backed by uncomprehending and authoritarian national educational bureaucrats, minimized the risk. In this context action led either directly or indirectly (because of the inept use of repression) to the flowering of a larger student movement. When *22 mars* promoted a building takeover, the Nanterre Dean closed down the campus for a time, accrediting the power of Cohn-Bendit and comrades. Then, on April 30, eight Nanterre students, including Cohn-Bendit and two of his closest collaborators,were arrested for distributing leaflets at a Paris *lycée*. When the offenders were summoned to appear before the Rector of the entire University of Paris, Nanterre life became constant agitation, and the Nanterre Dean closed the campus down again.

By summoning Cohn-Bendit to appear at the Sorbonne and simultaneously closing the Nanterre campus, the authorities gave *22 mars* the opportunity and incentive to appear on a national stage. On May 3, the Nanterre movement, led by *22 mars*, marched en masse to the Sorbonne. Rector Roche, acting on a tip that neo-Fascist *Occident* commandoes intended to attack the Nanterre parade, then called in the police. Using their customary brutality, Paris police eventually evacuated the court of the Sorbonne, arresting 550 students and carting them off to jail. Since an operation large enough to lead to the arrest of 550 people could hardly pass unnoticed in the dense society of the Latin Quarter, a rapid mobilization of Parisian students followed. Students and police then went head-to-head on the streets of Paris, rocks flying from one side, tear gas and clubs being deployed on the other. The "Events of May" had officially begun.

After May 3, student mobilization was lightning fast. Roche closed the Sorbonne, giving Parisian students little to do but protest and prepare for a mass demonstration which UNEF had called for May 6. The *Syndicat National d'Education (Supérieure)* (SNE [sup]), a union of young university faculty and research workers with Leftist tendencies, called an unlimited strike of its own. University administrators and the government responded by further repressive activity. On May 4, the courts quickly processed and convicted fourteen students (seven for pre-May activities, seven for the Sorbonne action itself). All received heavy sentences. And Alain Peyrefitte, the Minister of Education, labelled the SNE [sup] strike as "illegal." It was on May 6, however, that student rebellion became open warfare. The UNEF demonstration, after much speechifying, turned into a long cortege from the Faculté des Sciences (at the old Halle aux Vins in rue Jussieu) into the Latin Quarter, aimed straight at waiting police. The police again responded with clubs, tear gas and anti-riot grenades. This time, however, the student parade answered back en masse with cobblestones and other projectiles, inflicting considerable damage. Guerrilla warfare in the Latin Quarter went on for hours, leading to several hundred new arrests and the treatment of at least 700 in hospitals. The actions of the police—clearly informed by an anti-student hostility which went far beyond carrying out orders—created much new public support for the student cause.

By May 6, the government's strategy was crystal-clear. As with the miners in 1963, so with the students in 1968, intimidation and repression were the regime's primary responses. However, intimidation and repression, when deployed against a protest movement as deep-seated as that of Parisian students in May, coalesced and motivated the movement even further. When the government moved even more troops into the battle zone, the student rebels acquired street-fighting skills to greet them. Combat became more intense. The government's obvious determination to beat down the student movement by force without considering any of its grievances nourished growing public support for the student cause. The student movement spread to the provinces as well. As *Le Monde* put it, on May 11, "in order not to lose face the government is driving itself up a dead-end street. After having rather casually suspended courses at the Sorbonne, then cancelling them, then arresting the students who were demonstrating there, the powers-that-be are now demanding an end to a protest movement which was provoked by their own decisions."[9]

The worst was still to come. On the evening of May 10, in response to the swaggering presence in the Latin Quarter of thousands of police and CRS, word spread among students to "occupy" the Quarter. In a flash barricades went up across central arteries, including three immense walls constructed across Boulevard St. Michel. The barricaders used whatever fell to hand for their purposes, automobiles, cobblestones, building materials from construction sites, even trees which were summarily cut down. Occasionally, student zeal gained the upper hand over military wisdom, as in the rue Gay-Lussac, where an immense barricade was erected which was to block off any possible exit from the area by its defenders later on. The police held back until 2:00 A.M., when they received the order to clean out the area. Battles of position occurred, thereafter, from barricade to barricade, as the police first assaulted student defenders, then disassembled the barriers. Fires burned throughout the night, over a thousand students were wounded, while 400 policemen needed medical attention. The entire skirmish, which lasted until dawn, was broadcast over the radio, incident by incident, for all of France to hear. Also broadcast were attempts by internationally famous scientific figures (Laurent Schwartz, for example) to mediate, attempts which the government rejected.

9. *Le Monde*, 11 May 1968.

Contrary to a great deal which was written about the May-June crisis at the time, neither the PCF nor the CGT disliked massive social crises per se. However, they did both dislike massive social crises which fell outside their control. It was an important part of the Marxist-Leninist tradition to regard social movements and mass organizational activities which emerged outside the purview of party and union as unreliable, and more often than not, likely to enhance the fortunes of class enemies. Thus, as the May-June 1968 crisis developed, both the PCF and CGT insisted, with all of the resources at their disposal, that the upheaval ought to proceed along the strategic and political lines which they themselves had been projecting, each in its own way, for many years. Given the relatively weak position of the PCF in the student world, this insistence on the part of the party was bound to be ineffectual while simultaneously alienating the student movement further from French Communism. For the CGT, with its substantial power to shape events in the labor market, the situation was to be much different when, later, the working class entered the lists.

The PCF responded first to the student revolt by trying to channel it in certain directions. In the party's view, student protest within the university would be very useful to the extent which it could expose the priorities and shortcomings of the Gaullist regime's educational policies. Thus, early in May, both the PCF and CGT were quick to proclaim that the central issue which the students were raising was "the democratic and modern reform of the university and of education."[10] The student movement had exploded because of the neglect and perversion of French education by Gaullism, the monopoly caste, and their joint economic strategies. In this context, the government's repressive response to such just grievances was outrageous and provocative. Thus the PCF acted, to the extent of its limited capacities, to impose the "democratic reform" line in the student world to give some order to what looked like an inchoate, if deep-seated, revolt.

The other, vastly more publicized, aspect of the PCF's response to the student movement was its strident, and somewhat out-of-control, denunciation of student "Leftist extremists." None other than Georges Marchais set the tone on May 3 in *L'Humanité*:

> As always, when the union of democratic and working-class forces progresses, *groupuscules gauchistes* agitate everywhere. They are particularly active among students. At Nanterre, for example, one finds Maoists, the JCR [the *Jeunesse Communiste Révolutionnaire*, a Trotskyist pro-Castro group led by a number of ex-PCF youth-movement militants], the *Comité de liaison des étudiants révolutionnaires*, also Trotskyists, anarchists and diverse other groups more or less folkloric in nature.

10. See Georges Séguy, for example, in a press conference, 7 May, cited in *Le Peuple*, 15 May–15 June 1968.

Despite their contradictions these *groupuscules*—a few hundred students—have unified into what they call the March 22 Movement, led by the German anarchist Cohn-Bendit.

Not satisfied with the agitation they carry on among students—agitation which is against the interests of the mass of students and favors fascist provocations—now these pseudo-revolutionaries have become presumptuous enough to give lessons to the working-class movement. . . .

These false revolutionaries must be energetically unmasked because, objectively, they are serving the interests of the big capitalist monopolies and Gaullist power.[11]

Jean Dubois, of the CGT's Paris region (and a Communist) was even more hysterical. *Gauchisme* was "an arm, and a dangerous one, which the bourgeoisie used to get the labor movement off the track and to facilitate the use of repression against it. . . . Make no mistake about it, we are faced with a vast organized operation with powerful resources at its disposal, with the complicity of the *patronat*, regime and police, whose roots are in China, in Latin America, but also in America in the offices of the CIA."[12] The Union of Communist Students, which held back from the early student confrontations, issued a communiqué denouncing the various grouplets in different terms: "the *gauchistes* take the government's blunders as a pretext and speculate on underlying student discontent to attempt to block the functioning of the universities and prevent the mass of students from working and passing their exams. . . . Thus these false revolutionaries behave as objective allies of Gaullist power and its policies, which hurt students as a whole, and primarily those whose origins are most modest."[13]

The PCF's response was dictated by an urgent desire to see a certain division of labor prevail in the organization of protest in France. It was all to the good for students to expose the evils of Gaullist policies in the sector of society—the educational system—where they lived. By doing so, they would contribute to popular mobilization against the regime which might contribute to a developing United Front. However, were students, or student activists, to step outside such a sectoral perspective and begin posing as a vanguard for change in the society as a whole, then the PCF was obliged to unleash its anger. Yet this was exactly what the student-based *gauchiste* groups hoped to do, to turn the student movement towards insurrection and to provoke a revolutionary crisis in France which would short-circuit the PCF.

The PCF's desire to steer the student movement in a moderate "sectoral

11. *L'Humanité*, 3 May 1968.
12. Cited in Michel Johan, "La CGT et le mouvement de mai," *Temps Modernes* (August-September 1968), p. 370.
13. In *Partisans* (May-June 1968), p. 23.

process" direction and its thunderous denunciations of the *gauchistes* were, then, designed to isolate the *gauchistes*. The party worried that, to the extent that *gauchistes* became prominent in general student disruptions, some of the social groups which the PCF had been courting into an anti-monopoly alliance (which eventually were supposed to be the support for a new United Front) would be alienated from the Left. The danger of student *gauchisme*, to the PCF, was that it risked upsetting the PCF's own strategic plans. Moreover, the PCF knew that if, through some unforeseen course of events, the *gauchiste*-student revolt combination actually succeeded in precipitating a serious social crisis calling the Gaullist regime into question, the absence of firm United Front arrangements on the Left to propose as an alternative might lead to serious political setbacks for the Left. It is also clear that PCF attacks on *gauchistes* in the student movement stemmed from fear that *gauchiste* appeals might touch responsive chords within the PCF's own base. Denouncing *gauchistes* as provocateurs and as agents of the bourgeoisie was, in large part, meant for internal PCF consumption, to generate inner-party cohesion against *gauchiste* propaganda.

The PCF did invoke a broader theoretical context to justify its response to the student movements and to *gauchisme*. To the PCF, the student revolt was only part of a much more important change in French society, connected with the development of state-monopoly capitalism in France, involving a gradual shift in the political and social allegiances of the *couches moyennes* (middle strata). Because of the strategies of the monopoly caste, intellectuals, students and large parts of the middle strata generally faced a process of proletarianization. As this process moved forward, the ideological hold of the ruling classes over the *couches moyennes* became increasingly more tenuous. The final outcome of this process would be the detachment of such groups from their prior ties to ruling elites and their alignment on the side of the working class. As Laurent Salini of *L'Humanité* wrote, "the growing strength of the working class, its ever greater influence throughout society, its more affirmative role, the progress of the aspiration towards socialism" meant that "we are confronted with political mutations in the middle classes."[14] It was foreseeable, from this point of view, that problems between workers and students might arise in 1968, however. The process of the radicalization of the middle strata was only partially completed at this time. Students, whose class identification had formerly been *bourgeois* and *petit bourgeois*, were still insufficiently detached from their former class identities to have anything more than an abstract knowledge of the realities of working-class existence and thus tended to observe and approach workers in a paternalistic way. Given this, students were open to *gauchiste* extremism and anti-Communism. To cite

---

14. Salini, *Le mai des prolétaires* (1968); Réné Andrieu, *Les Communistes et la révolution* (1969), pp. 92–94; Réné Andrieu, *Choses dites* (1979), pp. 168–170.

Salini again, "it remains for them to understand that the working class is the motor and leader in this struggle. Being unable to understand this, students may oppose the working class."[15] The problem with this theoretical understanding was that the PCF foresaw only two possible class outlooks for groups such as intellectuals and students, either pro-ruling class or pro-working class (and thereby pro-PCF strategy). Middle strata, as they suffered proletarianization, would become proletarian in outlook. In this vision there was no room for a coalition between workers (and their vanguard, the PCF) and intermediary strata which allowed for legitimate differences in perspective between such groups. Theoretically, then, the PCF had still not de-Stalinized its understanding of French society enough to be able to understand the necessary dynamics of the cross-class anti-monopoly alliance which, strategically, it was attempting to build. In May 1968 the cost of this was a paroxysm of overdriven anti-student rhetoric which further set back the possibilities for the PCF to re-establish some degree of hegemony in the intellectual and student world.

As things happened in the early days of May, however, the PCF's initiatives had little hope of success among students. That the crisis was directed "to a democratic reform of the university" may, in fact, have been true, objectively, but this did not deter student activists from having much more grandiose visions. The mass of students, once aroused, probably did want to change society overnight, probably did believe that this was possible, had no interest in the logic of the PCF's strategy and very little understanding of the complexity of the world around them. The PCF had little or no organizational clout to make its view known among students. Finally, the natural leaders of the student movement (in the absence of an effective PCF presence) were the *gauchiste* groups the PCF was so intent upon denouncing. The ultimate result of Communist attacks on *gauchistes*, then, and especially attacks as virulent as those made by Georges Marchais, was to promote exactly the kind of student movement which the PCF least wanted to see, led by *gauchistes*, profoundly anti-Communist, and dedicated in a strident way to becoming the new vanguard of French workers in making a revolution in France.

From Students to Workers: The Great Strike of 1968

The night of the barricades, May 10–11, was a key turning point, the event which caused the focus of May-June 1968 to shift from students to workers and which brought the Gaullist regime to the edge of disaster. The obvious intention of the government to break the student revolt by force and the brutality of police action in the Latin Quarter obligatorily brought opposi-

---

15. Salini, p. 106 ff. On the PCF and May, one might consult George Ross, "The May Movement in France," *New Politics* (Fall-Winter 1968).

tion forces to new positions. The government could not be allowed politically to deal with protest movements in such a repressive way. The
regime's determination to beat down the students had to be checked by the
mobilization of non-student forces. The most important, and the first to
act seriously, were the unions.[16]

As early as May 9–10 the CGT and CFDT had begun negotiating with
student leaders with a view to promoting working-class support for the student revolt. Given the CGT's distaste for the leaderships of UNEF and
SNE(sup), a feeling which was amply returned, and given the impossible
demands which Alain Geismar of SNE(sup) and Jacques Sauvageot of
UNEF had made—involving trade-union submission to the student leadership and its positions—the negotiations had failed.[17] The barricades
changed things, however, especially for the CGT. The CGT Confederal
Bureau, in touch with CGT organizations in Paris by telephone, met continuously throughout the night of May 10–11. And, as the government's
repressive path became completely clear with the last stages of warfare in
the Latin Quarter, the Confederal Bureau put the entire CGT organization
on urgent alert "to follow events and Confederal directives in the hours to
come," in other words to be prepared to mobilize the rank and file in
response to a strike call which was imminent.[18] The next day the CGT called
for a twenty-four-hour strike for May 13.[19] Representatives of student
organizations, enchanted with the thought that they themselves could call a
general action without the CGT and, perhaps, succeed, held back from
commitment for a time.[20] The CGT, in turn, informed them that they could
do what they wanted, but that the CGT was going forward with its general
strike plans with them or without them. Quickly thereafter the CGT and
CFDT came to agreement about details for the proposed action. France's
two largest labor organizations were determined to go through with a
general strike. In these circumstances UNEF, SNE(sup) and even the
Fédération de l'Education Nationale had to join in the strike call. A joint
declaration from all of these organizations was therefore made public, appealing for strike action,

> in the name of the solidarity which unites students, teachers and
> workers against police repression, for the amnesty of the convicted
> demonstrators and for the cessation of all legal, administrative or uni-
> versity punishment of them, for trade-union and political liberties
> and for the achievement of . . . common aspirations—democratic
> reform of education in the service of working people, full employ-
> ment, transformation of the economic system by and for the people.[21]

16. *Le Peuple*, 15 May–30 June 1968, p. 15.
17. Interviews with CGT officials; Georges Séguy, *Le mai de la CGT* (1972), pp. 19–21.
18. *Le Peuple*, p. 15.
19. Ibid., p. 16; Séguy, *Le mai de la CGT*, p. 23.
20. Eugène Descamps, *Militer* (1971), p. 113.
21. *Le Figaro*, 13 May 1968.

Evidence about interaction between CGT leaders and the PCF within the PCF *Bureau Politique* around the question of the advisability of this strike call is sparse and anecdotal (Roger Garaudy submitted his version in 1978-1979, and we have heard corroborations of it in interviews with certain CGT leaders).[22] Four CGTers were members of the *Bureau Politique* at that point—Frachon, Séguy and Krasucki from the *Bureau Confédéral*, plus Georges Frischmann, Secretary-General of the Postal Workers Federation. Major figures in the *Bureau Politique* opposed the strike call, Georges Marchais in the first instance, and Waldeck Rochet. Frachon and Séguy insisted upon the call, however, and managed to make their positions prevail.

The strike call began what was to be a change in dramatis personae in the crisis. No longer were the May events simply a confrontation between students and the Gaullist regime. Unions were informing the government that it could continue its repressive course only by risking a major confrontation with the working class. The government understood this almost immediately and beat a hasty retreat. Prime Minister Pompidou, who had been on a trip to Afghanistan to this point, announced that student arrests were "to be re-examined" (forgotten), the Sorbonne was to be re-opened (which led to its occupation by students after the May 13 strike), and police presence in the Latin Quarter drastically reduced. In effect, the Prime Minister admitted that the government's tactics to that point had been unwise (an admission which, by making scapegoats of the police, did not please the police at all).[23] Pompidou was, of course, a politician of some skill. He believed that he was negotiating a huge trade-off to end the crisis. The government's liberalism would take the edge off student protest, on the one hand, while a huge, and tightly-controlled, one-day general strike led by the CGT, which Pompidou correctly judged to have its own interest in ending the student revolt, would allow everyone to retire in dignity.

It was true that, in the words of Lucio Magri, "the students had earned this enlargement of the struggle with great difficulty by succeeding in imposing on parties and trade unions first the rectification, then the reversal, of an attitude of hostility and reserve via a series of brutal confrontations. . . ."[24] There could be no doubt that the CGT's decision to act represented a tactical shift on the part of the Confederation and the more reluctant PCF about the student crisis. On the one hand, the student

22. See Roger Garaudy in *Rouge*, 21 May 1978, and *Non-Violence Politique* (November 1979).

23. See Paul Gillet, "Inside the Prefecture," in Posner, ed., p. 166-167. Pompidou's action was a disavowal of the police which led to serious discontent within police ranks which, when connected with long-standing police wage and hour grievances, created some doubt about the reliability of the police until the government judiciously granted some of the police's salary demands.

24. Lucio Magri, in *Les Temps Modernes* (August-September 1968). Magri's articles on May, translated from Italian, were perhaps the most intelligent independent Left political pieces on May to appear.

movement, completely out of control, had become troublesome. It risked compromising longer-term CGT and PCF mobilization plans towards a new United Front. This being the case, PCF and CGT, given their inability to control events in the student world, had no choice but to shift the scope of the crisis towards areas where they did have control. If, in the process, they could humiliate the government, so much the better. The general strike call could only be interpreted in this way. The CGT hoped to drown the student revolt in a much larger action in which the CGT would play a determinant role. If the May 13 action proved successful, party and trade union could hope that the government would be frightened enough to make concessions to the students which might, in turn, get students off the streets, back to classes, and away from the *gauchistes*. In the process, as well, the Confederation could hope that strike mobilization might give a hefty boost to working-class militancy. André Barjonet, still a high CGT official on May 13, later wrote "the CGT thought that all would stop there, that there would be a good day of strikes . . . and a good demonstration."[25] These thoughts were not confined to the CGT. André Jeanson, President of the CFDT, noted that "for many of the organizers of the demonstration it also marked the end of the events themselves."[26]

May 13 was an incredible success, involving the largest demonstrations to that point ever organized against the Gaullist regime—600,000 to 800,000 people in Paris alone.[27] The general strike was not total, but the strike call was well enough obeyed to make the action successful.[28] Georges Séguy and the CGT Confederal Bureau, with their CFDT and FEN counterparts, shared the front rows of the parade with Geismar and Sauvageot, the *gauchiste* SNE(sup) and UNEF leaders and, much to Séguy's chagrin, Cohn-Bendit. Except for this minor humiliation, however, there were few unpleasant moments for the CGT. The trade unions' parade marshals kept events well under control and the huge demonstration in Paris was disbanded, in disciplined fashion, at Denfert-Rochereau, just as the unions had ordered.[29]

Under the surface, however, May 13, far from ending the May Events, was to be a powerful catalyst for turning them in a new, more complicated and, for the regime, more serious direction. May 13 was an object lesson. The students had fought the regime until it had been obliged to back down.

25. Barjonet, in Labro, pp. 164–173.

26. André Jeanson, in Posner, ed., p. 144.

27. *Le Monde*, 15 May 1968; Bauchard and Bruzek, p. 75.

28. In sectors with a strong CGT organization the turnout was good. This was the case on the railroads, in the PTT and among northern miners, although less true, interestingly enough, at Renault. In general a majority of workers in the public-service areas of the public sector followed the strike orders, while workers in the private sector were less eager to follow. Paris transport workers, a good barometer of general strike support, struck at fifty percent.

29. A small student march led by Cohn-Bendit immediately afterwards, supposedly on the Elysée palace, was prevented by police from crossing the Seine.

This lesson was easily transferable to the labor market. For years workers and unions had gotten next to nothing from either the government or the *patronat*. Yet the hard struggles of 1967 and 1968 had demonstrated that there existed considerable militancy at the rank-and-file union level. May 13 was what was needed to prod French workers to action. Two years of hard union mobilization, facilitated by CGT/CFDT cooperation, were about to pay off.

On Tuesday May 14, a lightning-quick rank-and-file movement at Sud-Aviation in Nantes led to a sit-down strike in which enraged activists imprisoned the plant director in his office. Sud-Aviation-Nantes had been in continuous ebullition in 1967 and 1968. The issues of the sit-down in May were the same as those unsuccessfully promoted earlier,[30] including the key one of payment for reduced working time in the economic downturn.[31] The general problem, which had been a consistent CGT/CFDT focus, was the slump in aviation and Gaullist economic policies which had created it. Yet Nantes was a special place, over and above this.[32] *Force Ouvrière* in Nantes, unlike FO anywhere else in the private sector of the economy, was quite militant, imbued with a lively and long-standing anarcho-syndicalist tradition, one which was quite strong, moreover, at Sud-Aviation. This, plus a strain of Trotskyist unorthodoxy in the Sud-Aviation CGT, made the plant unusually volatile. Militant young workers, who had been the first to suffer from the plant's difficulties, provided a rank and file eager to follow such a militant leadership.[33]

On the next day, May 15, Renault at Cléon went out. Cléon was one of the government's exemplary regional-planning efforts, constructed far out of the Paris Red Belt to get away from the CGT, at least in part. Because of this, Cléon was staffed with young workers, many fresh out of the country-side, subject to unremittingly hard labor-discipline and, in 1967–1968, serious unemployment threats.[34] Ironically, because the Renault direction had succeeded in one of its decentralization goals, that of weakening unions, at Cléon the discontent which built up among young workers was badly channelled by regular labor institutions, a fact which increased the risk of wildcats.[35] Cléon had not joined in the May 13 action. But the local union had scheduled a plant action for May 15 around the social security decree issue, plus local questions, the most important of which was the Renault management's use of short-term contracts to keep young workers

30. *Le Peuple*, 15 May–15 June 1968, pp. 6, 11.

31. Georges Lefranc, *1944–1968*, p. 233.

32. *L'Humanité*, 16 May 1968.

33. See Yannick Guin, *La commune de Nantes* (1969), p. 37 ff.

34. See Diverse authors, *Notre arme c'est la grève, la grève chez Renault Cléon* (1968). This work, which has no offical author (perhaps in the spirit of May) is the product of Left union-ists at Cléon; see also Jacques Frémontier, *Renault: la forteresse ouvrière* (1975).

35. Lucien Rioux and René Backmann, *L'explosion de mai* (1968), p. 253; Bauchard and Bruzek, p. 78. Rioux and Backmann is probably the best single recounting of the May strikes.

in line. On May 15, the unions went through their usual rituals. They demanded three times that delegations be received by plant directors to discuss the issues. Three times, as per usual, they were turned down. This time, however, ritual was violated. The unions, which had intended only to generate rank-and-file awareness of the issues, found, to their great surprise, that a rank-and-file movement ied by young workers had followed up their protests to the management with a chain-reaction action on the shop floor. Work stopped throughout the plant, to begin with, and the workers then proceeded to begin a sit-down strike, similar to the one at Sud-Aviation.[36]

By Thursday May 16 a phenomenon of contagion was evident. Renault-Flins went out and the plant was occupied. The sociology and structure of Flins were close to those at Cléon.[37] Renault-le Mans also went out. There the movement was a direct extension of the labor unrest which had first broken out in 1967. On the same day the strike spread throughout the aviation industry and began to touch parts of the electronics industry. By May 16, the early scenario of the great strike of 1968 was clear. Industries most affected by the downturn of 1967–1968 and most sensitive to European and international competition were the targets. Actions began over long-standing unresolved issues, usually local, around which unions had been agitating for some time. Young, often non-union, workers sparked and spread the movements. Once action had been organized, it ran up against the intransigent responses from employers which had also characterized the recent period. In the changed context of May, however, such a response inflamed conflict rather than intimidating it. The result was an explosion of labor struggle which, for two days or so, took even the trade unions by surprise.[38]

The spread of action to Renault-Billancourt on May 16 involved a basic shift in the dynamics of the May strike, however. The strike at Billancourt began like those of the two days previously, with one fundamental difference.[39] The Billancourt unions, although initially wary of the action, shifted their ground and went ahead themselves to promote and organize the sit-down. And when one speaks of unions at Billancourt, one means the CGT. Thus by the emergence of the Billancourt movement, after two days of observing rank-and-file movements, the CGT had decided to deploy its vast resources to promote a very large strike. (Although only after Georges

36. Diverse authors, *Grève à Cléon*, pp. 16–18.

37. See Diverse authors, *La Grève à Flins*, another collective essay by Left unionists.

38. Rioux and Backmann, who are quite reliable, claim that the unions began to take control of things within twenty-four hours of the news of the Nantes-Sud Aviation occupation; Rioux and Backman, p. 313.

39. *L'Humanit'e*, 17 May 1968.

Séguy and other CGT leaders had again overcome the reticence of Marchais and Waldeck Rochet.)[40] The CFDT reached the same conclusion at about the same time.[41] From this point onwards, only two days after the initial wildcats, the growth and spread of the strike was to occur primarily because of mobilization undertaken by union organizations themselves. The unions, and most importantly the CGT, were not at all reluctant, once a certain threshold of rank-and-file enthusiasm had been passed, to build a massive strike movement. Indeed the CGT's determination to do so, once it had made a positive judgment about the climate at the rank-and-file level, was the main reason the great strike of 1968 was as powerful as it was.

The methodical way in which the strike developed after May 16 was clearly marked by the organizational power of the CGT. The Confederation began preparation in earnest on May 15 by calling the National Confederal Committee into emergency session. On the same day the CGT Confederal Bureau circulated a leaflet in which its intentions were made clear.

> Workingmen, workingwomen . . . at the call of your unions act without delay, gather together in your places of work, participate in the formulation of demands and of modes of action in your plants, your industrial branches and your regions.
>
> The CGT will take all of the responsibilities and initiatives necessary for organizing your action in order to insure the necessary coordination for it and to give it the depth and the power which will carry all before it.

The leaflet was replete with a Confederal warning about *gauchistes*, "*petits-bourgeois* who slander the labor movement and have the incredible pretension to teach it lessons."[42] On May 16, the CGT issued another call to strike which clearly underlined its intentions to push the strike as far as it could be pushed and mobilize its organization to do so.[43]

In this context, bringing out the Renault-Billancourt workers was designed to trigger industrial conflict throughout the important Paris metals sector. By Friday May 17, the strike was all over Paris.[44] The next step was

---

40. During these two days, extended debate about what to do took place between members of the PCF *Bureau Politique*. Waldek Rochet, Secretary-General of the party, was against a major strike movement because no Left political solution (i.e., no United Front) existed should the strike lead to a major social crisis. Waldeck Rochet favored, rather, the CGT taking the strikes in hand to limit their effect. It took the powerful arguments of trade unionists in the *Bureau Politique* (Séguy and Krasucki, for the most part, although Georges Frischmann of the PTT Federation was also on the *Bureau Politique*) about rank-and-file conditions and the CGT's outstanding grievances to overcome Rochet's reticence.

41. Descamps, *Militer*, p. 115.   42. *Le Peuple*, 15 May–15 June 1968, p. 21.

43. Ibid., p. 23.   44. *L'Humanité*, 18 May 1968.

to "nationalize" it. This the CGT did, as always, by calling out transport workers, in particular the *cheminots*. The railroad strike, beginning in the heavily CGT (and PCF) Rhône and Paris regions, spread quickly throughout the entire railway system.[45] Local transport was shut down simultaneously.[46] The railroad strike was not only a nationalizing tactic, it was also a device to ensure that the strike survived its first weekend, May 17 being a Friday. By Monday, the effects of the transport strike would be evident everywhere in the country, goods necessary for production would cease to be delivered, while public transport would cease to deliver the workers needed to produce. The May 17 spread of the strike into public-service areas of the public sector (electricity, gas and the post office) had the same goals. Here the CGT could draw upon the longstanding indignation, and the results of its own agitation, against the government's niggardly public-sector incomes policy. New additions to the strike on Monday, mainly in large private-sector industry which could not function without transport and services, demonstrated the success of the CGT's weekend survival tactics. Peugeot and Alsthom in Franche-Comté, Michelin in Clermont-Ferrand, almost the entire textile and rubber industries, Citroën in Paris, all shut down. By May 20 the strike was growing geometrically.[47] At its height it would involve almost the entire French working class.

The CGT had not anticipated the explosion of May-June any more than had other French union organizations. The May-June strike, like all massive strike movements in modern French labor history, occurred because the mysterious factors which made up the climate at the rank-and-file level—of which official union action was only one among many—all converged towards action in May. However, with the rapid spread of the great May-June strike, workers and unions replaced students as the major actors in the crisis. To be sure, the student revolt continued (largely because the strike shut off all normal activity in France), imagination came to power in small areas of Paris, the *Commune Etudiante* flowered in the Latin Quarter and intellectuals talked and wrote incessantly about the massive changes in human history which "their" movement represented.

45. Ibid.
46. Annie Kriegel, one of the more astute authorities on the PCF, claimed later that "neither the strike at Renault Cléon nor the agitation at Renault Flins would have been enough—even by the contagion which they fostered, even with the support of the CFDT—to lead to a generalized strike, if the party had decided otherwise. Only the mobilization of the powerful Federation of railroad workers . . . directed by Communists for decades—and that in Paris of the RATP unions . . . could bring other corporations out in their wakes" (Kriegel, *Les Communistes français* (1968), p. 244).
47. Peugeot, Michelin and Citroën were all notoriously anti-union employers. Thus the outbreak of serious strike actions in such places indicated the depth of rank-and-file support for the strike. In each case (Peugeot, Michelin, Citroën) open union activity of any kind would have been, in ordinary circumstances, cause for immediate dismissal.

Still, after May 16, the student revolt became a sideshow on the great strike. What then became important was that the shape and nature of the strike, insofar as they were controllable, were largely in the hands of the CGT. What happened to the strike industrially was to be largely the CGT's doing. And the political uses to which the strike was put was also in the CGT's hands. For nearly a month of French history, then, and one of its more tumultuous months, the CGT was to be *maître du jeu*.

The CGT's first tactical task, as of May 17, was to extend the strike while, at the same time, bringing as much of it under the Confederation's control as possible. In this case, both the CGT and the CFDT calculated that it would be almost a week, until May 22 or so, before the strike had reached its fullest extension. After that point the outcome of the strike—negotiations or not, and around what issues—would take precedence. However, early decisions about how to build the strike would have very great importance later on how the strike was settled. Thus Georges Séguy, the CGT's new General-Secretary (Benoît Frachon had retired from the post at the 1967 Congress, to assume the new post of President of the Confederation), announced to the National Confederal Committee on May 17 that no national general strike was to be called. "For the moment our tactic and our strategy is to extend the strike 'from below.' " The strike had begun from the rank and file with assemblies of workers, discussions of demands and slogans and the election of local strike committees. "There has already been the establishment of leadership, responsible to the workers themselves for its acts and decisions. This is the best form that we could give to the struggle of the working class."[48] Continuing to follow the form in which the strike began by promoting local strike committees had the advantage of maximizing the possibilities for rank-and-file support, critical in being able to carry the strike through to a successful conclusion and also very useful for deepening contact between CGT militants and the rank and file. Beyond this, calling a general strike from the Confederal level would have involved problematic negotiations with the CFDT about its form, and the certainty that FO would not have gone along, thus weakening the strike movement. Finally, and most importantly, building a movement whose decision-making locus was local would present definite bargaining advantages when negotiation time came around. Negotiations would, in all likelihood, be carried on at the top between union general staffs, the government and the *patronat*. For such general staffs to be able to assert, with some credibility, that the final decision on bargaining offers lay not with them, but with rank-and-file strike committees, meant that government and *patronat* would be prodded to come up with acceptable offers lest rank-and-file committees decided to carry on the strike in the event

48. *Le Peuple*, May-June 1968, pp. 27-28.

that concessions were inadequate. The Confederation, in refusing a general strike call, was therefore setting up a situation in which the advantages of national negotiations and decentralized local struggles could be cumulated.

Of course, the CGT fully intended to gain and keep control over the general directions of the strike, despite such decentralization. Thus, the Confederation's most important initial concern in the days after May 17 was to make sure that CGT militants ran as many locally elected strike committees as possible. Georges Séguy's summary of the Confederation's perspective on developing the strike is most illuminating in this respect.

In truth, to organize the outbreak of the strike and to lead it to victory our actions were inspired by a conception with which CGT militants are familiar since it follows from the experience of all our past struggles.

Consult the workers on demands and slogans for action, not in a neutral fashion but by giving them all the necessary elements to allow them to decide in full knowledge of the situation.

Place the movement under their vigilance and their control by the election of strike committees directly responsible to the strikers, in such a way that any operation from the top down against the strike cannot succeed.

Promote unity-in-action . . . at all levels . . . without foregoing what can be done immediately because of mass support. . . .

Avoid all which might cause the movement to become unpopular among other categories of working people in cities and countryside.[49]

In short, the CGT desired a decentralized strike which would function in accord with the Confederation's own desiderata. Locally elected strike committees dominated by CGT militants would center the discussion of demands and slogans around themes set out by the Confederation. *Gauchisme* and any other interferences with such plans were to be struggled against. Finally, the strike was to observe the mass perspectives by now second nature to the CGT. It should do nothing which might offend less militant sectors of the working class and those non-working-class groups likely, other things being equal, to be sympathetic to a "reasonable" strike.

Towards what goals was the strike to be directed? The CGT's answer was crystal-clear. The strike's purpose was to win major concessions on a whole series of long-standing trade-union demands, essentially those around which the CGT and CFDT had been agitating since 1966. The May 17 Confederal Committee concluded its work by announcing that the CGT wanted:

1. The immediate abrogation of the 1967 Social Security Decrees.
2. The satisfaction of fundamental wage demands and the conclusion

---

49. Ibid., p. 116.

of real collective agreements which will ensure the rights and living standards of workers.

3. The reduction in the length of the work week without reducing salaries, plus lowering the age of retirement.
4. A genuine policy of full employment which guarantees work and resources.
5. The full and free exercise of trade-union activity at the firm level and its legal recognition.[50]

Local strikes were to agitate for these general goals plus locally derived grievances.

All of this was, of course, predictable from the CGT's prior behavior and fit perfectly within what we have called the CGT's relative autonomy relationship with the PCF. The Confederation was behaving as a trade union, with due regard for the long-standing material grievances of the working-class rank and file in the labor market. Its only "political" concerns, and these were very indirect, at least at early points in the strike's development, were to see that the strike duly respected the mass mobilization criteria which it felt important for building the largest possible movement of public protest against the "regime of the monopolies," public protest of an economic kind which would, hopefully, be translatable into support for a political United Front (in the right circumstances and with skillful political work by the PCF). During the first week of the May strike, the CGT simply acted to develop action in accordance with tried-and-true French union practices for building large strikes. Generalizing a strike in France always meant persuading immense numbers of workers to stop work almost simultaneously. In most strike situations in French history, the CGT (and other unions who faced the same environment) had never been able to assume a sufficiently generalized rank-and-file eagerness to strike to trust that spontaneity would lead to an instantaneous national exodus from work. Traditional strike development tactics thus involved a series of organizational techniques—often with a tinge of "forced march" about them—to ensure that lukewarm rank and filers, and lukewarm sectors of the labor force (without whose participation any general action would fail) moved off the job. In many instances such tactics involved militant activities, backed by whatever rank-and-file fervor existed, to present an "off-balance" majority with a strike fait accompli—surrounding the plant with pickets, for example, to keep workers from entering. If working-class discontent was profound, as it was in May 1968, once workers found themselves out on strike they would quickly find good reasons for striking. But until they found themselves on strike, it made tactical sense for unions to take nothing for granted.

In the heated and unrealistic atmosphere of mid-May, in which much of the French intellectual community was convinced that power might, and should, fall into *its* hands, a great deal was made of the CGT's insistence upon stressing material strike demands to the exclusion of other, and especially political, issues. It was indeed true that the CGT made no attempt (beyond its usual efforts to connect material demands with broader points about the connection between Gaullism and monopoly capitalism) to urge the strikers to take to the streets in order to smash the state.[51] It was also true that the most general form of the strike, the sit-down, at least theoretically offered an ideal setting for political discussion among workers. While, in a minority of cases, such sit-downs were mass phenomena and did involve a great deal of discussion and debate (in which CGTers and Communists participated eagerly along with others), more often than not the sit-downs were *cadre* actions (since they were the best means to shut down a plant) in which plants were occupied by skeleton crews of pickets and maintenance workers. In such cases, and they were legion, most of the strikers probably stayed home and observed the crisis unfolding, with sympathy, to be sure, on radio and television.

One thing about which the CGT was resolute, however, and that which caught the attention of intellectuals involved in the student movement most easily, was the prevention of contact between strikers and student *gauchistes. This* kind of politicization was not to the CGT's taste, to say the least, as Geismar and Sauvageot were to learn when they tried to lead 1000 students to "liberate" Billancourt from the "revisionists." A *cordon sanitaire* of CGT and other Renault militants met them and informed them, in no uncertain terms, that the Renault workers were quite able to understand the world on their own.[52] Here CGT concern to prevent contact between *gauchistes* and its own rank and file, which included a vast campaign by the CGT organization to portray the *gauchistes* as "agents of the ruling class," involved considerable CGT fear that the Confederation might lose control over its own supporters in the heat of the crisis.

The thrust of much anti-CGT criticism in May was that the CGT, by focusing on bread-and-butter demands, was de-politicizing a potentially revolutionary working-class uprising. There is a great deal of evidence, however, that, at least during the first two weeks of the strike, the bulk of the nine million or so strikers were themselves primarily interested in the satisfaction of such material demands. The majority of strike movements, including those which emerged as wildcats—i.e., spontaneously from the rank and file—emerged around local issues which had been the object of trade-union agitation for months, or in some cases, years. In the words of

51. This is the point of Marc Johan's analysis "Le PCF et les évènements de mai," in *Les Temps Modernes* (August 1968), p. 359.

52. See Weber and Bensaid, p. 189; Magri, pp. 29–30; Jean-Marc Coudray in Lefort et al., *La brèche,* p. 116; Diverse authors, *Grève à Flins,* p. 12 for discussions of the CGT's political role, from a *gauchisante* perspective.

Rioux and Backmann, perhaps the best contemporary chroniclers of the strike, "the strikers themselves fought to settle old scores, to obtain the solutions to problems which had been up in the air for years. It is difficult to find any hiatus between their position and the CGT line."[53] Such rank-and-file concern with bread-and-butter questions was most deeply felt in just those sectors of the work force where the CGT was strongest, among semi-skilled factory operatives.[54]

The non-politicization stance of the CGT on the strike was complicated.[55] From the very first days of the strike Georges Séguy and other Confederal leaders insisted again and again that the Confederation's job was "not to conduct this movement to an eventual political conclusion. For if we have a sense of the responsibilities which are undoubtedly ours, we have a sense equally of the responsibilities which are . . . those of the parties of the Left."[56] As events revealed, this was simply not a statement of passivity with respect to the tasks which naturally fell to political parties. Throughout the May-June strike, the CGT tried to use its powers over the control of the strike to urge the parties of the Left to agree on a Common Program for an alternative to Gaullism. As Séguy wrote, long after the events, "given such a powerful movement, it ought to have been possible . . . to push towards the victory of a Left alternative. One sole condition had to exist: an entente, on clear grounds, between the two large Left parties, the PCF . . . and the Socialists."[57] In fact throughout the events the Confederation attempted to bargain its potential politicization in exchange for the conclusion of a United Front Common Program of the Left. The CGT was willing to "become political" in May, but only in support of a new United Front. And in the course of the May events it consistently demonstrated this. On May 19 the Confederal Bureau met with the PCF *Bureau Politique*, concluding that "the power of the popular movement calls for the urgent conclusion of an accord between Left political formations on a Common Program of government. . . ."[58] On May 20, the CGT met officially with the FGDS (the non-Communist Left Federation) leadership. Here, of course, agreement on the necessity for a Common Program was extremely difficult to achieve, indeed impossible.[59] And these were only two instances, from among many, in which the CGT attempted to urge upon the political Left negotiation to produce a Common

53. Rioux and Backmann, p. 313.

54. This is one of the more important generalizations of Pierre Dubois et al., *Grèves revendicatives ou grèves politiques?* (1971).

55. See, for example, Raymond Aron, *La révolution introuvable*, p. 147; Coudray, in Lefort et al., *La brèche*, p. 118.

56. *Le Peuple*, May-June 1968, p. 28.

57. Séguy, *Le mai de la CGT*, p. 48.

58. Ibid., p. 49.

59. *Le Peuple*, May-June 1968, p. 40; Séguy, *Le mai de la CGT*, p. 61.

Program.[60] In essence, then, the CGT was using its control over the shape and nature of the great strike of 1968 as a lever for ultimately political purposes.[61] Such a tactic cut in two directions, of course. Should the non-Communist Left and Center decide to promote a non-Frontist solution in the crisis, the CGT could severely compromise its success by holding the strike down to material demands or even by ending the strike. Were a Common Program to be agreed upon, in contrast, the CGT might well have been willing to use its strike resources to see to its implementation.[62]

Any strike strategy, even the relatively apolitical one decided upon by the CGT, was bound to have powerful political implications for the student movement. The emergence of a huge strike, in itself, drowned the movement, reducing it to the status of a local Parisian event, a fact which student militants, whose optimism about making a revolution in France had become boundless, were certain to resent. The strike, in itself, reduced the chances of student-worker contact—the major hope of the student *gauchistes*—simply because the tasks involved in organizing and carrying on strike operations were so demanding that trade-union militants had no more time to worry about the university situation.[63] In response to all this, *gauchiste* groups became more extreme. As Gilles Martinet noted, "from the beginning of the events the leaders of the front line of the 'movement' were persuaded that the politics of the Communist Party made revolutionary victory impossible. Thus they sought . . . to lead 'exemplary actions' and to provoke a *prise de conscience* in the largest possible number of students and workers."[64] *Gauchistes* therefore moved, once the strike took control over events out of their hands, to try to promote a situation in which the CGT lost control over its troops, by exemplary actions which would make the situation revolutionary again. This desperate strategy put leaders of the student movement on a collision course with both the CGT and PCF. As a result, one already lively subplot to the May-June events, conflict between PCF, CGT and the *gauchistes* became even more ex-

60. On May 18, Waldeck Rochet stated "it is time to see to the constitution of a popular government of democratic unity," the first step towards which being "the hammering out of a Common Program," (see Waldeck Rochet, *Les enseignements de mai-juin* [1968], p. 29). There were heated and complicated discussions during this week between the FGDS and the PCF. Little is known about their content except that they ultimately failed.

61. See George Ross, "May Movement," *New Politics*.

62. It would have been interesting to see just how far the CGT would have been willing to politicize the strike in the event of Left unity, since such politicization would have involved very great risk to the CGT, whatever the outcome.

63. Sit-downs, of course, involved setting up twenty-four-hour-a-day teams to man occupied plants, maintain order and, where the occupations were massive, to provide the occupiers with an appropriate agenda of daily activities. All of this, of course, had to be done in addition to regular union meetings to plan tactics and keep in contact with events elsewhere in the strike. Rioux and Backmann, p. 287.

64. Gilles Martinet, *La conquête des pouvoirs* (1968), p. 32.

travagant. *Gauchistes* vilified the CGT "bureaucrats" and their Communist "masters." In turn CGT and PCF spokesmen spared none of their brutal rhetoric and applied a lot of real muscle, on the *gauchistes*. We have already mentioned the abrupt response which the Renault-Billancourt CGT (plus, it must be said, Renault-Billancourt workers) made to the Geismar/Sauvageot student expedition to the Billancourt gates during the second week of the strike.[65] Later in the same week the CGT blocked a move by Leftist students (which the CFDT favored) to take over the ORTF (radio-television) headquarters in Paris.[66] Then, when the government exiled Cohn-Bendit from France—Cohn-Bendit was a West German national—not only did the CGT not protest the action, it further alerted its entire Paris organization to keep workers away from a UNEF and SNE(sup) mass protest demonstration against the expulsion.[67] Indeed, on the day of the Cohn-Bendit demonstration, which ended with some of the more ardent protestors trying to burn down the Paris Bourse, the CGT called its own counter-demonstration to keep workers otherwise engaged. *L'Humanité*, in the meantime, had taken to calling Cohn-Bendit the "German anarchist" who "slanders Communists and insults our party." In response to this, in part, student paraders had taken to chanting "we are all German Jews."

Hysteria and extremism aside, the PCF and CGT both had sound political reasons for assuming such a strong anti-*gauchiste* posture. The threat that French workers might abandon their historic allegiance to the PCF and CGT was small, if nonetheless real. Party and union, each in its own way, had invested years of patient and arduous effort to build political and social alliances between different groups which might, at some future point, lead to a Left majority and a United Front in France. *Gauchisme*, if it could be seen as a serious movement, represented a threat to these emerging alliances. Large numbers of French men and women who had an interest in serious social change nonetheless had an even stronger interest in such change occurring in an atmosphere of order and regularity. It was absolutely imperative for both the PCF and CGT, therefore, to dissociate themselves as much as possible from *gauchisme*, on the one hand, and to isolate the *gauchistes* on the other.[68] In addition, *gauchiste* extremism presented both party and union with a long-sought-after opportunity to

---

65. Where contact was made the results were not always what the students expected. One worker, interviewed by a journalist about the student visit to Renault, commented, "when the students came to see us the other day, they said that they were for the workers but that the trade-union leaders were all jerks [*tous des cons*]. One doesn't say that to workers who have been trade unionists for eighteen years." *Nouvel Observateur*, 22 May 1968; *Le Peuple*, 15 May–15 June, 1968, p. 22.

66. *Le Peuple*, 15 May–15 June 1968, pp. 15, 24, 27; Descamps, p. 115–116.

67. *Le Peuple*, 15 May–15 June 1968, p. 49.

68. Séguy, in *L'Humanité*, 21 May 1968.

demonstrate that they were no longer raving Bolsheviks eager to seize power at the first possible moment (an image which PCF history, anti-Communist propaganda and real events in the Cold War period had solidified in French public opinion). In May-June the Gaullist regime had proven itself unable to maintain order. The CGT, as the main actor in the strike, therefore stepped in to present itself as the guarantor of another kind of order, the order and dignity of a responsible and militant working class. In the words of Georges Séguy, "public opinion, upset by troubles and violence, saw in the CGT *la grande force tranquille* which emerged to reestablish order in the service of the workers."[69]

Gauchisme was an easier problem for the CGT to deal with than was the CFDT. As could have been predicted, the great May-June strike exacerbated tactical differences between France's major union organizations to the breaking point. The CGT moved to prod the strike, in true mass fashion, towards spectacular top-level negotiations, *à la Matignon* of 1936, between unions, *patronat* and government, hopefully to deal humiliating blows against both the regime and employers. The CFDT was also interested in high-level negotiations but, in keeping with its own tactical biases, had strong feelings about pushing local strike movements to the utmost possible limit. Developing trade-union power and control *within the firm itself* was a goal which the CFDT and CGT shared, but one upon which the CFDT placed much greater weight than the CGT.[70] More important, as the strike went on CFDT leaders and militants began to preach "worker's control" (*autogestion*), and "structural reform" without making clear what they were talking about. The CFDT's hazy new ideological commitments and its alleged sympathies towards *gauchisme* on the shop floor led Séguy and other Confederal spokesmen to attack the CFDT and its "vague ideas." "The movement, under the vigilance of the workers, is much too powerful to be stopped by hollow formulae such as 'self-management,' 'reforms of civilization,' 'plans for social and university reform,' and other inventions which all amount to the relegation of immediate material demands to the background."[71]

Accusing the CFDT of relegating immediate material demands to the background meant, of course, that the CGT insisted upon pushing these demands to the foreground, indeed that this was the way in which the CGT desired to shape the great strike. Here the CGT was simply continuing basic strategic orientations from the pre-1968 period. But the fact that the CFDT had begun to talk, however vaguely, of demands other than the immediately material was significant. The CFDT was not creating such new demands out of whole cloth, nor was it borrowing them entirely from *gauchistes*. There were real yearnings in parts of the working-class base for unions to include new, more qualitative issues in their action platforms,

69. Descamps, pp. 116 ff; Rioux and Backmann, p. 241; *Combat*, 22 May 1968.
70. Descamps, pp. 115–122.
71. See *La Peuple*, 15 May–15 June 1968.

demands about authority in the workplace, the nature of work itself, the structuring of production around Taylorist methods. For various reasons, the CFDT chose to allow such new demands to filter into its trade-union practices. In contrast, the CGT had a theoretical map of the industrial situation which filtered out such demands. This theoretical map, which the CGT and PCF shared, saw the primary contradictions of workers in the labor market in wages-and-hours questions, i.e., in economist ways. It was unquestionable that workers themselves ranked immediate material demands very high in their lists of action priorities. Thus the CGT was, in part, reflecting this ranking in its behavior. However, the CGT's unwillingness to consider the possibility that other questions might also be on workers' minds was a serious problem, one which the May-June 1968 crisis brought to public attention in spectacular ways, but also one which was to persist for many years to come.

Along these lines, to a limited but important extent, the issue of workers' control did emerge in the strike. If there was a model situation in which such control issues did come to the fore it was in plants, or in professional settings, where the "new working class" (technicians, engineers, intellectuals) was in a relatively powerful position. Such situations were much rarer than observers writing at the time made out (partly because most such observers were new working class in social terms and were themselves caught up both in the *autogestion* fervor and in the anti-CGT feeling of their peers), and far from being a major factor in the strike. But they caused the CGT much concern.[72] And well they should have, since they announced a profound theoretical and strategic weakness on the part of the CGT (and the PCF itself). They were part and parcel of a long-germinating crisis of France's middle strata due to the structure of French economic change and to Gaullist modernization. The inability of the PCF and CGT to theorize about a genuine cross-class alliance which granted different allies a degree of social autonomy (and therefore did not foresee non-working class groups simply adopting the positions and grievances of the working class) had been patent, as we have seen, long before May-June where the situation of intellectuals and students was in question. The problem of *autoges-*

---

72. At the Donges oil refinery, *cadres* and technicians began to run the firm. In certain Nantes plants, groups began to prepare the complete revision of work rules. Similar phenomena occurred at Alicatel-Montrouge, Rhône-Poulenc at Vitry, Perrier near Paris (where "workers' control" stemmed from the fact that the factory was contracted to produce hospital supplies, a service which the strikers decided to continue), the research center of EGF, the Institut Pasteur, the Atomic Research Centers—Saclay in particular—at Thomson-Houston in Bagneux, among others. The "self-management" thrust was much more common among the workers of professional associations (doctors, writers, etc.) and in universities among *chercheurs* and *assistants*. See Serge Mallet, *Nouvel Observateur*, 22 May 1968; Weber and Bensaid, p. 168; Jean-Marie Vincent in *Les Temps Modernes* (July 1968), p. 105; Rioux and Backmann, p. 436; Martinet, p. 70; *Nouvel Observateur*, 7 June 1968, p. 12; Dubois, *Grèves revendicatives ou grèves politiques?*; Henri Pesquet, *Des soviets à Saclay* (1968); Alfred Willener et al., *Les cadres en mouvement* (1969).

tion and "new intellectual workers" for the CGT, evident in May-June, came from the same type of theoretical error.

Grenelle and Its Sequels

As the great strike moved into its second week, all key actors held back waiting for their tactics to work. The government, waiting for the strike to *pourrir* (rot away) and leave the unions stranded, was careful not to take any action which might provoke the strikers. The CGT, the key union actor in the strike, waited on two possible outcomes. Either the Left would come to an agreement on a United Front and Common Program, or the government and *patronat* would agree to the spectacular negotiations at the top which had been the Confederation's goal for years. The Left had only a limited amount of time to put itself together, in the Confederation's calculations, because the May strike, like all other strikes, had a life of its own which had to be respected, hence a moment when the CGT could count on its fullest extension, at which point negotiations would be best undertaken (which the CGT foresaw around May 22). On the other hand, the government had every incentive to move to negotiations, rather than to let the strike drag on too long, out of fear that the Left might actually get itself together. In the meantime, the CGT ran the strike very carefully. Essential services (gas, water, electricity, food supplies, communications) were carried on at a level adequate to prevent general panic.

By the middle of the second week of the strike secret talks between the CNPF and CGT, and the government and the CGT had begun.[73] The CGT and CFDT, despite their disagreements, began to get their dossiers in order. Then, on May 21, Benoît Frachon announced that the CGT was prepared to "sit down at the table for discussion if anyone offers to discuss with us, but in that event two things might happen: either our immediate demands are satisfied and the strike ends, or this is refused and the workers will decide to continue their movement. No one will be able to prevent them from carrying it on. . . ."[74] Frachon's warning that negotiations, if they came, would have to give the strikers what they wanted or else they would not end the strike was to turn out a more credible threat than even Frachon knew. Nonetheless, the next day the CGT, CFDT, other unions, the CNPF and the government announced their readiness to negotiate.[75]

73. Bauchard and Bruzek, p. 88; Jean Raymond Tournoux, *Le mois de mai du Général* (1969), pp. 87, 138–143; *Le Monde*, 25 May 1968.

74. *Le Peuple*, 15 May–15 June 1968, p. 45.

75. The context in which this willingness to negotiate was made public is worth noting. It occurred on the eve of a motion of censure of the government's conduct in May submitted by the parliamentary opposition. Thus in a small but important way the unions' announcement that they considered the government an *interlocuteur valable* could be seen, and was seen, as an act of support for the regime. It was a particular source of encouragement for the Gaullist majority, which had begun to show signs of disintegration by this point. In fact, two Gaullist deputies did resign rather than vote support for the government (Edgard Pisani and René Capitant, both "left-wing" Gaullists).

The government's move towards negotiations, in which Prime Minister Pompidou (seconded by his chief aide-de-camp Jacques Chirac) played the central role, was its ultimate attempt to restore order in the May situation. If negotiations could be satisfactorily concluded and the unions prompted to send their troops back to work, relatively normal circumstances would return and the remains of the student revolt could then be dealt with. At this point, however, Pompidou's boss, General de Gaulle, intervened to upset the Prime Minister's plans. For his own reasons, the General chose May 24, the eve of the Grenelle negotiations, to impose his presence as "arbiter of national destiny," say the last word about the crisis, and return France *sur la bonne voie*. The General's arbitrator, above-the-mêlée, pose was his favorite stance, and had worked often in the past. This time the arbitrator informed the French that what the May crisis was *really* about was a general desire for the French to have greater "participation" in social institutions. This, of course, was a long-standing Gaullist homily (viz. the schemes for *l'association capital-travail* announced in the early 1950s) which had been conveniently forgotten since 1958 in the euphoria of Gaullist modernization.[76] In order to allow the French to express this desire in a constructive way, the General proposed a referendum on the desirability of increased participation in factories, regions and the university. In May 1968, however, the referendum-plebiscite device for subverting discontent did not work. In the General's own eloquent words, "J'ai mis à côté de la plaque." Participation, as a general concept, solved no one's specific problems. De Gaulle's intervention fell flat. And everyone knew that, at such a critical juncture, the total failure of what had been the regime's ultimate trump card meant that Gaullism was in serious political trouble. The Pompidou government, which had envisaged the negotiations at Grenelle to be the beginning of the end of the crisis, found its tactics overshadowed and conditioned by a major political crisis which some people were beginning to see as open-ended.[77]

Negotiations began at the Ministry of Social Affairs, on the rue de Grenelle, on May 25, the second week of the strike. Present, besides Pompidou and Chirac (and one other Minister, Jeanneney), were delegates of the CNPF and the PME (the small businessmen's association), representatives from agricultural workers' unions, plus delegates from six different trade-union organizations, the CGT, CFDT, FO, CFTC-Maintenue, FEN and CGC. The CGT and CFDT had a common list of outstanding grievances dating from the accord of January 1966, upon which there had been

76. See Jean Touchard, *Le Gaullisme 1940–1969* (1978), pp. 280–282, for the elaboration of this analysis.

77. At this point the Gaullist majority in Parliament began to worry about its future, while high civil servants began to consider the possibility of a change in regime (opening contact with certain Left figures). Opposition leaders began to foresee brighter days ahead as well. According to Philippe Bauchard, François Mitterrand, known as a shrewd politician, "hesitated and envisaged throwing in his lot with the students. Pierre Mendès-France dissuaded him."

some coordination during the strike, but otherwise there had been little or no joint preparation by the unions for the talks.[78] The relative weight of the various participants was soon clear, however. As Eugene Descamps, then Secretary-General of the CFDT (and therefore not likely to overrate the CGT's role) wrote later in his autobiography, events turned on the "two Georges"—Séguy and Pompidou—with Chirac serving as the Prime Minister's *homme à tout faire*.[79]

After an opening statement by Benoît Frachon warning government and *patronat* again that they had better come across or the strike would not end,[80] Séguy took the floor to outline the CGT's strike goals. Most important, in order of priority, were the abrogation of the 1967 social security decrees, a general wage raise, including a massive raise in the minimum wage, new guarantees of wage and employment security, a progressive reduction in the length of the working week and lowering of retirement age and, finally, new legal guarantees for trade-union rights on the firm level.[81] Séguy further demanded full payment for days spent on strike. The other unions followed with their own list of priorities. Here the CFDT differed with the CGT in placing the legal guarantee of union rights in the firm at the top of its list.[82] Moreover, only the CGT and CFDT demanded the abrogation of the 1967 social security decrees. It took several hours of mutual posturing—including ritual speeches by government and *patronat* about the economic costs of conceding—before the first break occurred. The minimum wage was pushed up to 600 francs a month (a full thirty-five percent increase) while the agricultural minimum was abolished and agricultural workers brought under the general minimum. Very quickly thereafter the infamous *abattements de zone* (regional variations on the minimum wage) were done away with. Then things slowed down. The government refused, on principle, to scrap its public-sector incomes policy, but was willing to allow branch-by-branch public-sector negotiations (which began almost immediately and led to sizeable public-sector wage increases). Then,

78. Martinet, p. 21.

79. Descamps, p. 60.

80. *Le Peuple*, 15 May–15 June 1968, p. 57.

81. The central demands (as cited in *Le Peuple*, ibid., p. 58) were: General wage and pension raises; No minimum wage less than 600f a month and a proportional increase in the buying power of families, aged people, invalids, etc.; Abolition of regional wage disparities; Abolition of age and other wage discriminations which effect . . . youth, immigrant, female labor; A contractual sliding scale tying wages to the evolution of the cost of living; Guarantee of resources and employment security; Progressive reduction in the length of the work week, without reducing wages; Lowering of the retirement age; Extension and guarantee of trade-union rights; Recognition of the trade-union section in the firm, pay for participation in union general meetings, space within the plant for trade union and sections, the right to hold union meetings in the plant, to put up posters and notices, to collect dues and distribute the union press within the plant; Immunity of union delegates . . . from victimization for union activity; Extension of power of the Enterprise Committees. . . .

82. Descamps, p. 117.

after great reluctance, the CNPF consented to certain private-sector raises, which almost all union delegates found insufficient.[83]

Before the start of the second day's negotiations, Pompidou made a round of private and separate conversations with the three major union leaders—Séguy, Descamps and Bergeron (FO). His purpose, of course, was divide and rule, thus he probed each leader for the soft spots in his bargaining position, hoping to find ways to cheapen the final bill for the strike. Nothing much is known about the Bergeron/Pompidou meeting, but, in any case, FO was not of determinant weight in the negotiations. According to CGT sources, however, Pompidou tempted Descamps of the CFDT with "an operation of an anti-CGT and anti-Communist nature,"[84] something which seems perfectly likely (Pompidou, that evening, was to try and tempt the CGT with an operation of "an anti-CFDT and anti-Third Force nature" to which the CGT, because of information from other sources, was more than sensitive).[85] Séguy's own recounting of discussions with Pompidou gives some sense of what the Prime Minister was up to. First of all, Pompidou tried to convince Séguy that France would be weakened economically if the CGT's demands were met and that this would profit the international, pro-Atlantic enemies of General de Gaulle's foreign policy. Séguy allowed that he had no sympathy for pro-Atlantic positions in foreign policy, but that the General's foreign policy had nothing to do with the CGT's strike positions. Then the Prime Minister tried to bargain an end to some of the (many) discriminatory measures which the state maintained against the CGT (refusals to allocate funds for trade-union schools which were mandated by law, etc.) against a softer CGT stand. Séguy's reponse was that, by right and by law, the CGT should not be discriminated against in any case. Thus there could be no question of connecting the end of such illegal discriminations to a softer CGT position.[86]

The second day of negotiations produced a governmental promise to submit legislation to Parliament reinforcing trade-union rights in the firm, after which the negotiations bogged down. At 8:15 P.M. on Sunday May 26, during a recess in negotiations, Séguy announced to the press:

> The discussions have taken a more severe turn . . . the government has yet to respond . . . to our questions about a guaranteed level of wages, about the reduction in the working week, about lowering the retirement age. On the other hand, it was clear on the decrees against social security: It does not intend to abrogate them. . . . We are going to bring the results to the workers. They will decide. . . .

83. See *Le Peuple*, 15 May–15 June 1968, pp. 119–121 and pp. 140–145, "Constat de Grenelle."
84. Séguy, *Le mai de la CGT*, p. 94.
85. Descamps, p. 120.
86. Séguy, *Le mai de la CGT*, pp. 100–102.

Frachon added, "Today we seem to be going backwards. We are going to let the workers in the factories know about the situation. The outcome of the negotiations will depend on whether the CGT's firm opposition and its decision to keep the workers informed are heeded. In the long run, this will be decisive."[87]

A day-and-a-half of negotiations had revealed the tactics of both sides in the talks. All of the governmental and patronal concessions to that point added up to classic divide and rule. They were aimed at dividing the strikers, giving in to demands affecting the lowest-paid workers, those in depressed regions and weak strikers in the private sector, while granting very little of substance to better-paid workers.[88] The promise to legislate greater union power at the firm level (which may have been one result of the Pompidou-Descamps conversation) was meant to buy off the CFDT, which had placed this question at the top of its list of priorities. In contrast, on all of the issues which the CGT had placed at the top of its list, the government and *patronat* were willing to give nothing—the social security decrees, the *échelle mobile* (which would have pegged wages directly to rises in the cost of living), the end of public-sector incomes policy, shortening the work week and lowering the retirement age. Here it is imperative to note that despite the endless commentary, at the time, about the CGT's alleged moderation, it was clearly the CGT which both government and *patronat* regarded as the most determined and dangerous defender of working-class interests.

The CGT's tactics were almost a mirror image of those of the government and *patronat*. The Confederation attempted to maximize its bargaining power by maintaining a threat that its mobilized rank and file would continue to strike rather than settle for insufficient concessions. Its position, from the beginning, had been that the strike had been called from below and, whatever happened at Grenelle, it would have to be ended from below by ratification of the results of negotiations at the base. As of the evening of May 26, then, when Séguy and Frachon spoke to the press, the CGT was in no way committed to urging the end of the strike on the basis of the meagre results of Grenelle achieved to that point. In fact, there is considerable evidence that the CGT was mobilized at the base to push the strike forward in those areas of the economy where the Grenelle results did not satisfy rank-and-file demands.

After midnight on May 26, however, the situation changed dramatically in rather mysterious ways.[89] After the press break of early evening, negotiations continued throughout the night until early next morning. At 7:00 A.M. the talks were concluded. Few new concessions had been made by government and *patronat*. Those which were made—partial payment of strike

87. *Le Peuple*, 15 May–15 June 1968, p. 60.
88. Ibid., p. 119; Séguy, *Le mai de la CGT*, pp. 106–107.
89. *Le Figaro*, 28 May 1968.

days, a vague promise to hold a conference in the near future to discuss the possibility of an *échelle mobile*, plus a very small change in the implementation of the 1967 social security decrees—were clearly directed straight at the CGT.[90] What had happened, in fact, was that, sometime after midnight, the CGT, which had, to that point, been the bastion of militant discussion with government and *patronat*, had quite suddenly decided to pack in the talks, in the process jettisoning major parts of its original bargaining agenda, including its insistence on the abrogation of the 1967 social security decrees. What had caused this startling about-face?

What had happened was that politics had intervened abruptly in the CGT's negotiating process. The CGT leaders at the talks had kept in constant touch with the PCF *Bureau Politique* during the talks through Georges Frischmann, leader of the CGT Postal Workers' Federation and the only CGT member of the *Bureau Politique* not directly involved in the negotiations. Frischmann apparently moved back and forth between the foyer outside the negotiating room and a café telephone, where he kept up with PCF deliberations at party headquarters. As Sunday evening progressed the PCF leadership had become more and more disturbed by political developments on the non-Communist Left. Plans were being made by non-Communist Left leaders, various student groups, including *gauchistes*, and the CFDT to hold a massive demonstration the next day at the Charléty stadium near the Cité Universitaire in Paris. The purpose of this demonstration, of which Pierre Mendès-France was to be the centerpiece, was, as the *Bureau Politique* understood it, to launch a political alternative to Gaullism which would exclude the PCF.[91] In response, the *Bureau Politique* sent word to CGT leaders at Grenelle that everything had to be done to block the success of Charléty. Translated into CGT action, this meant terminating the talks, and, if possible, winding down the strike soon thereafter. Without the mass strike, the atmosphere of crisis would rapidly dissipate, leaving the non-Communist Left without the social support necessary for the success of its initiative. For the CGT, this amounted to an abrupt about-face in strike tactics for immediate political reasons, an abandonment of relative autonomy, as we have defined it, in the heat of the crisis. It is, in retrospect, hard to understand. It is not hard to understand why, in a complex situation in which overreaction and miscalculation were rife on all sides, those CGT leaders who were also members of the PCF leadership might have seen Charléty as a dangerous threat to their party.[92] What is difficult to comprehend is the feeling by these leaders that such an abrupt change of line, which flew in the face of everything which they had promoted to that point, could work.

Since the strike had not been declared from the top, it could not be ended

90. Bauchard and Bruzek; Séguy, *Le mai de la CGT*, p. 108.
91. Tournoux, p. 144.
92. Séguy, *Le mai de la CGT*, pp. 106–107.

from the top. The workers had to be consulted on the results of Grenelle.[93]
This explains the substance of Séguy's statement to the press at 7:00 A.M.
on May 27:

> Our demands, which had long run up against the refusal of govern-
> ment and *patronat*, have been answered, at least partially.
> There remains much more to do, but the demands have been dealt
> with in part and that which has been decided is not negligible.
> However, we can give no response without consulting the workers.
> It is out of the question for us to give an order for returning to work,
> since we never gave an order for a general strike.[94]

The problems inherent in the CGT's shift became apparent immediately.
Arrangements had been made before Charléty interrupted Grenelle to take
the results of the talks immediately to the workers at Renault-Billancourt.
To begin with, Renault had not had a chance to catch up with the high
politics of early Monday morning. The Renault PCF, as a result of the unsatisfactory state of negotiations expressed at the press break on Sunday,
disseminated a strong tract urging Renault workers to *continue* the strike.
Indeed, Monday's *L'Humanité*, composed Sunday when the meagre results of Grenelle, and not Charléty, had been the concern, predicted the
strike's continuation. More important, the Grenelle results brought almost
nothing to the Renault workers, since those concessions which had come
from Grenelle were addressed primarily to low-wage workers in less
dynamic areas and sectors. Thus Séguy (who with Frachon and André
Jeanson of the CFDT had hurried to Billancourt directly from the rue de
Grenelle) had next to nothing with which to persuade the Renault work
force, already mobilized to continue striking, to change their intentions.
Séguy was the first union speaker in the great hall at Billancourt, presenting
the Grenelle accord with some enthusiasm. The rank-and-file response to
Séguy's urgings was less than enthusiastic, a fact of which Séguy himself
became aware as his speech went on.[95] It fell to Benoît Frachon, who
followed Séguy, to draw conclusions from this, on the spot. Frachon simply reversed the CGT's position, noting that "the accords . . . are going to
bring a degree of well-being to millions of workers who would never have
hoped for it . . . however . . . it is logical that for your factory this will appear derisory. Your program is serious and you ought to win a justified
success on your own demands from your bosses. . . ."[96]

The Confederation's Charléty-induced tactical shift was a mistake, then,
which the Renault incident proved. Here, as so many times before, it was

---

93. *Le Peuple*, 15 May–30 June 1968, p. 61; Lefranc, *1944–1968*, p. 251.
94. Séguy, *Le mai de la CGT*, p. 112.
95. Ibid., p. 108.
96. Frachon, in *Le Monde*, 26–27 May 1968; *L'Humanité*, 28 May 1968.

Benoît Frachon who, at the Administrative Committee's Monday meeting, made sense of the situation. Relative autonomy (our term, not his) was not something which could be dispensed with at a moment's notice, whatever the PCF decided. The general directions of CGT activity over years, and certainly over the days of the great May strike, had a momentum which could be disregarded only at the Confederation's peril, because it was the momentum also of the CGT's rank and file. Thus, by Monday afternoon, the CGT had again changed course.[97] In Séguy's retrospective words:

> We were convinced it was possible, through negotiations branch-by-branch already being carried out in the public and nationalized sector and soon to be carried on in the private sector, to win considerably better results than those at Grenelle.
>
> A precipitous movement to return to work would have deprived us of the possibilities of imposing new concessions on the *patronat* and government. The positive results of Grenelle ought to be a stimulant in the struggle to fill in their insufficiencies.[98]

The new line was to promote settlement on the basis of Grenelle where conditions at the base made this possible, while pushing strike action further towards greater concessions in those areas where the Grenelle conditions were insufficient.

Whatever the CGT did, however, the rejection of the Grenelle accords at Renault (and elsewhere) plus the total failure of General de Gaulle's intervention created the penultimate phase of the May-June crisis. On both Right and Left the credibility of the regime dropped disastrously. Everyone, except perhaps the PCF, came to believe, if only momentarily, that a critical political juncture which might involve a change in regimes was at hand. Civil servants began preparing a transition, to what they were not sure. More important for our own purposes, the non-Communist Left moved to capitalize on the situation, beginning at Charléty, without the PCF. The Charléty meeting itself verged on political hysteria. The general mood can be summarized by reference to the words of one speaker: "Today, all is possible, we can make the revolution." The general line of the meeting was that Gaullism was finished, the working class had begun to move away from its Communist affiliations to follow the lead of the true revolutionaries in the Latin Quarter, and the time had come to act decisively. Speakers from such ordinarily moderate organizations as the CFDT and *Force Ouvrière* preached the possibility of "workers' control" and "revolutionary structural changes." Particularly on display was André Barjonet, ex-collaborator of the CGT's economic research center, who had abruptly resigned his post in the heat of events to side with the student

---

97. Tournoux, p. 171; *L'Humanité*, 28 May 1968.
98. Séguy, *Le mai de la CGT*, p. 114.

movement. Barjonet told the crowd that the situation was such that events could be carried much farther than either the PCF or CGT were willing to go (Barjonet was also a Communist). Other speakers, inspired by Barjonet's presence—symbolic, they thought, of the mass disaffections from the PCF and CGT which were sure to follow—rose to new heights of rhetoric in condemning the PCF and CGT as revisionists and counter-revolutionary. More significant by far than all this was the magnetic presence of Pierre Mendès-France. Mendès refused to speak, but his purposes there were clear to anyone who understood the dynamics of French politics—which excluded, alas, most of the student audience in the stadium. Mendès represented the hopes of ambitious politicians on the non-Communist Left of capitalizing on the crisis at the expense of both the regime and the PCF.

François Mitterrand was the first non-Communist Leftist to take a concrete initiative after Charléty. At a press conference the next day he reflected on the situation which might follow the departure of de Gaulle, proposing that a "caretaker provisional government of the Left" be installed "to get the state going again" by answering the grievances of May and by organizing "the practical conditions for a presidential election." The PCF would not be excluded from such a government, but Mitterrand made no gestures at all towards the PCF's long-expressed desire for a Common Program.[99] While indicating his own willingness to head such a government, Mitterrand noted that "other men than myself could legitimately lay claim to the job. The first name which comes to my mind is that of Pierre Mendès-France."[100] The first thing which the newly elected President would do would be to call legislative elections. Mitterrand was cautious and vague. He sought to leave doors open to the PCF, but not the doors which the PCF wanted.

After Mitterrand's press conference, the Mendès-France balloon went up in earnest. The PSU came out for him as potential Prime Minister.[101] On May 29 the CFDT came out for Mendès. Eugene Descamps, CFDT Secretary-General, announced to the press that the CFDT was

> aware of the effort made by the Federation of the Left and the Communist Party in the last eighteen months. But the moment is of such seriousness that we are unable to see how these organizations could integrate the new forces and respond to their objectives. Confronted with the extremely serious risk of a political vacuum . . . it is apparent to our members and our trade-union cadres, in large majority, that Mendès-France is the man capable of guaranteeing the workers'

99. *Le Peuple*, 15 May–15 June 1968, p. 67.

100. Ibid.

101. Jean Daniel, *Nouvel Observateur*, 3 July 1968; Rioux and Backmann, p. 436; Gorz, *Temps Modernes* (August-September 1968); Labro, p. 183.

rights conquered in the firms in the course of these recent days, to work indispensable structural reforms. . . .[102]

During these brief few days of what looks, in retrospect, like political unreality rare even for the French non-Communist Left, the CGT did what it could to block the Third Force thrust. It called twelve different trade-union demonstrations in favor of the unsettled demands of the strike at different points in Paris at the time of the Charléty meeting. The demonstrations were successful. The next day the CGT began to move more positively, proposing to all groups on the trade-union and political Left a huge demonstration for May 29. Séguy's account of why the CGT proposed this demonstration makes the CGT's motives quite clear. The action was:

— to overcome government and patronal resistance to strike demands
— to open a concrete political perspective
— to allow those who were putting together, behind our back, a political maneuver which they mistakenly believed to be of great importance, to pull back in time.[103]

May 29 was to inform the Third Forcers that they had better move towards a United Front perspective, or else! If the Third Forcers did not repent, the demonstration would go ahead without them. Because the CGT did effectively control the allegiance of vast numbers of workers, the demonstration would prove publicly that the working class was not behind the Third Force initiative. It would also demonstrate publicly that the Left was deeply divided.

May 29 did not turn out to be the unified demonstration the CGT had hoped it might be. UNEF actually answered the CGT's unity letter, but was willing to join the demonstration only if it marched on the Elysée Palace—which was hardly what the CGT had in mind.[104] Other groups did not respond at all. Thus the CGT went ahead and issued a call on its own.[105] The results of the call were impressive indeed, in part because the CGT marshalled all of its resources to make them so—800,000 workers marched on Paris. Since the purpose of the march was political—to demonstrate that workers did not want a Third Force solution, rather a United Front—for the first time in May a CGT-directed action went publicly beyond the domain of strict material demands to call for a "socially progressive and democratic political change," shortened to the slogan *gouvernement populaire.* Two observers (Rioux and Backmann) not overly sympathetic to the CGT, commented on this politicization. "They did it reluctantly, one could feel that: it was a question on the one hand of responding to pressure from the base, on the other hand of not allowing

102. Bauchard and Bruzek, p. 115.
103. Séguy, *Le mai de la CGT*, p. 129.
104. Ibid., p. 131.
105. Ibid., p. 131.

themselves to be 'short-circuited' by allies of the moment who, confronted by the difficulties of the regime, were proposing an alternative."[106] Once again, the CGT had abridged its relative autonomy posture momentarily, although this time less dramatically than on the morning after Grenelle. In an atmosphere in which its main union ally, the CFDT, had already spoken out in favor of a Third Force political option, the CGT simply mobilized its base in favor of a United Front solution.

By May 30 a unique situation prevailed. The regime, since the General's *à côté de la plaque* speech and the failure of Grenelle to end the strike, seemed to hang by the thinnest of threads. In this atmosphere, it was inevitable that the strike would harden, since both strikers and their employers were waiting to see how the political situation would break. The Left responded to this in characteristic fashion. Non-Communist forces, attempting to capitalize on the revolutionary rhetoric of the student revolt, plus its anti-Communism, staked an early claim to the succession. The fatal flaw in its approach was its avid Third Forcism. The idea that seizing the initiative first would force the PCF to follow without having been granted even the minimal conditions which it desired (a Common Program or enough of one to save face) was illusory. The PCF had no choice but to try to block the Third Force move and, in desperation, oblige its promoters to shift back towards a United Front approach.[107] Thus, momentarily, the CGT brought out its troops in favor of a *gouvernement populaire*. The perception by many of an open-ended political crisis cut in other directions, of course. What had been seen as a fanciful student revolt which had the virtue of perplexing General de Gaulle, and an ordinary, if extremely large, strike, suddenly began to look quite dangerous to important segments of the French population. The students' rhetoric seemed unrealistic, and therefore not terribly serious, until it began to be aped by established politicians of the non-Communist Left. And the mobilization of PCF and CGT for a *gouvernement populaire* was not reassuring. Between May 26 and May 30 a "Great Fear" developed in France. However unjustifiable it was, given the facts, the Communist Party was set up, primarily by politicians of the Right, as the evil promoters of it all.

Conclusions: the General's Last Return

On the morning of May 29 General de Gaulle mysteriously left Paris, beginning what Pierre Viansson-Ponté later called "one of the most extraordinary poker plays in a career already particularly fertile in surprises." The General told no one, including his Prime Minister, where he was going, or why, except that he would end up at Colombey-les-Deux-Eglises to sleep

106. Rioux and Backmann, p. 605.
107. Viansson-Ponté, *Histoire de la République Gaullienne*, vol. I (1971).

and reflect. In fact, he flew first to Baden-Baden to discuss matters, probably military, with his old colleague General Massu. As the General intended, rumor spread quickly about his imminent retirement. All anyone knew was that he had promised to meet with the government the next day, May 30, and then to address the nation on radio. In retrospect, de Gaulle's drama was a tactical masterpiece. His mysterious trip was designed to coalesce *les peureux* into a party of order which he then could control. The main device for asserting control was to be his May 30 speech.

The speech was a coup, perhaps the General's last. De Gaulle was not quitting. The referendum, proposed in his earlier speech was to be cancelled. The National Assembly was to be dissolved and legislative elections held in June unless, the General added (referring to a "they" who could be none other than French Communists),

> they intend to frustrate the entire French people by preventing it from expressing itself at the same time as they prevent it from living, by the same methods that they prevent the students from studying, the teachers from teaching, the workers from working. These methods are intimidation, intoxication and tyranny exercised by strong armed organized groups and led by a party which is a totalitarian enterprise, even if it already has rivals in this respect.[108]

Next came the threat of repression. If, the General went on, this "situation of force" continued, "I will be obliged, in order to maintain the Republic, to take, in conformity with the Constitution, other courses than immediate consultation with the people by elections," in other words, the invocation of Article 16, which allowed the President to assume full power in an emergency. Finally, the General urged the French to organize "civic action" to aid the government (something which the Gaullists, who had a quasi-permanent "civic-action" arm, had already begun to do). "France . . . is menaced by dictatorship. They desire to force her to resign herself to a power imposed in national despair, a power which will essentially be that of . . . totalitarian Communism."

Behind all of this was political common sense contributed, in part, by Prime Minister Pompidou in last-minute talks with the General. The crisis had strained the nerves of the French population. More important, the Left was divided. Pompidou and the General judged, quite correctly, that the Left was in no position to present a credible alternative to the regime, therefore the regime had an opening to exploit. The General knew what the non-Communist Left, in its crisis-generated euphoria, did not know, that the PCF would not allow itself to be squeezed into the role of a political support group for non-Communist politicians. The PCF therefore needed ways to teach such politicians that United Frontism was the only strategic

108. *L'Humanité*, 30 May 1968; the entire speech is reproduced in *Le Peuple*, 15 May–15 June 1968, pp. 74–75.

path for the French Left. The regime needed a way out of the crisis. On and after May 30, these goals were complementary. Thus the General was gambling on the PCF and CGT to bail him out. The threat of repression (which could only be directed at significant organizations, thus the CGT, first of all) plus the election call both went in the same direction. The PCF, desperate to prove its republican loyalties, would be certain to shift immediately to an electoral mode. Moreover the CGT would be obliged to wind down the strike prior to the elections, since any militant strike promotion during the electoral period would provide evidence against the PCF's and CGT's republican claims for the Right to exploit. Finally, the General's crude equation of the PCF and *gauchisme*, which the politically sophisticated in France (and this included the General) knew to be complete nonsense, was meant in part to reinforce the PCF's already strong desire to isolate and smash student and other *gauchiste* groups. Thus during the pre-electoral period, the General hoped to count not only on the CGT ending the strike, but also on the PCF and CGT setting out, no holds barred, to beat down the *gauchistes*.

The General's judgements proved sound. Almost immediately after May 30, the CGT began the process of squeezing down the strike.[109] On May 31, Georges Séguy announced to the press that "in order to remove any uncertainty about the objectives which it is pursuing, the CGT declares that it has no intention of interfering with electoral consultation in any way. It is in the interest of the workers to be able to express their desire for change in the context of elections."[110]

CGT efforts to end the strike by national collective agreements, industry-by-industry, proved most successful in the public sector.[111] Here both the government and the CGT wanted a normal situation as quickly as possible, and government was willing to make concessions for this end. Both sides knew that the French, when confronted with the return of regular public services, would conclude that the crisis was over. Where the government sensed weakness in strikes, on the railroads for example, it took a harder line, but still ultimately gave substantial concessions.

When the return of public-sector workers was added to the return of those who had earlier accepted the Grenelle accord, the back of the strike, and the crisis, was broken. Renewed public services brought renewed goods and services for the French. The renewed availability of gasoline provided weekends in the countryside as a substitute for seizing power. Some sectors of the economy remained on strike, however, and the shifting situation altered the balance of forces in such areas, particularly in the metals, building, chemicals and rubber industries. Here, in just those sectors with

109. Lefranc, *1944–1968*, p. 242; Rioux and Backmann, p. 507.
110. Séguy, in *Le Peuple*, 15 May–15 June 1968, p. 121.
111. *Le Figaro*, 1 June 1968; Rioux and Backmann, p. 55.

the most militantly anti-union traditions, employers, who, at the height of the crisis, had been forced to accept untold indignities at the hands of their workers, began to fight back. Ending the strike with honor in such areas posed some problems for the CGT. Hardline employers resorted to old techniques (secret ballots of strikers held against union wishes, bringing in police to "protect the liberty to work," and so on).The strike at Citroën was ended in typical Citroën fashion, by a phony election called by the management followed by repression. Troops and "yellow" technicians were used by the government to end the ORTF strike in Paris as well (control over the media in a pre-electoral period being much more important to the regime than the civilities of ordinary negotiation—later almost all of those prominent in the ORTF strike were purged from their jobs). At Renault-Flins, where strikers had voted down Grenelle, the management refused any new concessions and tried the secret ballot method to get work started again. When the unions successfully blocked this, the management brought in 1000 CRS to evacuate the plant on June 5–6, in the name of "the right to work." The uncertainty of the situation provided an opening for *gauchistes* from Paris, led by Alain Geismar of SNE(sup) who arrived to "help the workers' struggle" and encourage the re-occupation of the plant, which the workers eventually did.[112] The coming of the students gave the CRS an excuse to give battle on the *gauchistes*, leading to a guerrilla conflict in the villages and fields around Flins in which one student was killed.

By early June the *gauchistes* had become what PCF and CGT had always called them, *provocateurs*. Their only hope as the situation changed was to undermine traditional working-class organizations and their strike-ending goals in order to re-launch the strike. Their strategy thereby was to block the elections from occurring and to reopen the crisis. The CGT's response to this was to denounce the *gauchistes* as de facto agents of the government.[113] While this may have been stretching things a bit far, it was now clear that the *gauchistes'* primary goal was to undermine the CGT, thus the CGT could hardly be blamed for taking a resolute stand against them. The entire CGT organization was therefore put on anti-*gauchiste* alert.[114] *Gauchistes* were, however, much easier to isolate from workers than was the CFDT. The CFDT's open Third Force politics in May had reduced communications between the two Confederations to near zero. But conflict between the two organizations over trade-union tactics persisted. The CFDT, in general, was much less willing than the CGT to subordinate the conduct of the strike to the political demands of the electoral campaign.

---

112. *Le Peuple*, p.85; Diverse authors, *La grève à Flins*.

113. Rioux and Backmann, p. 508; *L'Humanité*, 7 June 1968; *Le Peuple*, 15 May–15 June 1968, p. 95.

114. *Le Peuple* 15 May–15 June 1968, pp. 96, 104.

The CFDT also showed much too much sympathy, for the CGT's taste, for student *gauchisme*.[115]

The great strike of May-June 1968 therefore came to an end amid political and trade-union division. The end of the strike, however, did bring the end of the May events themselves. With the return to order after the strike, the government felt confident in cleaning up what remained of the student revolt. On June 13, it even banned several *gauchiste* organizations. To no one's surprise, neither the PCF nor the CGT protested. The strike terminated with unprecedented working-class successes, even if many of the unions' initial goals remained only partially attained. And despite the hardening of the strike after May 30, most strikers who stayed out after Grenelle did succeed in extracting larger concessions from their employers. Politically, the country moved uneasily towards the elections of June 23 and 30. The electoral campaign was most notable for the anti-Communist, anti-Left hysteria fomented by the government and majority. The electoral results—despite a last-minute agreement between the PCF and FGDS to exchange second-round support—were a major defeat for the Left, Communist and non-Communist alike.[116]

In retrospect, the interminable arguments about whether the PCF and CGT had rejected a revolutionary situation in May-June have lost their interest. Only if both party and trade union had moved towards insurrectionary activities would anything approaching a revolutionary situation have come to exist. And it is reasonably clear that had they been imprudent and impolitic enough to have entertained such a strategy, the effect would have been to unite the vast majority of French society against them, thus ending the May events by the isolation and possible destruction of French Communism and militant French trade-unionism. As party and union repeated again and again in their discussions of the Events the necessary unity of the French Left to propose any alternative to Gaullism in May was not present.

The PCF refused to budge one inch from the pursuit of its United Front strategy in May-June. The CGT, except for momentary and costly lapses (after Grenelle, May 29) into direct politics, shaped the strike as a labor mass organization with all of its resources and with its eyes on the dynamics of the labor market. As a trade union, it did try to make its labor-market strategy converge with the political strategy being pursued by the PCF.

115. Ibid., p. 125; an example of this noted by Georges Séguy was an alleged instruction from the CFDT leadership to its base to support non-Communist candidates in the first round of the elections no matter what the local circumstances.

116. The Left lost approximately six percent from the 1967 elections. The PCF won thirty-three seats, as opposed to seventy-three in 1967, the FGDS fifty-seven, as opposed to 118, the PSU lost its three seats. See *Cahiers du Communisme* (November-December 1968); François Goguel, "Les élections législatives des 23 et 30 juin 1968," *La Revue Française de Science Politique* (October 1968).

However, it, too, refused to budge from strategic and other determinations made years prior to May. Were party and union wrong? Not, it seems, in rejecting the revolutionary euphoria which seized French intellectuals during the Events. By maintaining their sang-froid the PCF and CGT may have saved the French labor movement from incalculable disasters. There is no question, of course, but that both the PCF and CGT misunderstood, and this from long years prior to May-June, what was happening to French students and intellectuals. And it is also clear that the CGT, solidly locked into a theoretical perspective on the dynamics of the French labor market which dictated strictly defensive, bread-and-butter unionism in May-June, overlooked the emergence of new kinds of rank-and-file needs in the great strike. But the May-June crisis was an incredibly complex event. Ultimately, the calculus of PCF and CGT had to be political. From the point of view of party and union, the factor lacking in this situation which prevented social crisis from becoming a change in regime was unity on the Left which gave the Communists their due. In the absence of such unity, which both the PCF and the CGT tried desperately to promote, in the heat of the crisis, the choice was between the course followed or the use of party and union resources to help a coalition of non-Communist Left and Center forces to come to power. Moreover, even the promotion of this latter alternative for the CGT would have carried with it the risk through politicization of compromising the possibility of major strike victories for the trade-union rank and file. In any case, both PCF and CGT judged that, in the absence of the kind of Left unity which they desired, it was vastly preferable to allow the regime to stay in power. The regime itself ultimately came to understand the Left's contradictions and was able to buy itself more time.

PART THREE

The CGT and the Rise and Fall of French Eurocommunism

Chapter 8

AFTER MAY

May-June 1968 did not "bring imagination to power in France." It did dramatically change the Fifth Republic, however. In the aftermath of May, General de Gaulle left the scene, never to return. The General's immediate successors subsequently attempted a number of important strategic changes, prompted by many of the issues which exploded in May. May-June brought a decade of stability to an end. After the crisis, France's political and social environment began to shift rapidly. For both the PCF and CGT, however, the events of 1968 were experienced as confirmation of the correctness of strategic directions set out earlier in the 1960s. For the party, May-June provided new incentives to intensify the United Front initiatives which it began long before May, leading it further down the road which we will henceforth call Eurocommunization. The CGT reacted similarly. In the new post-May circumstances, the Confederation remained resolutely dedicated to the relative autonomy posture which we have outlined earlier. Defensive conflict in the labor market around simple material demands was seen as the best way to create a broad front of labor opposition to the regime and *patronat* which, simultaneously, might be articulated with the evident malaise of other groups. If everything went well, such labor opposition would provide the backbone of social mobilization for a new United Front of the political Left. The CGT calculated that its defensive trade-union posture, so evident in the May-June crisis itself, was the best way to broaden and deepen the new rank-and-file militancy which surrounded it, and ultimately render this militancy convertible into political energy. In the immediate post-May period this meant that the CGT had to find ways to channel the more unorthodox forms of working-class protest which had emerged in the crisis period back towards the kind of defensive labor action which it desired. This meant also trying to channel the CFDT, which had become the trade-union champion of such new forms of protest, back into *la bonne voie*, as the CGT saw it. It involved as well trying to convince the

CFDT that working-class protest, in general, ought to be made convertible into support for a new united political front. All of this, it turned out, had to be attempted in a context shaped by new strategic initiatives from the regime desirous, for its own reasons, to reshape the French labor market in ways in which the CGT firmly rejected.

Strategies: the "New Society" and Left Union

As Jean Touchard noted in his lectures on Gaullism, in the decade after 1958 Gaullism-in-power had made a basic and profound choice.[1] General de Gaulle had long been aware, in his own original ways, of the basic flaws in French social relations and institutional life which made the French class conflict more explosive than that of many other capitalist societies. Indeed, in the General's years out of power he had often mused on "third roads" between capitalism and socialism, *participation, l'association capital-travail,* and so on. Yet after 1958 the General and his immediate advisors had chosen to put aside such musings and to concentrate on promoting national independence in foreign policy and rapid economic change, the former depending a great deal on the latter. The Gaullist regime, building on substantial foundations left by the Fourth Republic, had been quite successful in the economic domain. By the use of economic planning and state intervention in market mechanisms, the regime had sought to transform a relatively backward economy oriented towards colonial markets and protected against more aggressive and successful capitalist competitors into an open economy possessed of productive units of the size and structure necessary to confront powerful international rivals. In the process, France joined the ranks of the most advanced capitalist societies and acquired a reputation for economic dynamism, to the point where Gaullist economic policies became an export product in themselves. However, while economic change brought considerable change in social structure, it was achieved without any new attempts to include the working class and its organizations in defining its nature or in anticipating its social consequences. Post-World War II France had never developed the mechanisms of most other advanced capitalist societies for coordination—whether through highly institutionalized collective bargaining or political consultation—between the state, private employers and unions about basic economic options.[2] In essence, from 1947 onwards, workers and their organizations had been excluded from direct influence over the shape of modernization. Gaullism was not responsible for the "labor-excluded" modernization pattern of post-war France. Gaullism in power after 1958,

1. See Jean Touchard, *Le Gaullisme.*
2. The use of the term 'corporatist' in this context, recently resurrected in American political science, owes much to Philippe Schmitter. See Schmitter, "Still the Century of Corporatism," *Review of Politics* (January 1974); also the Schmitter-edited special issue of *Comparative Political Studies* (April 1977), on corporatism in advanced capitalist societies.

however, did nothing to change this pattern. Instead it demonstrated a pronounced preference for quasi-authoritarian methods for confronting class and labor-market issues—indicated clearly by its response to the 1963 Miners' Strike, the *Toutée Grégoire* procedures for public-service wage setting and the 1967 modification of social security by decree. It may be that General de Gaulle allowed himself to be persuaded by the universal myth of the 1950s and 1960s, that the famous expanding economic pie ultimately would solve all outstanding social problems. It is also certain that Gaullism was under considerable pressure from private-sector employers and technocrats, each for their own reasons, not to change relationships between the state, the private sector and labor. In any case, whatever the reasons for the regime's choice of strategy, it had paid a very high price for this choice in May-June 1968.

May-June caused General de Gaulle to return to his musings about *participation*. Ironically, this led to his downfall in the spring 1969 referendum on regionalization and the corporatist reform of the Senate. By 1969 most of the Left and the organized working class did not want *participation* of this kind, nor did it want any more of the General's plebiscitory referenda. It wanted real change. Moreover, parts of the Center and Center-Right, and particularly the hard core of *notables* who populated the Senate and local government did not want *participation* which would remove one of the sources of their power. Faced with such powerful sources of opposition, the General staked his Presidency on the outcome of the referendum. When the voters voted *non*, the General retired for the last time, in April 1969, to Colombey-les-Deux-Eglises.[3]

In the Presidential election which followed the General's abrupt departure, Georges Pompidou easily defeated Senate President Alain Poher, beginning the brief era which journalists came to call *Pompidolisme*. Pompidou did not take long to make clear that he had reached very different conclusions from May-June 1968 from those of General de Gaulle. The premise of their reflection was the same: modernizing economically with little regard for social costs was politically dangerous. Pompidou's conclusions, however, had none of the visionary third road pretensions of de Gaulle's. As the new President stated just after his inauguration, "my motivating idea [is] the transformation of social relations in France. It is unreasonable that in 1969 the relationships between *patrons* and wage earners should be those of endless conflict. We must establish new habits built around the spirit of, and respect for, contracts."[4] The specifics of the

3. In retrospect, it is interesting to note that Valéry Giscard d'Estaing also opposed the General on the referendum. The results were as follows:

| No: 11,943,233 | 53.17 percent of those voting |
| Yes: 10,515,655 | 46.82 percent of those voting |

4. *L'Express*, 9 July 1969.

new approach, promoted by Jacques Chaban-Delmas, Pompidou's first Prime Minister, involved creating in France a network of collective bargaining and contractualism between the state, private capital and organized labor similar to that which already existed in other advanced capitalist societies.[5] The architects of the new strategy (Jacques Delors, Chaban's "social" advisor, and Joseph Fontanet, Minister of Labor) were fully aware that the creation of a genuinely institutionalized network of collective bargaining in France would have to involve employer recognition of unions as socially useful organizations and as *interlocuteurs valables*.[6] It would also have to involve contracts of all kinds from which unions and their rank and file would gain real advantage, not only in terms of wages and hours, but also in increased control over the industrial environment and its evolution. Finally, the new approach had to have, for its success, a labor movement which wanted it to succeed, about which more later.

The new approach—labelled *la Nouvelle Société* by Chaban-Delmas in his September 16, 1969, address to Parliament—had, at its core, a revised approach to public-sector incomes policy, embodied in the so-called *contrats du progrès*. The *contrats du progrès* were designed to correct some of the more egregious faults of the *Toutée-Grégoire* procedures and therefore make contractually-sanctified wage restraint palatable to public-sector unions. To begin with, the *contrats* officially disengaged the government from any direct participation in public-sector negotiations. Instead each branch of the public sector was to be given a general *masse salariale* (a total figure for growth in remuneration) by the government, to be based upon projections both of general economic expansion and of the specific growth of productivity in the branch in question. Using this *masse* as a base, negotiations were to be undertaken directly between administrators of the branch and its unions about the actual allocation of this *masse* over the pluri-annual period to be covered by the contract. In theory these negotiations were to be totally open-ended and might involve, as agreed upon by the bargaining partners, the division of the *masse* between different categories of workers (and thus the wage hierarchy between job classes), and/or other goals such as worker training, shortening the work week, changes in the structure and process of work and so on. In short, unions were to be given new possibilities to intervene, through bargaining, in the

5. It should be noted that one of General de Gaulle's pet ideas, giving workers a token number of shares in the firms where they work—*actionnariat*—was carried out here and there, most spectacularly at Renault. It is clear, however, that this had none of the consequences hoped for by the General, those of dampening class conflict in particular. In fact, unions opposed the scheme, employers were only slightly less hostile, while the workers themselves were indifferent. Even on the level of the government it seemed as if the reform was meant more as a memorial to the General than as a meaningful change.

6. The regime clearly hoped that the post-May 1968 legislation legalizing trade-union presence at firm level would play a role in softening traditional *patronal* attitudes.

structuring of public-sector economic activity. Backing all of this, as befit the economic optimism which prevailed in government circles, was new governmental willingness to guarantee substantial and regular public-sector wage growth. In essence, to soften the pill of state-decreed *masses salariales*, the Chaban government was willing to consider not only a public-sector *échelle mobile* (automatic procedures which would keep wage growth ahead of inflation) but also important absolute wage growth beyond this. There was one catch. The government wanted to include limited anti-strike pledges in the *contrats*. In order to strike, unions would have to go through an incredibly cumbersome process of first renouncing the contract in a legally specified way, and then waiting through a three-month conciliation period before moving to action.[7]

Pedagogy was, in fact, the real core of *la Nouvelle Société*. Public-sector unions were to be brought into contractualism by real concessions in exchange for certain limitations on their traditional freedom of action. The hope was that, in time, such tradeoffs might become habitual, making the unions into newly reliable "social partners." The *contrats du progrès* were not meant to stand alone, either. Rather they were calculated to be the entering wedge of a governmentally induced process to restructure the entire labor market. To the degree to which the *contrats du progrès* generated new collaboration in the public sector, the government hoped that the private-sector *patronat* would take up the cudgel.[8] By 1969 such hopes were not without foundation, since the CNPF had taken a turn of its own towards greater contractualism even before May 1968, moderating somewhat the *patronat*'s traditional divine-right, anti-union perspectives along

7. For a succinct exposé of the *Nouvelle Société*, see Jacques Delors, "La nouvelle société," in *Preuves* (2e trimestre, 1970). The proponents of the "new society" were clearly inspired by some of the ideas of Michel Crozier [later expressed in his post-May book, *La société bloquée* (1970)]. To Crozier, class conflict was only a mask for the real problems of French society. What had really happened was that while France's infrastructure had changed very rapidly in the postwar years, perceptions of France by the French had not changed accordingly. The French therefore misunderstood their social world. The major consequence of such misunderstanding was that the French were ideologically, politically, and socially *backward* in relationship to their own national reality in ways which created serious barriers to further social change. Ultimately, the reasons for this were psychological. The French were *afraid* of change, and therefore clung, anachronistically, to well-tried, older views of the world. In the Delors-Crozier analysis, *economic* problems were easily resolvable. Other things being equal, successful economic expansion was inevitable. *Social* barriers, whose explanation was unrelated to economic life, might frustrate economic success, however. See also Jean Bunel and Paul Meunier, *Chaban-Delmas* (1972).

8. Already in 1967, as Prime Minister, Pompidou had begun pressing towards a new contractualism. At that point he invited the CNPF to consider negotiations with unions about a long list of problems. The CNPF accepted his suggestions on some issues, resulting in a negotiated accord arranging compensation for partial unemployment between the CNPF and unions (including the CGT, welcomed at the negotiating table for the first time since 1947). See Bernard Brizay, *Le patronat* (1975), pp. 125 ff.

the way. The regime's goal in all this was, of course, to institutionalize and regularize relationships between major social partners in the labor market *à l'américaine*. Included in this was also a strong desire to "de-statize" such relationships and thereby to limit the classic and crisis-provoking tendency for protagonists in French industrial conflict to turn immediately to politics for solutions, rather than bargaining amongst themselves.

If the regime was moved to change important aspects of its strategy as a result of the 1968 crisis, the PCF, in contrast, concluded from May-June that its strategy was perfectly appropriate. For French Communism, "after-May" was a question of further pursuing the implementation of the United Front course which had oriented all of its actions in the May crisis of Gaullism and monopoly capitalism in which the absence of unity on the Left had been the only barrier to important Left success. For the PCF, the longer-term causes of the crisis, connected with the growing stranglehold of French monopolies over French society and the consecration of personal power in the political sphere, remained.[9] The party therefore concluded that if it had been unable in May—even with powerful support from the CGT—to persuade the non-Communist Left to negotiate a Common Program, continuing crisis and continuing political polarization after May made ultimate success in its United Front quest quite likely.[10]

It did not take the PCF leadership long after the dust of May had subsided to issue a ringing reaffirmation of the party's strategy, in the important December 1968 *Manifeste du Parti Communiste Français, pour une démocratie avancée, pour une France socialiste*—the *Manifeste de Champigny*.[11] Despite all of its talk about the desirability of a Left Common Pro-

9. See Waldeck Rochet, *Les enseignements de mai-juin* (1968) and *L'avenir du Parti Communiste Français* (1970), ch. 1. See also Georges Marchais' report to the Nineteenth Congress of the PCF in *Cahiers du Communisme* (February-March 1970).

10. Here we must note that the PCF saw all of its actions in May-June 1968 as correct. Yet again there was no official recognition that anything was wrong in the party's dealings with students and intellectuals, despite the fact that the PCF's standing with, and hegemony over, the student / intellectual world had been further damaged by its positions in the crisis. The only dissident voice came from Roger Garaudy, long a *Bureau Politique* member. Garaudy, who stood up and made his disagreements public, had begun a theoretical movement away from the party's line. In his view basic social changes were occurring in and around the "scientific and technical revolution" which made intellectuals of all kinds and the intellectual worker into significant social actors on their own, both in terms of their size as a group and their economic centrality. Garaudy concluded, in Gramscian vocabulary, that what was needed politically was a new "historic bloc" of workers and intellectuals. Party spokesmen accused him of abandoning the PCF's central thesis of the working class as vanguard, an accusation which was not altogether wrong. See Garaudy, *Le grand tournant du socialisme* (1969). Garaudy, whose disagreements with the party grew acute during May, was in fact flirting with ideas similar to those of Serge Mallet in *La nouvelle classe ouvrière*. See also Robert Geerlandt, *Garaudy et Althusser* (1978). Ironically, it was Georges Marchais, whose anti-student excesses in May-June 1968 had been notorious, who emerged as Waldeck's *dauphin*. When Waldeck fell ill in 1969, Marchais became Secretary-General *adjoint*, then Secretary-General in 1972.

11. PCF, *Manifeste du Parti Communiste Français* (*Manifeste de Champigny*) (1969).

gram before 1968, the party had never indicated fully what it thought such a program should look like. The *Manifeste de Champigny*, as the first approximation of such a program, was bound to set the tone and structure of subsequent debate, and thus its contents had more than momentary significance. After a somewhat schematic theoretical introduction which purported to explain why a "large alliance of all social strata" against the "monopoly caste and its power" was possible, the main focus of the *Manifeste* was a programmatic definition of "advanced democracy," that state of affairs which could come to exist with the enactment of a Common Program by a United Left in power. Advanced democracy involved, first and foremost, removing levers of power from the monopoly caste and transferring them to the people. Economically, this would take extensive nationalizations in finance and industry, plus democratic planning which would use existing state resources and the newly expanded public sector to orient economic life towards the goals which the people desired. The new public sector would be "democratically managed," a term which meant, among other things, greatly expanded trade-union power over corporate economic activities. Politically, the *Manifeste* foresaw a series of measures to move France away from personal power back towards parliamentarism (which included proportional representation). Pious commitment to the expansion of civil, political and economic liberties was then voiced. Next, the *Manifeste* proposed a number of foreign-policy options, deliberately vague (with a neutralist tone) in an area where Communist–non-Communist disagreement was largest. Finally, the *Manifeste* asserted that advanced democracy could open the way to a "peaceful French road to socialism." Presumably what this meant was that if a United Front government did what the PCF desired it to do, a transition to socialism would be hastened. Yet what such a peaceful, French transition to socialism would look like, and how it might be worked, were not matters which the *Manifeste* helped to elucidate.[12]

The PCF did not have to wait long to demonstrate the firmness of its strategic commitment. In the 1969 Presidential election the non-Communist Left attempted, once again, to promote a Third Force outcome. Gaston Defferre was first in the lists as a Socialist candidate (as he had been in 1963–1964). This time, however, the Socialist apparatus and Guy Mollet supported Defferre (François Mitterrand having fallen out with the Socialists and the FGDS having fallen apart as a result of May-June

12. Likewise, the proclamation of the *Manifeste* meant to reassure potential allies, that French socialism could be built and maintained in a multi-party regime which would guarantee full political and social rights to all who obeyed the law, was foggy in the extreme. Everything depended upon what the PCF thought socialism would be. And in 1968 the PCF still clearly regarded the USSR and the Eastern European popular democracies (which, after all, had started their painful histories as "multi-party regimes") as socialist. Moreover, the party was still committed to a "dictatorship of the proletariat," even if multi-party, as necessary for the socialist stage of development.

1968). It seems clear that the Socialist leadership had judged that a United Left candidate could not win and that it would be better, in such circumstances, to allow Alain Poher (the Centralist Senate President who had acted as President in the interim period after de Gaulle's resignation) to confront Pompidou. The PCF was unwilling to go along either with Defferre or with the deeper sense of the Socialists' action. Rather quickly after May-June 1968 the PCF felt obliged to teach its familiar lesson to the Socialists yet again—*rien contre les Communistes, rien sans les Communistes*. To do so, the party decided to nominate its own candidate, none other than the venerable Jacques Duclos. Duclos turned out to be a formidable campaigner, and the tactic worked even better than expected. Duclos came close to Poher in the first round (21.5 percent vs 24 percent) while Defferre could do no better than five percent. For the runoff, the party, after its notable claim that Poher vs Pompidou amounted to *bonnet blanc vs blanc bonnet*, urged abstention. Sure enough, the figure for abstentions was unusually high (30.9 percent).[13] The Socialists could hardly avoid the implications of this. Whatever the (large) inner reservations of Socialist leaders, the Socialists very soon thereafter began their long voyage towards a Left Common Program.

The PCF had long realized that it had to change important aspects of its presentation of self to hasten the conclusion of Left Unity. Up to 1968 such steps had involved concessions to the ideals of democratic pluralism in the future "peaceful French road to socialism." By condemning the Soviet invasion of Czechoslovakia in August 1968, the party began to move in a qualitatively different direction. Not only did it publicly break its unblemished record of solidarity with Soviet foreign policy but for the first time it also criticized the Soviet Union (to the point where Jeannette Vermeersch, widow of Maurice Thorez and a fervent defender of old orthodoxies, broke with the rest of the *Bureau Politique*). In time it became clear that the party's gesture was more limited than, at first, it had seemed, as the PCF leadership supported the subsequent "normalization" of the Prague regime, even playing an important role in the international Communist movement—at the Moscow Conference in June, 1969—in persuading its European colleagues to admit that this normalization was an internal Czech affair (despite the well-known fact that normalization was carried out from the Soviet Embassy in Prague with a huge apparatus of Soviet administrators backed by Warsaw Pact troops).[14] However ambiguous the gesture was, it nonetheless was an important new departure for the PCF towards reconsideration of the Soviet Union and the Soviet model.

13. Interestingly enough, the CGT declined to support any candidates officially in the first round.

14. See Roger Garaudy, *Toute la vérité* (1972); Garaudy's insistence on denouncing the role which Georges Marchais had played in all of this was the straw which broke the camel's back. He was allowed his say, in a totally glacial atmosphere, at the PCF's Nineteenth Congress in 1970, then removed from the *Bureau Politique*. This was the last major PCF purge.

The CGT: 1968–1972, the Aftermath of May

The central slogan of the 1969 CGT Congress, *Pour un Syndicalisme de Masse et de Classe*, indicated that the CGT, as well as the PCF, intended to continue after May along the same lines as it had before. The Confederation had many reasons to be satisfied about the results of May-June. The great 1968 strike had won a major victory for unions and workers. Moreover the CGT had been the central factor in May, and it had taught the non-Communist Left the critical lesson of the need for Left political unity around a Common Program.[15] If the Confederation faced a very annoying upsurge in *gauchisme* in and after May-June (an upsurge which the CFDT seemed to find unobjectionable), it also benefited from a substantial membership increase (400,000 +) after the crisis.[16] In short, nothing in the May-June 1968 events led the CGT to reconsider its basic strategy of relative autonomy and mass-and-class labor-market action. Nonetheless, May-June 1968 had modified the context within which the CGT was to act. First of all, the government's *Nouvelle Société* offensive, directed, as it was, to the creation of new patterns of class collaboration in the labor market, was a direct provocation to the Confederation. If the CGT's mass action perspectives were directed towards forming a broad social alliance of protest which, on occasion, gave CGT activity a moderate allure, the CGT was also determined to crystallize class consciousness among the workers and others it tried to reach. The regime's new strategy was aimed at breaking down those very boundaries around the working class which the CGT was determined to deepen and perpetuate. On quite another level, the CFDT, with whom unity-in-action had been suspended as a result of profound disagreements in May-June, seemed determined to advance its own trade-union fortunes by promoting hyper-militant local struggles which flew in the face of the CGT's basic mass action criteria and which, moreover, were clearly aimed at undermining CGT power in the labor movement. The CGT, therefore, had to concern itself with the CFDT's "deviations" not only to stop them, but also, if possible, to regenerate CGT-CFDT unity-in-action on the basis of the CGT's mass-and-class action desiderata. This latter task had become all the more urgent given the PCF's sense that Left unity and the long-awaited Common Program were not far off in the future. Without unity-in-action between the CGT and CFDT it would be immeasurably more difficult to promote the mass working-class mobilization of protest needed to provide the social underpinnings of Left unity.

15. See Georges Séguy, *Le mai de la CGT*.
16. Figures for the CGT membership, given at CGT Congresses, are as follows:

1961	1,602,322
1963	1,722,294
1965	1,939,318
1967	1,942,523
1969	2,301,543

Underlying the CGT's option for strategic continuity at this point was a momentous decision. Events leading up to May-June and May-June itself indicated an important intensification of labor-market conflict in France, moreover one which seemed likely to continue into the near future. Workers were noticeably more militant, unions, including the CGT, were reinforced by an influx of new members and supporters, and the capacities of the labor movement as a whole to act on its environment grew.[17] By choosing strategic continuity, the CGT decided to use its influence to shape this new militancy in tried-and-true ways. Its labor-market goals, unchanged by May-June, were to promote defensive, bread-and-butter union action which would, in theory, unify the broadest possible spectrum of workers and others in opposition to the regime and *patronat*. The ultimate purpose of this, beyond the obvious one of maintaining and, if possible, improving working-class living standards, was to help in creating a mass oppositional front which might be translatable into Left political unity and success. As we have noted time and again, relative autonomy for the CGT was not neutrality in politics. However, the new militancy brought with it certain new rank-and-file concerns about authority in the workplace and the making of basic economic decisions. In the context of such new concerns, the CGT's option meant the exclusion of other possible courses. In particular, the incidence of new rank-and-file demands, plus the increase in union influence might have been turned towards expanding union and rank-and-file power in the workplace itself and towards opening up and democratizing union organizations. In a very different situation, to be sure, the Italian labor movement, led by the CGT's Italian counterpart, the CGIL, chose this course as a response to the Italian "hot autumn" and its aftermath.[18] For the CGT such a course would have meant taking new steps towards greater autonomy from the PCF and politics. In vague and inchoate ways, this was what the CFDT was urging. Given the CGT's ties to the PCF and, more important, given that both party and union analyzed the post-May situation as politically propitious in dramatically new ways, the Confederation's commitment to a labor-market posture congruent with the PCF's United Front plans was reinforced, rather than changed, by May-June. From its behavior in May-June the CGT had acquired major new increments of power and influence, which might, theoretically, have been used to adjust, or even reorient, the Confederation's relationship to the party. In fact, the existing relationship emerged from May-June more solidified. Because of this, it followed that the CGT would attempt, ultimately, to channel the new mobilizational energy revealed in May towards politics, rather than

17. See also on the international nature of the labor-market mobilization of the 1960s and early 1970s, Colin Crouch and Alessandro Pizzorno, eds., *The Resurgence of Class Conflict in Western Europe* (1978), 2 vols.

18. See, on the Italian situation, Georges Couffignal, *Les syndicats italiens et la politique* (1979).

towards changed union practices. In the longer run, this choice was to have its costs.

Campaigning Against the "New Society"

Contractualism *à l'américaine* required, in France, in addition to a willing *patronat* and state, trade unions who would separate their goals of basic social change from their daily behavior as loyal social partners. The Chaban government was not naive enough to believe that the CGT would go this far. The government's choice of the public sector as an entering wedge for contractualism was not only dictated by necessity, but also by strategy. If the CGT had large union power in the private sector, it was far from hegemonic in the public sector, especially among civil servants where it was, in fact, quite weak (it was stronger, however, in the service-industry area of the public sector, particularly at *Electricité et Gaz de France*, on the railroads, in the coal mines and in the PTT). Thus, if it played its cards properly, the government could hope for success if it negotiated *contrats du progrès* primarily with the more moderate unions present in the public sector, *Force Ouvrière* and the FEN, for example, plus the rump CFTC, and perhaps even the CFDT. With very real bargaining concessions to offer such unions, the government might get enough union signatures on its contract proposals to carry out its program despite CGT opposition. Its tactics, therefore, were to attempt to isolate the refractory CGT in opposition, negotiate *contrats du progrès* conferring real benefits on public-sector workers with "softer" unions, and hope that favorable terms of the contracts would ultimately sap rank-and-file CGT support for opposition. If all of this worked, the CGT might find itself obliged to choose between a serious loss of rank-and-file support in the public sector or capitulation to the new contractualism.

The stage was set, therefore, for a serious confrontation between the CGT and the *Nouvelle Société*. The CGT was not against contracts and negotiations, per se, of course. No successful trade-union organization could oppose such things. But, as we have noted before, the CGT viewed contracts as short-term treaties between implacable class enemies, treaties which momentarily consecrated working-class victories which might be renounced at any future point either when new issues arose or when working-class forces had gathered new strength. The government's contractualism and the CGT notion of negotiation were on a collision course, then. The government desired precisely to restructure the French labor market in ways which would eliminate union perspectives on contractualism such as those held by the CGT. To the CGT, this desire presented a basic threat to its self-understanding as a mass-and-class organization and to its fundamental class-forming and maintaining goals.

The Chaban government moved full steam ahead, and with a great fanfare of publicity, to implement the *contrats du progrès* program in the fall of 1969. It was wise enough to begin its campaign with a contract carefully negotiated far away from CGT mobilizing power, among lower-level civil servants (which was a category including teachers, and thus involved large numbers of people). All union Federations excepting the CGT accepted the accord and signed it, strike-limiting clauses and all, without problem. The government's next move was in *Electricité de France*, however, and here conditions were very different. In EDF long-standing rank-and-file discontent and CGT power coincided, making it the logical place for the first real battle over contractualism. Thus in mid-November 1969, as the *contrat du progrès* was first being discussed, the CGT promoted an unusually sharp movement among EDF workers, two days of work stoppages which seriously cut electricity supplies, with all of the disruption which this involved (in the process obliging the CFDT EDF Federation to act much more militantly than it desired). The government responded in kind, sending in legions of police to open generating stations and accusing the CGT of promoting "subversion by any and all means." The Paris metro was shut down, causing immense traffic jams, while the loss of current shut down businesses and caused loss of domestic heating. Public discomfort was such, on two very cold November days, that the CGT Federation was obliged to stop the strike earlier than expected, but the general conflict was engaged nonetheless. The government responded by negotiating a three-year *contrat* with EDF which all EDF unions, except the CGT, signed. The CGT did not disarm, however. In January 1970 it took the unprecedented step of calling its own referendum of EDF workers about the accord while pouring all of its EDF resources into the referendum preparation. Sixty percent of EDF workers voted in the referendum, while fifty-four percent of those voting opposed the contract.

The new contractualism then became a war of attrition between the government and the CGT. In other areas where its strength allowed—the SNCF, the Paris metro, the mines and the PTT—the CGT pulled out all stops to frustrate the *contrats du progrès*. The government soldiered onwards, nonetheless, comforted by the thought that as long as the CGT campaigned alone, governmental policies stood a good chance of success. For a time, in fact, the CFDT did not side with the CGT—indeed, as Jacques Delors was fond of pointing out, the idea of the *contrats du progrès* was first suggested by the CFDT in the earlier 1960s. Eventually, however, the CFDT slid towards the CGT's position. In a context in which CGT-CFDT unity-in-action began to renew itself (although the two Confederations continued to have quite spectacular public disagreement, their limited unity pact was updated in December 1970) the government's position was weakened. By late 1971, the *Nouvelle Société* was losing some of its larger pretensions. No-strike clauses in the *contrats du progrès* were quietly disappearing. The multi-year aspect of the *contrats* was progressively toned down to the point where de facto annual negotiations became the rule.

Then the notion of the governmentally-decreed *masse salariale* came under attack. Here what happened was that as public-sector negotiating periods approached, CGT-CFDT strikes and strike threats occurred in order to force the hands of government in setting the global figure for remuneration growth closer to that desired by the two Confederations. In effect, this amounted to a regular process of pre-negotiation by protest and response which called the original conception of *masse salariale* into question. Finally, in the spring of 1972 the Chaban government was forced to resign, largely because of opposition to it from more conservative sectors of the majority. With its departure the reformist sense of mission behind the new contractualism left as well. The forms of contractualism were to be carried on, as we will see. But the grandiose plans which motivated the introduction of the *Nouvelle Société* were abandoned.

Unity-in-Action and Shaping the Labor Market— the Belle Epoque of the CFDT

Promoting the kind of mass-and-class labor protest which it desired through unity-in-action with the CFDT was perhaps the most important pillar of CGT strategy, after as before May-June 1968. Here, as we have already seen, the CGT had to face endemic tactical differences with the CFDT. In the years before 1968, while the CGT was turning towards mass-and-class activities to unify the labor movement, the CFDT found itself drawn to exactly those kinds of union actions which the CGT disliked most. This divergence in tactical views was true primarily because the CFDT was relatively weak both in membership and sectoral implantation compared to the CGT, facts which led the CFDT towards efforts in those areas and types of struggle which the CGT, given its strategic goals, tended to neglect. Beyond this the decentralized internal structure of the CFDT, which existed partly by design, partly because the CFDT was a young organization engaged in new organization building, lent itself to the kinds of parochial local struggles which the CGT tried to transform into mass actions. In any case, the CFDT's resolute promotion of hyper-militant local actions and its openness to new rank-and-file demands annoyed the CGT prior to May-June and exasperated it during the 1968 crisis. Moreover, the CFDT's enthusiastic support of the student movement and its tolerance towards *gauchisme* in May-June, plus its participation in the Charléty Third Force operation in May, had led to a virtual cessation of communications between the two Confederations in and after the crisis.[19]

The years immediately following May-June brought no quick resolution to outstanding CGT-CFDT differences. To the CGT, local union action

19. Thirty-seventh Congress of the CGT, Vitry-sur-Seine, November 1969, *compte rendu in extenso*, Document d'orientation, pp. 463 ff.

was to have a mass orientation, and thus be comprehensible to non-involved workers and sympathizers. This meant insistence upon classic strike methods, peaceful and orderly work stoppages, disciplined picketing and so on. It involved opposition to illegality and violence—against property and persons, especially machines and bosses—to sabotage and to minority *grèves bouchons* (actions in which a small number of critically placed workers tied up production and forced large numbers of otherwise uninvolved workers to quit working). It also meant confining strike demands to defensive questions of wages, hours, and working conditions, while avoiding narrow local issues and high philosophy about the quality of work and workers' control. In situations in which strikes could be generalized from local movements to broader constituencies (which, of course, the CGT was delighted to do, providing its criteria for methods and demands were met), the CGT pressed for negotiations at the highest possible level—talks with a peak employers' association, with the CNPF, or with the government itself. To the CGT the more powerful and visible strikers' adversaries were, the more a confrontation would be useful for mobilizing other labor actions.

Conducting actions once they were possible was one thing. Cultivating a rank-and-file climate which would make actions more likely was another. Here, too, the CGT had firm ideas about how to proceed which the CFDT did not share. The keystone of CGT policy in this area was the *journée d'action*, at branch, sector or even national levels. The *journée*, which involved elaborate advance preparations for one day of striking and demonstrating, would, when promoted regularly and efficiently, prime continuous agitation at the union base, or so the CGT thought. Beyond this, however, the *journée* tactic had a (not-so-) hidden agenda. Given the nature of the *journée* exercise, slogans and demands would ordinarily be pitched at a high level of generality, often containing a political message of some kind, either direct (against government policies) or indirect (calling for the formation and strengthening of an anti-monopoly alliance). Thus the CGT intended the *journée* tactic to face in two directions at once—towards the working–class rank and file, for the purposes of mobilization, and towards non-working–class groups with incipient or actual grievances against the status quo who might be encouraged to more active opposition by the spectacle of a strong working class speaking its piece clearly in public.

For the CGT such considerations were not abstract statements of principle. They were the goals of trade-union unity-in-action, indeed of trade-union action *tout court*. The CGT desired, therefore to convert the CFDT (and as much as possible of the rest of French organized labor) to such goals. In this area, the immediate post-May 1968 years did not bring great success. Indeed, it seemed as if the CFDT, as it moved leftwards both in union and political terms—in large part impelled by the effects of earlier unified action with the CGT—became even more determined to develop action perspectives distinctive from, and contrary to, those of the CGT. In fact, it took over two years before the dust of May-June settled enough for the two Confederations to agree, even formally, to relaunch unified action. When agreement came, in December 1970, it involved simply a list of common priorities for union demands, saying nothing about how the two Confederations might achieve their common goals.[20] And it quickly became evident that the CGT and CFDT profoundly disagreed about how to struggle to achieve their first joint priority—wages and working-class power. The CFDT had adopted quite a radical stance on wage bargaining which aimed at the reduction in wage hierarchies between different job classifications,[21] a position which ultimately led Georges Séguy to lash out at the CFDT for its "dangerous theories . . . which suggest to ordinary workers that engineers, *cadres* and technicians are class enemies. . . ."[22] Beyond all this, however, the CFDT systematically slighted the CGT's most cherished unity tactic, the *journée d'action*. The CFDT had long felt that *journées* were not very good ways to cultivate rank-and-file militancy, being ritual occurrences which, by using up substantial amounts of union energy, tended to become substitutes for real struggles. In addition, the CFDT knew full well that the CGT saw *journées* with double vision as both union actions and quasi-political mobilizations. The CFDT wanted no part of such political activities. In the 1968–1972 period, then, the CFDT consistently refused to play the *journée* game.

20. The general areas of priority, in the order listed, were:

1. Wages and buying power—the *SMIC, échelle mobile*.
2. Reduce retirement ages and raise pensions.
3. Creation of monthly hour for trade-union meetings in firm.
4. Reducing length of the work week.
5. Employment security.

Working conditions, mainly those of assembly-line work, were added in 1971. By this point both unions and the CPNF had begun to worry about what appeared to be a revolt of "OS," semi-skilled factory operatives.

21. The "hierarchy" issue, which was, by necessity, at the core of any union campaign to negotiate wage raises, divided the two Confederations into the mid-1970s. The CFDT's position was that union wage campaigns should have, as one major goal, the diminution of hierarchical differentiations between job categories. It thus advocated that negotiated wage raises should be uniform amounts across the board—everyone, regardless of job classification, receiving the same amount. This, of course, would have had the effect of raising lower salaries faster than higher, and of thus flattening out differences between the salaries of different job ratings. The CGT was much less egalitarian on this issue, advocating instead uniform percentage wage increases which would leave the hierarchy intact. Here see Claude Durand et al., *La grève* (1975), pp. 334 ff. Also *CFDT Aujourd-hui* (January-February 1976), "Les rapports CFDT-CGT" ; and *Syndicalisme-Hebdo* (CFDT) (September 1970), "Remettre en cause la hiérarchie."

22. Georges Séguy, Thirty-eighth CGT Congress, *compte rendu in extenso*, 1972, p. 16. It should be noted that on this question the CGT eventually changed *its* position.

Differences between the two Confederations were most acute on the level of local action, however. The pattern of industrial conflict in the immediate aftermath of May (up until the *Lip* strike of 1973) resembled that of the months immediately preceding the May crisis. There were lots of strikes, especially in 1971 and 1972, on the firm level which, because of the issues which prompted them and the ways in which they unfolded, tended to remain local, without generalization.[23] Most were traditional wage-and-hours movements which, because of the relative lack of effective trade-union unity-in-action at higher levels, were played out where they began. However a certain number of them occurred in regions or industries threatened by decline or shifts in market structures, and/or among job holders who were relatively underorganized by unions and relatively more oppressed in their work—women, immigrant workers and OS (*ouvriers spécialisés*, the lowest official job classification in industry). Moreover, many of these movements posed new grievances of an *autogestionnaire* type, about firm-level economic decision-making, authority in the plant, the quality of work, the effects of economic decisions on the structures of local communities, and so on. On top of this, there was a strong tendency on the part of *patrons* involved to react with intransigence to such movements and even, on occasion, with repressive measures, lockouts in particular. In such an environment, in which memories of May were fresh, some local movements turned extremely militant, resorting to illegal and sometimes violent strike tactics—sit-down strikes sometimes accompanied by the *séquestration* of bosses. Incidents of industrial sabotage occurred here and there as well.

Where local actions went beyond the boundaries of mass-and-class propriety, the CGT disavowed them or tried to channel them back towards more acceptable practices. It was also clear that the CGT was reluctant to get too involved in the "revolt of the marginals" (women and immigrants), such movements being easily isolatable and manipulable by labor's opponents.[24] In general, prudence and decorum were serious concerns for the CGT. In contrast, the CFDT saw such movements, including the more unorthodox among them, as new opportunities to make its mark. Often, then, it seized upon such actions and pushed them to their limits of local hypermilitancy. And it resolutely refused to filter out new rank-and-file concerns about qualitative issues. In a whole series of highly-publicized, quite long and often quite extreme local strikes the CFDT came to the fore, condoning and even advocating tactics and demands which ran directly counter to CGT mass criteria. Here, to list only a few such strikes, the CFDT was prominent in the long OS strike at Renault-le Mans in 1971,

---

23. Here one should consult Durand, *La grève*, which is a detailed survey of a number of strikes in 1971 (which was the largest strike year, excepting 1968, in a decade).
24. Ibid.

Pennaroya, les Nouvelles Galeries de Thionville and le Joint Français in St. Brieuc in 1972 and, of course, Lip in 1973.[25] In time, and much to the CGT's annoyance, the CFDT acquired intense media attention and a new reputation for being the most militant wing of French organized labor.[26] More important than this, disagreements between the CGT and CFDT became ever more open and profound.

By 1972 (ironically, the year when *Union de la Gauche* was finally worked out) it looked as if a new pluralism had been solidified in the opposed labor-market perspectives of the CGT and CFDT. Edmond Maire, the soon-to-be Secretary General of the CFDT, could well assert in 1970, that "unity-in-action is inevitable from now on," but, in fact, conflict over labor-market strategies and tactics predominated in the relationships between the two Confederations. Unity was not absent, especially on the level of certain Federations, but it had few of the dynamics leading to strategic rapprochement—on the CGT's terms to be sure—which the CGT desired. As the CFDT changed it moved away from the mass-and-class perspectives which the CGT advocated. And to the degree to which the CFDT refused to cooperate in CGT-style tactics—*journées d'action*, attempts to focus local conflicts outward towards the rest of the working class and upwards towards higher level negotiations—such tactics became difficult to implement. In labor-market terms then, "after May" was quite painful for the CGT. At a moment when, for both trade-union and political reasons, the CGT wanted unified action on its terms rather strongly, its relationship with the CFDT made this impossible.

The CGT and Open Politics: Producing Mass Support for Left Union

By 1968, as we have seen, the CGT's relative-autonomy posture had become well adjusted to the PCF's United Front offensive. The CGT, as a mass organization, chose its strategic option from observations of circumstances prevailing in the labor market and at the trade-union base. Then, from the several possible courses which the Confederation could extrapolate from such observation, it chose those which would best advance the PCF's political goals. Throughout most of the 1960s this did not involve much direct politicization of CGT action. The CGT's calculation was simple: mass, public and continuous defensive labor mobilization against the *patronat* and the regime was the most important thing which the CGT

---

25. *L'année politique et sociale*, 1972, p. 144. From the early 1970s the "social" section of *L'année politique* was edited by René Mouriaux, perhaps *the* outstanding authority on French unions. Thus far from being a dry work of reference, it is an indispensable source of information and interpretation. See Durand, *La grève*, p. 236 ff; also Jacques Capdevielle, et al., *La grève au Joint Français* (1975); Danielle Kergoat, *Bulledor* (1975). See also *Syndicalisme-Hebdo* (CFDT), "Action syndicale et légalité" (September 1972).

26. The differences between the Confederations were less questions of relative militancy than of tactical appreciation.

could produce, both for its supporters as workers and for the political chance of the Left. On the other hand, the CGT, relative autonomy or not, never abandoned a degree of *direct* political activity although it rarely, if ever, engaged in direct politics in the old transmission-belt ways which the relative-autonomy posture had replaced. The CGT's self-definition as a mass-and-class organization left room for some politics. In the mass, the French working class was politically diverse, at least in terms of partisan identification. As a class, however, French workers had common interests which included certain broad political outcomes and excluded others. As long, therefore, as the CGT refrained from direct partisan political activities and stuck, more discreetly, to speaking for general working-class interests, as it perceived them, it felt that its political expressions were legitimate. It should be said, of course, that this general posture was not invented by the modern CGT, but had origins stretching back into the nineteenth century.

In any case, by the mid-1960s the CGT had made its own class political positions crystal clear. *Union de la Gauche*, consecrated by a Common Program signed by major Left parties, was in the broad interests of French workers. Prior to May 1968, the Confederation had repeatedly urged the political Left to sit down and negotiate a Common Program and its insistence on such negotiations in the heat of the May-June crisis was to change only in the direction of greater insistence. Already, at its 1967 Congress, the CGT had discussed, in ways which replicated the PCF's rhetoric embarrassingly closely, the need for a "true democracy, against domination by the monopolies," together with the need for "democratic nationalization" of the principal *secteurs-clés* of the economy.[27] Nationalizations had reappeared in CGT programs in 1963, in fact at its November 1969 Congress, it took further steps (again replicating the PCF in its *Manifeste de Champigny* of a year earlier) by adopting a general program of nationalizations as the "decisive means to realize economic and political democracy." This program not only listed the *secteurs-clés* which the Confederation wanted nationalized, but set out the criteria which it used to decide this list and suggested how new nationalizations should work (*gestion démocratique*).[28] From this point onwards the CGT was not only to

27. CGT Thirty-sixth Congress, Nanterre, June 1967, *compte rendu in extenso*, document d'orientation, p. 419 ff.

28. CGT Thirty-seventh Congress, p. 473 ff. The industries in question were the same as those of 1967: credit, commercial banking, insurance, iron and steel, petroleum, atomic energy, dominant groups in electronics, chemicals and pharmaceuticals, machine tools, aeronautics, aerospace, armaments, automobiles and the merchant marine. The various branches of credit were chosen because the ability to mobilize capital would be critical to an advanced democratic government. The others followed from one, or any, of three criteria:

1. Centrality in economic activity, by size and / or strategic place in the economy;
2. Centrality for the creation of new technologies; and
3. Economic or financial dependence on the state.   *(continued next page)*

urge a Common Program on the political Left but also presented its own program as one major element for the Left to consider in its negotiations. When one reads the *Manifeste de Champigny* and the CGT's nationalization document side-by-side, the logic of the Confederation's action becomes clearer. The CGT document was only directed towards matters where a trade-union confederation could be said to have legitimate interests, primarily in the area of democratizing the economy, whereas the PCF *Manifeste* ranges much wider, but where the two documents address common questions they take almost identical positions. In this general area, then, what the CGT felt to be in the class interests of French workers was virtually the same as what the PCF was urging on the rest of the political Left. Here, then, the CGT was acting as a trade-union complement to the PCF, adding its considerable weight to that of the PCF for a certain kind of Common Program.

While the CGT would urge Left political parties towards unity as often and as insistently as it might, what happened was ultimately only for political parties to decide between themselves. The CGT's option for a Common Program, and for a particular kind of Common Program at that, had another immediate, dimension connected with the Confederation's hopes for trade-union unity-in-action. The CGT's shift on unity-in-action strategy in the early 1960s involved a new willingness to agree on matters where immediate agreement was possible, primarily on labor-market action. Its general unity perspective was more grandiose, however. The Confederation hoped to work outwards, over time, towards broader agreement with its unity partners—in particular the CFDT—on appropriate political goals for the working class. And in this area, along with that of strategy and tactics for labor-market action, the CGT was very busy with the CFDT in the years immediately following May-June 1968. Aside from a thunderous, incessant and rather harsh campaign against *gauchisme* and, more specifically, against the CFDT's real and imagined *faiblesse* for *gauchisme*, the bulk of this activity went towards trying to bring the CFDT around to agree both on the general necessity for a Common Program of the Left and on the desirability of the kind of Common Program advocated by the CGT.[29]

Gestion démocratique was to involve:

    1. Specified relationships between nationalized firms and government (via planning—a democratic plan would be created, in whose elaboration workers would participate, at all levels, through their unions, with the plan being discussed and adopted by parliament);

    2. Relationships on the firm level (involving a tripartite *conseil d'administration*—Government appointed members, trade-union representatives and representatives of consumer groups—which would have ultimate responsibility and appoint direct managers).

29. That the CGT would declare war on *gauchisme* was inevitable after May-June 1968. It solved the problems of *gauchisme* in its own ranks, which had never been severe, by coopta-

Here, from the CGT's point of view, the same irony which marked CFDT labor-market attitudes existed in its politics. Internal CFDT change, plus the momentum of CGT-CFDT unity-in-action and the effects of May-June 1968, strongly pulled the CFDT to the Left, away from the reformism of the CFTC and the early CFDT. But in the political, as well as the trade-union, realm, the CFDT moved Left in ways which distinguished it even more sharply from the CGT, rather than bringing it closer. May-June 1968 consecrated *autogestion* as the CFDT's central conceptualization of social change, without the Confederation being very clear about what *autogestion* involved. The CFDT's political shift was made more obvious at its 1970 Confederal Congress, when the Confederation statutorily committed itself to class struggle and to the ultimate goal of a socialist society.[30] That the CFDT had set out to develop a political perspective to pose against that of the PCF and CGT was clear. More important for the CGT, the *autogestion* model being sketched out by the CFDT was based on a logic very different from that which the CGT foresaw at the core of a Left Common Program. Debate with the CFDT over politics became an urgent task for the CGT, therefore, not only for the general purpose of pulling the CFDT away from *autogestion* (which CGT leaders labelled, rather intolerantly, as anti-Communist), but also for the more immediate purpose of bringing the CFDT around to support of an imminent *Union de la Gauche*. This latter task was by far the most serious. Without minimal CFDT agreement to support a Left Common Program, it was likely that general working-class mobilization behind Union of the Left would be much weaker than it otherwise might be.

CGT-CFDT political debate in the immediate aftermath of May-June 1968 was rather undignified—of the "you-Stalinist-and-betrayer-of-the-hopes-of-May" vs "you-muddle-headed-reformer-agent-of-the-bourgeoisie" type so often characteristic of the French Left. When the smoke from the Events had cleared (after the CGT's 1969 Congress and the CFDT's Congress in 1970) the two Confederations decided to act more sensibly,

---

tion and repression. After May the CGT went out of its way to enroll young, militant workers and then to promote them rapidly to positions of responsibility. This policy, plus the fact that the CGT's strength and influence made it an obvious pole of attraction for the young and militant, limited *gauchisme* within the Confederation. Whatever *gauchisme* remained was dealt with harshly. As a result of all this, genuine *gauchistes* tended to gravitate towards the CFDT. Then the CFDT found itself bombarded with CGT hostility denouncing its softness on *gauchisme*. The problem of *gauchisme* in the labor movement eventually solved itself, however, given the internal incoherence and instability of the *gauchiste* movement. French Maoism continuously split after May. And, when the Cultural Revolution in China wound down to its perplexing halt, with the shifts in Chinese politicies which followed, French Maoism became a failing business. Trotskyism continued to prosper in the French student world, although much less in the labor movement. But, as the seventies moved on, French Trotskyism, in form and content, behaved much like the PCF.

30. Descamps, *Militer*, gives a good description of the Congress' preparation.

however, agreeing, in an unprecedented step, to prepare full statements of their views on social change and socialism for exchange and general discussion. The CGT began, in the spring of 1971, with "Themes for Reflection on the Perspective for French Socialism and the Role of Trade Unions."[31] The CFDT responded with "For Democratic Socialism, a Contribution by the CFDT."[32] There then followed considerable coming and going in various publications until both Confederations rested on their positions at their respective Congresses (CGT, 1972; CFDT, 1973).[33]

The CGT's initial contribution to the great debate contained few surprises. French workers needed socialism, political parties were the ultimate vehicles for defining and working such change, but the CGT, as a mass-and-class organization, had its word to say. Collective ownership, *gestion démocratique*, democratic planning, and extensive political democracy were the core of socialism. To get there a Common Program of the Left was necessary, at whose center would be a number of nationalizations to be enacted when the Left came to power, which it would with the creation of a cross-class anti-monopoly alliance. This first step, if carried out properly, would open the road to socialism. The CFDT, criticizing this document (while judiciously remarking its close relationship to the PCF's *Manifeste de Champigny*) first objected that the CGT seemed much less interested in discussing either capitalism or socialism than in an immediate *Union de la Gauche* and its programs. It then zeroed in on the absolute priority given by the CGT to the transformation of formal property relationships from private to public which, asserted the CFDT, would not be sufficient, in itself, to "suppress alienation, domination and establish new and different social relationships." The main focus of the CFDT's argument was, however, on the insufficiency of the CGT's vision concerning actual change in the relations of production in advanced democracy and socialism. As against the CGT's nationalization goal the CFDT counterposed a model of *autogestion* "in priority" (changing the relations of production), and decentralization (in addition to property over industry), both economic and political. It also questioned the CGT's recognition of the hegemony of political parties in social change and its allusions to the "socialism" which already existed (i.e., the USSR). The CGT's continuing participation in, and defense of, the World Federation of Trade Unions, which was domi-

31. *Le Peuple*, 16–30 April 1971. "Themes" is also reprinted in Henri Krasucki, *Syndicats et socialisme* (1972).

32. *Syndicalisme-Hebdo* (CFDT) (November 1971).

33. See "Nos premières réflexions sur les positions respectives de la CGT et de la CFDT," *Le Peuple*, 15 December 1971; Krasucki's series of eleven articles in *La Vie Ouvrière*, nos. 1430 to 1441 (26 January to 12 April 1972), also in *Syndicats et socialisme* ; "Analyse critique du document CGT," in *Syndicalisme-Hebdo* (CFDT), no. 1366 (4 November 1971). See *Syndicalisme-Hebdo* (CFDT) (15 May 1973), for Maire's report to the CFDT Congress on such questions.

nated by Moscow and assumed, as its main task, the defense of trade-union arrangements as they existed in the Socialist Bloc, could not pass the CFDT unnoticed.

The debate quickly became what the French eloquently call a *dialogue des sourds*. The CFDT profoundly disagreed with the CGT's views. *Autogestion*, democratic planning, and decentralization were the only ways to begin correcting the three primary evils of capitalism—economic exploitation, authoritarian domination and alienation. To the CFDT, when schemes for change did not address all three of these issues simultaneously, any socialism which might result risked being exploitative, authoritarian, and alienating (viz. the Soviet Union). The CFDT's position had immediate implications which connected with its labor-market strategy and tactics. For the CFDT a viable strategy for social change had to be connected directly with trade-union activity. This meant connecting day-to-day working-class struggles to *autogestion* demands, so that workers might begin to take control over their own lives even as they fought with employers in the short run over material demands and sought political change. Thus the CFDT was not prepared to support a *Union de la Gauche* structured around a series of reforms to be enacted at the top, around nationalizations and *gestion démocratique*. Such an approach, if it did promise certain improvements, did not go to the heart of things. As Edmond Maire asserted to the 1973 CFDT Congress, "substituted for the objective of workers' control, the term 'democratization' means above all achieving a greater degree of participation in the running of a system whose deep nature will not be fundamentally changed."[34] A strategy of structural reforms aimed at changes legislated at the level of the national state to be promoted by electoral mobilization simply neglected the level of rank-and-file mobilization for apprenticeship in direct democracy which the CFDT felt to be essential. Without this added dimension of activity, the CGT's program, if enacted, would reinforce statism, probably to the detriment of democracy, or so thought the CFDT.

In return the CGT attacked the CFDT for gravely underplaying the interrelated questions of changing property relationships and political power. Without realistic answers to such questions, workers' control was a "slogan." As Henri Krasucki noted, "in order to manage, in whatever ways, *auto* or not *auto*, one has to have something to manage. For the moment, workers have nothing."[35] Furthermore, the CFDT's *autogestion* perspective dangerously overlooked the vast complexity of advanced industrial societies, which necessitated state coordination and national-level decision-making. Krasucki also noted that the CFDT had no real notions about how to prepare the ground for its proposed form of socialism. According to the

34. Maire, *Syndicalisme-Hebdo* (CFDT) (May 1973), p. 91.
35. Krasucki, *Syndicats et socialisme*, p. 27.

CFDT vision workers would begin building *autogestion* within capitalism and somehow, magically, end up with full *autogestion* in socialism. Yet how all of this could happen, in a society where conditions were far from ripe for socialism, was not addressed by the CFDT. The CGT, through Krasucki, then tried to outline ways in which trade-union independence would be maintained in advanced democracy despite the new administrative and other powers which unions would acquire in *gestion démocratique*. Finally, and in some ways fatally (since it confirmed all of the fears of the CFDT), Krasucki vigorously defended the achievements of "socialist" societies (the USSR in particular) and the ways in which trade unions assumed responsibilities within them.

Trade-Union Difficulties vs Political Successes

In the "after-May" period, then, the CGT's record was mixed. It did play a major role in warding off the spectre of class collaboration presented by the regime's *Nouvelle Société* offensive. Yet the CGT had much greater ambitions than this, most of which were frustrated in the period. Its unity-in-action goals, which were the lynchpin of its post-1963 trade-union identity, were for the most part unachieved. It hoped that from the humble beginnings of agreement with the CFDT on a list of general trade-union concerns in 1966, broader unity—on, or close to, the CGT's own terms—about trade-union labor-market strategy and tactics and political questions might be built. In these areas the "after-May" years were difficult. The CFDT was not buying the CGT's appeals. Indeed on politics and labor-market methods the CFDT seemed even more dedicated to defining its positions in opposition to those which the CGT desired. By its 1972 Congress, then, the CGT faced a situation in which the CFDT, the wind in its sails, systematically encouraged local hypermilitancy around demands which the CGT considered heretical, at the expense of mass action. Moreover, after May the CFDT became every journalist's favorite innovative and dynamic trade union (excepting, of course, PCF writers) while the CGT was portrayed as moderate, stodgy and hidebound.[36] In the political sphere the CGT-CFDT debate seemed only to have led the CFDT to sharpen its *autogestion* analysis and in the process gave opponents of *Union de la Gauche* new ammunition. Indeed, if one paid attention only to commentaries of the time and disregarded deeper realities, one would have concluded that the CFDT was rapidly on the way to replacing the CGT as the principal axis of French organized labor. The CGT knew that this was very far from the case, to be sure. But the fact that the CFDT was blocking progress towards the kind of

36. Here, whatever the facts, there is also no question but that much press and analytical comment was motivated by anti-CGT and anti-Communist feelings, plus the hope that the CFDT might make breakthroughs in the union movement which would undermine the CGT's status as the primary axis of French organized labor.

mass, pro-Common Program labor mobilization which the CGT wanted to see was bad enough.

Difficulties for the CGT in the labor movement were eclipsed by important political changes, however. As the PCF had anticipated, *Union de la Gauche* and a Left Common Program were both realized in the immediate "after-May" years. Moreover, in cadence with this political success, the PCF took great pains to modify and modernize its theoretical understanding of the world around it.

The long story of Left unity, recounted by many, need not detain us here.[37] Suffice it to say that a decade of obstinate political work by the PCF finally paid off. The Socialists reacted to the lessons of 1968 and 1969 and turned, beginning at their 1969 Congress, towards the essential tasks of rebuilding their own party and constructing unity-in-action with the PCF. The SFIO changed its name and its leadership (with Alain Savary replacing Guy Mollet as First Secretary) at this point and declared that Left Union was henceforth to be the "normal axis of Socialist strategy." The idea of a Common Program was also accepted, although the new party proposed, first of all, a period of public debate on outstanding issues of difference between forces of the Left (by which the Socialists meant primarily the positions of the PCF on civil liberties).

It took some time for actual *Union* to be negotiated. The Socialists, who were at an historic low point politically in 1969, understandably desired to reconstruct their own organization before entering into any firm relationship with the much-stronger PCF. In particular the PS wanted to integrate the non-Socialist participants of the late FGDS into the new party. Thus in 1970–1971 the participants in François Mitterrand's *Convention des Institutions Républicaines* were incorporated. In addition, at the important Epinay Congress of 1971, François Mitterrand assumed the leadership of the *Parti Socialiste*. Mitterrand, who had built his entire Fifth Republic career around Left Union, reaffirmed the PS's commitment to unity and indicated, again, that the PS desired to stabilize its internal workings before concluding a Common Program. Mitterrand clearly wanted to hold off program-making until the last possible moment before the scheduled 1973 election campaign. Throughout all of these long months of delay the PCF hammered constantly at the PS to sit down and bargain seriously. On the electoral occasions which occurred during this period (in particular a number of important by-elections in 1971 and in the 1971 municipal elections) the PCF deployed considerable effort to block, and if possible humiliate, local Centrist factions within the PS and the ambitious Third Force plans of Centrist Jean-Jacques Servan-Schreiber.[38] Simultaneously, the

37. See Robert Verdier, *PS-PC* (1973); Jean Poperen, *L'unité de la gauche* (1977).

38. JJSS took over the Radicals in 1970 with the notion that there was space in the political center to try Third Forcism again, using the Radicals as the linchpin of a Socialist-Centrist alliance. In his attempts he used all of his patented Kennedy-style modernism plus all of his

PCF mounted a massive public relations campaign, led by the party's new Secretary-General Georges Marchais (the campaign was called *en direct avec les Communistes*), in which PCF leaders toured the country holding open meetings where they explained advanced democracy and answered often hostile questions. The party's major step to pressure the PS was, however, the publication in October 1971 of *Changer de cap*, a "contribution to a Common Program for a Left Union government," in fact a detailed elaboration of the *Manifeste de Champigny* in which statements of intent and direction became specific proposals for legislation and action by a United Front government.[39]

Negotiations between the two parties took a serious turn in the spring of 1972, despite a skillful attempt by President Pompidou to split the parties apart by a sudden referendum on broadening the Common Market.[40] Finally, on the evening of June 26, 1972, the negotiations were concluded successfully. The general framework long urged by the PCF, beginning with the *Manifeste de Champigny*, reappeared in the new "Common Program for a Government of Left Unity."[41] At the core of the Program's proposals for democratization were a series of nationalizations (fewer than the number originally proposed by the PCF, but still including credit, insurance, and nine major industrial groups), democratic planning, income redistribution, reforms of political structures (again, fewer than originally proposed by the PCF), extended civil and economic liberties, *gestion démocratique* for the public sector, plus some quite vague and often neutralist foreign-policy proposals (on such issues the two parties were still very far apart).[42] Years of Communist work had paid off. A United Front coalition had been created.

The final approach of Left Unity brought with it important changes in

---

publicity-gathering skills and resources. It was the wrong time, however, and he succeeded mainly in splitting the Radical party, from which split came the *Mouvement des Radicaux de Gauche* which ultimately signed the Common Program in 1972. JJSS never found a political space, except as a *notable*, and found himself, instead, a ministerial chair in the first Chirac government in 1974. He lasted only a few days there.

39. PCF, *Changer de cap* (1971).

40. The referendum, also meant to shore up the regime's sagging electoral support, failed on both counts. The PCF urged its votes to vote *non*, the PS urged its to abstain.

41. PCF, *Programme commun de gouvernement* (1972).

42. For the PCF, expanding the public sector was the transformational key to the Common Program and the center of its political strategy. See George Ross, "A New French Popular Front," in the *Socialist Register, 1977*. The issue will reemerge powerfully in chapter 9 of our text. On the economics of it all for the PCF see "Programme commun et nationalisation dans l'industrie," *Economie et Politique*, no. 216–217 (July-August 1972); M. Decaillot, "Programme Commun, le contenu novateur de sa base économique," *Economie et Politique*, no. 219 (October 1972); Philippe Herzog, "Chiffrer le Programme Commun," *Economie et Politique*, no. 221 (December 1972); A. Cousin and F. Nerval, "Les nationalisations au coeur de la logique économique du Programme Commun," *Economie et Politique*, no. 222–223 (January-February 1973).

the PCF's theoretical perspectives. Up into the late 1960s the PCF's theoretical vision had been a tangled mess founded on Lenin's *Imperialism*, adumbrated by Stalin's contributions and the Russians' 1950s analysis of state-monopoly capitalism, topped off by the unfortunate pauperization texts of Maurice Thorez. The gist of this strange mixture was that monopoly capitalism was in constant terminal crisis. In its critical agonies this system made the situation of workers and *petits bourgeois* even more unpleasant. This situation, in time, was bound to lead to an alliance of *petit-bourgeois* groups behind the working-class vanguard for change, and, ultimately, for socialism. The hypotheses of growing proletarianization of middle strata and deepening *immiseration* of the proletariat underlay this analysis, in ways which had always been inappropriate to the realities of PCF United Front reformist politics, but which had become even more inappropriate in the post–World War II years. Economic growth, the great expansion in "new-middle-class" occupations, the relative stagnation, in numerical terms, of the industrial working class, the mammoth introduction of science, technology, and education into the work process, and significant changes in consumption and lifestyle patterns all made a vision of society based on the superexploitation in satanic mills of factory operatives who would one day take to the streets and overthrow capitalism unrealistic. The PCF's theoretical baggage, in other words, was rather light. And, by the 1960s, it made the party appear more and more hidebound and tied to old (often Soviet-created) schemas. Thus the large corpus of theoretical work which the party undertook in the later 1960s was not only an important attempt to bring the PCF up to date in its mapping of the social world. It was also an important public and internal step away from the Thorez years and Soviet theoretical hegemony and, from another vantage point, a further step in PCF de-Stalinization.

The new "state-monopoly capitalist" analysis was developed primarily by the Economic Section of the Central Committee and by the team of economists involved in *Economie et politique*, an important party journal. The stage of state-monopoly capitalism ensued historically as monopoly capital was forced to use and manipulate the state even more completely to counteract the tendency of the rate of profit to decline. With this new situation came new problems for the cutting edge of capitalism. The open political role which the monopoly caste was obliged to take to promote the policies which it needed for survival exposed the state even more as an agency of the bourgeois class. Liberal and bourgeois-democratic ideological masks were dropped in the process, creating an endemic crisis of political legitimacy for monopoly capital at that very moment when monopolists most needed political security, hence the resort, in France, to new and more precarious forms of rule such as personal power. Moreover, state-monopoly capitalism was forced to exist atop a profound contradiction. As economic units become larger, more complex, and more dependent upon a polyvalent labor force, in other words as the socialization of production proceeded, the private appropriation of surplus value appeared even more constraining and wasteful to ordinary people. The material resources (productive machinery, science and technology, human talent) existed to create abundance and eliminate degrading work and social roles. Yet state-monopoly capitalism could not allow consumption to rise beyond a certain point, allow public services and amenities to grow or to deploy the resources of science and technology in the full service of human potential because rates of profit would be threatened.

The new theory brought with it a new social map. Between the industrial working class and the bourgeoisie now lay, in addition to old intermediary groups (peasants, *boutiquaires* and liberal professionals), a whole panoply of new *couches intermédiaires* thrown up by advancing capitalism: white-collar workers, engineering and technical workers, lower level *cadres* (administrators), intellectuals. Two things were important about these new intermediary strata. First of all, they had their own social interests, separable from those of the working class. Secondly, their lives and work tended to make them move sociologically closer to workers. With workers they shared the common condition of *le salariat*: loss of power and control in work, and increasing subjection to cost-cutting and productivity-raising strategies on the part of their monopoly and state employers. Thus although the bulk of incumbents in *couches-intermédiaires* roles were not workers, per se, since they did not actively produce surplus value, their general conditions brought their interests closer to those of workers.

What was of decisive importance in state-monopoly capitalism was the huge shortfall between the objective and human capacities which existed as the socialization of production progressed, and the barriers to the utilization of such capacities presented by the rule of monopolies. From this emerged a vision of change towards socialism motivated less by negative rebellion against utter misery (the old view of the PCF) than by growing awareness that only socialism could release the human potential which monopoly rule blocked. Moreover, the map of social classes sketched out by the new theory created new perspectives on how such change could occur. State-monopoly capitalism increased social pluralism, on the one hand, while on the other bringing underlying strata and classes closer together in terms of interests and aspirations. The industrial working class remained the most exploited group, and therefore the most revolutionary. But the processes which were at work among new intermediary strata, who had their own interests and goals, allowed members of these strata to understand better both the revolutionary feelings of workers and the need for change. In general, the possibilities for a cross-class anti-monopoly alliance were being greatly enhanced by the very processes engaged by monopoly capital in its quest for survival. The new theory thus pointed towards a socialism, premised on struggle within monopoly capitalism, which would be one of abundance and human self-realization rather than the socialism of accumulation which inspired the Soviet model. In addition, it foresaw the necessity for such struggle to be carried on *pluralistically*. The PCF could no longer expect non-working–class groups to submit their interests to the vanguard working class. Rather this working class had, as its main task, creation of an alliance which recognized the specificity of interests of all groups concerned. In other words, the new theory promised change away from the PCF's traditional *ouvrièrisme*. The potentiality for a cross-class anti-monopoly alliance was produced daily by the workings of state-monopoly capitalism. Its realization, however, was up to the PCF. Implicit in the theory (which was codified in a mammoth PCF political economy manual, published in 1971–1972)[43] was the message that the party had to do much more than defend different groups against suffering. It had also to demonstrate to them what a future without state-monopoly capitalism might be like. In doing so the party had to be prepared to embrace new issues of alienation and liberation of all kinds. As of 1972, however, it was enough that the new analysis gave the PCF additional reasons to be optimistic about the success of *Union de la Gauche* and its own strategy.

43. See PCF, *Traité d'économie politique (manuel): le capitalisme monopoliste d'état*; also George Ross, "The New Middle Classes, French Marxist Critiques," *Theory and Society* (March 1978).

Chapter 9

THE BRIEF LIFETIME OF
UNION DE LA GAUCHE, 1972–1977

The reader will have to forgive a certain unorthodoxy in the exposition of what follows. The reason is that the years between 1972 and 1977, from the creation of *Union de la Gauche* to its collapse on the eve of the 1978 general elections, were very strange both for the French Left and for the French labor movement. The PCF and CGT, together with other important actors, lived things *as they seemed* during this period. Simultaneously, behind their backs other processes played themselves out. The PCF's long-standing United Front policy seemed destined, finally, for success. However, as the critical 1978 elections approached, what looked like success for the PCF's policies turned, increasingly, into triumph for the Socialists, placing the PCF in a terrible dilemma. Moreover, the CGT's goals in the labor movement seemed to be crowned with success as well—the CFDT progressively abandoned its "unorthodox" labor-market activities and the entire labor movement moved towards mass protests of a kind which would mobilize political support for the Left against the regime. However, for the CGT, and for the French labor movement as a whole, such success involved, in time, an overpoliticization and generalization of trade-union action which progressively left unions disarmed against the effects of the most serious economic crisis of the post–World War II period. Ironically, as *Union de la Gauche* seemed to move from strength to strength, both the PCF's Eurocommunization and the CGT's relatively autonomous trade-union strategy were failing. Things as they seemed were promising. But things as they were were nearly catastrophic, as events of the summer of 1977 made clear. But before this clarity came, there were two separate histories in these years. One was experienced day-to-day. The other, built on deep misunderstandings and fed by unintended consequences, happened at a much deeper level.

The PCF and UNION DE LA GAUCHE

For the PCF, *Union de la Gauche* worked relatively well from 1972 to 1974. Neither major partner in the *Union* was optimistic enough about the other to believe that the progress of their alliance would be smooth. The belated publication of parts of the July 1972 Central Committee discussion of the Common Program (in Etienne Fajon's *L'Union est un combat* in 1974, about which more later) indicated that the PCF leadership mistrusted the PS profoundly, but placed considerable hope in the dynamic of Left *Union* as a corrective for the PS's "right-wing social-democratic" tendencies. And the PS clearly intended not to allow itself to be locked into a political logic decided by the PCF. Moreover, the Common Program, in its generality and abstraction, swept numbers of political disagreements between Communists and Socialists under the rug. Nonetheless, the signature of the Common Program in June 1972 announced the opening of a prolonged electoral campaign in which Left Unity had to be played to the hilt, no matter what differences between Left partners remained unresolved. The legislative elections of March 1973 were the first opportunity for the Left to test its new approach with the voters and the first occasion for the Left to win back the parliamentary support which it had lost in the crisis-dominated elections of June 1968. The results were promising. The Left regained its 1967 electoral strength and then some, the PCF maintained its usual Fifth Republic level of electoral appeal, the Socialists began to revive electorally and the Center found itself even more squeezed between the Majority and the Left (which was exactly what the PCF desired).

The PCF did paint itself into something of a corner in the months after the elections by its contradictory reaction to the general fervor provoked by Soviet censoring and persecution of Alexander Solzhenitsyn. While lamenting that the Soviets were unwilling to publish Solzhenitsyn, the party noisily denounced what it claimed was an anti-Soviet campaign around the issue, this thoroughly vitiating the timid liberalism which was, in fact, its position on the question. Timid liberalism, and not the heavy-handed approach of the anti-Soviet campaign, was the party's general line in this period, however. In the fall of 1973 (perhaps in part as a response to the coup in Chile which, everywhere in Western Communism, led to an increased recognition of the need for solid Left unity and large mass support),[1] Georges Marchais published *Le Défi démocratique*, which was designed both to explain the PCF to outsiders and as a text for internal party education, and which was perhaps the PCF's first fully-fledged Eurocommunist document.[2] At about the same time the PCF took the unprecedented step of opening up much of its internal life to two investigative journalists (Harris and de Sédouy, the authors of the screenplay for the

---

1. In Italy, of course, it contributed to the adoption by the PCI of the "historic compromise" strategy.

2. Georges Marchais, *Le défi démocratique* (1973).

controversial film *The Sorrow and the Pity*), who visited cells, section meetings, factories, party schools and interviewed a wide variety of party leaders to produce a book—*Voyage à l'intérieur du PCF*—which, despite a clear lack of enthusiasm for the PCF on the part of the authors, portrayed a party full of new energy, self-criticism and desire for new openings to the world around it.[3]

The new *Union de la Gauche* and the PCF had, in fact, very little time to digest the elections of 1973 before they found themselves in the middle of another decisive electoral campaign. After months of rumors about his health, Georges Pompidou died in April of 1974. And while the majority began to tear itself apart over the succession (Chaban-Delmas and Pierre Messmer, among others, fighting over who would be the Gaullist candidate, amid Machiavellian intrigues by Jacques Chirac, with Valéry Giscard d'Estaing skillfully promoting his own non-Gaullist candidacy) the Left proceeded, without controversy, to designate François Mitterrand. In this, and in the campaign which followed, the PCF's energetic support for Mitterrand and its willingness to grant Mitterrand considerable room for political maneuver was decisive. Mitterrand did very well in the first round of the election and came within a fraction of a percent (with 49.2 percent of the vote) of defeating Giscard in the runoff. The success of the Left was within the Left's grasp.[4]

Two years of nearly constant electioneering and two years of relative Left harmony gave way, in the autumn of 1974, to conflict and acrimony, in large part initiated by the PCF. There were two major reasons for this. First of all, the period after the 1974 Presidentials, because it was relatively free of electoral occasions (cantonal elections, the next major electoral mobilization, were not scheduled until 1976) allowed space for fine tuning in the balance between the two major parties of the Left. The development of Left Unity from 1972 to 1974 had revealed certain trends which both the PS and the PCF had to take into account. Secondly, this brief non-electoral interim allowed both parties some time to adjust their inner mechanisms in anticipation of the major battles which lay ahead—the various events which would cumulate in the 1978 general election campaign.

By autumn 1974 it had become quite clear to parts of the PCF leadership that despite the party's new, open presentation of itelf, despite its new theories, despite its evident rallying to Eurocommunist ideas, despite its new cross-class alliance goals,[5] *Union de la Gauche* was benefiting the PS

3. André Harris and Alain de Sédouy, *Voyage à l'intérieur du parti communiste* (1974).

4. See FNSP, *Les élections présidentielles de 1974* ; also *Cahiers du Communisme* (May 1974, June 1974).

5. In this respect the PCF had shifted its alliance slogan and goals in the spring of 1974 to *L'union du peuple de France* in an evident attempt to appeal to Gaullists. The party judged, quite correctly, that the Gaullist coalition was shaky. As a result it began to pitch its appeal, partly by deploying a more strident nationalism, to sectors of Gaullist support (the Gaullist working-class vote in particular) who might be prepared to shift their political allegiance. See *Cahiers du Communisme* (September 1974).

more than the PCF. The trend had first been suspected in the Presidentials. Of the thirteen million votes cast for Mitterrand, party electoral analysts could, at best, count five to five-and-one-half million of them as PCF voters. Still, the Presidential format allowed of a certain ambiguity in interpreting the others (i.e., they might not have been pro–PS). No ambiguity was possible, however, in interpreting a series of by-elections in the autumn of 1974. If at first the problem seemed to be that the PS was winning the bulk of support which was shifting Left as *Union de la Gauche* made its mark (already a serious issue for the PCF), the by-election results showed that the PS was also beginning to attract new support from the traditional PCF electorate itself.

Electoral balance between the two major parties was only part of the question. As was quite predictable, what looked to be the remarkable recovery of Socialist political fortunes seemed also to be creating internal political changes in the PS. François Mitterrand has been remarkably reticent about the Common Program in his Presidential campaign, for example. Then the PS continued to open itself to new political currents, broadening the already wide spectrum of opinion in its midst, but, as of 1974, more and more in directions which made the PCF uneasy. The elaborate spectacle prepared by the PS in the fall of 1974 (the *Assises du Socialisme*) to incorporate Michel Rocard and his PSU followers into the PS was a warning.[6] Rocard had never approved of Left Unity and was widely regarded as a Third Forcer by PCF leaders. The ritual incantation of *autogestion* at the *Assises* looked, to PCF observers, like a coverup, an opening to the Right. The PCF's guard went up further as the Socialists made a quite heavily publicized attempt to construct party sections in factories, a direct challenge to the PCF on its home grounds. The eviction of the CERES (the leftish *Centre d'études et recherches socialistes*) faction from the PS leadership at the 1974 Congress did not help. By isolating the PS's Left, Mitterrand was putting himself in a position of much greater tactical freedom vis-à-vis the PCF. At about the same time Rocard (who was labelled the PS "dauphin" by the Press) and Jacques Attali, two analysts with distinctly technocratic propensities, emerged as Mitterrand's main economic consultants. In all this, the repeated insistence by Mitterrand and others about the need to reequilibrate the Left—i.e., make the PS stronger than the PCF—was not reassuring to the PCF. There did seem to be a certain logic in what the PS was doing. By accumulating new political resources and by limiting the power of its own left wing the Socialist Party seemed to be preparing for a political confrontation with the PCF over the policy directions of *Union de la Gauche*. In a context in which the new President of France, Giscard d'Estaing, was making pious vows about "re-

6. The *Assises du Socialisme* also included the CFDT, something which worried the PCF even more.

formism" and talking about the need for a "recentering" of French politics, the PCF could not exclude the possibility that a renewed PS might well be tempted eventually towards a Center-Left arrangement with Giscard.

In response to all of this, the PCF moved to take protective action, beginning at its Twenty-first Party Congress of 1974. The exact nature of the events which led to the PCF's tactical change at this point is unclear, since debate within the PCF *Bureau Politique* is a closely guarded secret. The most striking public event was the drastic change in the original Congress proposal in the course of Congress preparation. The original proposal submitted for debate by the Central Committee was full of rosy optimism about Left Union. The proposal finally adopted by the Congress was much less optimistic and profoundly critical of PS intentions to reequilibrate the Left in its favor. Beyond open concern about reinforcing the PCF, particularly on the shop floor, the Congress adopted a new perspective on its own strategy within *Union de la Gauche*, entitled *Union du peuple de France*, which was quite *ouvrièriste* in outlook and considerably less oriented towards the creation of a cross-class anti-monopoly alliance than earlier statements.[7] The shift in perspective was clearly the product of profound strategic conflict within the leadership and in the party more generally. The leadership current behind Georges Marchais, the proponents of the Common Program and Left Union, were pushed onto the defensive by their opponents, led by Roland Leroy. Indeed there is considerable evidence that Leroy and his allies organized in a quasi-fractional way through the party press and different party Federations where they had personal power bases to have the original Congress proposal rejected and replaced by something more skeptical of Left Union.[8] Whatever the specific circumstances, however, from the holding of this Congress in October 1974, for almost a year the PCF attacked the PS with a vehemence rarely seen since the Cold War.

The debates at the 1974 Congress clarified the motivation of the "polemic," as it came to be called. At its core was one powerful notion. Only a strong PCF, clear about its purposes and based on strong working-class support, could carry *Union de la Gauche* through to the kind of victory

---

7. PCF XXIe Congrès (Extraordinaire), *Cahiers du Communisme* (November 1974).

8. Some indication of this opposition can be seen in the transcript of Georges Marchais' report to the Central Committee meeting of June 1972, which followed the signing of the Common Program (published in 1974, interestingly enough, in Etienne Fajon, *L'union est un combat* [1974]). The abrupt change in Marchais' public positions from *Le défi démocratique* to extreme vituperation of the Socialists within a few weeks was further evidence, as was the accession of Roland Leroy to the editorship of *L'Humanité* at this point. See also Victor Fay, "Au XXIe Congrès du PCF, raidissement tactique," *Critique Socialiste* (January 1975); Pierre Naville, "A propos des contradictions entre le PC et le PS," *Critique Socialiste* (March-April 1975); J. C. Poulain, "Sur l'accord des trois partis de gauche," *Economie et Politique* (March 1975); "Querelles à gauche," *Projet* (April 1975).

which would guarantee *real* change. This notion had implications both for the inner life of the PCF and for its relationship with its Left partners. Internally, Communists were put on clear notice that they had come to expect too many magical results from unity at the top with the Socialists in the two years after 1972 (i.e., that the party leadership had been taken in by the fact of unity, to the point where it neglected the PCF's important role, at the base, of making sure that unity went in the proper directions—although the leadership did not go through any elaborate *autocritique* at the Congress). Too much euphoria about unity per se, if continued, would lead the party away from the kind of work at rank-and-file level which was necessary to keep the PCF from becoming a support group for the Socialists. What was necessary, first of all, was for the party to reinforce and deepen its working-class base, making sure, in the process, that workers in general were aware of the profound differences which existed between the PCF—the "party of the working class"—and the PS. Here the PCF was clearly worried that the PS might begin to eat away at the PCF's political base in a serious way. Asserting the specificity of the PCF, in contrast to the PS (which was "reformist"), was the remedy; hence the campaign, begun at this time, to form large numbers of new factory cells. Also decided at this point was the creation of a special *Grande Entreprises* section of the Central Committee under *Bureau Politique* member Jean Colpin to monitor and enhance PCF activity in forty-three large factories.[9] The rather strident self-assertions of the PCF in several strikes and industrial protests, particularly in the course of 1975, were part of this.[10]

Directed outwards towards the Socialists, the PCF's attacks were meant as a not-so-polite warning to the PS that *Union de la Gauche* was not a license for the PS to hunt new supporters from among the PCF's flock. Nor should the PS nourish illusions about the possibility of relegating the PCF to subordinate status in the coalition. The general message of the PCF, directed both to its own base and to the PS, was that the Socialists had begun to deemphasize support of the Common Program in the interests of diminishing the PCF's support—reequilibrating the Left was not what Left Union was about; bringing the Left to power around clear sup-

9. This *Grandes-Entreprises* section, chaired by Jean Colpin, connected the Central Committee directly to party organizations (cells, sections) in forty-three large firms across the country.

10. Here the party, most often through the activity of the *Grandes-Entreprises* section of the Central Committee, took direct leadership in strike actions. On occasion high party officials, including Georges Marchais, appeared at strike sites to urge the workers on and mark the party's presence in struggle. More to the point of our study, the party shifted a number of important party members whose work had been in the CGT back to party tasks (Aimé Albeher, CGT leader at Renault who was made head of the Renault-Billancourt party section, being only the most public case). That the CGT leadership was unhappy about all of this, and that Georges Séguy in particular did not like it, was well known.

port for the Common Program, then implementing the Program to the fullest, was.

Behind all of this was a reassertion of the core of the PCF's United Front strategy. The PCF wanted *Union de la Gauche* to strengthen the Left in the country generally, so that it would come to power electorally and implement the Common Program. Furthermore, it wanted the momentum of *Union* to move the PS to the left, towards what the PCF understood to be a genuine commitment to socialism (and, of course, away from the PS's reformist social democracy). Finally, the PCF wanted *Union de la Gauche* to increase the relative power of the PCF *within* the Left coalition. If all of these conditions were met, then the Common Program could be carried out in those ways desired by the PCF, a process which might, the PCF thought, begin a peaceful transition to a *socialisme aux couleurs de la France*. The period 1974–1975 was a good time, given the absence of any immediate electoral occasion, to remind the Socialists what the PCF had in mind.[11] François Mitterrand had become, in Marchais' harsh words, *sûr de lui et dominateur* and the PS had hinted at a shift to the Right. The one-sided polemic which occurred, then, was meant to bring the PS back to the logic of Left unity as the PCF saw it.[12]

The polemical storm then ended as abruptly as it had begun, in the summer and fall of 1975. At this point the PCF shifted quite dramatically towards its fullest wave of Eurocommunization yet.[13] Most importantly, the party (finally) began to remove the Soviet albatross from around its neck. Sustained criticism of the lack of civil liberties in the Soviet Union was the first major step (all the more remarkable, in fact, if one reflected back for

11. The publication of Fajon's *L'union est un combat* in 1974, to which we have referred, was a key part of this campaign to alert the party rank and file about the dangerous propensities of the Socialists for "reformism."

12. The polemic was really a harangue by the PCF. The Communists, Georges Marchais especially (Marchais' real public forte, alas, is the castigation of enemies), attacked relentlessly, while the PS, especially François Mitterrand, played the role of a dignified and wronged suitor. The PS rode out the storm of petulance which it knew would come to an end. To the extent to which the PS responded, it raised issues which fell outside those raised by the PCF. In 1974–1975 Portugal was useful for this. The PCF gave complete support to the sectarian strategy pursued by Alvaro Cunhal and the PCP in the Portuguese revolution, support which allowed opponents of the PCF (in the right-wing press in particular) material for a field day of "speculation" about what the PCF might do were it allowed to approach power, given its affection for the minoritarian attempts to seize power and capitalize on the collapse of Portuguese fascism by the PCP. The *Repubblica* affair of the summer of 1975 (in which PCP unionists shut down a leading Socialist newspaper because of its political line) added fuel to the fire. Here the fact that Georges Séguy, after a visit to Portugal, announced that the affair was one of simple trade unionism (the paper was shut down because of the material grievances of its workers), did not help.

13. Undoubtedly there had also been shifts and reconsiderations at the highest level of the PCF, with Georges Marchais (who was, in fact, at the time a very cautious "liberal" at heart, but who was obliged to go along with the *durs* of the *Bureau Politique* when they gained the upper hand) and Paul Laurent gaining a temporary advantage.

only a few months, to the party's strange position on the "anti-Soviet campaign" around Solzhenitsyn). The party began acknowledging and protesting against the harsh treatment of political dissidents in the USSR, even to the point of participating in public meetings on such questions (for example, on the treatment of Leonid Plioutch) which it had not organized itself. When French television screened a film showing a forced labor camp for political deviants in Latvia, the party acknowledged and strongly condemned the existence of such camps. Again, when French television showed Costa Gavras' film *The Confession* (made from Arthur London's "novel" about the Slansky trials in Czechoslovakia in the early 1950s), Jean Kanapa, the party's foreign-affairs spokesman—and a very close friend of Georges Marchais—recognized the extent to which the anti-Titoist show trials had been fabricated by Stalin to eliminate real or imagined "nationalist" enemies in Eastern Europe.[14] The party's shift on such issues was neither occasional nor purely tactical, as broad and often painful internal debate in the party demonstrated. From this point onwards until the Twenty-third Congress in 1979 the PCF criticized internal Soviet practices on civil and political liberties as vigorously as anyone else. Clearly, however, the PCF's own Stalinist past was seen by party leaders as a barrier to increased electoral support for the PCF and for *Union de la Gauche*. Sharp criticism of Soviet behavior was one oblique way of approaching the problems posed by this legacy. The publication of *Vivre libres*, a long document declaring the party's commitment to the extension of civil and political liberties in France, was another.[15]

The PCF did not confine "de-Sovietization" to denunciations of the lack of democracy in the Soviet Union.[16] It also took certain measures to disen-

14. The fact that Kanapa was in a position to initiate a PCF self-criticism was, of course, highly significant. Kanapa had, during the dark days of the Cold War, been one of the PCF's most rabid pro-Stalinists. In charge of intellectuals for the Central Committee (Jean-Paul Sartre, at one point labelled him an *intellectuel-flic*), Kanapa had been charged with enforcing the Jdanov line on cultural matters. Indeed the "Eurocommunization" of Jean Kanapa—who was in charge of the Central Committee work group which prepared the Twenty-second Congress in 1975–1976—is, in many ways, symbolic of the tortured and incomplete path of change of the PCF as a whole. Here the very moving article on Kanapa after Kanapa's death in 1978 by Francis Cohen is well worth reading. See "Jean Kanapa, un homme sans relâche," in *Nouvelle Critique* (October 1978).

15. PCF, *Vivre libres* (1975); see also Pierre Juquin, *Libertés* (1975).

16. It is vitally important to note here that the PCF restricted its criticisms of the Soviet Union to the political sphere, while continuing to praise Soviet and Eastern European progress in the economic and social spheres. To the PCF Soviet and Eastern European societies were *socialist*. The problems which existed were superstructural. Progress had been made in most areas, but political development towards democracy had fallen behind, due to Stalinist deformations. The vital question of the relationship between Soviet social structures and such political deformations were not asked. The PCF's unofficial "vanguard" on such questions was Jean Elleinstein, an historian of the Soviet Union and vice-director of the PCF's *Centre d'études et recherches marxistes* (CERM). See his *Histoire du phénomène stalinien* (1975) and his four-volume *Histoire de l'URSS* (1975). For a more official, but quite similar analysis, see Jean Kanapa's address to the PCF's party school in *France Nouvelle*, 12 December 1977.

gage itself from Soviet international hegemony. The circumstances surrounding this change emerged mainly from Soviet insistence, of long date,
on convening a Conference of European Communist parties to condemn
the Chinese, and, as the 1970s moved on, to reassert control over growing
Eurocommunist deviance. The Yugoslavs and Italians had, for quite some
time, dragged their feet about the convening of this Conference, and in
1975, the PCF publicly joined them. In fact, a series of bilateral meetings
between the PCF and PCI about this and other issues first gave rise to
media speculation that there were phenomena worthy of the label Eurocommunist. In any case, severe tensions between the PCF and the Soviet
Communist Party developed almost immediately, to the point where
Georges Marchais refused to attend the 1976 Soviet Party Congress.[17]
Then, when the delayed Conference was finally convened (East Berlin,
June 1976) the PCF, PCI and the Yugoslavs led a concerted fight to block
Soviet attempts to condemn the Chinese and produce a single strategic
communiqué (which would have implied a unified international strategy).
Georges Marchais, who played a central role in the Conference, pointedly
commented afterwards that "conferences such as this one don't appear to
me to correspond any more to the needs of our time." Further, "any
elaboration of common strategy for all of our parties is henceforth absolutely excluded." Marchais concluded by sternly warning the Russians
against interference in the unfolding of PCF strategy.[18]

The third, and most important, aspect of PCF de-Sovietization was, of
course, strategic and theoretical, involving the abandonment of the Soviet
model for socialism. By the mid-1970s the party had already moved quite
far in this direction, as we have seen. Its most decisive step, nonetheless,
was taken at the February 1976 Twenty-second Congress. For here the
party dropped—finally—its historic commitment to Soviet theories of the
state and social change by officially abandoning the notion of "proletarian
dictatorship."[19] The PCF's official allegiance to the "dictatorship" notion
was the anchor of its remaining ties to the Soviet model. Abandoning it
meant, then, that the "peaceful, democratic road" to a *socialisme aux couleurs de la France* was henceforth a road which had no foreordained conclusion. To the degree that the Congress discussed reasons for the change,
its discussions were interesting. "State-monopoly capitalism" had altered

17. It was most ironic that Gaston Plissonier substituted for Marchais. The irony follows
from Plissonnier's internal role in the PCF leadership as one of the strongest pro-Soviet voices
in the secretariat. Plissonnier joined Enrico Berlinguer on the podium to speak in favor of international pluralism in the world Communist movement.

18. *L'Humanité*, 1 July 1976.

19. See, for the Congress debate, *Cahiers du Communisme* (February-March 1976). For opposing views see Louis Althusser, *XXIIe Congrès* (1977) and Etienne Balibar, *La dictature du
prolétariat* (1977). In addition to a relatively small number of Communists who actually opposed the change, larger numbers resisted the ways in which the proposal for change was made
and/or worried that the change left the party without an articulated theory of the state under
socialism.

the conditions for passage to socialism. In effect, according to the party, the progress of democracy and the further development of state-monopoly capitalism were incompatible. Thus to the degree to which the PCF led the struggle for greater democracy in France it would be undermining monopoly power. At the end of struggle for *la démocratie jusqu'au bout* lay socialism.

In all of this lay buried a decision by the PCF's leadership to "Italianize" the party in answer to the problems of reequilibration of *Union de la Gauche* raised in the difficult months of the anti-Socialist polemic of 1974-1975. The PCF knew that it had to attract a degree of new support—particularly from the *couches intermédiaires*—both to generate the political resources needed within Left Union to counteract growing Socialist strength and to augment the general strength of the United Left. Eurocommunization and Italianization were the party's responses. These processes did involve de-Sovietization in its different aspects—not simply a new face to the outside world. The leadership had also made a clear choice to transform the PCF from a cadre to a mass party. It had relaxed recruitment requirements, reduced the intensity of demands on militants at the base and promoted an opening up of debate and discussion at cell level to make the party more attractive to potential new members, particularly to members of the urban *couches intermédiaires*. Aided by the favorable climate created by Left Union, this choice had begun to pay off by the Twenty-second Congress. By 1976 the party's membership had reached upwards of 500,000, with Georges Marchais announcing the party's goal as a million members in the near future.[20] Moreover, if the party's campaign to

20. Here one runs across the classic problem of knowing what membership figures actually mean. The PCF itself, in fact, has rarely known how many active members it has had. Its statistics indicate how many cards are delivered to cell and section level and "placed" in members' hands at annual ceremonies of the *remise de cartes*. How many placed cards actually involve regular dues-paying members, and how many of these are active in party life, cannot be ascertained, although it is considerably less than the number of cards placed. To complicate things even further, the party has not always been truthful about such things, although there is reason to think that, by the 1970s it had ceased earlier forms of exaggeration. In any case, the figures given by Jean Elleinstein in his book, *Le PCF* (1976), are probably as good as one can find.

Number of membership cards delivered/placed

Year	Delivered	Placed
1961	407,000	300,000
1964	407,000	300,000
1966	425,800	350,000
1969	454,640	380,000
1972	456,640	390,000
1973	471,000	410,000
1974	500,900	450,000
1975	556,170	491,000

Source: Ellenstein, *Le PCF*, pp. 96–97.

reinvigorate its network of factory cells had been successful after 1974, this broader mass focus had also, by 1976, begun to change the socioeconomic profile of PCF membership to give increased relative weight to such *couches nouvelles*, as the party desired.[21] More generally, the party's membership profile became ever younger and ever more weighted towards post-1968 recruits. De facto, then, a process of de-Stalinization was at work here as well, as the generations of militants and members who had been conditioned by the Stalin-Thorez years became numerically fewer and less important.[22]

Eurocommunization was, then, the PCF's answer to the threat of political imbalance in the Left. As for the other main aspect of PCF strategy, bringing a properly balanced *Union de la Gauche* to power in the 1978 general election, the world seemed on its side. The majority in power had begun to be plagued with serious economic difficulties by 1973–1974 (inflation, rising unemployment) which widened after the energy crisis of 1974 into the most refractory downturn France had experienced since the 1930s. It took some time for the dimensions of the new situation to become clear, but when they were—a two-decade–long period of relatively steady economic expansion had ended—the regime found its political problems compounded. Since the regime had been in power continuously since the late 1950s it could not help but bear the political brunt of the economic crisis. Moreover, the measures which it took to counteract crisis did not work. Under Jacques Chirac as Prime Minister (1974–1976) the government tried to buy time while waiting for an upturn which would bail the majority out. Under Raymond Barre, who succeeded Chirac in 1976, austerity politics which increased unemployment and hardship for numerous social categories succeeded in diminishing public support for the regime, without ending the crisis. In this context the Left's policies, in particular the measures foreseen in the Common Program, became more credible, at least momentarily. Moreover, the regime had long since fallen victim to the effects of longevity in power. The very existence of an alternative went quite a distance towards rendering this alternative attractive. In any case, after the difficult moments of polemicizing in 1974–1975, the Left's stock began to take off. Faced with this, existing divisions in the Majority (which had originally been divisions between "clans" which were held together by common need for General de Gaulle) became divisions about strategy. President Giscard d'Estaing, concerned both to subordinate the Gaullists

21. Elleinstein, ibid., ch. 6. See also Jean-Paul Molinari, "Contribution à la sociologie du PCF," in *Cahiers du Communisme* (January 1976); Jacques Derville, "Les Communistes dans l'Isère," in *Revue Française de Science Politique* (February 1975); François Platone et Françoise Subileau, "Les militants communistes à Paris," *Revue Française de Science Politique* (October 1975).

22. See Anne Andreu and Jean-Louis Mingalon, *L'adhésion* (1975); also Thierry Pfister and André Laurens, *Les nouveaux communistes aux portes du pouvoir* (1977).

and disaggregate the Left, presented himself as a reformer and proposed to "govern in the Center" (see his manifesto, *La Democratie française*, 1976). His hope for the long run was that *Union de la Gauche* would fall apart and the Socialist would slide back to a Third Force posture. The Gaullists, seriously menaced by Giscard's initiatives, regrouped in the RPR (*Rassemblement pour la République*) around Jacques Chirac in the fall of 1976 to advocate firm Left-Right confrontation to defeat the "Socialist Communist enemy" under a banner decorated with classic Gaullist slogans— nationalism, order, etc. Suspicion deepened between the two conflicting wings of the Majority with Giscard's careful and persistent efforts to undermine the État UDR (the "Gaullist State," so-called because of the degree of Gaullist control over major administrative bodies created by fifteen years of continuous rule). In short, as the Left's fortunes grew, the Majority slipped ever deeper into a mire of acrimony and disputation.

In contrast to the Majority's infighting, the Left seemed both united and serene in its unity. Opinion polls showed a steady rise in support for the Left and the credibility of its programs. François Mitterrand and, to a lesser degree, Georges Marchais began to appear as statesmen, in contrast to Giscard, who looked inept, and Jacques Chirac who looked overquerulous and a bit irresponsible. The Left's unity was reinforced by electoral success first in the cantonal elections of 1976 and then in the municipal elections of March 1977. Indeed, on this occasion, *Union de la Gauche* was, for the first time, *majoritaire*. Everyone knew, of course, that people used different criteria for their vote in national legislative elections, when the course of national policy was at stake, than they did in local elections, when protest was less costly. Nonetheless, by the springtime of 1977 the likelihood of Left success in coming to power was greater than it had been at any time since 1944.

The CGT: towards Trade-Union Success?

In the immediate "after-May" years, the CGT had labored in difficult circumstances, as we have seen. From 1972 to 1977, however, events shifted dramatically to favor the Confederation. In fact, by 1977 the CGT found itself in what seemed to be a more successful position than any it had known since 1947. The *Nouvelle Société*, seriously weakened prior to 1972 as we saw in the previous chapter, was resoundingly defeated. The CFDT abandoned most of what the CGT felt to be its errant ways in the labor market and rallied to action perspectives which were much closer to those advocated by the CGT. Finally, if the CFDT did not "come around" completely in the political realm, it did soften some of its earlier positions, obliged, as it was, by a changing environment to behave in a fashion which the CGT found much more comfortable. On all fronts, then, the difficult labors of "after May" began to pay off in the mid-1970s for the CGT.

The Death of the New Society

We left the *Nouvelle Société* threatened and weakened with the fall of the Chaban government in 1972. The Messmer government which succeeded it (lasting until the Presidential elections of 1974) scaled down contractualism, above all abandoning Chaban's grandiose talk about changing the general shape of the labor market in France through it. It continued, nonetheless, to promote extended contractualism in the public sector as the only promising method of promoting an incomes policy which it had in hand. The CGT plus events had, then, defeated the Chabanist reformist thrust. What the Confederation faced now was the less spectacular, but still serious problem of the public-sector contractualism which remained. Here, as in many other areas, economic developments favored the Confederation's aims. The limited public-sector contractualism which survived after 1972 depended, for its success, on predictable, stable economic growth. Stability went first, when, by mid-1973, inflation began to reach very high levels. In response, the government concluded that cost-of-living plus real wage increases embodied in public-sector contracts were inflationary, a conclusion which the CNPF, fearful of the exemplary effect of public-sector wage settlements, publicly shared. In consequence the governmentally calculated *masses salariales*, which were the center of branch-by-branch public sector negotiations, got smaller and smaller. In effect, the Messmer government was making public-sector workers responsible for general inflation while violating commitments to contractualism made during the Chaban years. More conservative "manager-state" responses replaced reformism as the main motivation for public-sector contractualism. It was inevitable, in this context, that trade-union cooperation would be undermined.

By 1973 significant strike action in the public sector had returned, largely in sectors where the CGT and CFDT had important mobilization power. Strikes were almost always promoted immediately prior to offical negotiation periods (and at any other moments when discontent allowed them as well) as a method of "pre-bargaining" by labor protest the determination, by government, of specific *masses salariales*. In addition, the CGT and CFDT refused to sign proposed contracts. The branch level *journée d'action*—the CGT's preferred mass tactic, it will be remembered—also returned in the public sector. From 1973 onwards conflict in the SNCF, at EGF, the Paris Metro and among Post Office workers (where *Force Ouvrière* was also strong) was endemic. Beginning in 1974 further government retrenchment deepened such conflict. To begin with, government fears of inflation cut down the size of contract offers and, on occasion, the length of time which they were to cover. Then, worsening economic conditions—the crisis—pushed certain public-sector branches to attempt changes in work (technology and different work schedules) to increase productivity and/or actual cutbacks in personnel. On the railroads this led to severe and recurring strikes. In the Post Office such tactics set up a very long (and, from a union point of view, not terribly successful) strike in the fall of 1974. Usually the CGT led such actions, followed by the CFDT (although FO was important in the PTT strike). Regular public-sector movements of one kind or another continued through 1977.[23]

The government's room for contractual maneuver declined drastically after 1973, first because of inflation and then because of recession. Where possible, however, the government tried to hold on, relying on the faithful collaboration of less militant unions. The willingness of such unions to sign whatever the government presented them with—*Force Ouvrière* in civil-service jobs turned itself into a professional contract-signer in this period—allowed contractualism to be carried on formally amid conflict in areas where the CGT and CFDT had power, and with more substance in those parts (primarily among functionaries) where FO and FEN were pre-dominant. Since the *fonction publique* included not only civil servants per se, but teachers as well (the FEN, with several hundred thousand members, was the largest single union federation in France) the government's room for maneuver was not inconsiderable. There was little hope that *Force Ouvrière* would see the light, since it had made contractualism its central strategic premise, but there was some hope that FEN might be moved, and this is what the CGT set out to do. What the Confederation desired was to bring the FEN within the orbit of CGT-CFDT unity-in-action. This, by ex-panding such unity, was desirable in its own terms. FEN collaboration with the CGT and CFDT was all the more desirable, however, given that FEN represented several hundred thousand members of the *couches in-termédiaires* whose mobilization in opposition to government might have an important spinoff in terms of political support for *Union de la Gauche*. Thus tempting the FEN into united action with other unions became an im-portant CGT objective, as the Confederation's *Document d'Orientation* for the 1975 Congress indicated.[24]

Extra-special CGT efforts to promote common action with FEN must

23. Here one might consult Pierre Dubois, *Mort de l'état patron*. See also *Le Peuple*, 15–30 November 1974, "La politique dite contractuelle en question." In 1974 in the spring (when the government offered only 2.5 percent raises and then only for a four-month period), the CGT and CFDT refused contract offers and led actions on the RATP, SNCF and at EGF. In the fall of 1974, there was further action on the SNCF and at EGF, plus a very long PTT strike (on which one should consult CFDT, Fédération des PTT, *Des idiots par milliers* [1975]). In 1975 CGT and CFDT refused accords on the SNCF, at EGF, and the PTT, and in the *fonction publique*, with strikes in all of these areas except the civil service, in addition to full-fledged *journées d'action* at EGF, and on the RATP and SNCF. In 1975 the same routine was fol-lowed, except that on March 9 there also occurred a one-day national civil-servants' strike in which everyone participated: CGT, CFDT, FO, FEN, and the CFTC. On all of this one might consult George Ross, "Gaullism and Organized Labor, Two Decades of Failure?" in Stanley Hoffman and William Andrews, eds., *Two Decades of Gaullism*.

24. CGT, Thirty-ninth Congress, 1975, *compte rendu in extenso*, p. 584.

have influenced the teachers, but the evolution of government policy after 1976 was undoubtedly a more powerful lever. In early 1976 the Chirac government, assailed by economic crisis, offered the *fonction publique* a very bad contract, leading to a national warning strike in which not only FEN, but also FO and the rump CFTC joined the CGT and CFDT. Nonetheless, all three moderate organizations ultimately signed a revised contract. The straw which broke the camel's back for FEN was the first *Plan Barre* in the autumn of 1976 (after Chirac had been replaced as Prime Minister by Raymond Barre). Opting for severe austerity, the Barre government virtually shut down contractualism in the public sector by decreeing a wage standstill. This, on top of serious new threats to job security in education (due both to demographic changes and to government-sanctioned reduction of teaching personnel) was what forced the FEN to "see the light" on contractualism. FEN participated in the huge *journées nationales* of October 1976 and May 1977. In addition, it made its opposition to government policies crystal clear. By the springtime of 1977, then, contractualism in the public sector was nearly dead—even FO could be heard, faintly, protesting. The CGT, aided mightily by *la crise*, had won its long battle against public-sector "class collaboration."

Shaping the Labor Market—CGT/CFDT Unity-in-Action

As of 1972 the CGT and CFDT were in almost total disagreement about the structure of trade-union action in the labor market—the CGT insisting upon mass-and-class perspectives to no avail as the CFDT continued to pursue hypermilitant local strikes whenever and wherever they were possible. Here, too, much was to change in the CGT's favor. To begin with, the kinds of local struggle which favored the CFDT's tactics were to decline drastically after 1973. This, plus a slight shift in the CGT's own tactical perspective, was to allow the CGT to take the initiative in local strikes of a mass kind. Simultaneously the CFDT began to moderate its own tactical views. Finally, all of these factors plus economic crisis pushed CGT-CFDT protest back towards the *journée d'action* approach which the CGT consistently advocated.

Political and trade-union change did not coincide in 1972. *Union de la Gauche*, to the degree that it affected relationships between the CGT and CFDT, made them worse, at least in the short run. The CFDT continued to promote the kind of extreme local militancy which had so strained its ties with the CGT in the "after-May" period. It continued to philosophize about *autogestion*. And it refused to entertain the idea of supporting the Common Program. Indeed, perhaps the most spectacular of all CFDT-led local actions exploded at the Lip watch factory in Besançon in the spring and summer of 1973.[25] At Lip, the CFDT transformed a local conflict

---

25. On Lip, the best sources are *Nouvel Observateur* and *Politique Hebdo* over the summer and early autumn of 1973. In English, see Peter Herman, "The Lip Movement in France," in

about the shutdown of a mismanaged plant into a media event which involved the Lip workers taking over the factory and producing watches without any management at all. Ultimately, the government was forced to move in and bail out Lip (although not before the drawn-out struggle came dangerously close to ending Lip's existence for good). Charles Piaget, the CFDT leader at Lip, became a national celebrity, perhaps France's first hero of *autogestion*. And the CFDT and CGT at Lip were at loggerheads from beginning to end of the action.

Ironically for the CFDT, Lip, the most publicized of its hypermilitant local actions, also turned out to be the last really important one. Times had begun to change. Several things, occurred, to begin with, in the ideological field around the CFDT which had been so marked by May-June 1968. First of all the *gauchisme*, in its various forms, which had sought out the CFDT as a logical trade-union attacking point, ran out its course. Third Worldist *gauchisme*, Maoism, and Castroism, simply declined.[26] Other *gauchiste* currents, Trotskyism in particular, came more and more to have union perspectives not that dissimilar from those of the PCF and CGT. One source of action stimuli for the CFDT, moreover one which had pushed strongly towards local hypermilitancy, began to dry up, then. At the same time the "new-working–class" energies which had fueled May-June in the intellectual world and which had in part, filtered into the CFDT afterwards, began to shift away from the Confederation towards either the PS, *Union de la Gauche* and politics, or towards single-issue social movements— against nuclear power, for ecology, for women's liberation, and so on. Not that the movement for *autogestion* disappeared, but it diversified away from its point of production focus of May-June 1968 towards other, often

---

Working Papers for a New Society (Fall-Winter 1973). For a less sympathetic treatment see Bernard Brizay, *Le patronat* (1975), pp. 199 ff.

26. As an issue dividing the CGT and CFDT, *gauchisme* had only one more major flareup, in 1975 around the issue of CFDT tolerance for *gauchiste* organizers in the army. During 1975 local organizers in the army attempted to form unions at army bases, stressing strong anti-militarist ideological positions. The government arrested the organizers, and then proceeded to a search of the CFDT's Paris offices to ascertain the extent of central CFDT involvement. The CFDT, invoking the CGT-CFDT accord, then asked the CGT to join in a protest against the government's action. The CGT refused, even when the CFDT threatened to demonstrate alone. What was most at issue was the CFDT's apparent agreement with the anti-military line of the *gauchistes*. The CGT was unwilling to countenance in any circumstances any connection between the mass of organized labor and such political views. Anti-militarism ran directly contrary to one of the basic premises of the PCF's *Union du peuple de France* perspective, that the Union of the Left favored real French independence, for which a sound, albeit democratized, army was necessary. The CFDT's actions in the army risked compromising the Left's nationalist credentials, which the PCF and CGT judged critical for making electoral appeals to those social and political groups (independent producers and wavering Gaullists) who might make electoral victory possible. The CGT eventually consented to a joint CGT-CFDT demonstration on the issue of trade-union liberties, in which the question of unions in the army was avoided. See *Le Peuple*, 1–15 February 1976; *L'Humanité*, 4 December 1975.

more personal, areas. Most important for the CFDT, the economic crisis of the mid-1970s had begun to exercise determinant effects on the shape of workers' actions. Higher and higher levels of inflation made bread-and-butter issues of wages, hours, and working conditions more salient. Growing levels of unemployment worked in the same direction. Such things, compounded by an accentuation of trends towards the elimination of less profitable firms—often concentrated in specific regions—and "runaway" shop phenomena associated with the multinationalization of parts of French capital, brought defensive trade-union perspectives back to the fore with a vengeance. In themselves, these developments favored CGT perspectives on labor-market action, as the new rank-and-file qualitative concerns championed by the CFDT since the late 1960s seemed less important, however momentarily. The economic crisis was to become the central preoccupation of *both* Confederations, however.

The CGT had, historically, a tendency to use the word "crisis" promiscuously—French capitalism had been in continuous crisis since 1944, while the "crisis of state-monopoly capitalism" had been going on since 1968. But the crisis of the 1970s was not simply "crisis-discomfort for French workers" (the usual sense of the word as used by the CGT) but crisis-disaster. With the onset of the first major depression-like economic downturn since the late 1940s, the CGT had to face major new tasks. First of all, the Confederation had to do ideological battle with the controllers of the French economy to make its understanding of economic developments heard by the working-class rank and file. Secondly, the CGT had to translate its crisis analyses into action. These two processes, taken together, were to lead the CGT to preempt the leadership of militant local strikes from the CFDT. This, in turn, cut the tactical ground out from underneath the CFDT's feet.

Because of the crisis the regime and the *patronat* were obliged to begin shifting their ideology away from the Keynesian "economic growth solves all problems" optimism of earlier years. The post-war boom was over. Regular, if grudging, concessions to workers and unions on wages and other benefits, could no longer be projected into the future. Increasingly the new message from *patronat* and regime was "we are all in this together and now we must consent to sacrifice and austerity for the national good." This meant, in fact, that workers could look forward to stagnating living standards and substantial employment insecurity. In the face of this new ideological offensive, the CGT had to act to prevent workers from accepting such new analyses.

The CGT's new crisis analysis began appearing with great regularity even before the petroleum problems of 1973. In March 1973, (in *Le Peuple*) Jean-Louis Moynot, CGT Secretary charged with economic research, concluded after a long and thoughtful examination of the "Mansholt Plan" (Mansholt was a Common Market official who advocated zero growth) and the gloomy works of the Club of Rome that the monopoly caste was clearly looking for a new way of justifying its policies in new economic circumstances. Underlying social groups had to be persuaded to stop expecting regular income growth and to accept sacrifice via class collaboration. Because capitalism was in crisis, Moynot asserted, capitalists had to seduce workers towards an understanding of things in which "society" was threatened so that a new consensus on retrenchment could be achieved.[27] With the oil crisis, however, it was not simply the works of gloomy bourgeois intellectuals which had to be counteracted. It was governmental and patronal policies. *Non à l'austérité* was the Confederation's slogan. It contended, with regard to the oil crisis, that the energy situation was as much a fabrication of the oil multinationals as of the OPEC countries and that behind the oil issue lay a more general crisis of state-monopoly capitalism. As the *Document d'Orientation* of the 1975 CGT Congress explained, the crisis was international, caused by the *dérèglement* of world capitalism in which multinational firms (U.S. and West German, for the most part) played the major roles. It went on:

> In France, the crisis has the same basic causes as in other capitalist countries. The economy is dominated by a small number of giant financial groups which grow richer and more powerful to the detriment of workers and the nation. Policies carried out over the years, whose essential purpose has been their profits and the reinforcement of their positions nationally and internationally, have thrown the country into crisis.
>
> The political power of capitalist feudalities cannot effectively struggle either against unemployment or inflation. Far from getting at their basic causes, this power wants to make the workers pay the costs of crisis and seize the occasion to accelerate capitalist concentration by eliminating small, medium and sometimes even large entreprises. Redistribution of industry consists primarily in putting the country's resources and the financial and political means of the state at the disposition of industrial and financial groups which can, potentially, be of multinational size.[28]

The CGT knew full well that the route which it had to take to persuade French workers that its analysis of the crisis was correct wound through actual working-class action. And here it was that the CGT was finally able to still the CFDT's labor-market unorthodoxy. In essence, what the CGT began to do in later 1974 was to promote and seize upon local struggles—which sprung from the same ground as those earlier utilized by the CFDT, ground now fertilized, of course, by economic crisis—around the

27. Moynot, in *Le Peuple*, 1–15 March 1973.
28. CGT, *Congrès national, 1975*, p. 579.

general and mass lessons contained in its crisis analysis. Workers were to refuse austerity, working-class living standards were to be protected and the "dismantling" of French industry in the interests of multinationals and the monopoly caste was to be prevented. In essence, the crisis led the CGT to reconsider the mass possibilities of local strikes of the kind which the CFDT had earlier used to its own ends.[29] Whereas the CFDT had turned such local actions to extreme militancy and to new fields of battle to promote notions of *autogestion*, the CGT now turned them towards confirmation of the Confederation's views of the crisis. Any local struggles whose origins could be laid at the crisis' door (and there were very few which escaped such a broad net) deserved CGT attention and help. In exchange for this the leaders of many such local struggles found themselves fighting out local issues and broadcasting the CGT's crisis analysis.

Much of the original impetus for this shift on the part of the CGT came from the PCF. As we have noted, in the fall of 1974 the PCF shifted its own tactics towards polemic with the PS and towards new attempts to deepen party support in the workplace. The party's central goal was to regenerate and expand its network of workplace cells, a process which would be hastened, thought the party leadership, if Communists in factories visibly took the lead in militant local struggles. This led to party efforts to pry numbers of important party members in industry—particularly in large plants—away from a primary focus on trade-union activity through the CGT towards direct PCF action. For example, Aimé Albeher, CGT leader at Renault in Paris, was shifted to the job of coordinating party work at Renault. There were aspects of the party's efforts at this point which caused friction between it and the CGT, in particular between Marchais and Séguy. Arbitrarily moving important militants from union to party work was difficult for the CGT to accept. Even more difficult to accept were party attempts to create strident local actions to demonstrate the party's devotion to workers, actions which were not always thought through from the point of view of developing broader struggle. In time, however, the CGT was able to see the utility of such newly militant local struggles when carried on under its own aegis, and integrated into its mass strategic perspective.[30]

---

29. See *Le Peuple*, 1–15 May 1973, for a striking justification of such changes in action at Renault.

30. The workings of the PCF Central Committee's *Section des Grandes Entreprises* which was directly tied to forty-three large firms, did not make the CGT leadership happy either. It is difficult to know, in fact, what relationships, if any, were established between the *Section* and the CGT. It is likely that Colpin did deal with Krasucki and, perhaps, Séguy, through the *Bureau Politique*, but there was no general contact between the two organizations, although certain CGT National Secretaries did attend the Section's meetings (not necessarily to be guided by them, however). The possibility that the party might try to manipulate the CGT through the *Section* was clear, and CGT leaders, including Séguy, were not happy about this. It is quite possible that Séguy opposed this within the *Bureau Politique*.

Throughout 1974 and 1975, then, the CGT tended to eclipse the CFDT in its advocacy of militant local action. Such action was rife, despite the general refusal of private-sector employers to negotiate, their eagerness to resort to repressive tactics and the relative rarity of concessions.[31] Many of the tactics which the CGT had earlier stigmatized when the CFDT sanctioned them (sit-down strikes, primarily) the Confederation now found perfectly acceptable. The bulk of the more spectacular local actions recorded in these years took place, effectively, in sectors most touched by the crisis—heavy vehicles, iron and steel, aviation, textiles, the press, and printing.

How much the CGT had changed its attitudes towards local struggle was best illustrated in the long strike of CGT *Fédération du Livre* workers against the "dismantling" of the *Parisien Libéré* by press magnate Baron Amaury. The causes of the *Parisien Libéré* strike were similar to those of numerous other actions in the press and printing where the introduction of new technology, "runaway shops" and the crisis all took their toll. Indeed, in the printing industry a number of very long sit-down strikes led by the CGT occurred. *Parisien Libéré* began with a sit-down. Quite quickly, however, it turned into a virtual war between the strikers (led personally by Henri Krasucki, CGT Secretary in charge of *revendications* and member of the *Bureau Politique* of the PCF) and Amaury. With his plant taken over Amaury tried first to have the paper printed in Belgium, a move which was blocked by the solidarity of Belgian printers and transporters. Then Amaury managed to set up two clandestine "yellow" printing operations around Paris. Since distribution circuits were fully unionized, he then was obliged to set up his own network of distribution, with his own non-union drivers and unmarked trucks. This, in turn, led to intensive CGT detective work and, ultimately, wild chases through the night around Paris, with CGT strikers trying to seize the *Parisien Libéré* trucks and stop distribution (trucks were actually burned on occasion). The conflict dragged on for months and months, piling up, in the process, a mountain of litigation for unfair labor practices on both sides. Ultimately the CGT won a victory of sorts which allowed a dignified end to the conflict but not without a sizeable loss of jobs.

In all of this the CFDT's ultra-militant, anti-mass tactics simply disappeared. Skirmishes on the leadership level between CFDT and CGT over union tactics continued into 1974, but by the middle of this year the CGT had successfully reclaimed the mantle of militancy which the media had earlier awarded to the CFDT.[32] That the CFDT was also changing its mind

31. For CGT thoughts on the increased use of patronal repression see two works by Marcel Caille, CGT National Secretary responsible for legal questions, *Les truands du patronat* (1977) and *L'assassin était chez Citroën* (1978). The CGT and CFDT made the issue of employer repression central in their joint campaigns during 1975 and 1976.

32. See, for example, André Berteloot, another Confederal Secretary of the CGT, in *Nouvel Observateur*, 1 April 1974.

about its earlier practices became clear in the revised version of the CGT-CFDT unity-in-action pact which was negotiated in the early summer of 1974.[33] In this accord, for the first time the two Confederations agreed not only on the general objectives of their actions in terms of demands and concessions, but also about the methods of action appropriate for achieving these objectives. And the phrasing of the "methods-of-action" section of the accord indicated that the CFDT had indeed moved much closer to the CGT than it had been earlier on such questions. *Gauchisme* was condemned roundly and mass action was praised.

The CGT's "victory" over the CFDT on the question of union tactics had other dimensions as well, as the shape of major joint actions mounted by both Confederations increasingly indicated. The *journée d'action* returned to the scene. Branch-by-branch *journées* in the private and public sectors emerged as central mobilizing devices once again beginning in the fall of 1973. Moreover, general, interprofessional Days, with their full regalia of short local strikes, mass demonstrations (the standard march from Nation to République in Paris) and speechifying—in short, everything which Edmond Maire and colleagues had castigated as impotent in the early 1970s—became a quasi-permanent feature of France's union life.[34]

In all of this there seemed to be a profound, and pro-CGT, logic. As crisis emerged, beginning in 1973, the shape and demands of local strikes changed. Movements which the CFDT might earlier have exploited *à la Lip* became defensive wage-hours-working conditions struggles which the CGT could coordinate, under mass slogans such as *halte à la vie chère, négociations*, and *non au démantèlment*. The increase in general CGT mobilizing power which followed this obliged the CFDT to take the CGT's insistence upon certain unity-in-action tactics such as *journées d'action* much more seriously. Things moved even further as the crisis deepened and installed itself, seemingly for the long haul. Local strike actions, except in the public sector, became more and more difficult to promote. Employers ceased negotiating and resorted to repression whenever local movements did occur. This process, plus serious unemployment, dampened the desire of local militants to risk anything more extended than short symbolic protest. In this context Days of Action became the only tactic which unions could deploy to make their presence felt and keep up the spirits of the rank and file. As the crisis deepened, then, working-class discontent channelled itself more and more towards short, symbolic mass protests of the Day form, in which large numbers of workers could act without the risks involved in major, extended workplace confrontation. And, as the crisis deepened,

33. For the entire text, see *Le Peuple*, 15 July–15 August 1974.

34. There were full-fledged national Days on December 4, 1973, December 12, 1974, September 23 and December 7, 1975, October 7, 1976 and May 24,1977. During this period branch-by-branch Days occurred much more often.

journées became ever larger and ever more politicized in reaction to government austerity programs. Indeed, the last two major *journées* of 1976 and 1977 (October 1976 and May 1977), both directed primarily against the *Plan Barre* I and II, were immense outpourings of working-class anger. Each, in its turn, was the largest working-class action since May-June 1968.

Unity-in-Action and Alliance Politics

The labor-market successes of the CGT after 1972—burying the *Nouvelle Société's* contractualism, changing the CFDT's tactical mind, seducing the FEN into opposition—were undeniable and important, and not only for purely trade-union reasons. The CGT had chosen its labor-market strategy, after due consideration of the realities of the workplace world, to complement the PCF's United Front goals. With *Union de la Gauche* finally a reality, the CGT's hidden agenda in the labor market was, of course, to promote the kind of social (and ultimately electoral) mobilization which would bring the Left to power. Labor market activity of the mass-and-class kind promoted by the CGT was the major axis of such mobilization. However desirable such mobilization was for its indirect political effects—getting workers to protest against the crisis and governmental policies which hurt them—there remained a great deal more which the CGT could do to further the cause of the United Left.

As we have had occasion to remark, the CGT, although relatively autonomous from the PCF, did not eschew *all* direct politics—its self-definition as a mass-and-class organization left room for some political activity. After 1972 the CGT's direct political activity acquired new urgency. Once the Common Program was signed, it became the central focus of direct CGT political concern. Generally, this meant that the CGT disseminated, where possible, a new and powerful message. Specific trade-union actions, although of decisive defensive importance for workers, could not, in either the shorter or longer runs, lead to real solutions for working-class problems. Such problems could only be solved with the election of a United Left government and the implementation of the Common Program. It was in this direct political area that the CGT's successes after 1972 were more limited.

Of course, the CGT went to great lengths to persuade its own rank and file of the logic and virtues of the Common Program. The problem was in communicating this message to workers outside the CGT's orbit of influence. Here the CGT hoped to use the channels opened up by labor-market unity-in-action, in the first instance with the CFDT. Were the CFDT to be persuaded to share the CGT's views on these essential questions, it might then bring its own rank and file into the Common Program fold. This in itself would be important. It might also create a momentum which would extend beyond the CFDT, towards the FEN, for example. Here the CGT had to face the old debate with the CFDT about *autoges-*

tion. The CFDT believed that real change could only begin at the work-place, through struggles for *autogestion*, and that without such beginnings, national-level reforms would bring little new. The CGT wanted to persuade the CFDT of the desirability of new nationalizations, *gestion démocra-tique*, democratic planning, and the rest of the Common Program. In this task the Confederation failed completely, despite a full array of private and public attempts to persuade, seduce and harass the CFDT into submission. The CFDT went as far as support for François Mitterrand in 1974, and never hid its general sympathy for the Left. But it would not support the Common Program, nor *Union de la Gauche*. In this domain, unlike that of labor-market action, the CGT had no major sources of leverage over the CFDT. The CFDT would not budge.

In more subtle ways, however, the post-1972 years were not without their direct political returns for the CGT. By the 1970s it had become traditional for unions, including the CGT, to squeeze down labor-market activity dur-ing pre-electoral periods. The most obvious reason for this was that in-dustrial conflict during elections was easily interpreted by critical sectors of the electorate as interference in the electoral process, interference which might weight heavily on the chances of those political forces which unions favored. For the CGT such policies had become doubly important begin-ning in the 1960s as the Confederation came to understand more fully the need for it to demonstrate its devotion to the democratic process with more energy. After 1972 these reasons were even more compelling. Dampening down labor-market conflict during elections in order to create a smooth climate for voting was consistent with the CGT's position that working-class problems could not be solved by labor-market action alone, but depended, for their solution, on political change to be brought by *Union de la Gauche* through the implementation of the Common Program. In this realm, of course, the CGT had real power. If it did not have sufficient organizational resources to decree the action which it desired in the labor market, it did have sufficient resources to veto action of which it did not approve. Thus once it decided to clear the industrial decks for electoral mobilization it was able to do so, for the most part, particularly since no other union force (and especially the CFDT) was willing to place *Union de la Gauche* in electoral danger by intemperate behavior. In the abstract, all of this may seem trivial. But the period after 1972 was one of near constant electoral activity. In 1973 (general elections), 1974 (presidentials), 1976 (cantonals), and 1977 (municipals), France went to the polls. More impor-tant, each of these electoral confrontations was understood by everyone concerned as a step in the gradual progress of the United Left towards the general elections of 1978. In effect, then, after 1972 union action was reg-ularly conditioned by the occurrence of electoral contests, so that periods when electoral mobilization overshadowed labor-market concerns for the CGT and other unions became a regular fact of life. Thus what the CGT could not obtain from its union partners directly, support for *Union de la Gauche*, it did obtain indirectly, to a degree, by the ways in which the incidence of electoral consultation impinged on trade-union life. Whether other unions supported the Common Program or not, the logic of political life after the signature of the Common Program obliged them to participate in a periodic mobilization of the rank and file for electoral occasions.

The consequences of economic crisis after 1975 likewise favored the CGT's direct political goals. Drastically increased employment insecurity made other than symbolic local strike actions extremely difficult to promote once the crisis had set in. As a result *journées d'action* became an ever more important axis of both the CGT's and CFDT's tactics. *Journées*, on whatever level they occurred, cut the risk to rank-and-file participants, since they involved only short-term work stoppages and had primarily symbolic purposes. If the logic of a crisis labor market led towards *journées*, then, it was also true that *journées* tended to be more political in nature than ordinary strikes. In the public sector *journées d'action* were political by definition, directed, as they were, against the manager state. Private-sector branch-by-branch *journées* were less so, but by their generality they pointed towards political solutions for branch and sector problems. Beyond this, beginning in 1975—but particularly after the summer of 1976, when the Raymond Barre government was installed—government actions to deflate the economy and enforce austerity on the working class naturally became the central target of all *journées*, at whatever level and in whatever sector. To the degree to which government policies became the focus of union concerns, then, the crisis had the effect of politicizing almost all union activity, which automatically came to oppose such policies and demand different ones. In such a context it was much easier for the CGT to disseminate the message that the logical alternative to governmental anti-crisis (and anti-working class) policies was working-class support for the Common Program. Anyone who witnessed the huge national *journées* of October 1976 and May 1977 could hardly have avoided being struck by the centrality of political concerns expressed by strikers and demonstrators. Hundreds of thousands of *manifestants*, organized in parades by professional branches, shouting *Union, Action, Programme Commun* told the story in very concise form.

Things as They Were?

The events of summer 1977 began to reveal the history of unintended consequences which underlay what looked, to that point, to be the undivided success of the PCF and CGT. After the March 1977 municipal elections, in which a United Left won a clear majority of the votes cast, *Union de la Gauche* turned to a new page in preparation for the decisive general elections scheduled for March 1978. The first important task in this preparation was the up-dating of the 1972 Common Program, begun in the summer of 1977. The *actualisation* talks, as they were called, led, ultimately, to a complete impasse. The day-to-day unfolding of these discussions is not our concern here, but the results are. Conflict between Socialists and Communists centered on critical questions of the extent and nature of nationalizations, measures for income redistribution and defense policy. On defense policy, both parties had changed their positions since 1972 (when, in fact, the original Common Program had papered over differences with vague language) and moved much further apart, although here, after hard talks, a compromise agreement was within reach when the talks broke down.[35] On income redistribution—primarily the issues of the minimum wage and capital gains taxes—the PCF negotiators wanted a substantial raise in the minimum wage (to 2400 francs per month) which the Socialists opposed, while on capital gains taxation the PCF wanted to maintain the strong measures of the 1972 program with the Socialists insisting on milder policies.

Nationalizations were the real stumbling block. The 1972 Program had called for the nationalization of credit, insurance and nine central industrial groups. At the outset, the PCF desired to extend the list of groups to include iron and steel and the Peugeot-Citroën group in automobiles on the grounds that both were dependent on injections of state capital to maintain their positions. The Socialists refused this, and the PCF negotiators were ultimately willing to compromise on the issue of expanding the nationalization list. The real problem arose when it came time to define the meaning of "industrial group." The groups in question were all industrial conglomerates, with vast holdings not only in their main field of industrial activity, but in numbers of other, and often unrelated, fields as well. The PS negotiators insisted that a reasonable interpretation of group would involve only the parent company. The PCF insisted that group meant the entire package of parent company plus affiliates (*filiales*, in French). From this point of departure, in which the two major parties (the

---

35. Here the PCF's springtime 1977 change of defense policy should have indicated the difficulties ahead for the Left. From the 1972 Common Program, which proposed a standstill in the *Force de Frappe* and its ultimate liquidation, the PCF moved to support the nuclear deterrent, provided that it be deployed in complete independence from established military blocs—the famous *stratégie tous azimuts* (advocated as well by certain Gaullist military thinkers) in which French missiles and bombs would be targeted against all potential attackers. It is unclear why this step came at this moment, although several complementary reasons are obvious. First of all, Giscard had begun sliding France back toward NATO, a fact which displeased the PCF and, the party thought, also might displease parts of the Gaullist electorate. Secondly, the PCF suspected, on good grounds, that the Socialists, through the Socialist International, were toying with the idea of resurrecting a European Defense Community. The Socialists themselves had also changed their position on defense policy since 1972, now advocating that a referendum on the question of the *Force de Frappe* be held after the elections.

Left Radicals, who basically wanted no nationalizations at all, were used by the Socialists against the PCF position) were very far apart, some concessions were made, but no agreement could be reached.[36] In essence, the Socialists, using a narrow reading of the vague language of the 1972 accord, backed away from their 1972 commitments. Although they never admitted this change publicly, their argumentation in favor of retreat, based on the new vulnerabilities of the French economy caused by the crisis, admitted it implicitly. The Communists, in contrast, entered into the negotiations with the intention of making the Common Program even stiffer, by extending the list of nationalizations. And, while PCF negotiators were willing to bargain on their desires to strengthen the Program, they were not willing to compromise on their reading of the 1972 Program. In their perspective, the crisis of the French economy provided an ideal moment to begin a substantial change in the structure of accumulation in France. Important changes in the shape of income distribution were possible only if a *seuil minimum* (minimum level) of new nationalizations were enacted.[37]

What was essential in all of this, besides the real disagreements, was the inability of the two major parties to bargain towards a compromise solution. On the evening of September 27, 1977, *Union de la Gauche* collapsed. The *actualisation* talks broke down without conclusion, with each major participant blaming the other for rupture. "Things as they seemed"—the sometimes happy honeymoon of Left Union—had come to an end. It took a divided electoral campaign, in which attacks of the major Left parties against one another were vastly more prominent than a general Left offensive against the regime, and ultimate Left electoral defeat, to begin uncovering "things as they were."

The immediate question of rupture, why compromise was impossible to negotiate, was easy enough to answer. To begin with, one must refer back to the expectations which the PCF had for the dynamics of Left Unity. *Union* was to strengthen the Left within France to the point where the Left became an electoral majority, while simultaneously pulling the Socialists to the left within the coalition (i.e., bringing them closer in perspective to the PCF), and, finally, strengthening the PCF relative to the Socialists within the Left. The PCF based its hopes for success in these three interrelated realms on the following calculations: the Common Program, in a setting of economic and political crisis for the regime, would appear as a plausible alternative to a majority of Frenchmen, and, in particular, to critical strata in the "new middle classes" whose electoral allegiance would put the Left "over the top." Advocacy of the Common Program, in itself, would pull

36. Here see Robert Fabre's book, *Toute vérité est bonne à dire* (1979).
37. The only full version which we have of the negotiations is Pierre Juquin's book *L'actualisation à dossiers ouverts* (1978). Although Juquin, one of the PCF's negotiators, was not neutral, the fact that no other participants in the talks have denied his version of things makes the book a reasonably credible source.

the Socialists leftwards. More important, however, the PCF expected that the rapid process of Eurocommunization and "Italianization" which it had begun, haltingly, in the 1960s but accelerated in the 1970s, would attract important new support to the party itself, especially among the groups which the party called "ITC"—engineers, technicians, *cadres*—the bulk of the *couches intermédiaires* towards whom the PCF's state-monopoly capitalist analysis turned in the early 1970s. This new support—which would make the PCF itself a mass party composed of a cross-class anti-monopoly alliance of groups—when added to the PCF's traditional base, would ensure that the PCF would remain the political motor of *Union de la Gauche*. Because of this the PS would be obliged to follow the PCF's political leads which would, in turn, pull the PS to the left.

The *Union de la Gauche* did move from strength to strength after 1972, with each electoral confrontation. By the springtime of 1977, after the municipal elections, everything pointed towards a Left victory in 1978. Growth in Left strength had overwhelmingly benefited the Socialists, and not the PCF. And, partly because of this, the center of gravity in the Socialist Party stubbornly refused to move leftwards. In fact, beginning in 1974 (when the PCF had initially reacted to Socialist policies for reequilibrating the Left) the Mitterrand leadership had taken a number of steps to minimize the strength of Left tendencies within the PS (primarily by removing the CERES group from any position of influence) and therefore minimize the likelihood of leftward movement. It had also begun to re-evaluate a number of its Common Program commitments in the light of new Socialist analyses of France's economic crisis coming from a number of the PS's technocrat-economists such as Jacques Delors, Michel Rocard and Jacques Attali. In general, however, François Mitterrand was preparing himself, by endowing his leadership with near complete autonomy, in anticipation of the strategic conflicts which he knew were in the offing with the PCF. In all of this, the PCF's own strength, as demonstrated in various electoral consultations, stagnated.

What was really at issue in the summer of 1977 was a serious and growing imbalance in political resources between the PS and PCF. *Union de la Gauche* had worked in the PS's favor: the Socialists had, as a result, not moved to the left in the ways in which PCF had hoped that they would, and, in the *actualisation* talks these two processes had eventuated in important Socialist retreats from their commitments of 1972. Alas, for the PCF, the Left appeared well on the way to power in the summer of 1977. This situation therefore posed fundamental problems. The PCF's entire United Front strategy was premised on the PCF's possession of superior reserves of political resources to its partners, so that, if and when a United Left came to power, the PCF would have the last word on the shape and implementation of the Left government's policies. Without such a reserve of resources, the PCF knew that it would face, once the Left came to power, the difficult choice of supporting policies of which it would not approve or acting publicly to break up a governmental coalition. Either way it stood to lose. And, for better or worse, the one thing which the PCF did not want to become was a support group for the social-democratic policies which the Mitterrand leadership seemed ever more inclined to favor.

Confronted with what looked to be an almost completely blocked future, the PCF decided to take a perilous path. Since it could not count on having the power vis-à-vis the Socialists to implement the Common Program as it desired after a victory of the Left, it decided to try and force the Socialists, *in advance of the elections*, to agree to the kind of program which the PCF wanted. Compromise in the summer 1977 *actualisation* talks was thus impossible to achieve because, on the one hand, the PS, weighing its new strength relative to the PCF, felt able to push for an edulcorated Common Program while, on the other, the PCF was determined to prevent any such edulcoration from occurring. To compensate for its own relative weakness, the PCF had only one weapon. But this weapon was a very threatening one indeed! The party could assume the risk of breaking Left Unity just at the point when the Left seemed about to succeed. The PCF's (desperate) calculations were, then, clear. The Socialists, who wanted more than anything to come to power, would have to choose between giving in to the PCF in order to win electorally or refusing to give in, at the risk of definitive rupture and the almost certain electoral defeat which such rupture would entail. When the Socialists chose not to give in, the electoral and political fate of *Union de la Gauche* was sealed.[38]

The difficult circumstances of summer 1977 were one thing, the deeper reasons for their existence were another. Here the contrast between things as they seemed and things as they were was clearest. The events of summer 1977 were, more than anything, an admission of strategic failure by the PCF. The expanding base of political resources which the PCF needed to ensure its leverage within *Union de la Gauche* depended upon the success of the party's efforts at Eurocommunization. The party had moved towards Eurocommunism primarily to expand its base of support beyond its traditional, primarily working-class, limits. From Eurocommunization the PCF envisaged the construction of a cross-class, anti-monopoly alliance in and around the party, *à l'italienne*. At the heart of the PCF's new social-alliance goals were openings towards the *couches intermédiaires*—engineers, *cadres*, technicians, intellectuals, white-collar employees—openings based on the new modernist face which the PCF believed itself able to present. The PCF's failure along these dimensions was the ultimate cause of its in-

---

38. It is a legitimate, although rarely asked, question (at least outside the PCF) why François Mitterrand and the Socialists were so reluctant to give in more than they were. Undoubtedly reasons of principle, electoral calculations and misjudgments about the intentions of the PCF were mixed up in this posture.

ability to sustain its own United Front politics as the general election of 1978 approached.[39]

Analyzing the causes of such a profound strategic failure, uncovering the logic of things as they were after 1972, is a difficult task. To begin with, we must keep in mind that, with regard to new social alliances, both the PCF and the PS had the same strategic goal—to recruit "new middle-class" support. PS and PCF were therefore fighting for the political allegiance of the same social categories. And in any such fight, the PS was bound to have certain a priori advantages. To begin with, the PS's natural social bases and political proclivities were much closer to those of the new *couches intermédiaires* of advanced capitalism than were those of the PCF. Social-democratic reformism, as an ideological point of departure, was bound to be more comfortable to new intermediary groups, as they moved leftwards, than the more orthodox and strident Marxism of the PCF. And the PS was, basically, a party of the middle classes, with all which such a social base implied in terms of lifestyle and cultural preferences, not to speak of ways of perceiving the world and presenting such perceptions in words. The PCF, in contrast, was primarily a working-class party with, moreover, the strong handicap in wooing new middle strata which an *ouvrièriste* past—not altogether gone—presented.

The contrast between the PCF's past and that of the PS raises another point. In the Fourth Republic, French social democracy had established a very dubious record of unprincipled compromise with Center and Right political forces in order to acquire ministerial posts which had involved support for anti-working–class social policies and brutal colonial warfare. However, the later 1960s brought an important break with this past. The SFIO bowed out, along with the leaders who had been responsible for its sinuous and rather degrading post–World War II policies. The new PS had a new leadership, a considerably different internal balance of forces, new analyses and new rhetoric. The break in the PS's history which occurred in the 1969–1972 period allowed the Socialists to renew their appeal in ways which were much more difficult, both internally and externally, for the PCF to do. And here it must be said that the new PS proceeded skillfully in its appeals to the new middle strata. The PCF had emerged from May-June 1968 on the wrong side of the vast malaise which had caused the May-June crisis in the world of students and intellectuals. The PS could therefore make good use of the slogans and hopes of this world in its attempt to win their allegiance, as the adoption by the PS of the notion of *autogestion* indicated most clearly. The PS, in the process of regrouping, was also able to make space, even at very high levels in the party, for newcomers from such

39. Ironically, the PCF *had* managed to shift its recruitment towards greater "new middle-class" membership in the post-1968 period. Its broader base of support, in particular electorally, had not followed this, however.

groups. Its success in attracting new middle-class support was therefore obvious by the mid-1970s.

The relative failure of the PCF in this realm cannot, however, be written off solely by listing the advantages which the PS had from the start. For the PCF was somewhat aware of the PS's head start and was attempting, in what it did do, to compensate for it. In essence, the failure of 1977 was the failure of the PCF's own, tragic history. The PCF's hopes for a new cross-class anti-monopoly base of support did not materialize because the new social groups which the party desired to attract did not feel comfortable, by and large, in giving their allegiance to French Communism. The processes of Eurocommunization and de-Stalinization in the PCF had come too late in time and had been too limited in their scope for the party to make a plausible appeal to the *couches intermédiaires* whose help the party needed to carry out its United Front goals. The party had begun to take its distance from the Soviet Union and the Soviet model for socialism in a serious way in the mid-1970s. It had begun, haltingly, to recognize that real problems of civil and political liberties existed in the Socialist bloc. It had begun a profound conversion towards accepting the likelihood of, and need for, political pluralism in the French Left and in any future French socialism. But all of these changes had been undertaken only as *Union de la Gauche* became a political reality (with the exception of the commitment to pluralism, begun earlier, but only really affirmed convincingly with the abandonment of the "dictatorship of the proletariat" in 1976).

Moreover, the party's past and the ways in which it began to change even in the 1970s—it gave the impression of making concessions on fundamental questions of liberty and democracy primarily because it wanted to present itself as a plausible ally for other Left parties, and not out of profound conviction—could not help but create reservations among new middle strata. The PCF claimed to be democratic in its own life, yet the entire process of Eurocommunization and de-Stalinization was promoted from above, by the party leadership. And while the leadership had clearly initiated some important internal PCF changes, encouraging more debate and discussion at the base, such changes had not been substantial enough to match the party's claims for itself and, moreover, they had been decreed from the top in the first place. The PCF still carried on its relationships with the outside world—as evidenced by the brutal polemic with the Socialists in 1974–1975—and its internal conflicts (the Garaudy case could not be forgotten) in ways which were much too reminiscent of a too-recent past. Beyond this, the PCF in the 1970s continued to pay a huge price for its disastrous strategic misjudgments vis-à-vis intellectuals in the 1950s (especially around the crisis which brought de Gaulle to power), the early 1960s (around the Algerian War and, later, around "Italian" and "Chinese" deviations in PCF student organizations) and in May-June 1968. Opinion polls and other evidence indicated, by the mid-1970s, that the PCF had begun to change its popular image, that Cold War anti-Communism was gradually subsiding and that parts of the French electorate were less fearful of the PCF than they once had been. But from such evidence to the cross-class coalition which the party needed to succeed in its United Front goals of the 1970s the distance was very great.

For the PCF until summer 1977, things had seemed promising indeed. Things as they were were tragic. For in fact, the PCF *had* begun a long, complicated voyage into the uncharted waters of Eurocommunism. But the party had started out on this voyage much too late, and with too little wind in its sails, to achieve the goals which it had set for itself in the United Front campaign which began in the early 1960s and terminated so abruptly in summer 1977. The PCF of the 1970s was a victim of its own history and, more importantly, of its own inability and unwillingness to confront and understand this history. The Stalin era had left the PCF with a complex and weighty legacy. However, rather than examining this legacy and acting in accordance with the results of such an examination, the PCF had avoided and buried the problem of Stalinism. For this the party leadership of the 1950s, Maurice Thorez most of all, bore responsibility. The Twentieth Congress of the Soviet Communist Party in 1956 had presented an ideal opportunity to begin a change of direction. Unlike the PCI and Palmiro Togliatti, the PCF and Thorez had rejected this opporutnity. The premise of any ultimate United Front success for the PCF was thorough de-Stalinization, well enough advanced so that the PCF's United Front allies and, above all, the new social groups upon whose support the PCF's strategic hopes depended, could count on its completeness. Instead, the PCF took its course of late, incomplete, and halting de-Stalinization only *simultaneously* with the late stages of the United Front offensive of the 1970s. By 1977 the PCF faced a situation in which it did not have the resources to carry out its politics. The reason for this was that, earlier in time, the PCF had not taken the necessary steps to create the politics which might have led to the accumulation of these resources.

The contrast between things as they seemed and things as they were was not confined to politics. The CGT, beginning in the late 1950s and early 1960s, had developed a new model for its relationship with the PCF, a model which we have labelled relative autonomy. This model had been created to allow the Confederation to redevelop its mass trade-union credibility after the distortions of the Cold War years. It aimed at establishing a new division of labor between PCF and CGT in which CGT labor-market action would be autonomous and *ultimately* complementary to the PCF's political goals, ultimately in the sense that the CGT would pay scrupulous attention to the realities of the working-class world on the shop floor before choosing its fundamental strategic axes. As we have seen, the Cold War problems of enforced, direct, one-to-one correspondence between the PCF's day-to-day political desires and CGT activity—which, at the height of the Cold War, had threatened the CGT's very survival—had been satisfactorily resolved by this reorganization of tasks between party and trade union. Still, the notion of complementarity, even with studious reference to the situation in the labor market by the Confederation, admitted of a variety of interpretations. In general, the meaning which the CGT attached to relative autonomy was bound to correlate with the PCF's primary strategic choices. Beyond this, the CGT's specific translation of this general choice into trade-union practice was bound to change over time as the PCF's strategy unfolded from stage to stage. Finally, as we saw in our analysis of the May-June 1968 situation, the entire notion of relative autonomy might well be called into question, in the heat of a major crisis when, to the CGT leadership, the Confederation's general *position de classe* seemed to dictate closer and more direct identification with Communist goals. Thus even if the extreme politicization of the transmission-belt years seemed gone forever for the CGT, there remained considerable room for greater or lesser politicization of the CGT within the ill-defined boundaries of its new relative-autonomy role.

The decade of the 1960s, that is to say the early years of the PCF's modern United Front offensive, demonstrated the benefits which might acrue to the CGT from its redefined relationship to the PCF. In the PCF's eyes, mass working-class mobilization of a classic, labor-market–based, defensive type was what was needed to provide the social foundations of mass mobilization which would, in turn, fertilize the ground for the creation of Left Unity. Thus the CGT was free to promote new, non-sectarian, unity-in-action arrangements with other unions and working-class labor-market action of all sorts. In the process the CGT was able to reconstruct its public image as a genuine trade-union organization and not the labor-market arm of French Communism, gaining membership and mobilization power at the same time. And, to the degree to which renewed protest in the labor market exposed the priorities of the Gaullist regime and the connections of this regime with the French *patronat*, important political messages were also communicated to rank-and-file workers. The signature of the Common Program in 1972, however, marked the beginning of a new stage in the unfolding of the PCF's United Front thrust. In consequence, the shape of CGT behavior began to change.

The consecration of Left Unity with the Common Program meant that the electoral success of the Left, probably in the 1978 general elections, became the priority of the PCF. Whereas in earlier years trade-union action, in and of itself, had been understood as complementary to, but separate from, the PCF's quest for a firm alliance of the Left in the political sphere, after 1972 (and particularly after the Presidential elections of 1974), the eyes of both party and union began to focus more narrowly on the same objective, victory in 1978. *From this point mobilizing workers for Left electoral success became as important as day-to-day trade-union action for the CGT.* As we have observed, after 1972 day-to-day trade-union action increasingly came to carry a complicated network of messages to workers. Trade-union struggle in itself was important, but, in itself, it could bring no lasting solution to the problems of workers. Only the victory of *Union de la Gauche* and the implementation of the Common Program promised such solutions. The CGT's new marching slogan, *Union, Action, Programme Commun,* graphically illustrated this shift, which was facilitated by an economic crisis of such depth that it made mass symbolic (and hence political) union activities the major recourse of the CGT and other union organizations. As the Left entered the home stretch towards the 1978 elections, the change in the CGT's behavior became increasingly marked. The Confederation slipped progressively, albeit quietly, towards greater politicization.

The shape of the CGT's politicization in the 1970s was very different, however, from the transmission-belt excesses of the Cold War years. Whereas in the transmission-belt period the CGT had mobilized directly and immediately for the PCF's day-to-day purposes, in the 1970s the relatively autonomous CGT became the trade-union ally of an entire political coalition and its programs. The CGT became vehemently and vocally pro–*Union de la Gauche* and pro–Common Program. As a result the CGT was not exposed, as it had been in the Cold War years, to extreme isolation and an onslaught of anti-Communism. Still, politicization was politicization, whether sectarian or ecumenical. As such, it carried with it definite risks. Increasing CGT stress on the priority of Left political success over labor-market action inevitably worked to draw the attention of the working-class rank and file away from base-level trade-union problems towards a vision of salvation through politics. The Common Program tended to become the magic solution to all outstanding issues.

To the degree to which such a shift in emphasis by the Confederation was successful—and, as we have noted, almost everything conspired towards its success, including union actions, the economic crisis, and the extended and intensive pre-electoral fever which seized all of France from 1975 onwards—the rank and file was bound to be relatively demobilized for ordinary trade-union purposes. And this was true whether the Left won or lost the upcoming elections, but true in different ways, depending upon the outcome. If the Left won, the situation which would almost certainly have followed such a victory, involving attempts to implement the Common Program in a setting of severe economic crisis, would have demanded subtle perceptions of new circumstances from rank-and-file unionists. After thirty years of hostile governments, ordinary workers would have been sorely tempted to ask for as many concessions as possible from a Left government. Yet for any such government to survive, these same ordinary workers would need a sophisticated understanding of the relationship between a Left government's policies and immediate bread-and-butter concessions, and considerable self-restraint.[40] To the degree to which support for the Common Program became a ritual incantation which transcended shop-floor realities—and there were many disturbing signs that this was the case, as in particular it was clear that most rank and filers had only the most elementary understanding of the logic of nationalizations as applied to specific branches of industry—such sophisticated understanding was actually being blocked rather than developed. If the Left lost, a different, but equally difficult, situation could be anticipated. Left defeat would mean victory for the existing majority and, in all likelihood, an intensification of policies of austerity, industrial relocation and high unemployment. In such a context rank-and-file militancy would be tremendously important. Yet such militancy would have to be reconstructed, after the elections, from the ground up, in so far as the relative neglect and diversion of rank-and-file activity had followed pre-electoral politicization. Moreover, were the high hopes built up by such politicization dashed by defeat, the task of reinvigorating rank-and-file life would be doubly difficult because of the demoralization which would certainly ensue.

Direct politicization was only part of the problem. To the degree to which the CGT had carried on ordinary labor-market action during the post-1972 years, the strategy and tactics of such action, chosen to be complementary to the political situation, had also been seriously distorted. In its powerful concern to defeat the new contractualism emanating from the public sector (a concern which spilled over onto CGT action in the private sector as well) the CGT had created a very delicate balance which, at any moment, could move against its best interests. In the struggle against the new contractualism the CGT had repeatedly engaged its full union power in actions to transcend the concessions which the state and private employers were prepared to offer contractually. And, quite often, such struggle led to partial successes in which employers were obliged to concede more than they had intended to originally. However, when such partial successes were codified into reformulated contracts the CGT usually refused to sign. Other unions were less reticent. *Force Ouvrière*, for example, in a clear effort to capitalize on what it saw as the CGT's tactical mistake, turned itself into a professional contract-signer during these years. The problem in all of this was that those unions who signed the contracts (and the CFDT, at Federation and other levels, often joined FO) were often able, thereafter, to claim responsibility for the employers' concessions which, in fact, CGT mobilization had made possible.

More dangerous, perhaps, were the effects of the CGT's determination to generalize the nature of labor-market–action demands so that they represented the broadest possible level of mass concern and had, as their ultimate object, negotiations at the highest possible level (branch-level peak-

40. See Serge Christophe Kolm's astute analysis in *La transition socialiste* (1977).

employers' associations, the CNPF, the government). Here again the Confederation's concern had been to promote union action which would lead to spectacular public concessions from employers around highly general questions which were easily translatable into political conclusions. One result of this quest for generality was that rank-and-file workers progressively found the CGT to be less in touch with the issues which really mattered to them—a feeling which became particularly acute in the crisis after 1975 as the CGT pulled out all stops to deploy the *journée d'action* tactic. The CGT's flight towards generality was especially ill-advised in certain sectors of the French economy (metals and electronics, for example) where the *patronat* had learned certain new lessons after May-June 1968. Divine-right perspectives in such sectors tended to disappear, to be replaced by more "American" techniques of management. Experiments in work reorganization became common, as did complex human-relations personnel methods and changes in the assigned functions of foremen on the shop floor. Foremen, instead of being primarily disciplinarians, assumed the task of being conduits of communications from workers to managers and vice versa on grievance and other questions, thus to an important degree supplanting trade-union delegates.

With such subtle changes in management approaches to shop-floor problems (which were often accompanied by more sophisticated anti-union tactics) emerging simultaneously with the CGT's efforts to displace rank-and-file attention upwards from shop-floor concerns towards high generalities in a context of deepening economic crisis it was not surprising that the CGT itself began to suffer certain organizational difficulties. The Confederation's membership began to stagnate. In effect, in terms of active workers, membership actually began to decline slightly, as the numbers of retired CGTers grew relative to the total Confederation membership. The problematic evolution of CGT membership was evident from the Confederation's own figures, announced as follows at different Congresses:

Congress	*Membership*
33rd (1961)	1,602,322
34th (1963)	1,722,294
35th (1965)	1,939,318
36th (1967)	1,942,523
37th (1969)	2,301,543 (including 243,641 retired)
38th (1972)	2,333,056 (including 271,637 retired)
39th (1975)	2,400,000 (approx. 300,000 retired)
40th (1978)	2,400,000 (approx. 300,000 retired)

The usual reservations about these figures are in order (as with all French union-membership figures, the numbers refer to the number of membership cards distributed, and not to the meaning of such distribution, i.e., whether the cardholder paid dues regularly). Even in their uninterpreted form, however, they clearly indicate that the CGT growth of the 1960s had stopped in the 1970s. At Congresses in the 1970s Confederal leaders still talked optimistically about the CGT's "campaign for three million," but the campaign to increase union membership had clearly begun to fail by 1977. Growing Confederal concern about the financial state of the organization corroborated an hypothesis that membership had, in fact, begun to decline. Yet another indication of organizational difficulties were relative CGT losses in professional elections. The losses were not enormous, but enough to generate considerable concern.[41] Over all, then, the CGT's trade-union independence—to the degree which it had been painfully created out of the wreckage of the transmission-belt years—was seriously undermined in the years after 1972. The Confederation's understanding of relative autonomy was not sophisticated enough to withstand the feverish politicization of everything and everyone touching *Union de la Gauche.*

41. Voting percentages in professional elections (*comité d'entreprises*) follow:

		CGT	CFDT	FO	CGC	Non-union
Election 74	T	42.7	18.6	8.3	5.3	15.7
	C1	49.0	19.4	8.1	0.4	14.3
	C2	25.5	19.4	9.2	17.1	19.1
	C3	7.8	11.0	3.3	36.6	23.7
Election 75	T	38.1	19.6	8.4	5.7	19.0
	C1	44.6	20.2	8.6	0.4	18.2
	C2	20.8	19.0	8.4	18.1	21.6
	C3	3.6	11.3	7.4	36.0	22.5
Election 76	T	41.5	19.1	9.3	5.3	14.6
	C1	47.9	19.8	9.0	0.4	13.9
	C2	25.0	19.0	11.1	15.9	16.5
	C3	8.2	11.2	7.6	37.5	17.8
Election 77	T	37.4	20.2	9.0	5.4	18.8
	C1	43.5	21.0	8.0	0.6	17.8
	C2	20.2	19.2	9.1	16.9	22.3
	C3	7.1	13.1	7.8	34.2	22.0

Source: *Travail Informations, Ministry of Labor each year.*

Key: Total vote = T
    College 1 = C1—Workers and white collar employees (operatives)
    College 2 = C2—Foremen, technicians (includes *cadres* where fewer than twenty-five exist in the firm)
    College 3 = C3—*Cadres* (where more than twenty-five in firm)

N. B.: *Comités d'entreprise* are mandatory for firms with *more than forty-nine employees,* they may exist in firms of smaller size, but only if they, at one time in the past, employed more than forty-nine. Thus only about one-third of the French labor force votes in the above elections. In addition, individual *comités d'entreprise* are elected once every *two* years, thus each year's election figures indicate results only for those firms where elections occurred. Despite such problems, the above results provide the major indicators for unions of their support, given the fact that membership figures indicate, for the most part, activists. We have excluded several smaller unions from the tables.

The Confederation became, in sequence, a trade-union support organization for *Union de la Gauche*, a posture which, in turn, led to contradictions which were certain to weigh heavily on the Confederation's future. The split-up of Left Unity in summer 1977 created yet another set of contradictions for the CGT, further compounding the difficulties which the post-1972 years had already created. The PS-PCF rupture demoralized a working class which had been led to expect Left victory and major change. Worse still, the rupture confronted the CGT leadership with a terrifying new choice to make. Should it assume a "hands-off" position in the dispute between the two Left parties in the hope that they could come to agreement between themselves before it was too late? This choice would neutralize the CGT's resources in the PS-PCF dispute but it had the advantage of respecting the CGT's relative-autonomy posture. Or should the Confederation mobilize itself and its supporters on the PCF's side in the hope that such a mobilization might be decisive in producing new concessions from the Socialists? The Confederation could claim some "legal" justification for choosing the latter course, since its own longstanding programmatic commitments were very close to those from which the Socialists had retreated in the *actualisation* talks. Yet such legalistic grounds for defending the PCF were too transparent for a CGT whose own programs were often near-direct translations from those of the PCF and whose leadership was overwhelmingly Communist. Thus if the situation after 1972 had led the CGT towards over-politicization of its union activity in support of Left Union, the circumstances which developed after summer 1977 threatened to move the CGT backwards in time towards a posture resembling that of the transmission-belt years. In an atmosphere heavily charged with anti-Communism, in which unity-in-action was already tenuous with the CFDT and in which the CGT's labor-market practices in the post-1972 period made it vulnerable at the base, the risks involved in such a regression were obvious. Yet did not the CGT's *position de classe* dictate the assumption of such risks? The electoral campaign of 1977–1978 was to demonstrate how vulnerable the CGT's relative autonomy was to crisis-engendered political calculations.

Chapter 10

THE RECKONING: 1978

Sometimes events provide more eloquent analyses than academic abstractions. For the PCF and the CGT the momentous events of 1977–1978 are of this kind. By 1978 it had become clear that the PCF's United Front strategic initiative, which had begun in the early 1960s, had totally collapsed. This collapse, and the confused attempts by the party leadership to find another strategic perspective to replace *Union de la Gauche*, led to an unprecedented explosion of discontent and self-criticism in the party. In all this, the contradictions of the party's history plus those of the incomplete processes of Eurocommunization of the 1970s came together in a graphic summary of the dilemmas of French Communism. The CGT was unable to escape the trauma of these times, either. Its strategy and its relationship of relative autonomy with the party both collapsed. What occurred in the calamitous year of 1978, then, had almost the value of an experiment for this study. In 1978 the central actors in our story themselves proceeded to discuss and analyze the very things which we have described in earlier pages. The PCF had to face its own failures, the CGT likewise. Then both party and union had to devise ways to act in a very uncertain future.

The Election of 1978

The PCF's electoral campaign after the night of September 22, 1977, was shaped by the contradictory unfolding of its United Front strategy. The party leadership had hoped that the Socialists would react to the threat of Left disunity brandished by the PCF in the *actualisation* (updating) talks by conceding on key points. The Socialists refused. The PCF therefore felt obliged to act on its threat. In the autumn of 1977 the Communists could still hope that the Socialists would, in time, change their positions, as the March 1978 elections drew closer and the likely electoral costs of Left disunity became clearer. In an effort to hasten this end, the PCF launched a brutal and strident campaign against the Socialists, reminiscent of earlier "class-against-class" and Cold War diatribes against the "right-wing social democrats." Communist spokesmen, Georges Marchais in particular, blamed the PS for the failure of the Program negotiations and tied this to a Socialist "turn to the right" often, in turn, connected with an alleged *rapprochement* between the PS and the German Social Democrats. The ultimate logic of such attacks was, to be sure, to undermine prospects for Left victory. The PCF hoped that this logic would not be followed to its conclusion—perhaps a compromise could be reached—but it was prepared to carry it out.[1]

It was on the level of social alliances that the PCF faced the most unpleasant realities. Since 1972 it had failed to make any real progress towards the cross-class base of electoral support upon which its United Front strategy hinged. Beyond this, however, Socialist success had actually begun to threaten parts of the PCF's traditional electoral base. To confront this situation the PCF devised campaign tactics worthy of a Hollywood western. It began to draw all of its wagons in a circle around its working-class supporters to protect them from the Socialist Indians. Primarily, this involved centering the party's electoral appeals on issues which were felt most strongly by workers and the poor—discourses on poverty and misery, the outrageous luxury of the rich, the urgency of raising the minimum wage, erasing unemployment, protecting people against the immediate economic consequences of the crisis (blocking evictions and repossessions, for example), and, in general, advocating policies to "soak the rich." Such an approach, when coupled with the attacks on the Socialists for having caused the Left split, was designed to deprive the PS of any Left legitimacy among the PCF's traditional base of support which it might have acquired over the years of *Union*.[2] And, in fact, given the Socialists' own pressing need to concentrate their electoral fire on Centrist and new middle-class segments of the population, the PCF's approach did make it very difficult for the Socialists to touch much of the PCF's working-class vote. It had the fault, however, of rendering the PCF's appeal virtually incomprehensible to anyone but workers. In essence, the PCF reacted to the longer-term

1. It is technically correct to claim—as a number of observers have done—that the PCF was willing to lose the 1978 elections, if one insists upon the important caveat that such a will to lose held true for only *one* of the PCF's tactical scenarios, the one in which the Socialists refused to concede what the Communists wanted.

2. One of the things which had happened, and of which the PCF became rather painfully aware in the 1977 municipal election campaigns, was that the Left "protest vote" which had gone to the PCF for years because no plausible other Left group existed had begun to loosen. *Union de la Gauche* had the effect of legitimizing the PS as a Left force (largely because of the PCF's work, it should be said) and as this process matured, segments of the protest vote which had come to vote PCF not because of pro-Communist commitment, but because of "Left" feelings, slipped towards the PS. Re-firming up PCF support among protest voters by depriving the PS of its Left credentials—denouncing its *virage à droite*—was one of the PCF's goals during the electoral campaign.

failures of its social alliance strategy by renouncing its cross-class alliance goals during the electoral period. Instead, it assumed a defensive posture and fell back upon many of the tried-and-true reflexes of *ouvrièrisme*.

The campaign, like the *actualisation* talks, became a stalemate. The PCF never stopped attacking the PS. Neither the PCF nor the PS spent anywhere near the ammunition against the existing majority which they used against one another. Indeed, things reached the point where the Communists threatened that, unless the PCF's electoral results counterbalanced those of the Socialists, and/or the Socialists gave in on program, the PCF might withhold support from leading Socialists in the second round of the elections, a threat which promised total electoral disaster. The Socialists did not budge on what counted to the PCF. Why they did not is a matter worth speculating about. Undoubtedly, for some time, the Socialist leadership judged the Communist posture as a bluff, reasoning that the PCF really wanted to come to power and, to do so, it would eventually soften its stand to reforge unity. Beyond this simple calculation lay questions of ideology and principle. The Socialist leaders, impressed by the depth of French economic problems, were much less willing to confront the costs of major structural reforms than were the Communists. They were committed to a substantial amount of welfarist type of change. But their essential goal, insofar as it ever became clear, was probably the promotion of a mild degree of public ownership in France in order to regenerate French investment and growth—capitalist growth. That the Socialists were more aware than the Communists that the economic logic of the Common Program overestimated the amount of orderly economic change which might flow from strictly national structural reforms and underestimated the complexity of the international division of labor (and the likely vengeance which this division would take on determined structural reformers in France) is clear. Most importantly, the Socialist leadership had no desire to be caught up in the logic of change which the PCF proposed. Beyond all of this, Socialist electoral calculations worked in the same direction. Socialist leaders believed that the PS would be better able to appeal to the critical three to four percent of the floating new middle-class vote—allegedly intimidated by the fear of change and of the PCF—if it took its distance from the PCF. Most interestingly, the entire campaign took place against a background of public-opinion polls which consistently pointed to a Left victory, disunity or not.

Two desperate gambles were played out to the end. The Communists were banking on the fact that anticipation of the costs of Left disunity would force the Socialists to give in on program. The Socialists believed, in contrast, that Left disunity would not prevent Left success.[3] When the results of the first round of the election (March 12, 1978) came in, it was

3. For a brief account of the campaign as experienced by a Paris PCF cell, see George Ross and Jane Jenson, "Life in a French Communist Cell," *Canadian Dimension* (November-December 1978).

obvious that both parties had lost their bets. If one included the vote of extreme Left and ecology groups, the Left had not done badly, winning a plurality of the votes cast.[4] When projected ahead to the March 19 runoff, however, the results indicated that there would not be enough support for the Left to win a parliamentary majority. Communist efforts to punish the Socialists for their "right turn" were mildly rewarded nonetheless. The Socialist vote, which the PS and the polls had expected to be twenty-six to twenty-seven percent of the first round total, stuck at 22.5 percent. The Socialists had anticipated breakthroughs not only towards the political Center, but also into the PCF's electoral base, neither of which occurred. The critical three to four percent of middle-class voters in whose hands both Socialist success and the election's outcome depended had switched back to support of the existing Majority at the very last moment. On the Left, the PCF had succeeded in protecting its own base.

Communist cells and sections talked a good deal about the party's "victory over social democracy" between the two election rounds, by this meaning the party's ability to conserve its usual electoral strength (20.5 percent) during a difficult time. The talk was hollow, however. Party militants knew first hand that the party's soak-the-rich campaign had made Communist candidates unpalatable to non-working–class voters, a fact which had hurt PCF candidates in constituencies where only a combination of working-class and other votes could have placed them in the runoff (the case in many urban settings, especially Paris). Defeating social democracy seemed even more hollow because the party had lost its larger gamble by failing to force the Socialists to give in on program. This failure placed the party in a delicate situation for the runoff. Were it to carry out its earlier threats not to support better-placed Socialists in the second round, electoral disaster for the Left and an absolute impasse for any future United Front plans would be certain to follow. Yet none of the issues of principle posed by the party in the electoral campaign had been resolved. Predictably, principle gave way to shorter-run concerns. On the day following the first round the PCF and PS signed an agreement to exchange support without negotiating new arrangements on program. Militants found this puzzling. If the PS-PCF split had not been based on profound disagreement, then why the split at all? If the split had been based on principle, then why the last minute accord? In any case, bad blood between the rank and file of the two parties ran too deep to allow for a week-long joint campaign with any enthusiasm. The outgoing Majority therefore moved in for the kill, mounting an intense propaganda barrage in which crude anti-Communism was given pride of place. By the evening of the second round, only the size of the Majority's victory was surprising. Although the real division of the vote

4. For election statistics, see *Le Monde*, "Les élections législatives de mars 1978," *Dossiers et Documents du Monde* (March 1978). See also the special issues of the *Revue Française de Science Politique* on the 1978 elections (December 1978); and *Cahiers du Communisme* (special number on the elections, 1978).

was quite close (less than one percent) the Center-Right coalition returned to power with a substantial majority of seats in parliament.

These events placed the CGT in an extremely difficult position. As we earlier remarked, the Confederation had maneuvered itself unwittingly into a trade-union cul-de-sac even before the PCF-PS split. In the interest of Left political success after 1972, the CGT had stressed politics over trade unionism overall, and the very general over the point-of-production-specific in the trade-unionist sphere. By 1977, whoever won the 1978 elections, it was clear that the CGT was in trouble. Were the Left to win, the over-simple pre-electoral politicization of union life and the over-generalization of trade-union demands would have found the CGT ill-prepared to generate the sophisticated rank-and-file trade-union support for a Left government which such a government would have needed. Were the Left to lose, the Confederation would find itself equally ill-equipped to regenerate the rank-and-file oppositional union activity which would be needed to deal with a reinvigorated Majority bent on increased austerity and industrial redeployment. The split on the Left made things much worse, however. If the CGT did not use its resources on the PCF side of the split, it might forego possibilities of influence which could prove decisive. If it did so intervene, the risks were huge. Direct support for the PCF would compromise the CGT's mass appeal, carefully reconstructed in nearly two decades of relative autonomy from the PCF. It might also cause internal difficulties. There was also a strong possibility that a part of the CGT's base would be unwilling or unable to follow the Confederation in such an intervention. Finally, CGT aid for the PCF would almost certainly undermine unity-in-action with the CFDT.

What the CGT would do was a foregone conclusion, of course. It was simply a question of how far the CGT was willing to go towards open support for the PCF. The CGT's first major statement after Left rupture deploring the split and reaffirming its long-standing commitment to the Common Program, was issued by the *Bureau Confédéral* on September 22. Then, on September 26, the Confederation held a press conference on the issues in conflict. Jean-Louis Moynot, armed with several industry studies prepared by CGT Federations, argued quite convincingly that, were one to accept the Socialist position on the nationalization of subsidiaries (the PS initially argued against taking over anything but the actual stock owned by a nationalized mother company unless this was more than fifty percent of a *filiale*), the purpose of nationalization, "to give ourselves the means for real change," would be defeated. Henri Krasucki, who presided, discussed the CGT's own commitment to the Common Program, noting that the CGT had advocated a Common Program long before the political Left had negotiated one. It was an indelicate coincidence that both Moynot and Krasucki were Communists, with Krasucki a member of the *Bureau Politique*. What was not coincidental was the fact that the CGT took the same position on nationalizations as the PCF. Confederal spokesmen could argue, technically correct, that the CGT had reached this position independently, after long CGT deliberations and the duly consecrated decisions of CGT Congresses. The identity of PCF and CGT positions spoke louder than such technicalities, alas.[5]

The CGT *Commission Exécutive* of October 3–4 generalized the Confederation's position. A minimum level of nationalization was the absolute prerequisite for the kind of change which the CGT desired to see, and only such a *seuil minimum* would create the economic leverage needed to implement the long list of redistributive and other reforms contained in the Common Program.[6] Once again PCF and CGT positions on the *actualisation* dispute were virtually identical. However the Confederation's declaration on the issue did not pass the Executive Commission unanimously. The vote, 90–2, was overwhelming, but the presence of more than eighty Communists on the Executive Commission made this automatic. The two negative votes were significant. The CGT leadership was dividing along partisan lines. Pierre Carassus (a Paris Departmental Union Secretary and CERES militant) contended that the Confederation had never officially adopted the specific position on the nationalization of *filiales* which the leadership was promoting (the leadership claimed the opposite, of course, and probably with reason). Claude Germon, editor-in-chief of *Le Peuple*, the CGT's official magazine, agreed. With Germon, the CGT leadership was falling into a trap of its own making. Germon had been parachuted onto the CE and towards *Le Peuple* as a *Socialiste d'office* (token Socialist) to demonstrate the pluralism of the Confederation, a long-standing CGT practice. Germon, however, had come to be tempted by higher ambitions of a political kind. Angling towards a Socialist seat in parliament in March 1978, Germon proved very willing to become the leader of an extremely small, but very vocal, Socialist faction in the CGT which began to manifest itself as soon as the CGT leadership began taking the PCF's side in the Common Program split.

Public disunity in the CGT became, therefore, a fact in the Confederation's life, to be magnified beyond all proportion by the media in the months which followed. The ploy of promoting open Socialist opposition in the CGT was a shrewd one by the PS (there being no reason to doubt that Germon's activities were coordinated with PS leaders). By cracking the facade of unity in the CGT, the Socialists could hope to discredit the Confederation's attempt to intervene in the PS-PCF dispute. By openly speaking as Socialists in the CGT, and by openly accusing the CGT leadership of pro-Communist partisanship on nationalizations, Germon and friends automatically drew attention to the CGT leadership's attachments to the

5. See CGT *service de presse*, Communiqué no. 327–377; and *Le Peuple*, 1–5 October 1977, pp. 2–7.

6. *Le Peuple*, 16–31 October 1977, p. 2.

PCF. At the very least, this could rekindle an anti-Communism which would diminish the CGT's capacity to act. In turn, all the CGT leadership could do was to accuse the Socialists of constituting a "fraction" within the CGT while asserting that its own behavior was guided only by prior CGT mandates and not by partisan considerations (also true, technically, but sufficiently jesuitical as truth to be transparent to observers less convinced of the objectivity of the CGT's own self-perceptions). By trying to shift the debate away from substance to procedure, however, the leadership opened itself up to external charges of being anti-democratic, of attempting to control dissenters by organizational power (an accusation which Germon nurtured by demanding with insistence that CGT publications be opened up for *tribunes libres* on the issues).[7] The leadership was caught. It did not like living with a pro-Socialist fraction in its midst, yet, for obvious political reasons, it could do little to limit it.[8]

Solemn deliberations at the top of the CGT about its position on nationalizations had their purpose, of course. They were a necessary prelude to an attempt to mobilize the trade-union rank and file around the Confederation's positions in the *actualisation* dispute. The main vehicle for this, as decided by the Executive Commission on October 18, was to be the dissemination, accompanied by meetings and assemblies, of a manifesto entitled *Il faut que vive le programme commun*.[9] The mobilization campaign proved difficult, however. In effect, the CGT had to confront the consequences of its own work since 1972, plus those of the split on the Left.[10] Everything, including the CGT's strategy and tactics, had led the rank and file to expect miracles from Left political success in 1978. The focus on this had been so complete, however, that ordinary workers had come to feel that issues such as nationalizations—even of their own firms—were the business of politicians, unconnected with the daily logic of working-class life. With all hope resting on the shoulders of politicians, and the politicians falling out in complete discord, rank-and-file response was demoralization. It proved very hard, then, for the CGT to mobilize demoralized workers to demand reforms which they did not fully understand.

Whatever the problems in mobilizing the base, the CGT leadership

7. See, for example, Germon and Krasucki in *Le Peuple*, 1–15 January 1978.

8. As the electoral campaign wore on, the problem became more serious. Every time CGT leaders appeared in the general public to make their positions known they had to face questions about the new "opposition" in the Confederation. The standard answer was that the CGT was an independent class-and-mass organization which had long ago decided (in 1935, in fact) that there should be no place for political "tendencies" within it. Séguy was sufficiently vexed by all of this that he was moved to write a long article in *Le Monde* defending the Confederation's position, see *Le Monde*, "Remous dans la CGT," 28 January 1978.

9. *Le Peuple*, 1–15 November 1977, pp. 3–5.

10. A careful reading of the *Commission Exécutive* discussion of January (*Le Peuple*, 1–15 January) shows clearly the anxiety of *Commission Exécutive* members about the problems which the Confederation's campaign was encountering at the base.

judged the political situation too serious to restrain its initiatives. The next step, in December, was to organize an official CGT delegation to all of the Left parties. At this point the National Confederal Committee (CCN) adopted an important new statement about its political independence, entitled *Pour le changement*. The statement claimed that the CGT was independent of other organizations because it defined its own positions and programs in its free and statutory deliberations. "Factions" threatened this independence (another slap at Germon) because they "crystallized positions and falsified democracy and collective life." The CGT's independence was not neutrality, however. It had a right to speak in the class interests of workers. Indeed, it had done so in pushing Left parties to unite and sign a Common Program. It therefore considered itself part of the Left alliance, but as a "trade-union organization with its own responsibilities . . . . By its nature as a mass organization, its actions are to be situated on a different plane from those of political formations." Discord on the Left which threatened a Common Program whose formulation had been, in part, the CGT's work, was therefore the CGT's business. On the basis of its own trade-union specificity and its own programs, then, the CGT resolved to try and persuade the Left parties to mend their rift.[11]

The ironies in the CGT's position were compounded by this statement. The CGT was reasserting its independence of partisan affiliation in order to clear the way to intervene further in the PCF-PS dispute on the side of the PCF. There were two dimensions to this intervention. First of all, the CGT genuinely hoped to sway the PS on the issues, primarily on nationalizations.[12] Secondly, if this proved impossible, the CGT hoped to persuade workers that the PS had betrayed the Common Program, therefore helping the PCF in its electoral campaign. The statement on independence, together with all of the talk advanced in support of it, might have unintended consequences, however. Raising the issue of trade-union independence to use it, de facto, for partisan ends, was the best way to bring CGTers themselves—including Communists—to begin thinking anew about the question of independence and its real meaning in CGT practice.

The CGT's interviews with the leaderships of all three Left parties—PCF, PS and Left Radicals—ended predictably. The CGT and the PCF saw eye to eye on so many things that the communiqué following their meeting went to great pains to stress the one major issue on which the two

11. *Le Peuple*, 1–15 January 1978, pp. 45 ff.

12. At a later point in the campaign (February) the CFDT proposed a compromise on nationalizations which fell between the PCF and PS positions. In response, the PCF bent over backwards to announce that it was ready to deal on the CFDT position (see *L'Humanité* in February whenever the CFDT is discussed) while there was a serious attempt on the part of the CGT leadership to reopen the issue on the Left as part of a common CFDT-CGT initiative. The CFDT refused to go this far, probably because the PS was unwilling to discuss the nationalization issue further, and the question was dropped.

organizations were not in official agreement, defense policy.[13] In contrast, the interview with the PS turned up all of the predictable disagreements, all of which the CGT solemnly communicated to its rank and file. In addition, François Mitterrand had the unfortunate tactlessness to comment to Georges Séguy that "when I see you I see the PCF," which had the effect of cementing solidarity between CGT representatives, including the three Socialists. In all, the political situation was not changed by the CGT visits with the Left parties. This did, however, give the CGT new reasons to detail its disagreements with the PS.[14]

As the election came closer, the CGT's situation began to deteriorate in new, if predictable, ways. In particular, relationships between the CGT and CFDT virtually collapsed. Conflict over politics between the two partners reopened old differences over trade-union strategy and tactics, at a crucial point in time when the CGT desired a new affirmation of unity. During a long and stormy meeting between the two leaderships in early January 1978, Edmond Maire of the CFDT stated the obvious: "we fear that you share the position of the PC, that your theme is no longer *union*, and that your intervention has for its objective to force the Socialist Party to accept Communist proposals."[15] Maire's remarks on the trade-union situation were of greater significance, however. According to the CFDT Secretary-General:

> Our *Bureau National* has projected the basis of our future activity on the basis of self-criticism of the past years.
>
> Social struggles have not been up to the demands of the situation, and we have not been able to mount really articulated action. As a result, the *patronat* has got off free. National, interprofessional "Days" haven't helped develop activities on an industry level, the only locus of action which brings the bosses to the negotiating table. . . .
>
> There has been a general underestimation . . . from which follows the necessity for general industry-level mobilizations to overcome employer resistance, whatever the outcome of the elections.[16]

The CFDT was reacting to CGT behavior on two different, if interrelated, levels. Politically, the CFDT leaned towards the Socialist position in the Common Program argument (although much more discreetly than the

13. The CGT had not changed its position on defense policy—which was essentially that of the 1972 Common Program—after the Kanapa/PCF report on defense of spring 1977. Thus party and union officially disagreed on defense.

14. "Bilan et perspectives après les rencontres CGT-partis de gauche," CGT Commission Exécutive, 20 December 1977. See also "Déclarations du Bureau Confédéral," *Communiqué no. 20* (18 January 1978).

15. Excerpt from the CGT's internal bulletin (unofficial) reporting the January 11, 1978, meeting. See also Edmond Maire's speech to the CFDT Construction Federation, 13 January, which is similar in tone and content, CFDT *service de presse*, 13 January 1978.

16. Maire, in CGT bulletin.

CGT leaned towards the PCF).[17] The CGT wanted the CFDT to commit itself to national-level trade-union action before the elections—designed, in part, to reinforce the PCF's position—and the CFDT was not about to buy this.[18] With less at stake politically, the CFDT was also able to reconsider the situation from a trade-union point of view. In part, the CFDT was able to recognize some of the more general failings of trade-union action in the years prior to the election—its overgeneralization and overpoliticization. It concluded from this that its long-standing objections to CGT action biases were correct, that *journées d'action* did not pay, that more local-level mobilization was needed. It went even further, however. In a report to the CFDT National Council later in January, Jacques Moreau, the CFDT's political secretary (and, by far, the CFDT leader most disliked by the CGT), proposed reopening the question of unity-in-action with *Force Ouvrière* and a turn towards renewed contractualism. What came to be called the *recentrage* (recentering) of CFDT action had begun. The CFDT had calculated that the CGT was completely immobilized by its ties to the PCF. As a result, there existed new openings for the CFDT to take trade-union initiatives which would strengthen its position vis-à-vis that of the CGT.[19]

In effect, the CFDT was beginning to move away from unity-in-action with the CGT on the CGT's terms. The CGT's long, hard-fought campaigns against the CFDT's strategic and tactical heterodoxy, campaigns which had resulted in considerable CGT success by the mid-1970s, were being nullified, largely because of the CGT's mistakes after 1975. And as long as the CGT felt obliged to follow the electoralist course which it had set for itself in 1977–1978, there was nothing which could be done about the CFDT's shift.

How deeply committed the CGT leadership was to the PCF's political concerns became crystal clear later in the month of January. Georges Séguy, in a speech in the Paris *banlieue rouge*, urged workers openly to vote PCF. The speech caused a furor, and not only outside the CGT. Séguy had either "compromised the CGT's independence," or the CGT leader was finally being open about the CGT's real posture, the reactions depending upon which political side commentators were on. In response, Séguy and others produced the classical justification for his remarks: when Séguy urged workers to vote Communist, he was speaking as a Communist and not as Secretary-General of the CGT. The controversial nature of such a justification was obvious, even to many Communists. Georges Séguy, however, was neither an irresponsible nor a foolish man. One could only conclude therefore that his speech had been considered at the highest levels of the PCF beforehand and judged to be worth the risks to the CGT which it

17. See Maire, speech to CFDT Construction Federation, p. 4 ff.

18. On the CGT-CFDT meeting of January, see *Le Monde*, 13 January 1978; *Le Matin, Les Echos, Le Quotidien de Paris*, 12 January 1978.

19. On the *rapport Moreau* see *Syndicalisme-Hebdo* (CFDT) (January 1978).

entailed. Nothing could have better symbolized the CGT's dilemmas in these difficult months. The CGT *Bureau Confédéral* had not been consulted about the advisability of such a speech, even though it was certain to cause trouble for the Confederation. When things came down to the wire, the independence of the CGT, such as it was, mattered less to the leaders of the PCF than the likely (and probably marginal) effect on the CGT rank and file of the Confederation's Secretary General appealing to them to vote Communist!

Crisis in the Party

Thoughtful Communists were well aware that the Center-Right had not won the 1978 elections, but that a divided Left had lost them. This, in itself, enjoined self-criticism in the PCF. The party's obvious strategic failure provided further incentives. Moreover, the end of the electoral campaign marked the end of nearly a decade of United Front mobilization. Springs drawn taut by years of constant effort could finally be relaxed. Thus the PCF's post-election period was bound to be a time for reflection. Alas, the PCF has never been very good at analyzing things past in open debate. The analysis of the elections presented by the *Bureau Politique* immediately following the defeat illustrated this. It was also a provocation to parts of the PCF rank and file. According to the *Bureau Politique* the split on the Left which led to the Left's defeat was entirely due to the Socialists and their "right turn." In contrast, the course followed by the PCF had been consistently correct.[20] In essence, the leadership's analysis fell into a long and traditional line of self-justificatory pronouncements designed to sweep important issues under the rug. The problem, this time, was that many rank-and-file Communists knew better. Tired homilies about the irreproachable farsightedness of the PCF might work when the party was mobilized to the limit. In the aftermath of the 1978 elections, however, they sparked an explosion of discontent unprecedented in French Communist history.

At cell and section levels in certain areas the leadership's version of what had happened would not wash. Instead, a vast amount of questioning began, initially about the party's strategy and tactics. Had the last-minute electoral accord with the PS been wise? What of the soak-the-rich campaign and its implicit recognition that the PCF had failed to build any cross-class social alliances in the 1970s? Would the party be forever stuck in a working-class political ghetto? If this was a danger—and 1978 indicated that it might be—then how would the party ever accumulate enough political resources to be the vanguard of a peaceful transition to socialism? Had the party done the right thing in splitting with the Socialists in 1977 (very few militants disagreed with the party's analysis of the situation as of sum-

20. *Le Monde, L'Humanité,* 22 March 1978.

mer 1977; this was rather a question about the tactics which it had chosen to cope with the situation)? Should the party have agreed with the Socialists in 1972 in the unclear ways in which it had? Both those who had favored and opposed the abandonment of the dictatorship of the proletariat in 1976 (most favored it, of course) agreed that the change had left the party without a coherent theory of the capitalist state to guide its action. And many in the party close to, or in, the trade-union movement, were upset with the ways in which the CGT had been used to further PCF goals during the campaign.

The discussion was confused, fraught with internal contradictions and cross-cutting points of view. Despite this, it very quickly opened up a whole new realm of controversy. Once questions about important strategic errors had been raised, it was logical to ask *why* they had been made and *how* they had been made. Who was responsible for the mess of 1978? When this issue was raised, a number of militants uncovered certain disquieting continuities in PCF decision-making. Why had the *Bureau Politique* made all of the critical judgments in the electoral period with little or no broader party discussion? Why had the rank-and-file been consistently placed in a situation where its only option had been to ratify choices in whose making it had played no role?[21] On quite another plane, why did the Central Committee almost always act like a rubber stamp for the *Bureau Politique*? Why were major party occasions—Congresses and Conferences—still ritual *grandes messes* rather than open and free discussion?[22] And why were the delegates to such occasions still elected by de facto cooptation from above?

Debate on strategy and inner-party life soon raged out of control, largely because of the leadership's insensitive responses to it. *L'Humanité* refused to acknowledge that serious controversy existed and steadfastly refused to

21. For example, the party's shift in defense policy, undertaken with no general debate. Then, of course, the Twenty-second Congress had dropped the dictatorship of the proletariat clause in the statutes without sufficient discussion (remember, it was first announced to PCF militants by Marchais on television!) Another good example was the publication in 1974 of the minutes of the June 1972 *Comité Central* (see Fajon, *L'union est un combat*).

22. The *grande messe* rituals are not difficult to describe. Major party occasions are usually organized around a "project" which the leadership sends out before the occasion is convened. What is prepared in advance at the base, however, is not conflictual discusion, for the most part, but ritual speeches in support of the project. Then at the Congress (or Central Committee) the leadership's spokesman reads a long report which contains or proposes the project. Most of the rest of the time is spent in "discussion" which consists essentially in prepared speeches from delegates giving their specific reasons for believing that the project is correct (for example, "the workers at Renault agree with the report of Georges Marchais for the following reasons;" ". . . we have talked long and hard in the Federation of Hauts-de-Seine and it is remarkable how well the lines of action set out in the project speak to our needs," and so on). To be sure, there are exceptions to this. But habits of ritual are so deeply ingrained in the party's behavior that the exceptions have to be encoded in the rituals, so that only insiders can understand them. All of this, of course, goes for *public* occasions. Closed meetings, Central Committees, and *Bureaux Politiques* may be different.

print any but the most orthodox commentaries. It did grant that the party was engaged in "discussion," indeed it congratulated the party for being so engaged, but its readers would have been at a total loss to know what such discussion was about had they not turned to other sources of information. In fact, largely because the party press was closed to them, critical Communists began publishing discussion of their party in non-party publications—*Le Monde, Politique Hebdo* and *Le Nouvel Observateur* among them, none very high on the leadership's list of desired reading. When the leadership finally realized that something was going on, it responded with hackneyed clichés which everyone involved knew to be false—only a "handful" of people were protesting out of 600,000 Communists, the critics were all "intellectuals," and so on. And it was quick to remind this "handful" of "intellectuals" that it was against party rules to air dirty linen outside the party. The disciplinary effect of this was somewhat vitiated, however, when Georges Marchais, in an absolutely necessary gesture to the outside world, indicated that there would be no expulsions of members.

Leadership attempts to deny the substance of debate only made the situation worse. The first round of discussion had occurred mainly at rank-and-file level. What followed, however, was the entry of several well-known Communists into the public lists. Jacques Frémontier, editor of *Action* (a Central Committee journal directed to workers in large firms), resigned his position over a rather scandalous—and, as it turned out, expensive—affair of censorship by the party leadership of an electoral pamphlet on civil liberties which he had put together.[23] At about the same time, Francis Cohen, an astute older militant not known for his risk-taking, published a strongly critical piece on the party's electoral strategy in *La Nouvelle Critique*, perhaps the PCF's most prestigious journal (of which Cohen was editor).[24] Next, the PCF's two best-known heretics, Right and Left, let loose in *Le Monde*. Jean Elleinstein, the party's leading "liberal" deviant, was first with some obvious thoughts—the party's alliance strategy had failed, the split with the Socialists was perhaps unwise (or unnecessary), and basic changes in the party's internal life were long overdue.[25] Next, from the Left, came the thunder of Louis Althusser who, in four articles, condemned the party's strategy, its organizational life, its ideological posture and its relationships with the masses.[26] Then, sprinkled here and there in the pages

23. The pamphlet had originally been covered with photographs illustrating political oppression in the USSR, West Germany (the *Berufsverbot*), and Chile and had been printed up in more than a million copies before Gaston Plissonnier had ordered it scrapped. A second edition was scrapped at a similar stage of preparation before the leadership was finally willing to allow a third to appear which restricted its photographs to France. See *Le Monde*, 21 April 1978.

24. *La Nouvelle Critique* (April 1978).

25. *Le Monde*, 13, 14, 15 April 1978.

26. *Le Monde*, 25, 26, 27, 28 April 1978. The Althusser pieces were very quickly published in book form: see Louis Althusser, *Ce qui ne peut plus durer au PCF* (1978).

of *Le Monde* were the very well-informed articles of Thierry Pfister, *Le Monde*'s writer on the French Left, who had obviously become a letter box for dissatisfied Communists. Almost simultaneously there appeared two unofficial and highly critical books by respected Communists who had every intention of remaining in the party and fighting the issues which they had raised through to a conclusion.[27]

Much of the fracas of the first post-electoral month was really directed at producing some sensible and comprehensive answers to obvious questions from the party leadership at the April Central Committee which was the first after the election. Here, in a long report, Georges Marchais conceded nothing to protestors, adding insult to injury by labelling the critics as potential liquidators of democratic centralism, eliminators of the distinction between the vanguard and the masses, destroyers of the working-class character of party leadership, and more. Beyond this, Marchais' report reiterated the *Bureau Politique*'s earlier statement, claiming once again that the Socialists had been the exclusive villains of the election piece and that the PCF had been correct every step of the way.[28] By caricaturing the protestors, the leadership wanted to conjure protest away, and, given the chaotic nature of debate in the party, this was a possibility. Certain federations, notably Paris, were consumed with controversy, while others were relatively quiet. Moreover, the debate came almost exclusively from local, as opposed to workplace, cells. This was partly because local cells had little to do after the elections except to reflect, while workplace cells had to continue their shop-floor business as usual, and partly because workplace cell members traditionally protest in the PCF "with their feet" (by ceasing to attend meetings and do party work) rather than with words.[29]

The Central Committee did not make the crisis disappear, however. From the exemplary action of PCF "big guns" (Althusser, Elleinstein, et al.) revolt shifted towards long petitions and collective letters, often in *Le Monde*, signed by numbers of rank-and-file party members. On May 17, *Le Monde* published an open letter from 100 activists demanding a new discussion of the elections, while noting that the Central Committee's deliberations had not been very useful in this respect. On May 20 came a similar petition from Aix-en-Provence signed by 300 Communists clearly announcing that the revolt was not simply Parisian. Then on May 25 the party was asked by a number of well-known scientists and intellectuals to rethink its relationships to the intellectual world. By the autumn of 1978, protest had turned towards demoralization and disaffection. At the same time the party leadership had become mired in strategic and tactical confusion. Incessant

27. See Gérard Molina and Yves Vargas, *Dialogue à l'intérieur du parti communiste* (1978); and Jean Rony, *30 ans du parti* (1978).

28. *L'Humanité*, 28 April 1978.

29. Whatever the reason for these differences between local and factory cells, they did provide some ammunition to the leadership in its campaign to portray the protesters as "intellectuals," since local cells were where the "intellectuals" lived.

and often outrageous polemics against the Socialists, a defensive and rather nationalist opposition to the expansion of the Common Market (motivated, in large part, by immediate electoral concerns—the first general elections to the European Assembly had been called for June 1979) an appeal to Communists to work towards *union à la base* (although with whom and for what remained unclear) and injunctions to stern vigilance against an "anti-Communist campaign" did not, taken together, amount to a clear political perspective.[30]

With party strategy completely blocked—United Frontism without allies is difficult, especially with the PCF doing everything it could to destroy its key potential ally—an already complex inner-party crisis became even more complicated. In a crablike way (i.e., by walking sideways) the leadership began to concede a few points. It would acknowledge no mistakes in the electoral period, but it hinted that the Twenty-third Congress, expected in spring 1979, might relax the rules to allow more open discussion in the party press.[31] And Central Committee Reports (followed by other party publications) began to talk—rather mysteriously, in fact—of the *retard* which the party had suffered in 1956. The likelihood of a reexamination of the PCF's postwar history was broached, then, if only, ironically, to pin part of the blame for 1978 on the late Maurice Thorez (who certainly deserved it).[32] Likewise the party leadership gave its official imprimatur to a book of essays on the Soviet Union (*L'USSR et nous*) by five PCF Soviet specialists so as to generate a deep discussion of the failings of the Soviet model for

30. In effect all of this amounted to a return to the line pursued for several months after the Twenty-first Congress in 1974–1975, in which the *union du peuple de France* was first promoted. The resort to nationalism represented a refusal of the party leadership to abandon its belief (which had caused considerable trouble during the election campaign) that a wholly national strategy was possible in France, disregarding changes in the structure of European capitalism and the emergence of transnational economic actors. The PCI took a diametrically opposed line, which led it to a very different appreciation of social democracy. See the PCI Theses for its Fifteenth Congress, *Unità* (February 1979).

31. Legally, the party press was opened to *tribunes libres*, in which anyone could contribute their thoughts, only in preparation for Congresses. Changing the rules for this to allow such *tribunes* more often (when the Central Committee deemed an event important enough to open up a *tribune*) was one of the proposals for change contained in the *projets de thèses* for the Twenty-Third Congress, see *L'Humanité*, 13 February 1979. Changing the rules did not amount to as great a concession as it appeared, however. The party apparatus could easily control which letters were published, leaving it still in control of the shape of debate.

32. At the same time, the party-sponsored Institut Maurice Thorez began to produce some new and honest reflections on the PCF's history, based on the PCF's Archives and other new sources. The first such work has been mainly on the inter-war period, and it demonstrated a new openness to acknowledge the determinant voice which the Comintern and the Soviet Party had on the shaping of the PCF. See *Cahiers de l'Institut Maurice Thorez*, no. 25–26, "Le PCF et l'Internationale Communiste" (2e trimestre 1978); and ibid., no. 28, "L'Internationale syndicale rouge," by Jean Charles, (4e trimestre 1978).

socialism.[33] Another book, *La condition féminine*, sparked a similar debate about the PCF's failings on issues of women's liberation.[34] Not that the questions of feminism and the USSR were unworthy of consideration. Indeed, discussion on both topics was long overdue and very important. On the other hand, it was clear that such discussion—which, the leadership knew, would attract the energy and attention of many of those in the party who had been most upset after the elections—would be useful in diverting rebellious sentiment.[35]

With the Twenty-third Congress on the way, the party crisis was progressively institutionalized. Rebels continued to grumble, while the leadership kept granting them small concessions for which they had not asked, rather than what they really wanted—a free and open discussion of party strategy. At the same time the entire party apparatus was mobilized in a class campaign to disseminate *bonnes paroles* about how open and how changing the PCF was.[36] Nonetheless morosity and *attentisme* afflicted the party. The Twenty-third Congress would clearly be a critical event.

The PCF's post-1978 election crisis would take years to resolve, but by early 1979 its basic issues had been amply clarified. Strategically, the party had been unable to accumulate the resources it needed to see its United Front strategy through to a successful conclusion. The party's failure to build the Italian-style cross-class alliance which its theory and strategy had both recognized as necessary was what needed to be explained. Any such explanation would have to confront the PCF's modern history without indulgence. French social democracy had fallen to pieces in the fifties and

33. Alexandre Adler, Francis Cohen, et al., *L'URSS et nous* (1978). Discussions of this book within the party met with considerable resistance in some areas and were eventually shut down in early 1979. Beyond this, discussions were strictly limited to the Soviet Union. The same critical perspectives were not applied to other Socialist countries, so that when Vietnam invaded Cambodia, the PCF gave it total support, creating confusion in the party itself and opening the PCF's positions to ironic and acerbic commentaries from the outside. Ultimately Georges Marchais and the leadership pronounced that the PCF's evaluation of Socialist countries was "globally positive," closing the inner-party debate by fiat. See *L'Humanité*, 13 February 1979, Marchais' introduction to the *projet de thèses* for the Twenty-third Congress.

34. See Yann Viens, et al., *La condition féminine* (1978).

35. Intellectuals continued to be a real problem for the leadership, to the point that, in early December 1978, the *Bureau Politique* felt obliged to hold a two-day meeting with 400 selected intellectuals (including the leading *contestataires*). See the relatively honest reproduction of debates in *L'Humanité*, 4 December 1978; also *Le Monde*, 5 December 1978. At the same time the party leadership muzzled the editorial group of *Nouvelle Critique* when it tried to publish articles by *contestataires*. The October *Nouvelle Critique* had a series of articles on "Société, parti, richesses du pluriel," which was to have a second part published in November. It was this second part which was suppressed. See *Nouvelle Critique* for November for the editorial group's discussion of this censorship. Certain of the scheduled pieces mysteriously turned up in *Nouvel Observateur*.

36. See the singularly unedifying book by Paul Laurent, the leader of the "liberal" group in the *Bureau Politique*, *Le PCF comme il est* (1978).

sixties, in ways which might well have allowed the PCF to rebuild its own fortunes by recruiting new social support. Yet nothing of the kind had occurred. Instead, French Social democracy rose again, beginning in the late 1960s, with the PCF presenting the PS with the major vehicle for revitalization: *Union de la Gauche*. It was not simply the *retard* of 1956 which caused this failure, although 1956, taken as the symbol of the failure of the PCF to de-Stalinize at the right time, would be a useful point of departure. In any case, the PCF did fail to de-Stalinize and begin Eurocommunizing in time, and behind such huge abstractions lay much of the explanation for 1978.

The PCF's strategic contradictions were not unconnected with its other major set of problems, the clashes set up by Eurocommunization between the party's approach to the outside world and its internal life. In the 1970s the PCF had come to affirm that profound change in France could only come democratically, with the Twenty-second Congress' proposition that the party's new watchword be "democracy to the limit" (*la démocratie jus-qu'au bout*) representing a genuine turning-point. To the degree to which the party clarified its commitment to democratic change, however, it created serious problems for its own organizational life. The party's internal structures, burdened, as they were, by the profoundly Stalinist legacy of the Thorez years, changed much more slowly than its strategy. Even then, they changed only to the extent to which the leadership was willing to allow. Thus as opportunities for United Front success opened up in the 1970s, the gap between the party's external commitments and its internal procedures grew steadily until the crisis of 1978–1979.

Perhaps the most obvious underlying causes for the growth of conflict between the PCF democratic strategy and its internal life were PCF doctrinal changes. As the party refined its analysis of democratic change it abandoned much of the scorn with which it once treated "bourgeois" democratic forms to adopt a perspective which saw the expansion and deepening of such forms as a major part of the road to change. Accompanying such refinement came a new determination to denounce the lack of political and civil liberties in the Soviet Union. To the degree to which party activists took all of these changes seriously they could not help but begin subjecting their own party to some of the hard critiques which they were being taught, by this very same party, to direct at the rest of French life. Sociological changes in the PCF reinforced such ideological movements. As political prospects for the Left began to look up in the 1970s the PCF attracted large numbers of new members. The leadership's decision to make the PCF into a mass party led to more aggressive recruitment and a general relaxation in the PCF's once quite stringent recruitment standards. By 1978 the vast majority of PCF members had few political memories beyond those of the PCF's modern United Front offensive. The necessity of Left Union to promote a peaceful, democratic transition to advanced democracy, and then to a *socialisme aux couleurs de la France* was their catechism. The generation of older, workerist party faithful, once the backbone of the party, was now a minority. Moreover, a substantial minority of the party's new members were new middle class, bringing with them a strong sense of their right to be heard in inner-party life. Ideology, the changing structure of party generations and sociology all conspired to favor a crisis of democracy inside the PCF.

Paradoxically, the ways in which the internal structures of the PCF had actually changed contributed to the crisis. Internal de-Stalinization in the PCF started very late and proceeded haltingly. Extreme centralization around the Secretary-General and rigorous enforcement of the leadership's will through a core of permanent officials were both attenuated. The *Bureau Politique* became more collegial. But however collegial it had become, it still decided everything of importance with limited input from below, while the Central Committee and Congress remained pliable audiences. Party *permanents* remained the producers of rank-and-file ratification for policies in whose making the rank and file had played little role—in his *Le Monde* series Althusser called such *permanents* the *préfets* of the PCF. Upper-level party leaders, Central Committee members, Congress delegates, all were still elected from lists prepared at the top and limited to the exact number of nominees needed to fill the posts in question. Yet at the other end of the organizational spectrum, considerable care had been lavished to promote open and lively debate at the cell level (and, in certain federations, Paris in particular, on the section level), changes which the leadership had certainly encouraged. Thus the Eurocommunization of the PCF partially opened up the party's structures in ways which, in certain circumstances, made it extremely difficult for the leadership to control rank-and-file life. As long as the party was totally mobilized for the implementation of a strategy which everyone supported and understood—as had been the case in the 1970s—open discussion at the base tended to focus on the adaptation of the party's line to local circumstances. In circumstances when this was not the case, as after the 1978 elections, the new openness at the base created a *foyer* for questioning, systematic reflections and, on occasion, open rebellion. The events of 1978 were then, an important way station for the PCF in its Eurocommunization, both the product of earlier change and the bearer of new things. The party crisis involved a continual display of dirty Communist linen, while at the same time demonstrating a degree of rank-and-file vitality quite extraordinary in the PCF's history. In one way, the PCF needed such a crisis. Had things gone on as usual after the 1977–1978 election debacle, the PCF's credibility might well have been damaged even more irreparably than it had been. As it was, however, whether the resolution of the crisis would turn out positively or negatively was not clear. The ability of critics and rebels in the party to carry on, express themselves, and be listened to within the party was a considerable victory for Eurocommunization. Formal change within the party would have been hollow indeed if controversy and debate among Communists had not had a chance to develop. It was unlikely that in the future things would ever be as quiet within the PCF as they had been in most of the party's past. On the other hand what looked to be, in early 1979, the PCF leadership's turn towards a Left sectarian strategic stance, in which social democracy in general and the PS in particular were targeted as the party's major opponents, bode ill. It was not at all inconceivable that many of the internal gains of Eurocommunization might be rolled back. Time pressed, and the PCF had long since used up its alloted quota of major mistakes.

Self-Criticism in the CGT

The results of 1978 were as catastrophic for the CGT as they had been for the PCF, if not more so. The CGT had centered almost all of its trade-union strategy around the political prospects of *Union de la Gauche* in the 1970s. The Left's failure placed the Confederation in a critical situation, then. It had to change its ways in order to face the future, and, to change its ways, it had to own up to the consequences of its past mistakes. The task of self-criticism and change was made all the more complicated for the Confederation by the crisis in the PCF. The major problem which the CGT had to confront, however, was the fact that the Center-Right majority had won the elections. In the pre-electoral years governments had had to temper their economic policy goals in order to avoid creating new electoral difficulties for themselves. Ad hoc programs had been established to limit the spread of unemployment (particularly youth unemployment), for example, and certain ailing sectors of the economy (iron and steel, textiles, and shipbuilding, among others) had been propped up artificially by government subsidies. A tremendously costly unemployment compensation program had been prolonged, despite governmental and employer desires to change it, dangerously high social-security deficit had been allowed to grow, and so on. All of this had been done, particularly under Raymond Barre, in a context in which austerity was already quite severe. With the solid electoral victory of 1978, the Barre government and President Giscard d'Estaing were given several years of new space to calculate their policies (there being no major electoral occasion in sight before the Presidential election of 1981). Thus the CGT and other French unions could expect to face the full rigor of Giscard's "new liberalism" after the elections—continually rising unemployment, major attempts to promote industrial redeployment to create internationally competitive branches of French industry (with the corollary of liquidation for other branches), liberalism in the realm of prices, and policies for ending subsidies for ailing branches (iron and steel, textiles, and shipbuilding, among others, were to face Draconian and, in some cases, terminal, new situations in which entire regions in France would face the dole), attacks on established social-security and unemployment compensation arrangements, and more. In short, an offensive from government and *patronat* for economic "rationalization," the likes of which post–World War II France had never seen, was in the cards.

Prospects would have been sombre enough even had the CGT been in a strong position to deal with the new situation. But it was not, as we already know. In the pre-electoral years, the labor movement, prodded onwards by the CGT, had become overpoliticized, projecting solutions to outstanding union problems from Left electoral success. And for the CGT (and because of its pressure, the CFDT as well), trade-union action had been overgeneralized, at the same time. Both tendencies had pulled union organizations away from rank-and-file problems. On top of these distortions, of course, came those stemming from the election campaign itself. CGT-CFDT unity-in-action, the core of any effective trade-union response to the new circumstances, had been virtually destroyed by the effects of the campaign. Moreover, the trade-union rank and file, led by everyone, parties and unions alike, to expect major change from the Left, had been disillusioned and demoralized in dramatic ways by the split on the Left and its results. This, plus trade-union disunity, and the effects of the economic crisis itself, made mobilizing possibilities limited indeed. The crisis in the PCF posed very great indirect risks for the CGT as well. To the degree that Communists in the CGT followed the PCF leadership's official post-election line and devoted their energies to attacks on the Socialists, further divisions in the CGT, between the CGT and other unions, and in the trade-union rank and file were bound to follow.

In short, the CGT faced immense problems after March 1978. The general lines of what, logically, the Confederation had to do were clear. It had to find new ways to rebuild contact with its rank and file. It had to renew unity-in-action with the CFDT. Most of all, it had to rethink its ties to the PCF. The quasi-transmission–belt aberrations of the election campaign had to be undone. Relative autonomy, at least in the way in which it had been defined in the sixties and seventies, had to be reformulated. And the economic crisis had to be confronted.

The official remarks of the *Bureau Confédéral* immediately after the election did not indicate that logic was uppermost in the CGT leadership's mind, however. Georges Séguy, addressing the March 30 National Confederal Committee, while advancing a series of generally intelligent explanations for the Left's failure, turned towards attacking the Socialists as the villains of the piece. He then added, "for our part, we have nothing with which to reproach ourselves. In our trade-union role, we did everything which we could possibly have done to pressure Left Unity, its program, and to promote victory."[37] He proceeded to attack the CFDT for a "strategic reconversion which, in the guise of realism moves closer to the reformism

37. *Le Peuple*, 15–30 April 1978, p. 4.

which the CFDT finds in its colleagues of the West European trade-union movement" (an allusion to the CFDT's participation in the European Trade Union Confederation beside the German trade unions).[38] Essentially, Séguy was accusing the CFDT of the same "right turn" under German Social Democratic influence of which the PCF accused the PS. He concluded, however, by looking towards the Fortieth CGT Congress, scheduled for November 1978. He proposed that the Fortieth Congress should be "audacious, innovative, and conquering."

The CGT, unlike the PCF, had to face a major public occasion very shortly after the elections. Thus it had to make some basic choices very quickly after March and, as the Fortieth Congress began to take precedence over other CGT activity (preparations were begun in April and May of 1978), the Confederation began to take some striking new steps. That something was happening at the level of the *Bureau Confédéral* first became clear in a long lead article by Jean-Louis Moynot in *Le Peuple* in May, entitled *Between Yesterday and Tomorrow*. Here appeared a tone of self-criticism (and implicit criticism of the PCF as well, despite the fact that Moynot was a Communist) new in the CGT. Everything was scrutinized. The CGT's contribution to the failures of the Left in attracting new middle-class votes was questioned, along with the PCF's soak-the-rich campaign ("many engineers, *cadres*, and technicians believed themselves rich and therefore the targets of those who were not. . . ."). More important for the CGT, the Confederation had been unable to make its position on the necessity of structural reforms understood to the rank and file, such that the Left's demands for new nationalizations remained general and abstract. Furthermore, the CGT had not "been sufficiently understood on the necessity for, and role of, mass democracy." The CGT, in its positions on structural reform, had relied upon "old positions of the CGT fixed in the 1960s and even earlier." In its attempts to promote mass discussion the CGT had too often been reluctant to engage the rank and file fully and had, furthermore, been sectarian when genuine differences of opinion appeared. Finally, the CGT had not been sufficiently independent. Moynot concluded with several clear injunctions. The CGT needed:

Much more trade-union independence, much more CGT autonomy, especially on all those problems related to the profound changes of work and society.

Much more mass democracy in the life and discussion of our organizations.

And:

It is important to return to the concrete and the *quotidien* in trade-

---

38. Ibid., p. 5. This accusation was backed by a very aggressive letter to Edmond Maire by Séguy (ibid., p. 6).

union action . . . in order to make a qualitative leap in our activities in firms, on the shop floor, at all levels.[39]

This was strong medicine! That it was not simply isolated talk became more obvious as the *Bureau Confédéral* sat down to the serious work of preparing the Congress. Things were not the same as they had been. Certain non-Communist Secretaries who had earlier been content to blend into the Confederal Bureau's consensus began to take strong, sometimes public, stands in favor of change (such was the case most notably for René Buhl and Jacqueline Lambert). Even more important, Communists on the *Bureau Confédéral* were divided as they had not been in living memory. It would be wrong to see such divisions in terms of factions (as did so much of the non- and anti-Communist press) since alliances in the Confederal Bureau were issue-bound and changed with the issue. But the eight Communist CGT National Secretaries were in disagreement with one another not only about the ways in which the Confederation's recent past ought to be analyzed, but also about the relative weight which they ought to place on trade-union autonomy vis-à-vis the PCF and about the crisis in the PCF. As a result of these things new possibilities for discussion and policy choice arose in the Confederal Bureau.

In all of this the key figure was Georges Séguy. As Secretary-General Séguy had great influence over the directions taken by the *Bureau Confédéral*, and hence the CGT as a whole, to deal with this new situation. Séguy's position was objectively difficult. He was a member of the PCF *Bureau Politique* and obliged, therefore, to take cognizance of the rise of sectarian strategic inclinations within the PCF leadership. At the same time Séguy was responsible for the success or failure of the CGT as a mass labor organization. In the aftermath of the 1978 elections the CGT's situation was not promising, for all of the reasons which we have discussed. The CGT could follow new PCF sectarianism only at its own peril. On the other hand, Séguy knew full well that, to the degree to which the CGT did not follow changes in PCF strategy, the Confederation might play an important role in internal deliberations in the PCF about the advisability of such changes. There are many reasons to suspect that Séguy saw the post-electoral situation as one in which the relative independence of the CGT from the party might be enhanced. Moreover he may well have also concluded that an "opening up" of the CGT might play some role in unblocking the situation in the party itself. In any case, Séguy seems to have been affected by the great increase in internal conflict in the Confederal Bureau, often throwing his weight behind those who called for serious change. How far he would go in such directions, and how far the Confederation itself was open to change, was unclear, however.

Thus, at the top at least, the CGT was in a position to react very dif-

39. *Le Peuple*, 1–15 May 1978.

ferently from the PCF in the post-electoral period. Whereas the PCF leadership had barricaded itself behind attacks on the PS, calls to *union à la base* and appeals to the party to close ranks, the CGT might choose another course. And, as the *Bureau Confédéral* began to prepare its dossiers for the Fortieth Congress, in particular in its drafting of the Congress *Document d'Orientation* in the early summer of 1978, certain subtle changes began to appear. Prior to 1978 the Confederation had advocated a defensive trade-union stance vis-à-vis France's economic crisis which proposed regenerating popular consumption in the short run, with structural reform legislated by the political Left as its only longer term strategy. The new perspectives began to place more weight on the international nature of the crisis and began to cast doubt on the efficacy of union tactics which focused primarily on defensive struggle to restimulate popular consumption. Crisis-induced processes of industrial and economic change were under way in a setting in which political prospects for the Left were nil. In this context, were the CGT to continue its earlier line of defensive unionism plus political mobilization, it would effectively abdicate any influence over structural change in France to class enemies. The Confederation was thus obliged to begin thinking about a strategy in which industry-by-industry struggle to impose a different logic on crisis-induced changes than that proposed by capital and the state would be central. The terms *autogestion* (once the CFDT's "vague formula" but legitimized by the PCF in the 1977–1978 electoral campaign) and "industrial solutions" became prominent. The *Document d'Orientation* for the Congress opened up a discussion on such questions.[40] At the same time, debate on *conseils d'atelier*, new organisms of workers' control, went in the same direction. The initiation of new and serious attempts (by *journées d'études* at federation level, with Confederal help) to reexamine the economy branch-by-branch partook of the same logic, with the ultimate goal of generating action which responded to real rank-and-file problems in each branch.[41]

40. See CGT, *Commission Exécutive*, "Projet de document d'orientation" (27 June 1978).

41. Here it should be noted that the CGT, finally, had begun to reorient its international position. It had long been the major non-Communist union in the FSM (WFTU). In fact a CGT leader had consistently served as FSM Secretary-General over the years (Louis Saillant, then Pierre Gensous). By the mid-1970s, years after such a realization ought to have been made, the CGT began to realize that its ties to the FSM were more a liability than anything else. (The Italian CGIL had pulled away from the FSM long before this.) The crisis of the seventies made trade-union deliberation and action on a European scale an absolute priority. This was even more pressing for the Confederation because it risked being shut out of the *Confédération Européenne des Syndicats* (CES). The CES, dominated by the German DGB, remained something of an ad hoc body by the later 1970s, but was clearly the most promising vehicle for European trade-union coordination. It was composed of the European members of the CISL (World Federation of Free Trade Unions) plus members and ex-members of the Catholic trade-union organization, including the CFDT. The CGIL was a member, but DGB vetoes kept out the CGT, the Spanish *Commissions Ouvrières* (tied to the PCE), and the Portuguese *Intersyndical* (tied to the PCP). The FSM had become a burden for other reasons as

The preparatory documents for the Congress were more open and more questioning than those from the CGT's past, then. What followed their introduction was even more innovative, however. For the first time in the modern history of the CGT—and perhaps in the history of the French Left—all of the resources of the Confederation were given over to open debate and discussion. Beginning in September 1978, and lasting through the Congress, every CGT publication devoted itself primarily to publishing letters and other contributions from anyone within the Confederation who desired to express an opinion. To ensure that there would be no limits on such discussion, the *Bureau Confédéral* pledged that everything which was received would be published. Furthermore, literally thousands of meetings were held across the country, at every level of CGT organizations, to discuss the issues to be decided at the Congress. The entire CGT, from top to bottom, was turned into a discussion forum. And as anyone who had the energy to read through the huge number of contributions published in *Le Peuple, La Vie Ouvrière, Antoinette* and *Options* in the autumn of 1978 could attest, no subject, however taboo it had been in the past, was untouched. Under the general rubrics of analysis of the CGT's recent past and "what CGT do the workers need?" the CGT's positions during the election campaign, the power of the PCF in the Confederation, the role of different political currents in the CGT (the fraction-issue), the CGT's international affiliations and policies, the ways in which authority was distributed and exercised, all were examined and reexamined. On the question of politics, the conflict revealed in the letters was severe and open. Despite a degree of bitterness, however, the Confederal leadership's earlier positions were amply defended. This was predictable, to be sure. Much more important were the conclusions of contributors on other questions. The vast bulk of the letters underlined the necessity for the Confederation to put itself back into touch with rank-and-file trade-unionist concerns. The sense that the CGT had slipped away from the problems of ordinary workers was everywhere. And many writers urged the CGT to reanalyze the economic crisis, to look for new ways to cope with evident and crisis-induced changes in the

---

well. Long a transmission belt for Soviet goals, it refused to budge on questions of civil liberties in socialist countries and on issues of trade-union rights in the socialist bloc. At a moment when the CGT, by force of the development of *Union de la Gauche*, had become ever more sensitive to such issues (Séguy, for example, established direct contact with Charter 77 representatives on a 1977 trip to Czechoslovakia), something had to be done. The CGT leadership (Séguy and Krasucki, in the first instance) were reluctant to cut ties completely with the FSM, however. Thus the Confederation began to speak its piece openly with the FSM, in the hope that either the FSM would change some of its positions, or that the CGT's new stances might open up CES doors. Neither had occurred by 1979. Georges Séguy's speech to the FSM Congress of 1978 is well worthy of consultation to note the degree of CGT evolution on the FSM issue, however. See *Le Peuple*, 6–15 April 1978. And the CGT's newly critical positions caused Pierre Gensous to be removed from his FSM post (from whence he returned to the CGT *Bureau Confédéral* to replace René Duhamel at the head of the International Department).

work process on shop-floor level. In essence, the products of open discussion in the CGT were appropriate criticisms of the Confederation's activity.[42] And the CGT's open discussion in crisis demonstrated that there were few disadvantages and much to be gained from unrestricted debate.

The Fortieth Congress itself was full of contradictions. There was a new openness in the occasion, which we will presently discuss. The structure of the Congress was quite traditional, however. For example, despite the vast pre-Congress campaign to promote discussion, Congress delegations were chosen in the same old ways, which meant that Communists predominated in the electoral process and among the delegates. The Confederal leadership did prod lower levels of the organization to be more ecumenical in their choice of delegates. Thus there were greater numbers of *Socialistes d'office* and other categories *d'office* (Catholics, women, immigrants, etc.), but their attendance at Grenoble was often more tokenism—acceded to, in many cases, only after considerable pressure had been applied from above—than anything else. And the working of the Congress were still old-style *grandes messes*. Delegations had been mandated, before the Congress, to make set speeches in response to the preparatory documents. Thus despite urgings from the Confederal leadership that give-and-take on new issues was of great importance, the public side of the Congress was, for the most part, a series of set speeches of traditional kinds. Moreover the form of the Congress—2000 delegates meeting in plenary session most of the time—contributed more to solidarity rituals than to exchange. In effect, many of the innovative propositions of the leadership and much of the pre-Congress debate were submerged in Congress routine and, to a degree, political recrimination (Germon and other Socialists were prominent, as were numbers of sectarian responses from Communists). And, as usual, major issues of conflict were handled behind the scenes. Elections to the new *Commission Exécutive* and *Bureau Confédéral* proceeded by de facto co-optation yet again, although sometimes in bizarre ways. In one important incident, a well-known Communist, Georges Frischmann, was bumped at the last moment from the *Commission Exécutive* in order to make room for a non-Communist.

Continuities in form notwithstanding, the Fortieth Congress was innovative in content. Séguy's opening report was quite remarkable in this respect. Rather than the usual long recounting of the past and the state of the organization, Séguy set out several important new definitions of CGT purposes in the guise of themes for reflection.[43] Some of these related to

42. Certain *Bureau Confédéral* members, led by Henri Krasucki, had strong reservations about the debate period. That Krasucki's reservations were overridden clearly meant that Séguy threw his weight on the side of the "liberals." That he did so, in part, to influence the evolution of the PCF, is also clear. He may well have been working in this direction with the tacit, or even spoken, encouragement of Georges Marchais.

43. Such was not the case, alas, on the question of Europe. Here Séguy pushed the PCF's position against the enlargement of the Common Market as hard as he could.

serious day-to-day union problems (unity-in-action, the need for a massive new unionization drive, which he also proposed to other unions for joint consideration). Others involved CGT responsiveness to new rank-and-file concerns. One major section of the speech was devoted, for example, to CGT reactions to changes in the structure of work. Séguy roundly attacked what he called the productivist model of economic development (in ways which, five years earlier, would have been acceptable by the mainstream of a CFDT Congress) in which economic change tied to the need for capital accumulation led to the intensification and de-qualification of work. The CGT, Séguy suggested, ought to give more thought to confronting workplace alienation. Séguy was of course implying that the CGT in the past had focused unduly on issues of *quantity*—wages, hours, etc.—while overlooking issues of the *quality* of work. It should be the CGT's responsibility to struggle not only for better rewards from work, but also for a more humane model of work itself.

There was a powerful dose of self-criticism in Séguy's speech as well. To begin with, he said,

> we should ask ourselves whether our tendency to make everything contingent on the Left coming to power may have led us to underestimate the value of this or that concession which could be won in struggles from the coalition of government and *patronat*, or led us to minimize the importance of this or that compromise, or to denounce all accords which we refused to sign as intrinsically negative.[44]

Then he added a critically important phrase. "Trade-union struggle for material gains is, by definition, struggle for reforms, small, middle-sized and large." Here Séguy was raising three different issues simultaneously, all decisively important. First of all, he was recognizing the Confederation's responsibilities in the overpoliticization of trade-union action in the pre-electoral years. Secondly, he was suggesting that the Confederation's past policy on collective bargaining had been inadequate. It had been inconsistent for the CGT to struggle for concessions in the labor market and then to refuse to sign contracts proposed by employers, if the contracts had any value at all. Indeed, it was more than inconsistent to the degree that other unions, whose contributions to struggle had been less important, had thereby been able to assume the credit for union action simply because they were willing to sign. Yet Séguy was not advocating simple contractualism, as his third point indicated. What he was suggesting was that *certain structural reforms might be won by unions in labor-market struggle itself.*

The CGT had to get back in touch with the rank and file and its concerns. Clearly this was Séguy's primary concern. Struggle at the shop floor around a wide variety of issues, some of them new for the CGT, was the key to this. But such struggle had to have some relevant goal. To the degree

44. *Le Peuple*, Edition Spéciale, 40ᵉ Congrès, no. 2, p. 9.

to which the CGT had earlier posited political mobilization as this goal, to the degree to which it had dangerously neglected collective bargaining, tactics had to change. Were the CGT to shift its ground and point local and branch struggle towards collective bargaining, however, the question "bargaining for what?" arose. In particular the danger of a new thrust towards bargaining leading to class collaborationist behavior had to be addressed. The way out of this danger, and the way to correct the specific overpoliticization problems which had arisen in the years prior to March 1978—years in which electoral victory of the Left and nationally legislated reforms were seen as the *only* serious answer to working-class difficulties—was to develop a trade-union strategy of structural reform on the level of industry itself.

Here, without question, the Secretary-General was roundly condemning much of the Confederation's practices of the preceding two decades, practices based on the absolute dichotomy of defensive bread-and-butter unionism—the trade unions' task—and social change—the task of political parties, to whose success such defensive mobilization by unions might indirectly contribute. Implicitly Séguy was recognizing the fact that *Union de la Gauche*, as it had been projected and formulated, was based on an erroneous *grand-soir–électoral* strategy in which the CGT's dual role had been to behave in rather conventional trade-union fashion in the labor market while mobilizing workers politically to await a package of miracle solutions which would follow electoral victory. The new posture which he had in mind for the Confederation was less clear. The CGT should develop a specific program and strategy for social change, based on its trade-union position, in which step-by-step structural reforms of industrial life would be won through labor-market and other union action. As examples of what might be done, both Séguy and Jean-Louis Moynot cited the possibilities of struggle for *conseils d'atelier et de service*.[45] What seemed implied was a very great expansion in the scope of CGT activities in the direction of a neo-syndicalism modelled, perhaps, on the approach of the Italian CGIL (the Italian analogue to the CGT). In fact, Séguy was known for his admiration of the CGIL's policies in the 1970s. But he gave few precise indications of what he really had in mind to the Congress.

Finally, in a long concluding section on "our failings," Séguy directly raised political questions, questions about the PCF and the CGT in a veiled way, and about democracy in the CGT itself:

> It is well known that in too many cases the composition of our organizational leaderships doesn't always reflect the diversity of the CGT and the currents of thought running through it correctly enough. . . .

45. See Jean-Louis Moynot's speech to the Congress, *Le Peuple*, Congress Edition, no. 4, pp. 13–15.

We often encounter resistance to the political enlargement of the CGT, above all in cases where habits of working and leading have been formed between militants of the same political opinions. In these we hear answers like the following: 'It's simpler like this, no problems, we gain time, it isn't worth creating new difficulties for ourselves by introducing new opinions or new political views into the leadership.'

Don't such situations generate feelings of superiority, the sentiment that we are the unique repositories of revolutionary truth, intolerance towards different ideas, reticence towards democratic debate and even a certain unwillingness to promote women and the young?

Sometimes one opposes 'enlargement' to unity and to CGT cohesion, arguing that the appearance of disagreement in the CGT and non-unanimous votes at leadership levels would allow greater (anti-CGT) outside speculation.

This is how that our obsession with 'unanimism' comes to contradict trade-union democracy.[46]

The CGT leadership was talking a dramatic new language to the Fortieth Congress. One major aspect of this language was new stress on mass democracy, open debate plus full representation of all currents of working-class opinion. The other was the proposal of an entirely new trade-union strategy involving step-by-step union struggles, using union means, for structural reforms. René Buhl summed up this latter thrust in his closing address to the Congress. The crisis made such a new strategy inevitable.

For many years the CGT—justly—avoided mixing the economic realm and that of day-to-day demands. But today we face not only destructive political policies but also an economic crisis whose roots are profound. Whole industries, whole areas of economic activity, social services and culture are menaced with disappearance, purely and simply.

We must therefore struggle . . . against such policies and decisions while ourselves advancing solutions which will create a minimum number of durable economic guarantees. The only way to do this is for us to put forth our own industrial solutions by defining them in perspectives of democratic change, all the while realizing that we can obtain only partial results in this way.[47]

The contrast between the PCF's reaction to the 1978 election debacle and that of the CGT was striking. The PCF battened down its hatches against internal debate and while it too began to work strategic changes, they were clearly sectarian, a return to old-style *ouvrièrisme*. The CGT re-

46. *Le Peuple*, Congress Edition, no. 2, p. 14.
47. *Le Peuple*, Congress Edition, no. 7, p. 2.

acted very differently. First of all, it opened itself up to the broadest public debate over basic options which it had ever had in the months before the Fortieth Congress. Then, at the Congress, key leadership figures urged a dramatic new strategic orientation on the Confederation, moreover one which was in no way sectarian. To be sure, this new orientation was not out of phase with aspects of the PCF's self-reflection, in particular the party's stress on *union à la base* and the possibilities for "step-by-step" change. But the PCF's goal in using such terms was short-term, they were devices to be used to struggle against the PS. The CGT's new approaches might involve a serious redefinition of the meaning of trade-union activity and of the relationship of such activity to politics. What the leadership was proposing to the Fortieth Congress was a more genuinely independent CGT, in essence a major reformulation of what we here called relative autonomy. From the late 1950s through 1978 the CGT had seen itself as an organization whose trade-union activities were to be confined rather strictly to the defense of its rank and file in the labor market even if, ultimately, such defensive activities might also be complementary to the PCF's goals of political mobilization for a United Front. In the reformulation of CGT purposes suggested to the Fortieth CGT Congress this strict division between political and trade-union labor was called into question. Proposed was an intermediary level of struggle between the defense of rank-and-file interests and global political change, a level of struggle for structural reform in the productive sphere itself, which might involve redefining work, democratization of the workplace, workers' control of all kinds (the once-taboo word of *autogestion* now being used without hesitation). This intermediary level of struggle, offensive struggle for "industrial solutions," would also involve the development of specifically CGT economic analyses and overviews of the development of different industrial branches.[48]

There was place in this new perspective for a relationship of relative autonomy with the PCF. The CGT's new goal was not to take the place of political parties. Nationalizations and other major structural reforms could only come from a new political majority and legislation by the Left in power. Indeed, part of the motivation for the CGT's desire to change its strategic perspective came from the failure of the Confederation's campaigns to make new nationalizations plausible to ordinary workers in terms of the day-to-day logic of their work. Thus the new approach was designed, in part, to provide the connection, missing earlier, between global political programs and the workplace needs of workers. Nonetheless, the new course foresaw a major expansion in the scope of trade-union activity. If Relative Autonomy I was defensive unionism plus mobilization for global political

48. The first major manifestation of the new approach was in the Fédération des Métaux, with reference to the French iron and steel crisis. See *Le guide du militant*, CGT Féd. Métaux, no. 136 (November 1978), "Face à la crise de la sidérurgie. . ."

change, then Relative Autonomy II proposed a new level of offensive unionism between the extremes of the CGT's earlier posture, one which would seek to use collective bargaining, negotiations around issues of industrial redeployment and change, economic planning and whatever other points of access became available to the Confederation to work towards whatever progressive changes were possible, no matter what happened in the political sphere.

To be sure, there were no guarantees that the new course proposed to the Congress would be followed. As Edmond Maire of the CFDT commented cautiously, "There have been other ephemeral springtimes, and this one is only in its very first days."[49] To begin with, there were major questions about what the new course would mean specifically in terms of action. What had come from the podium of the Congress were very general declarations of intention, little more. More important, there were substantial internal barriers to the implementation of such declarations. Segments of the PCF leadership would almost certainly oppose such implementation and/or attempt to define new CGT action in terms which came closer to party goals. The majority of the PCF *Bureau Politique* was behind the party's own sectarian response to electoral defeat, even if the PCF leadership was divided. Séguy and Henri Krasucki were both members of the *Bureau Politique* and bound to be sensitive to party pressure, even if in different ways—Séguy being reluctant about the party's new course and Krasucki more enthusiastic. Such political differences between CGT leaders overlapped with differences of opinion within the *Bureau Confédéral* about trade-union issues and, in particular, about many of the new orientations announced at the Congress. It was quite obvious at the Congress itself that only certain CGT Secretaries promoted the new line, while others were conspicuous for their lack of reference to such things. Krasucki in particular was known to have been quite discomfited by the new openness of the Confederation evidenced in preparations for the Fortieth Congress and accepted it, in all likelihood, more as a safety valve for the difficult post-electoral period than as any permanent change in direction.

Differences at the very top of the Confederation about the scope and meaning of the innovations of the Fortieth Congress were only the tip of an iceberg. The weight of decades of habit at lower levels of the CGT organization in itself made the implementation of new perspectives problematic. Defensive, bread-and-butter unionism involved a tried-and-true routine which would be very difficult to change. Beyond this lay political problems. To the degree to which CGT actions and the PCF's line diverged in practice, Communist CGTers, (and the bulk of incumbent officials in

---

49. Maire's public response to the Fortieth Congress is most interesting. See CFDT, *service de presse*, "Intervention d'Edmond Maire au Congrès Régionale CFDT de Rhône-Alpes," St. Etienne (5 December 1978).

federations, department *and* local unions were Communists) would be placed in a contradictory situation. Communist CGTers who followed the party's line to the letter—the anti-Socialist, anti-"reformist" aspects of the PCF's post-electoral stance were, translated into trade-union terms, both anti-mass and anti–structural reform—would be very uncomfortable with the new course. Moreover, the new line to the degree to which it became fact, would involve a redefinition for PCF militants in the CGT of the strange personal bifurcation which they were all required to make between their identities as Communists and as unionists.

Clearly Edmond Maire was right in his "springtime" skepticism. The obstacles to CGT change were great. Beyond internal organizational questions lay the CGT's environment. Here there was little to be optimistic about. The effects on French workers of deepening economic crisis promised to make rank-and-file mobilization for anything, let alone for bold new initiatives, difficult indeed. The regime's electoral victory would inevitably bring with it an onslaught of new austerity and industrial restructuring making union activities of any kind even more difficult. And on top of this the CGT itself was in trouble, its membership declining and its financial situation, as a result, deteriorating. Much would depend on the strategic and tactical sense of the architects of the new course in the *Bureau Confédéral* and, above all, on the actions of Georges Séguy. The official line of the Fortieth Congress, was still, in 1978, very much a leadership formulation, unintegrated into the vital middle levels of the CGT organization and misunderstood at the base.

CONCLUSIONS

This study began with the assertion of an obvious truth: the close involvement of all Western trade unions with politics is an established fact. Such involvement comes in various shapes and forms—from North American business unionism and its indirect pressure-group activities, through the many varieties of social-democratic unionism with their partisan affiliations with social democratic parties, to the union movements which grew out of the Third International/Communist tradition. Our purpose has not been to reach conclusions about the desirability of trade-union participation in political life, nor about the desirability of any particular model for such participation. Such considerations we very happily leave to political philosophers, moralists and propagandists. The different models of trade-union involvement in politics, and the particular model which we have looked at in detail, are historical realities, all with profound roots in the complicated lives of different social formations. However it is clear that each specific formulation of union-political ties has its own peculiar combination of benefits and costs to workers, unions, political parties, and the structures of political conflict in the society where it exists. Moreover, within this general balance of costs and benefits of specific forms of union-political relationships, there also exists a broad range of particular costs and benefits attributable to the wisdom and/or foolishness with which real unions and parties carry on their day-to-day activities. The purpose of our work has been to detail such cost-benefit structures, over time, for the PCF and CGT.

PCF-CGT ties are perhaps the best example, among the union movements of the advanced capitalist world, of the unionism derived from the Third International/Communist tradition. What distinguishes such unionism from other types of party-union relationships is, of course, the decisive role played by the political party in the shaping of union strategies. As we have seen, however, if party predominance in union strategizing distinguishes the CGT-PCF relationship from that obtaining, say, in the relationships between social democratic unions and social democratic parties, it neither describes nor explains the content of CGT-PCF ties. Such tasks of description and explanation have been the undertakings of this monograph.

In general, it is crystal clear that the PCF's ties to the CGT have been the most important element in the PCF's ability to sustain its presence in French life since World War II. Without PCF power over the CGT the PCF would, in all likelihood, have become a relatively insignificant force in the shaping of modern French politics and society, with all that this would have entailed. In the shorter run, the CGT has served as the major source of working-class mobilization for different specific PCF projects. In more profound, and longer term, ways, the CGT has been a decisive tool in the PCF's attempts to promote and perpetuate certain basic popular perceptions of the shape of capitalist society as it has developed in France. While the modern PCF and CGT cannot claim exclusive responsibility for the continuing power of certain notions of class and class conflict in French life, the fact remains that PCF and CGT interventions in French social life have made an immense difference to the visions of social process held not only by French workers, but by intellectuals and elite groups as well. Without the PCF, and without the effective class-forming tool which the CGT has been for the PCF, French workers and others would, in all likelihood, understand their social relationships in very different ways.

Another thing is clear. If the class-forming role of PCF-CGT ties and actions is well demonstrated in modern French social history, the limitations of party-union relationships of the PCF-CGT kind are quite as obvious. To begin with, any partisan affiliation places limits on the union movement which accepts it, given the sociology of advanced capitalist societies. Labor movements are mass organizations which depend, for their immediate success, on their ability to solicit an ecumenical base of support, other things being equal. Moreover, specifically trade-unionist issues of maximizing working-class advantage in the labor market—job security, wages, hours, authority at the point of production—are different issues from those of the political sphere, they are fought out in different arenas and they have different rhythms of development. This does not mean, of course, that trade-union and political questions are unconnected—the universal involvement of Western trade unions in politics indicates that they are connected—but simply that they are not the same questions. Thus combining trade-unionist and political mobilization in union activities is problematic, if necessary. This is so, to begin with, because the labor forces of most advanced capitalist societies are, to varying degrees, politically pluralist. It is also so because mobilizing workers for two different purposes, trade-unionist and political, is more difficult than mobilization around strictly labor-market issues.

It stands to reason, then, that contradictions between mass union appeal and union partisan affiliation will be more acute the more a specific union movement considers mobilization for party political purposes as a central and urgent task. Here Western trade unions are very different in approach. North American business unions maintain a low political profile, if a partisan one, and pursue pressure-group tactics. Direct partisan affiliations vary greatly, of course. For most social-democratic union movements, however, partisan affiliation does not influence strictly trade-unionist day-to-day behavior in major ways (even if there are important exceptions to this generalization). The PCF-CGT model of party-union relations, which involves, as we have seen, an important component of trade-union strategic subordination to the political party, poses the mass-appeal/partisan-affiliation problem in the most evident ways. Insistence upon this model, primarily because of its benefits, automatically sets limits on the mass base of support which a union will be able to tap, however carefully the question of affiliation is handled. To the extent to which the PCF has attempted to deploy the CGT for political purposes, it has had the broad effect of limiting the CGT's potential mass appeal. The results of this, historically, have been obvious throughout our work. There has been a perpetual, if shifting, division of the total French union movement along somewhat partisan lines.There has been persistent disunity between different branches of the French union movement about how best to promote and protect rank-and-file working-class interests. There have been continual strategic differences between unions, often reflecting each one's desire to outflank the others as much as a general desire to advance working-class interests. All this, more generally, has placed serious limitations on the effectiveness of the total labor movement in the labor market. These results, in their turn, have had their inevitable effects on the shaping of French economic development, contributing to the relative inability of French organized labor to influence and participate directly in the shaping of important developmental decisions.

What is really important to assess are the results of PCF and CGT action, given such general limits. Have the PCF and CGT maximized the possibilities which their particular form of association seems to confer in the abstract? The answer is, unquestionably, no. There has been a consistent tendency for the PCF to oversubordinate the CGT to short-run political goals at the expense of the CGT's prospects for mass trade-unionist appeal. While the tendency has been consistent, however, it has varied in important ways in intensity and form. PCF-CGT relationships in the immediate post–World War II took on classic transmission-belt forms, with the party using its influence over the union to make CGT actions in the labor market correspond to PCF projects in the political sphere in direct one-to-one correspondence. In the peculiar circumstances of Resistance and Liberation, when an unprecedented degree of working-class unity around specific union and political goals existed, thereby reducing partisan tension at the

CGT's base and in the working class more generally, transmission-belt unionism may well have helped the PCF to succeed in consolidating its influence over the bulk of the CGT. In the very different circumstances of renewed partisan conflict which soon emerged, transmission-belt PCF-CGT relationships were one important cause of the renewal of destructive trade-union pluralism in France. Ultimately, in the catastrophic Cold War years after 1947, extreme transmission-belt party-union ties, carried on in sectarian ways in a Manichaean general setting, so diminished the CGT's mass appeal that their continuation in the early 1950s brought the Confederation to the brink of organizational disaster. It was at this juncture, in the mid-1950s, that party and union began to reevaluate their relationship.

Relative Autonomy and Eurocommunization

The beginnings of change from transmission-belt to relative-autonomy party-union ties predated the strategic changes in the PCF which ultimately created Eurocommunization. During the middle and later 1950s the PCF remained completely trapped in the strategic muddle which had plagued it during the Popular Front and post-Liberation periods. The party avowed a United Front domestic strategy and expressed its desires to construct new alliances with other political forces. The proximity of the Cold War, Budapest and the domestic political distortion attendant upon French decolonization made this hope a rather implausible one. But even if the outside world had been less hostile the PCF would have been ill-prepared to take advantage of any new opportunities. It had yet to take any distance from the Soviet model for socialism—the USSR was still the workers' paradise. It still held to neo-Bolshevik scenarios for revolutionary change—a United Front would, given correct PCF policies, lead to Popular Democracy, East-Europe–style which, in turn, would lead to a one-party dictatorship of the proletariat. Moreover the party's pauperization economic theory was increasingly beside the point in a France which had begun to participate eagerly in the general postwar boom of Western capitalism.

Operating within the environment created by such PCF strategy and theory, the CGT was limited in what it could do, despite the deemphasis on direct politicization initiated in the mid-1950s. This tentative degree of relative autonomy probably saved the CGT from further isolation and decline and indeed it allowed the Confederation to begin reconstructing a degree of union credibility. Yet the full possibilities of such reconstruction were blocked by the continuing isolation of the PCF. They were even more compromised by the regular political disasters suffered by the party and felt in the trade-union realm by the CGT, the events surrounding the Soviet invasion of Hungary in 1956, for example, and the crisis of 1958.

The Confederation's retreat from involvement in open politics back towards a more traditional trade-unionist focus on labor-market activity was also insufficient to regenerate significant union action because, despite this retreat, the CGT continued to share the PCF's theoretical perspectives. The CGT's use of Thorez's pauperization map of the social world led it to continue regarding other French union organizations as illegitimate "misleaders" of French workers. Thus if unity-in-action with these organizations was an absolute prerequisite for renewed mass labor struggle, the CGT continued to pose impossible conditions for its achievement, demanding a whole range of political, organizational and strategic changes from other organizations. Given that *Force Ouvrière* remained profoundly mired in its own Cold War posture and that the CFTC was only at the beginning of the changes which would turn it into the CFDT, it is doubtful whether any substantial unity agreements were possible in any case. Still, to the degree that any movement towards unity-in-action was conceivable, the CGT's own positions made such unity unthinkable.

The processes which eventuated in the PCF's experiment with Eurocommunization began in the early 1960s, in the immediate aftermath of the Algerian War. From this point, the party, presented with, and itself creating, a situation in which new United Frontism was possible, began to grant political, doctrinal and theoretical concessions to the outside world in order to present itself as a plausible United Front ally. The process of change was piecemeal—as befits change initiated by a desire to adapt to outside stimuli rather than change oriented by a new vision of practice—until the dust began to clear after the twin crises of 1968, the Events of May-June and the Soviet invasion of Czechoslovakia in August. The processes of PCF Eurocommunization had become significantly more coherent by the early 1970s, with the theory of state-monopoly capitalism, the PCF's changes in attitude towards allegiance to the Soviet model for socialism and Soviet foreign policy, movement towards the abandonment of certain basic Marxist-Leninist principles (the dictatorship of the proletariat) and attempts to Italianize the party.

It was this process of PCF change which made possible the golden age of the relatively autonomous CGT, which stretched from the mid-1960s into the mid-1970s. In this period the CGT, to increase its mass appeal, based its activity primarily on defensive bread-and-butter trade unionism structured around the Confederation's appreciation of the realities of the labor market. PCF theory, increasingly the state-monopoly capitalist perspective, encouraged this, to the degree to which it pinpointed the primary contradiction of French capitalism in the economic sphere. Only after the CGT had considered data from the labor market did it then choose between the several different plausible trade-union strategies which any given labor-market conjuncture created. At that point the CGT tried to seek out that specific union strategy most congruent with PCF goals in the political sphere. Here as well, PCF strategy and theory helped the Confederation. To the degree to which the PCF itself sought unity arrangements with other political forces and to the degree to which state-monopoly capitalist theory sanctioned such unitary attitudes, the CGT itself developed new and more creative approaches to other union movements, in particular the CFDT. An important degree of trade-union success followed.

Relative autonomy, if it was a necessary corrective for earlier PCF-CGT relations, did not resolve the mass-appeal–partisan-affiliation contradiction. The fact that Communists continued to predominate in CGT decision-making would have continually activated the contradiction, in any case. But, even beyond this, PCF politics still entered CGT deliberations in powerful, if less direct ways. To begin with, as we have just remarked, the ultimate choice between plausible labor-market scenarios was made by the Confederation with reference to PCF political projects. While this did not directly politicize CGT action, for the most part it did bias such action to favor certain outcomes in the political sphere as against the others. Beyond this, the CGT, as a union movement, even under relative autonomy did not assess the development of the labor market in a blindly empiricist way. Rather it used a specific theoretical map to distinguish the significant from the trivial. And, over the years, this map was virtually the same as that of the PCF. Relative autonomy, then, was limited autonomy, limited by perceptions of the social world shared with the PCF, perceptions which did orient CGT choices even in the labor market, and by an ultimate desire to develop a trade-unionist strategy which would, indirectly, advance PCF political fortunes. Moreover, even this definition of relative autonomy, with all its limitations, was violated in the direction of quasi-transmission–belt behavior in moments of extreme political crisis, as in May 1958 and at moments during the May-June 1968 events.

Relative autonomy is only a conceptualization of a certain *type* of party-union relationships. As such it is incomplete without further consideration of those elements of party and trade-union *strategy* which gave detailed content to these relationships. From the early 1960s both strategic dimensions had been well defined. For the PCF, the United Front offensive of modern times became the order of the day. For the CGT, mass-and-class trade unionism—the label was the CGT's own—was the goal. As specified by the Confederation the purpose of mass-and-class unionism was to promote very broad defensive union action, directed towards the creation of spectacular public movements involving large numbers of workers which might be translated into high-level negotiations with the government and with major peak employer's associations. As we have noted very often, mass-and-class unionism came replete with a preferred repertory of tactics of struggle, of which the *journée d'action* was the linchpin.

As practiced by the CGT, mass-and-class unionism consistently suffered from two major flaws. First of all, because it was ultimately oriented towards the production of the broadest possible front of working-class struggle around the most general of demands and, even beyond this, towards the encouragement of protest among non-working–class groups, it tended to dictate relative moderation in any specific workers' struggles. This was so because the Confederation saw broad working-class mobilization against general Gaullist economic policies and against the structures of Gaullist modernization as the core of the cross-class anti-monopoly social alliance which would bring a new United Front to power. Thus workers in any given conflict situation, through CGT mediation, were held responsible for the consequences of their actions not only for the working class as a whole, but for potential social allies of the working class as well. Hyper-militant local actions which brought with them the risk of disaggregation for this broad potential social front were therefore discouraged.

The second flaw was connected to this. Ironically enough, mass-and-class unionism contributed to the development of a major chasm between union action in the labor market and politics. The CGT saw union action as a defensive struggle for day-to-day material gains of the classic wages-and-hours kind. Anything which went beyond such limits was to be left for a United Front to change by coming to power. In essence, the mass-and-class perspective, by neglecting the prospects for broader action by *unions, in union struggle* to win social change for workers, led the CGT towards a narrow economism. One consequence of this, which the CFDT consistently pointed out in its debates with the CGT, was that the CGT neglected to take seriously a range of less economistic new rank-and-file concerns about authority in the work place, the structure of economic decision-making at firm and branch level and the organization of work itself which began to emerge in the later 1960s. Another consequence of this, in the political sphere, was that the structural reforms, primarily nationalizations, which the PCF proposed to change the day-to-day situations of workers in the workplace, came, in time, to be understood by these workers in abstract and general terms as changes which would be worked *for* them, by politicians, through processes which had little to do with their lives.

Despite these problems, however, CGT relative autonomy with its mass-and-class trade-union strategy worked quite well for more than a decade. Not far from the surface, however, relative autonomy was burdened with a fatal contradiction. The redefined PCF-CGT relationships perfected in the early 1960s involved an attempt to square the circle, to allow the CGT the necessary trade-unionist space to generate new mass appeal and working-class struggle while, at the same time, contributing to the success of the PCF's United Front political plans. The balance between these two goals was delicate at all times and depended ultimately on the stage of development reached in the PCF's United Front project. As long United Front successes remained far off in the future, the balance could be struck in favor of the CGT as a trade union with primary focus on the labor market, albeit behaving within the limits of the economist mass-and-class perspective which we have just described. But the balance in CGT relative autonomy was likely to shift towards politics to the degree to which the PCF actually succeeded in its United Front goals.

With the conclusion of the Common Program in 1972 and the creation of a plausible United Front poised to make a bid for electoral victory, such a shift began. After the signature of the Common Program in 1972, political mobilization became an ever more pressing concern for the CGT and the Confederation began, in consequence, to orient ever more of its union action towards deepening working-class support for the specific measures of the Common Program. If possible, the CGT also wanted to convince its union partners, the CFDT in particular, to do the same. Before the economic crisis of the 1970s began to hit hardest, up through 1975, say, this increased emphasis on politics proved relatively compatible with defensive unionism in the labor market. Even so, the message which the CGT desired to communicate through labor-market action changed somewhat. Workers were to mobilize for protest and strikes, to be sure. But they were also to be led to understand, rather urgently, that labor-market action could provide only temporary remedies to working-class problems. Real, lasting solutions could come only through the electoral victory of *Union de la Gauche* and the implementation of the Common Program.

Beginning in 1976, however, political mobilization began to displace trade-union action rather than to supplement it. In essence, this meant ever increasing CGT stress on the Left-electoral-victory-is-the-only-solution line at the expense of more orthodox trade-union concerns. Moreover, at the same time, in its purely trade-union actions the CGT pressed ever more urgently towards general, high level and publicly spectacular movements of the *journée d'action* type which, in their contents, progressively left rank-and-file concerns behind for electoral mobilization. It was during this period that the slogan *Union, Action, Programme Commun* became the CGT's marching song.

It would be very wrong to assert that conscious CGT decisions were the only factors in the growing overgeneralization and overpoliticization of French trade-union action after 1975. The highly charged political atmosphere which developed generally in France after the 1973 legislative elections created a setting in which such shifts in union emphasis seemed both natural and reasonable. In effect, France lived for several years in a constant state of preelectoral tension, leading towards the 1978 legislative elections which would be, everyone knew, the decisive moment for *Union de la Gauche*. Moreover, the CGT and CFDT were self-proclaimed participants in the French Left as well as trade unions, even if the CFDT never openly supported the Common Program. Whatever their *arrière-pensées*, both knew that 1978 represented perhaps the best chance the French Left had ever had to begin a process of transformative change in France. And both believed, each in different ways, that such transformative change was the privileged avenue towards solutions to French working-class problems. Beyond even this, a crisis-altered labor-market made rank-and-file union action, even of a defensive kind, much more difficult. Problems in generating workplace struggle thus abetted a shift towards symbolic demonstrations and politicization as central union tactics. In all, however, CGT decisions about how to shape labor action were very important. And rather than resisting tendencies to overgeneralize and overpoliticize union action, the CGT pushed such tendencies forward.

Trade-union politicization in favor of *Union de la Gauche* did not immediately cause the kinds of mass problems for the CGT which earlier and different kinds of politicization had. Ultimately, however, the convergence of such politicization with the narrow economism which we have asserted to be the first major fault of mass-and-class unionism was tremendously costly. After years in which the CGT had defined union activity in an economistic way, leaving social change to the politicians, it then tended to neglect day-to-day union activity in favor of politics. This was a guaranteed recipe for the simultaneous demobilization of the union rank and file in the labor market and for a type of politicization in favor of distant abstractions which rendered the logic of the Common Program incomprehensible to many workers. The results of this we have examined earlier. Whether the Left had won or lost in 1978, the CGT would have been ill-equipped to cope with whatever circumstances followed.

What is most important for us is to underline the fact that the CGT's mistakes in the mid-1970s were a direct product of the central contradiction in relative autonomy as it had been defined in the early 1960s. Relative autonomy simply did not allow the CGT enough trade-unionist space to resist the pressures for politicization which were bound to arise in the event the PCF's United Front political strategy moved towards success. This was no accident. In effect, relative autonomy had been designed to contribute to such success. The overpoliticization of the CGT in the mid-1970s, then, was, ironically, the trade-union side of PCF Eurocommunization. At the very moment when the PCF was reaching ahead in terms of doctrine and behavior towards a post-Stalinist reformulation of its identity, the CGT was moving towards a dangerous shift in the balance of its activities away from trade unionism and towards politics. In the event, the PCF's strategy was a losing one. Its implication for the CGT, turning the Confederation into a political support group for the party, were against the CGT's profound trade-union interests. The political failure of 1978 therefore obliged both the PCF and the CGT to reevaluate their respective strategic positions, as well as their mutual relationship. The situation was all the more dramatic because such complex reevaluations had to be carried out in the context of the most severe economic crisis which France had known since 1947.

Replacing Relative Autonomy?

As we have seen, crisis in PCF-CGT relationships was one of the underlying issues at the November 1978 CGT Congress. Even if the discussion was not formulated in the terms which we have used (relative autonomy, in particular), its themes were clear. The CGT had developed serious problems of overpoliticization and overgeneralization in the labor market and something had to be done about them. As the CGT approached the 1980s, however, profound disagreement within the Confederation about exactly how to replace relative autonomy persisted. There were two basic schools of thought on the subject. The first advanced a new kind of "proposition-force/industrial-solution" type of unionism, modelled on the policies of the Italian CGIL in the mid-1970s and proposing an autonomous, trade-union-based, structural reformism. The second, following the strategic re-evaluations of the PCF, proposed what looked like a new variety of trans-mission-belt relationship.

The rise of a "proposition-force" current around the Fortieth Congress is one of the more important changes in the CGT's recent history. Proposition-force ideas had antecedents within the Confederation in the mid-1970s, but the ideas did not really strike fire until the inadequacy of the CGT's pre-March 1978 practices became clearer.[1] The essence of this new position was that the CGT had to jettison relative autonomy and become a proposition force for industrial solutions in economic life itself, through struggle in the labor market and elsewhere. The primary focus of the new current was the economic crisis. Simple, defensive, bread-and-butter unionism directed against the symptoms of crisis—unemployment, inflation, industrial redeployment, cutbacks—would not be enough, in itself, to protect workers and regenerate union action. Moreover, waiting for change to come from the political sphere was also unreliable, if not dangerous, as the 1977–1978 experience demonstrated. Unions could either be acted upon by capital in the crisis, in which case the likelihood was very strong that workers' interests would be attacked in a flood of economic change, or unions could take the offensive to become a proposition force for industrial solutions to the problems posed by the crisis. The core notion of proposition-force advocates was that the crisis presented a new opportunity for unions to direct collective bargaining and union mobilization beyond simple wages-and-hours issues towards questions of authority and the shape of work in the firm, towards attempts to shape firm, branch and national investment policies and towards broader social reforms *as unions*.

Proposition-force approaches demanded innovative practices of the CGT. To begin with, the Confederation, and its rank and file, had to acquire new knowledge of the exact structures and dynamics of the French economy. The old CGT perspective of leaving economic decisions to capital—while, of course, constraining such decision-making processes as much as possible through defensive struggle—until the Left could come to

1. See, for example, Jean-Louis Moynot, "Luttes syndicales et bataille politique," in *Nouvelle Critique* (October 1973); and Moynot, "La crise sous nos yeux et son issue un peu plus loin, dans les luttes," *Nouvelle Critique* (October 1975).

power and dramatically restructure the accumulation process as a whole did not require such knowledge. Conflictual intervention in economic policy-making at all levels, in contrast, required a sound knowledge of the context within which policy was made. Efforts to acquire such knowledge were well underway by the later 1970s. On the Confederal level there were a series of long seminars on different branches of the French economy, ultimately leading to publications discussing the evolution of specific sectors.[2] Producing a CGT new map of the French economy also involved reexamining the international context of French activity. Proposition-forcers were also *autogestionnaire*. They did not see themselves as constructing any general CGT countermodel for the economy. Industrial solutions to crisis-created structural problems were to be the end product of the mobilization of rank-and-file workers. Moreover, actual union counter-propositions were to be combined with increases in rank-and-file shop-floor and sectoral power so that transformational consciousness would be deepened at base level.

Proposition-force unionism had profound implications for the recasting of CGT relationships with the PCF and politics. Because of its focus on the development of autonomous trade-union struggles for sectoral changes in economic life, it would clearly lead to a decentralization of social mobilization away from the almost exclusive focus on national-level political change

2. In 1978–1979, for example, the CGT Confederal Center for Economic and Social Studies held weekends of research on specific industrial groups such as Suez–St.-Gobain–Pont-à-Mousson, Rhône-Poulenc, and Empain-Schneider (dittoing up internal reports in their series of *notes économiques*). There were also Federal- and regional-level study and research meetings. Among the Center's offical publications sectoral discussion has had pride of place in the past couple of years. See, for example, CGT, Centre Confédéral d'Etudes Economiques, *études et documents économiques* as follows, *Perspectives et problèmes de l'énergie* (November 1977), *L'industrie française depuis 1958, un bilan accusateur* (February 1978), *Les industries de la construction* (April 1979), *Crise et solution pour la sidérurgie* (November 1979).

Another interesting recent development in this respect is the development of Federation-level research capabilities on industrial questions, usually by the employment of specific researchers. To an outsider the Federal-level presence of such capabilities might seem an obvious necessity. But the CGT Federations have rarely developed industrial research, working instead, when they have needed data and analyses, through the Confederal Center. At the same time the Confederal Research Center itself has been traditionally treated as a luxury whose main job was to find last minute bits of information or connections to support arguments arrived at without extensive inquiry. One can often judge the relative importance of specific services within the CGT by the political stripe of the Secretary in charge of them. In the case of the Research Center, the Secretary appointed was always a non-Communist. There have been two since 1947, Pierre LeBrun and Jean-Louis Moynot. LeBrun, as we have earlier noted, had Gaullist propensities which made it easy to disregard the Center, especially after 1958. Moynot, elected to the *Bureau Confédéral* primarily to fill a non-Communist "slot"—he was a Catholic and a *cadre*, joined the PCF *after* two years of *Bureau Confédéral* incumbency, largely as a result of his experiences in May-June 1968. In recent years the Research Center has greatly expanded its activities, although its role in CGT activities is still ill-defined.

held by the French Left through March 1978. Moreover, if the old relative-autonomy perspective left the implementation of change to political parties, proposition-force/industrial-solution unionism would appropriate at least part of the task of change for trade unions, deemphasizing the role of parties. As we have noted earlier, all of this amounted to a proposal for a form of neo-syndicalism, very different from the politico-centric vision of transformation so dear to the Leninist tradition. Taking proposition-force unionism seriously would oblige the PCF to take a different view of labor mass organizational activity, one in which the party's task would be much more as coordinator for decentralized and self-generating action at the base and in the CGT than as the setter of general strategic lines and as the ultimate recipient vessel of all labor-generated energy for a change.

In the aftermath of the Fortieth Congress it became clear that unionists following the strategic shift of the PCF had a very different route out of relative autonomy to urge on the CGT. As the party moved closer to its own Twenty-third Congress in May 1979, a pronounced return to strategic *ouvriérisme*, with a strong overlay of nationalism, was promoted by the leadership.[3] Ultimate adherence to United Frontism was reaffirmed, but for the foreseeable future the party's central task was to strengthen its own forces vis-à-vis the PS such that when the propitious moment came to renew contacts with the PS, the PCF would do so in a new position of strength. The party's central goal, to be accomplished through "struggle" and *union à la base*, was to deepen its power within the working class itself. The new strategic package, essentially a reformulation of the *union du peuple de France* line of the Twenty-first Congress in 1974, came wrapped up in a theoretical argument about the economic crisis. In essence, this argument contended that the economic crisis was *avant tout nationale* and could be attributed, in the last analysis, to specific policy choices of the regime and the monopoly caste. In order to ensure the success of French and other multinational corporations, the Giscardian regime was willing to undermine the integrity of the French economy by allowing certain essential activities to disappear in the interests of an international order in which multinationals would predominate. Giscard and the existing majority were, therefore, the proponents of a "strategy of decline." But they were not alone. Behind them were the German Social Democrats and the Americans. And, because of their ties with the German Social Democrats and their Europeanism, the French Socialists were also implicated. What the PCF proposed, via struggle and *union à la base*, was mobilization against industrial redeployment in France, and particularly against the dismantling of sectors of the French economy which would undermine the relative self-

3. For an overview of these events see George Ross and Jane Jenson, "Conflicting Currents in the PCF," in Ralph Miliband and John Saville, eds. *The Socialist Register 1979*, and Jane Jenson and George Ross, "Strategies in Conflict: The Twenty-Third Congress of the French Communist Party," in *Socialist Review*, no. 47 (September-October 1979).

containment of French economic life, hence the strong nationalistic side to the party's new appeals.[4]

The unionism urged upon the CGT by unionists following the PCF's new line was not difficult to describe. What the CGT ought to do, side-by-side with the party, was to struggle tooth and nail against any and all policies stemming from the strategy of decline which threatened French workers. This did not mean the simple defensive unionism of the past, however. The intent was more clearly political. The CGT was to be deployed in the labor market to increase the PCF's strength at the working-class base, and, in particular, to aid the PCF to redress the political imbalance between it and the Socialist Party. What this would involve, for the most part, would be CGT adoption of the strategy-of-decline analysis as the major orientation of its action. Were the CGT to do this, while initiating militant struggles against the consequences of Giscardian industrial policies, workers would presumably be taught lessons about the strategy of decline and learn to see the Socialists—and the CFDT—as allies of the regime. In general, then, this new PCF perspective advocated a unionism primarily oriented towards political mobilization, although political mobilization of a very different kind from that of the relative-autonomy period. Indeed, it looked very much like a return to a transmission-belt posture of the kind used between 1947 and 1949. Union action would not be directly political, since struggles would be directed at economic problems created by the crisis. But they would be directed towards persuading the union rank and file of the utility of an analysis of economic change held only by the PCF. To the degree to which this was successful, the rank and file would then turn to the PCF politically. And, clearly, the primary frame of reference would not be the specific rhythms of the labor market, but events in the political sphere, in particular the development of relationships of relative strength between the PCF and the PS. The PCF wanted to impose a highly partisan position on the CGT in the interests of increasing its own influence among workers. And to do this it was willing to oblige the CGT to pay the costs of such partisan identification in terms of mass appeal and possible unity-in-action with other union movements, the CFDT in the first instance. Thus as the PCF itself moved towards a *ouvriériste* strategy redolent of the Cold War and class-against-class periods in its past, it also desired to see the CGT resurrect the sectarian trade-union practices of this transmission-belt past.

CGT response to the breakdown of relative autonomy therefore involved intra-Confederal conflict about reformulating the Confederation's position. What was most interesting about this conflict, as the CGT began the 1980s, was the very fact that it existed. The PCF was not automatically able to impose its own desires. The long years of relative autonomy had created

---

4. See *L'Humanité*, 13 February 1979, for the *projet de résolution* for the Twenty-third Congress, entitled *L'avenir commence maintenant*.

their own contradiction. For important groups within the Confederation, relative autonomy had not been enough autonomy, and the problems to which relative autonomy had led could only be resolved by increasing CGT autonomy. Indeed, the persistent strength of the advocates of proposition-force unionism within the Confederation indicated the degree to which the relative-autonomy years had brought the issue of CGT independence to the forefront of concern. The positive side of the influence of the proposition-force current was important. But it meant also that the CGT could not make up its mind what to do, a fact which was represented in a number of zigs and zags in CGT action throughout 1979. Whether or not the Confederation would support the PCF's position on Europe,[5] the CGT's response to the government's steel crisis plan,[6] and unity-in-action with the CFDT

5. See *Le Peuple*, 1–15 April 1979 for the final text adopted by the *Bureau Confédéral* and the *Commission Exécutive*. The text does not support the PCF's position, and was the object of considerable internal conflict and discussion in the *Bureau Confédéral*.

6. The steel story was a long and complicated one. The government's steel rationalization plan, based both on the near bankruptcy of big steel in France and the EEC's crisis plan for steel (the "Davignon Plan"), proposed the elimination of tens of thousands of jobs and the devastation of certain traditional steel-making regions (the Longwy basin and the Denain area in the north). (See *Le Monde* during the first ten days of December 1978.) For a number of reasons, the CGT Metalworkers Federation responded to the crisis plan in a "proposition-force" way. Rather than simply resisting defensively, the Federation prepared a complex counter-proposal for restructuring the industry on different grounds without loss of employment. (Here see CGT, Fédération des Travailleurs de la Métallurgie, *Le guide du militant* no. 136 [November 1978], "Face à la crise de la sidérurgie, les solutions de la FTM-CGT pour une négociation immédiate.") Trade-union mobilization within the steel industry was undertaken around the proposals of the FTM "memorandum," with considerable success during early 1979. The CFDT, caught out by this CGT innovation, was itself obliged to prepare its own crisis "counter-Plan," much less well-researched and demanding than the CGT. (See CFDT Fédération Générale de la Métallurgie, *Avenir de la sidérurgie, propositions de la FGM-CFDT.*) The Minister of Industry was also caught short by this unexpected initiative and the skill with which it was executed, to the point where he had to consent to negotiations with the unions over the government's plan, a step which had not been planned originally. In order to pressure the Ministry and the companies in question who were to do the actual firing, the FTM-CGT planned a mass march of steel-workers on Paris for March 23 1979. It was at this point that pro-PCF forces in the CGT stepped in to change the direction of the steel campaign. The steel issue, connected to the EEC, was too good for the PCF to pass over in the context of the run-up to the June elections to the European Assembly. What PCF strategy proponents in the CGT wanted to do was to make the steel issue into a nationalist–anti-European one and turn it, if possible, against the PS and the CFDT. Control over the organization of March 23 thus shifted into the hands of pro-PCF forces in the CGT, largely through the organization power of Henri Krasucki, Confederal Secretary in charge of *revendications*. The political ambitions of André Sainjon, the new Secretary-General of the FTM-CGT may have played a role as well; Sainjon was elected to the PCF Central Committee at the May 1979 PCF Congress. The result of all this was that the content of March 23 was shifted towards the Europe issue and unity-in-action with the FGM-CFDT undermined, if not sabotaged. The anti-Socialist effect of the move was also somewhat undermined, however, when the PS came out in support of the march. In any case, the shift in emphasis of the CGT and the growth of trade-union disunity in steel undoubtedly helped the Minister of Industry to deal with the steel issue at a much

were issues which generated conflict within the CGT and led to inconsistent behavior.[7] As the 1980s began, then, the meaning of the CGT's Fortieth Congress remained quite unclear. If the fact that the Confederation did not submit immediately and completely to the PCF's attempt to redefine party-union relationships in a modified transmission-belt way was positive, conflict within the Confederation about future directions made the CGT's course of action confusing and difficult to follow.

Crisis and the Future

Union movements are not eternal. They are formed in specific historical circumstances which change, ultimately changing unions along with them. Contemporary union movements were formed in the Great Depression—when mass-production factory operatives organized—and in the various post–World War II "settlements" in which the basic socioeconomic equilibria of modern times were struck. Each national case differed from others, to be sure, both because the structures of the Great Depression and post-war settlements differed from society to society and because each national union movement had a different historical point of departure. In all cases, however, unions faced a changed capitalism in the post-1945 period. Vastly increased state intervention in economic life, characterized by Keynesian counter-cyclical demand management, the "welfare-state," and a massive dissemination of new goods and services to popular strata were its central characteristics. In the postwar boom which began in the 1950s, the ability of capital to provide regular increases in income and a new array of consumer choices to workers tended almost everywhere to promote a unionism mainly oriented towards wage gains and employment security. This was, of course, the period of the "end of ideology" in which the new pundits of Cold War capitalism announced that labor movements were no longer threats, but contented estates of the realm. French and Italian unions were much less tempted towards cooperation and relative quiescence, since, in both cases, because of the Cold War,

---

lower cost than otherwise might have been the case. No modifications of the steel plan were negotiated. The Minister instead offered substantial severance rewards to workers who offered to leave (50,000 francs, about $12,000). Trade-union disunity helped the Minister and the steel industry later when new contractual agreements were negotiated for steel.

The brief article by Philippe Zarifian, "Restructurer ou non," in *Dialectiques* no. 28 is of great interest, as is Zarifian's piece "Tactique de lutte dans la sidérurgie," in *Nouvelle Critique* (April 1979). Zarifian was the major architect of the original "proposition-force" approach in steel.

7. Unity-in-action with the CFDT almost came to an end in the later summer of 1979. It was clear, in the complicated events preceding and surrounding CGT-CFDT negotiations in September of 1979, that the PCF desired a breakdown in CGT-CFDT cooperation. One has only to read the incessant attacks on the CFDT in *L'Humanité* during this period to realize this.

the postwar settlement excluded them from any overt participatory role in the development of postwar events. In both cases this made for a different, more oppositional and combative trade unionism, as we have seen for the French case. But French and Italian divisions around the Cold War also made for a relatively weak trade unionism. But, in general, characteristic stable forms of trade unionism were established in the postwar settlements, even in Italy and France.

It is too early to be completely sure, but it may well be that the economic and social difficulties of the 1970s are part of a more general crisis of transition for advanced capitalism away from the predictable framework of the postwar settlement towards a new era. There are many signs of this. Cyclical problems *within* a relatively stable stage of accumulation are usually amenable to temporary resolution through the application of whatever fine-tuning mechanisms may be in vogue. Yet "stagflation"—unemployment, low growth, monetary instability and inflation—seems quite refractory to the fine-tuning mechanisms used successfully in the earlier postwar years. Keynesianism is everywhere questioned. Policymakers themselves generally acknowledge the end of the postwar boom and predict a future of austerity, uncertainty and high unemployment. Central features of the postwar settlement in different societies have come under increasing attack. The content of "bourgeois" politics has shifted rapidly rightwards, in the guise, quite often, of "returning to a free-market economy."

What makes us suspect that Western economies are facing something more than an ordinary, if prolonged, downturn within an economic framework which retains its central identifying features is the emergence of new economic forms and arrangements out of crisis. Symptomatic of these new forms and arrangements is the growing anxiety of national regimes about the place of their national economies in the international market and their desperate casting about for national policies which might promote comparative advantage in this market. The role of national economic endeavors, in a volatile international setting, in long-range policy calculations is displacing earlier concern for stability within relatively self-contained national economies. If we look carefully around us it is hard not to observe a qualitative leap in the internationalization of economic activity. The "catch-up" industrialization policies of the 1960s of France, Germany, Japan, and others, designed to place these economies on a competitive footing with the U.S.A. have, in fact, led to a cutthroat and, in many sectors, saturated international market. This situation has been further complicated by the oil problem, new sectoral competitiveness of non-Western newly industrializing societies, plus a general increase in the openness of advanced industrial societies to international economic movements. The most spectacular manifestation of change is, of course, the rise of the multinational corporation, with its unprecedented capacities to internationalize production as well as marketing. Increasingly multi-nationalization has become the strategy of major industrial entities which had earlier been primarily national in base and outlook. In all of this even the most sophisticated and advanced national economies have had to face the fact that they will be able to succeed in the future only to the degree to which they are able to find viable places in an interdependent international market. We have no label for the new stage of capitalist development which may be upon us. We have no idea how long transition to it, whatever it will be, will take. We have no adequate theorizations of the outline of transition or of the shape of the emerging new situation. Nonetheless, it is compelling to think that an important change in the structure of capital accumulation has begun.

Our major concern in concluding on this note is the meaning of such change for labor movements. First of all, beneath the surface of stagflation lie important modifications in the structure of national labor markets. Multinational capital, along with national capital possessed of international ambitions, now make investment and other decisions with an international labor market in mind. Jobs may be moved relatively freely from one advanced capitalist society to another, towards less-developed societies, or in both directions. Growing competition from capital in the so-called "newly industrializing countries" has directly undermined employment in sectors which had only recently been considered the preserve of advanced capitalism—steel, shipbuilding, and textiles—and this is only the beginning, with new threats in the production of consumer durable goods on the horizon. As a complement, crisis-related problems—profit squeezes, changing technologies, new competition—have prompted extensive rearrangements of patterns of employment within advanced capitalist societies, often to lower labor costs and/or to avoid unions. In some places this has involved geographical shifts in activities from region to region within countries. Almost everywhere it has involved the reorganization of work through rationalization and automation with their consequences of job re- and de-classification. Subcontracting, the extensive use of temporary and part-time workers and the introduction of women and immigrants into the workforce are other manifestations. In places where there exist openings for union-busting, new approaches to the art have developed involving the refinement of espionage on personnel, a booming market in private "consulting" for corporations on anti-union strategies, and the rise of company unions of one sort and another. The exact shape and extent of labor-market restructuring varies greatly from one advanced capitalist society to another, depending upon the nature of the specific economy and its place in the crisis. But the general process is clear. The redeployment of capital, occurring both internationally and within national boundaries, is changing the nature and location of the working class.

The danger in this for unions is obvious. Modern unions have been constructed around reasonably predictable social bases. Change in crisis has already altered, and threatens to alter even more, the actual social movement upon which trade-union existence depends. Traditional sources of class identity and unions' strength are menaced. As a result unions face new and unprecedented problems. As workers, particularly unionized workers, face threats to their skill levels and/or their jobs, tendencies towards "particularism," that is, the desire at the union base to protect *only* its narrowest interests or union pressures towards trade protectionism for specific sectors or even more broadly—often in terms of nationalism—has begun to appear in numbers of places. The search on the part of certain unions for new, quasi-"sweetheart" deals with employers to preserve certain jobs at the expense of others—often manipulating hard-won union conquests such as seniority in the process—is a manifestation of particularism, as well. Particularism may fragment labor movements of all kinds. For labor movements with strong coverage of their working classes guaranteed more or less by institutionalization, particularism may undermine the capacities of the movement to act in a coherent way in response to general economic trends. For class-oriented labor movements it may alter the shape of working-class outlooks in important ways. In the best of circumstances labor movements which seek to nurture class identity are obliged to walk a tightrope between tendencies towards a defensive rank-and-file consciousness oriented primarily towards a negative refusal to cooperate with the existing order and a more offensive perspective pointing towards positive change. Particularism can only accentuate the former at the expense of the latter, other things being equal. For weak, class-oriented labor movements—and the CGT is one of these—particularism may further weaken union capacities to act in a coherent way *and* promote defensive consciousness.

The multinationalization of important parts of capitalist production and the increased importance of the international market for national economies pose two separate and very complex new problems for unions. First of all, the emergence of multinational accumulation strategies as a general phenomenon raises quite starkly the issue of developing patterns of international union struggle. At present union movements remain profoundly national phenomena, a fact which makes it extremely difficult for one national movement to understand another, let alone set out concrete courses for international cooperation. The difficulty is further multiplied by deep-seated political differences between different national movements stemming from the Cold War. Indeed, the most substantial existing foyers of international trade-union contact, the International Confederation of Free Trade Unions (ICFTU), the World Federation of Trade Unions (WFTU), and the Catholic World Confederation of Labor (WCL) exist for largely *political* reasons and serve mainly to divide different labor movements from one another.

The second problem is equally complicated. Vastly intensified internationalization of capital accumulation carries with it the development of increasingly specialized national economies. The future will belong less and less to relatively self-sufficient national economic units, within which the whole range of productive activities will be carried on. Instead, the source of strength of any given national economy increasingly will be its ability to compete within a complex international division of labor. A nation's capacity to sustain a national standard of comfort and a full complement of domestic service activities will increasingly be geared to the competitive position of its dynamic sectors in the international market. The rising cost of imported raw materials only accentuates such tendencies by heightening balance-of-payments concerns. Thus any given national unit, even those presently best placed in the world market, must attempt to promote the development of internationally competitive economic activities, whether through attempts to prod the emergence of new dynamic sectors, to modernize those sectors which are actually or potentially well-placed in international trade, or through the encouragement of locally based transnational corporations.

National union movements are quite as subject to these trends as other economic actors. It is difficult to avoid the conclusion, therefore, that union movements will be ever more drawn towards concern with the specific nature of national economic decisions. "Industrial policies" of one sort and another are becoming questions of life and death for unions. They include not only what specific realms of economic activity will be promoted, but also which branches will be sacrificed. Enhancing national productivity and maintaining national costs within internationally competitive boundaries involve similar basic choices for unions. Traditional defensive union behavior, struggle in the labor market on bread-and-butter questions while leaving to capital and the state the task of making policy decisions, is becoming less and less adequate to the general tasks which unions face. To be sure, there is nothing inevitable about the exact nature of any new union involvement in questions of industrial and economic policy. But that such new involvement is in the cards is clear.

The third general crisis problem which unions must face is political. The recent years of crisis in Western capitalism have brought with them a significant shift to the Right politically, both in terms of the political composition of governments in power and in terms of the ideologies and strategies of the forces behind such governments. We cannot know yet how far this shift will go and what specific forms it may take. But we do know enough already to assert that most union movements stand to face a very different political environment in the future than they did in the past. With the end of the postwar boom governments can no longer count on steady growth and slow inflation to moderate social conflict and absorb the costs of regular wage increases. High inflation and slow growth, in contrast, place a premium on the development of de facto or de jure incomes policies, with or without union consent. The progressive abandonment of Keynesian demand management, the rise of monetarism and the new enthusiasm for a "return to market capitalism" are all threats to unions to the extent that they signify a willingness on the part of governments to abandon commitments to full employment and to support capital-induced labor-market restructuring. Communitarian appeals that "things have changed and we must now tighten our belts and share austerity" barely conceal offensives against working-class standards of living. Likewise, retrenchment of state expenditures involves attacks on many of the hard-won working-class conquests of the postwar settlement: social security, pensions, health care, education, housing, and other social welfare schemes are threatened.

All of this, taken together, represents a challenge to trade unionism unlike any since the Great Depression. The national union movements produced in the Depression and postwar years will be obliged to make major adaptative changes in response. A new, and quite different, trade unionism may well be the result. The CGT will not be exempted from facing these challenges. How is it likely to respond?

France is profoundly affected by changing labor-market structures. All French unions already have good reasons to be concerned about emerging particularism, about threats to employment in certain economic sectors where unions have traditionally been well implanted and about employers' strategies to undercut unions. In general, the French labor movement is weak in membership coverage, organizational and financial capacities and shop-floor power compared with other national movements. Historically, such weakness has not necessarily translated into a lack of rank-and-file militancy, however, or a low level of rank-and-file collective consciousness. Indeed, in part *because of* such weakness, French unions have tended to place an unusual amount of weight on tasks of ideological and political mobilization and on the cultivation of a militant climate at the base. By constantly maintaining the threat of rank-and-file explosions and of sudden working-class political pressure, French unions have thus tried to compensate for their organizational flaws. Even with this in mind, however, a period of great economic change such as the present creates major new problems. The constant and corrosive agitation of the CGT in past decades has been premised on a working-class structured in certain ways. Particularism and other crisis-induced changes undermine these structures. As a result, rank-and-file response to union initiatives, always difficult to predict in France, will become even more unpredictable. To the degree to which this becomes true, and in a context of much greater general economic constraint, employers and the state will be tempted towards more aggressive strategies which could verge on open union busting. Here the CGT has a critical role to play. For its own sake it must find new ways to recruit new membership and support. It must develop creative new responses to new rank-and-file concerns, which means that it must learn to identify such concerns. Thirdly, it must facilitate unity-in-action with other union movements, the CFDT in the first instance, but beyond the CFDT if possible.

The international side of the labor-market problem, created by the internationalization of production and the growing willingness of capital to view the entire international setting as its labor market, is a question of a different order. No national labor movement in the advanced capitalist world is as yet sufficiently aware of the dimensions of the new problems to be faced. The internationalization of union action will probably proceed, if it proceeds at all, by growing coordination of struggle between different national movements in the advanced capitalist world. Here there are certain very small signs of life, informal collaboration across national boundaries between unions in multinational corporations (in which some CGT unions are involved) and the European Trade Union Confederation. ETUC is the first major new attempt to promote general cooperation. But ETUC has thus far been dominated by the German DGB (*Deutsches Gewerkschafts Bund*) and the DGB has insisted upon certain political criteria for membership. These criteria have, to this point, excluded not only the CGT, but also the Spanish Workers' Commissions and the Portuguese *Intersyndical* (although not the Italian CGIL). In essence, the DGB has had a strong interest in pumping up social democratic union movements in Spain and Portugal, where it has invested a considerable amount of money and time, and to a lesser extent, in France, hence its strong anti-Communism.

The CGT, although perhaps the main victim of the DGB's political ambitions, has not thusfar been very responsive to the problem of internationalized action. The Confederation's posture in the mid-1970s symbolized its attitudes. It attempted to ride two international horses at once, applying for membership in ETUC while maintaining its position in good standing in the WFTU (where one of its own, Pierre Gensous, was Secretary-General). In 1977–1978, conscious of the difficulties of entering ETUC and motivated by growing displeasure at the obvious use of WFTU as a Soviet transmission-belt—WFTU was becoming a serious embarrassment to the degree that it insisted upon defending illiberal Eastern trade-union practices and opposing Eurocommunist changes in the West—the CGT began to loosen its ties to WFTU, but never to the point of disaffiliation. Séguy made a strong critical speech to the 1978 WFTU Congress which led to Gensous' resignation, but the CGT did not withdraw, as had, much earlier, the Italian CGIL (which became an "observer"). The CGT's reluctance to break with the WFTU is a good indicator of its true feelings on the internationalization question. The political unionism of the Cold War in which defense of the Socialist bloc had pride of place is still more important than developing European union cooperation in struggle against internationalizing capital. Thus the CGT faces the 1980s profoundly undecided about the international scope of union action. Should it be political in the traditional sense of the Cold War, a posture which would make participation in cross-national industrial struggles in Europe extremely difficult? Or should it opt for such cross-national action, in which case it will eventually have to take its distance from the unionism of the Socialist countries?

The second challenge for unions posed by the growing internationalization of economic life, that which follows from economic interdependence between specific capitalist societies, is even more profound. Production in many sectors—particularly, if not exclusively, those based in advanced technology—has become genuinely international. This means that specific national societies will lose much of the economic self-sufficiency which they earlier had, and that their economic success will depend increasingly upon an ability to conquer beachheads of comparative advantage in specialized activities. This fact explains the universal concern and anxiety of governments about "industrial policy." If specific economies do not develop internationally successful specialties, they will lose out, with disastrous consequences for the standards of living of their citizens and, ultimately, for the stability of their social orders. Unions, as important actors in these national settings, can avoid confronting these new realities only at their great peril. The direction and control of national investment is perhaps the central new economic issue arising out of the crisis.

As the decade turned, the CGT's response to all of these challenges, including that of a rightward shift in the politics of the French majority, was uncertain. Of the two alternatives presented to the Confederation, "proposition-force/industrial-solution" unionism seemed the most appropriate. The proposition-force approach promised to maximize prospects for sensitivity to new rank-and-file concerns, new outreach and unity-in-action with other union movements, the keys to the development of new militancy, broad rank-and-file mobilization, and successful opposition to anti-labor political trends. It also seemed more attuned to new realities of industrial structure and policy and the new international environment. There were strong barriers to its adoption however. Its strategic directions and the practices which they would involve were quite unclear, even to its most vocal advocates. This, in itself, was likely to create large obstacles to its progress in a CGT organization steeped in a decades-long tradition of defensive, bread-and-butter unionism. Beyond this, however, the advocacy of a very different perspective by the PCF and committed followers of the PCF's line in the CGT made it virtually certain that proposition-force unionism faced a long struggle to survive and thrive. Thus whether the CGT would eventually resolve its crisis through proposition-force/industrial-solutions innovations, through the PCF's post-1978 line, through some complicated amalgam of the two, or even through some very different option unforeseeable in 1980, was unknowable at time of writing.

The PCF's strategy-of-decline perspective, translated into CGT action, would be a course fraught with danger for the Confederation. The unionism which would result would be overwhelmingly defensive, almost *poujadiste*, and this would be likely to further stimulate particularism at the base. It would demonstrate little sensitivity to new rank-and-file concerns about authority in the workplace, the organization of work and the content of firm-level economic decisions. And its not-so-hidden political agenda, enlisting the CGT in the party's attempt to increase PCF strength vis-à-vis the Socialists, would make unity-in-action and CGT outreach operations towards the unorganized extremely difficult. The politics of the PCF position, with their vehement anti-social–democratic rhetoric, would not facilitate new relationships of international cooperation with Northern European social-democratic union movements either. It is the understanding of general capitalist reality embedded in the strategy-of-decline analysis which is most disturbing, however.

Theoretically, the strategy-of-decline perspective would lead the CGT directly to a strongly defensive nationalist posture. French economic activity of all kinds would be defended against further incursions by the new international order. It is, of course, clear that any sensible CGT crisis strategy would have to defend the integrity of these French economic activities which the Confederation considered vital for the kind of France which it desired to see. But the PCF's strategy-of-decline analysis makes no discrimination between economic change due to deliberate and incorrect governmental and employer *policies* and broader questions of the restructuring of an international *system*. In the strategy-of-decline perspective everything is caused by voluntary policy decisions. As a result, consideration of the shape of actual change in the structures of capital accumulation disappears. At first sight such a conflation of political and systemic analyses seems strange and counterproductive, the latter to the degree to which the perspective might lead the CGT to fight the wrong fights in the wrong ways. In fact, however, the "decline" perspective is informed by a sense of strategic desperation. To the degree that international economic interdependence becomes a fact and France becomes firmly enmeshed in a complex international division of labor, the linchpin of the PCF's traditional political vision, the possibility of constructing "socialism in one country," will become ever more unrealistic.

In this light what looks, at first sight, to be a simple, if very serious, crisis in PCF-CGT relations following the unfortunate 1978 elections may be, in the perspective of accelerating change in the structures of advanced capitalism, an historic switchpoint for both party and union. To be sure, relative autonomy did not work. Moreover, transmission beltism failed dismally in the past and is likely to fail quite as dismally in the future. Whatever the relationship between party and union may be in years to come, however, one of the basic premises of the entire French Leninist edifice, of which party-union relationships are one part, may rapidly be losing its validity. Orthodox perspectives on the transcendence of capitalism based on nineteenth-century views as crystallized and modified by the Soviet experience do not stand outside history. The strategic notion of "socialism in one country" has been at the very center of PCF projections of change from early in the party's history up through the Common Program of the 1970s. If contemporary economic change is rendering this notion less and less realistic, at least in its received forms, where does this leave party and union?

The logic of Eurocommunization, which the PCF was both unable and unwilling to follow through to its conclusion in the 1970s, led directly into the uncharted strategic waters of the new situation. "Big-bang" or *grand-soir* notions of change are increasingly unworkable, to the degree to which they imply an economic autarky whose instruments are rapidly disappearing with the internationalization of capital. Some form of step-by-step structural reformism must replace them. But step-by-step reformism cannot work if it does not cumulate into transformative change over time. Any new strategic perspective must therefore include new approaches to the problem of maintaining working-class victories in the flux of future political change while structuring such victories so that they create a broader base for further and broader victories at a later point. Otherwise something resembling social democracy will ensue, at best. A step-by-step strategy in France must, therefore, discover new ways of mobilizing ordinary people and keeping them mobilized for change. It is clear that, for the PCF, this must involve a considerable modification of its past insistence that all mobilizing activity must be focused towards change in the political sphere. New, sustained, and creative attempts to reconstruct civil society are an absolute prerequisite for successful navigation on the new course. That they must involve vast new installments of direct democracy as a supplement to the PCF's traditional, and almost exclusive, focus on the use of representative democracy as a tool for change, is clear. This desideratum has profound implications for PCF-CGT relations. The CGT *could* become a decisively important vehicle for the reconstruction of civil society and for direct democracy in work. But, to do so, it would have to be liberated from its historic task of focusing labor mobilization ultimately towards change at the level of the national state. Not, of course, that the CGT can, or should, become indifferent to the political sphere. In the present and future, however, its most useful contribution to change will be in the democratic mobilization of workers for step-by-step transformative change in work and economic life. Our conviction that this is true, of course, is the source of our obvious sympathy for the proposition-force/industrial-solutions initiatives being advocated within the Confederation at present. The new conjuncture has other implications as well. Both party and union must develop radically new approaches to a new international reality. Given growing international economic interdependence, even a step-by-step structural reform strategy for change must be prepared to cope with international reactions to progressive initiatives in France. Ultimately this can only be done by dramatically internationalizing strategic perspectives themselves. New alliances and new arrangements of cooperation, with progressive forces in other societies, especially other European societies, are imperative. Moreover, party and union must pursue such arrangements each in its own ways and within its own spheres of competence. Eurocommunism, now moribund, might, resuscitated, be a good place to start, to the degree to which it involved genuine strategic coordination between the PCF and the Italian and Spanish parties. A separate "Eurosyndicalism," involving the CGT, CGIL and the Spanish Workers' Commissions on trade-union questions, would be another. Beyond such beginnings, however, new links with Northern European social democracy and its unions (which among other things might prod the emergence of more progressive currents within social democracy) are clearly necessary.

Thus as the 1980s progress, the PCF and CGT, separately and together, will face circumstances in which the choices will be between holding onto the false comfort of past recipes which can no longer work, or moving forward into a very new world. Nothing guarantees that the right choice will be made. Indeed, the exact nature of the right choice is as yet unclear. How will transformative social change follow from step-by-step structural reformism? If neither relative autonomy nor transmission beltism is an adequate conceptualization of party-union relationships, what is the alternative? Can some variant of proposition-force/industrial-solution unionism succeed in giving real direct democratic content to *autogestion*? Can party and union adjust to the change in their strategic perspectives which the internationalization of capital demands? Should choice be avoided, and/or past recipes be retained, the danger of decline for both party and union could become real. This need not be the kind of dramatic decline—isolation, collapse of membership, diminution of mobilizing power—so long hoped for by their opponents. It is much more likely that party and union would maintain much of their present strength while ceasing to be plausible agents for social change. A very different scenario would await a party and union which made the right choice, however.

BIBLIOGRAPHY

Books and Documents

Adam, Gérard. *La CFTC*. Paris: Armand Colin, 1964.

_____ . *Le syndicalisme ouvrier en France*. Paris: Cours de l'Institut d'Etudes Politiques, 1969.

Adam, Gérard, Frédéric Bon, et al. *L'ouvrier français en 1970*. Paris: Armand Colin, 1971.

Adam, Gérard, and Jean-Daniel Reynaud. *La négociation collective en France*. Paris: Ed. Ouvrières, 1972.

Adler, Alexandre, Francis Cohen, et al. *L'URSS et nous*. Paris: Ed. Sociales, 1978.

Alexandre, Philippe. *L'Elysée en péril*. Paris: Fayard, 1969.

Althusser, Louis. *XXIIe Congrès*. Paris: Maspero, 1977.

_____ . *Ce qui ne peut plus durer au PCF*. Paris: Maspero, 1978.

Andreu, Anne, and Jean-Louis Mingalon. *L'adhésion*. Paris: Calmann Levy, 1975.

Andrieu, René. *Les Communistes et la révolution*. Paris: Julliard, 1969.

_____ . *Choses dites*. Paris: Ed. Sociales, 1979.

Andrieux, Andrée, and Jean Lignon. *L'ouvrier d'aujourd'hui*. Paris: Rivière, 1960.

Angeli, Claude, and Paul Gillet. *Debout partisans*. Paris: Fayard, 1970.

L'année politique en France. [later, *L'année politique, économique et sociale*]. Paris: PUF; annual, 1944–present.

Aron, Raymond. *La révolution introuvable*. Paris: Julliard, 1968.

Aron, Robert. *The Vichy Regime, 1940–1944*. London: Putnam, 1958.

Baby, Jean. *Critique de base*. Paris: Maspero, 1960.

Badie, Bertrand. *Stratégie de la grève*. Paris: Armand Colin, 1976.

Balibar, Etienne. *La dictature du prolétariat*. Paris: Maspero, 1977.

Balibar, Etienne, Guy Bois, et al. *Ouvrons la fenêtre, camarades!* Paris: Maspero, 1979.

Barbe, Philippe. "*Les grèves de novembre et décembre 1947*." Unpublished. Paris: Institut d'Etudes Politiques, 1952.

Barjonet, André. *Qu'est-ce-que la paupérisation?* Paris: Ed. Sociales, 1960.

_____ . *La CGT*. Paris: Seuil, 1968.

_____ . *La révolution trahie*. Paris: John Didier, 1968.

_____ . *Le Parti communiste français*. Paris: John Didier, 1969.

Bauchard, Philippe, and Maurice Bruzek. *La syndicalisme à l'épreuve*. Paris: Robert Laffont, 1968.

Baudelot, Christian, Christian Malemort, et al. *La petite bourgeoisie en France*. Paris: Maspero, 1975.

_____ .*Qui travaille pour qui?* Paris: Maspero, 1979.

Baudot, Jacques, and Jean-Marie Desmottes. *Conditions de vie et d'emploi des jeunes travailleurs*. Paris: PUF, 1968.

Belleville, Pierre. *Une nouvelle classe ouvrière*. Paris: Julliard, 1963.

_____ . *Laminage continu*. Paris: Julliard, 1969.

Bernoux, Philippe. *Les nouveaux patrons*. Paris: Ed. Ouvrières, 1974.

Billoux, François. *Quand nous étions ministres*. Paris: Ed. Sociales, 1972.

Blackmer, Donald, and Sidney Tarrow, eds. *Communism in Italy and France*. Princeton: Princeton University Press, 1975.

Bloch-Lainé, François. *Pour une réforme de l'entreprise*. Paris: Seuil, 1963.

Blondel, Charles. *Les syndicats des salariés en France*. Paris: Cours de l'Ecole Nationale d'Administration, 1956.

Blum, Léon. *Le problème de l'unité*. Paris: SFIO, 1945.

Bockel, Alain. *La participation des syndicats ouvriers aux fonctions économiques et sociales de l'état*. Paris: L.G.D.J., 1965.

Bodin, Louis, and Jean Touchard. *Front populaire*. Paris: Armand Colin, 1961.

Boggs, Carl, and David Plotke. *The Politics of Eurocommunism*. Boston: Southend Press, 1980.

Boissonat, Jean. *La politique des revenus*. Paris: Seuil, 1966.

Bornstein, Stephen. "From Social Christianity to Left Socialism: The Itinerary of the Catholic Labor Movement in France." Cambridge: Ph.D. dissertation, Harvard University, 1979.

Bouillot, François, and Jean-Marie Devisa. *Un parti peut en cacher un autre*. Paris: Maspero, 1979.

Bourdet, Claude. *Les chemins de l'unité*. Paris: Maspero, 1964.

Bourdieu, Pierre. *La distinction*. Paris: Ed. Minuit, 1979.

Bourdieu, Pierre, and Jean-Claude Passeron. *Les héritiers*. Paris: Ed. Minuit, 1964.

Branciard, Michel. *Société française et luttes de classe*. 3 volumes. Paris: Ed. Ouvrières, 1967, 1978.

Brière, Jacques. *Vive la crise!* Paris: Seuil, 1979.

Brizay, Bernard. *Le patronat*. Paris: Seuil, 1975.

Brousse, Henri. *Le niveau de vie en France*. Paris: PUF, 1962.

Brower, Daniel. *The New Jacobins*. Ithaca, N.Y.: Cornell University Press, 1969.

Bruhat, Jean, and Marc Piolot. *La CGT, esquisse d'une histoire*. Paris: CGT, 1966.

Bunel, Jean and Paul Meunier. *Chaban-Delmas*. Paris: Stock, 1972.

Caille, Marcel. *Les truands du patronat*. Paris: Ed. Sociales, 1977.

_____ . *L'assassin était chez Citroën*. Paris: Ed. Sociales, 1978.

Caire, Guy. *Les syndicats ouvriers*. Paris: PUF, 1971.

_____ . *La grève ouvrière*. Paris: Ed. Ouvrières, 1978.

Capdevielle, Jacques, and René Mouriaux. "Les militants de la CGT et de la CFDT." Unpublished. Paris: Institut d'Etudes Politiques, 1969.

_____ . *Les syndicats ouvriers en France*. 2nd ed. Paris: Armand Colin, 1973.

Capdevielle, Jacques, et al. *La grève au Joint Français*. Paris: Armand Colin, 1975.

Capocci, Armand. *L'avenir du syndicalisme*. Paris: Hachette, 1967.

Carrillo, Santiago. *Eurocommunism and the State*. London: Lawrence and Wishart, 1977.

Casanova, Jean-Claude. "La position des syndicats français dans l'économie politique." Unpublished. Paris: Faculté de Droit, 1956.

Caute, David. *Communism and French Intellectuals*. London: Macmillan, 1964.

Charlot, Jean. *Le phénomène Gaulliste*. Paris: Fayard, 1970.

Cheminots, Fédération Nationale des, CGT. *Les cheminots dans l'histoire sociale de la France*. Paris: Ed. Sociales, 1967.

Chombart de Lauwe, Pierre. *La vie quotidienne des familles ouvrières*. Paris: CNRS, 1956.

Claude, Henri, et al. *La IVe République*. Paris: Ed. Sociales, 1972.

Claudin, Fernando. *La crise du mouvement communiste*. 2 volumes. Paris: Maspero, 1973.

_____ . *L'Eurocommunisme*. Paris: Maspero, 1978.

Cohen, Stephen. *Modern Capitalist Planning: The French Model*. Cambridge: Harvard University Press, 1969.

Cohn-Bendit, Daniel. *Obsolete Communism: The Left Wing Alternative*. New York: McGraw-Hill, 1968.

Collinet, Michel. *Essai sur la condition ouvrière*. Paris: Ed. Ouvrières, 1951.

_____ . *L'ouvrier français, esprit du syndicalisme*. Paris: Ed. Ouvrières, 1951.

Colpin, Jean. *Communistes à l'entreprise*. Paris: Ed. Sociales, 1979.

Combe, Maurice. *L'alibi, vingt ans d'expérience d'un comité central d'entreprise*. Paris: Gallimard, 1969.

Confédération Française des Travailleurs Chrétiens (CFTC). Congresses, 1945–1963. Paris: CFTC.

_____ . *Unité syndicale ou unité d'action*. Paris: CFTC, n.d.

Confédération Française et Démocratique du Travail (CFDT). Congresses, 1963–1979. Paris: CFDT.

_____ . *Dialogues CGT-CFDT*. 2 volumes. Dittoed. Paris: CFDT, 1968.

_____ . *CFDT: textes de base*. Paris: CFDT, 1974.

_____ . *La crise*. Paris: CFDT, 1975.

_____ . *Les dégats du progrés*. Paris: Seuil, 1977.

CFDT, Fédération Générale de la Métallurgie, *Avenir de la sidérurgie*. Paris: CFDT, 1979.

CFDT, Fédération des PTT. *Des idiots par milliers*. Paris: Maspero, 1975.
Confédération Générale du Travail (CGT). Congresses, Comptes rendus *in extenso*, 1946–1979. Paris: CGT.
_____ . *Données chiffrées sur les femmes travailleuses*. Paris: CGT, 1977.
_____ . *Perspectives et problèmes de l'énergie*. Paris: CGT, 1977.
_____ . *L'industrie française depuis 1958, un bilan accusateur*. Paris: CGT, 1978.
_____ . *Pour un nouvel ordre économique international*. Paris: CGT, 1978.
_____ . *Des manufactures à la crise du Taylorisme*. Paris: CGT, 1978.
_____ . *Les industries de la construction*. Paris: CGT, 1979.
_____ . *Crise et solution pour la sidérurgie*. Paris: CGT, 1978.
CGT, Fédération des Travailleurs de la Métallurgie. *Le Guide du militant, face à la crise de la sidérurgie*. Paris: CGT, 1978.
Cotta, Alain. *La France et l'impératif mondial*. Paris: PUF, 1978.
Couffignal, Georges. *Les syndicats Italiens et la politique*. Grenoble: Presses Universitaires de Grenoble, 1979.
Courtois, Stéphane. *Le PCF pendant la guerre*. Paris: Ramsay, 1979.
Crouch, Colin, and Alessandro Pizzorno, eds. *The Resurgence of Class Conflict in Western Europe*. 2 volumes. London: Macmillan, 1978.
Crozier, Michel. *La société bloquée*. Paris: Seuil, 1970.
Daix, Pierre. *J'ai cru au matin*. Paris: Laffont, 1976.
_____ . *La crise du PCF*. Paris: Seuil, 1978.
Dale, Leon. *Marxism and French Labor*. New York: Praeger, 1954.
Danos, Jacques, and Marcel Gibelin. *Juin 1936*. Paris: Ed. Ouvrières, 1952.
David, Marcel. *Les travilleurs et le sens de leur histoire*. Paris: Cujas, 1967.
de Gaulle, Charles. *Mémoires de guerre*. Paris: Ed. Poche, 1959.
de Lattre, André. *Politique économique de la France*. Paris: Sirey, 1966.
Delilez, Jean-Pierre. *L'état du changement*. Paris: Ed. Sociales, 1977.
Delon, Pierre. *Les employés*. Paris: Ed. Sociales, 1969.
Desanti, Dominique. *Les staliniens*. Paris: Fayard, 1975.
Descamps, Eugène. *Militer*. Paris: Stock, 1971.
Detraz, Albert, et al. *La CFDT et l'autogestion*. Paris: Cerf, 1973.
Dimitrov, Georgi. *United Front Against Fascism*. New York: International, 1935.
[Diverse authors.] *Le Contre Plan*. Paris: Seuil, 1965.
[Diverse authors.] *Le grève à Flins*. Paris: Maspero, 1968.
[Diverse authors.] *Notre arme c'est la grève, la grève chez Renault Cléon*. Paris: Maspero, 1968.
Dolléans, Edouard. *Histoire du mouvement ouvrier*. 3 volumes. Paris: Armand Colin, 1953.
Dubois, Pierre. *Mort de l'état patron*. Paris: Fayard, 1975.
Dubois, Pierre, et al. *Grèves revendicatives ou grèves politiques?* Paris: Anthropos, 1971.
Duhamel, Olivier, and Henri Weber. *Changer le PC?* Paris: PUF, 1979.
Durand, Claude, et al. *La grève*. Paris: Armand Colin, 1975.

Duverger, Maurice. *Partis politiques et classes sociales en France*. Paris: Armand Colin, 1964.

Ehrmann, Henry. *French Labor from Popular Front to Liberation*. New York: Oxford, 1947.

_____. *Organized Business in France*. Princeton: Princeton University Press, 1957.

Einaudi, Mario, ed. *Communism in Western Europe*. Ithaca, N.Y.: Cornell University Press, 1951.

Elgey, Georgette. *La république des illusions*. Paris: Fayard, 1965.

_____. *La république des contradictions*. Paris: Fayard, 1969.

Elleinstein, Jean. *Histoire du phénomène stalinien*. Paris: Ed. Sociales, 1975.

_____. *Histoire de l'URSS*. 4 volumes. Paris: Ed. Sociales, 1975.

_____. *Le PCF*. Paris: Grasset, 1976.

Epistemon. *Ces idées qui ont ébranlé la France*. Paris: Fayard, 1968.

Fabre, Robert. *Toute vérité est bonne à dire*. Paris: Fayard, 1979.

Fajon, Etienne. *L'union est un combat*. Paris: Ed. Sociales, 1974.

_____. *Ma vie s'appelle liberté*. Paris: Laffont, 1976.

Faucher, Jean-André. *La gauche française sous de Gaulle*. Paris: John Didier, 1969.

Fauvet, Jacques. *Histoire du Parti communiste français*. 1st ed. 2 volumes. Paris: Fayard, 1964, 1965. 2nd ed. 1 volume. Paris: Fayard, 1977.

Fejtö, François. *The French Communist Party and the Crisis of International Communism*. Cambridge: Massachusetts Institute of Technology Press, 1967.

Fiszbin, Henri. *Les bouches s'ouvrent*. Paris: Grasset, 1980.

Fondation Nationale des Sciences Politiques. *Le communisme en France*. Paris: Armand Colin, 1969.

_____. *Les élections présidentielles de 1965*. Paris: Armand Colin, 1970.

_____. *Les élections présidentielles de 1969*. Paris: Armand Colin, 1972.

_____. *La politique des puissances devant la décolonisation*. Paris: Armand Colin, 1969.

_____. *Les élections législatives de 1967*. Paris: Armand Colin, 1971.

_____. *Les élections législatives de 1973*. Paris: Armand Colin, 1976.

Force Ouvrière. *Comment et pourquoi . . . les scissions*. Paris: Force Ouvrière, 1964.

Frachon, Benoît. *Au rythme des jours*. 2 volumes. Paris: Ed. Sociales, 1967, 1969.

Frémontier, Jacques. *Renault: la forteresse ouvrière*. Paris: Seuil, 1975.

Friedmann, Georges, and Pierre Naville. *Traité de sociologie du travail*. Paris: PUF, 1962.

Frischmann, Georges. *Histoire de la Fédération CGT des PTT*. Paris: Ed. Sociales, 1967.

Gallie, Duncan. *In Search of the New Working Class*. Cambridge: Cambridge University Press, 1978.

Gani, Léon. *Syndicats et travailleurs immigrés*. Paris: Ed. Sociales, 1972.

Garaudy, Roger. *Le grande tournant du socialisme*. Paris: Gallimard, 1969.

_____. *Toute la vérité*. Paris: Grasset, 1972.

Gaucher, Roland. *Histoire secrète du PCF*. Paris: Albin Michel, 1974.

Gavi, Philippe. *Les ouvriers*. Paris: Mercure de France, 1970.

Geerlandt, Robert. *Garaudy et Althusser*. Paris: PUF, 1978.

Giscard d'Estaing, Valéry. *La démocratie française*. Paris: Fayard, 1976.

Glucksmann, André. *Stratégie et révolution en France 1968*. Paris: Christian Bourgois, 1968.

Godfrey, Edward. *The Fate of the French Non-Communist Left*. New York: Doubleday, 1955.

Goëtz-Girey, Robert. *La pensée syndicale française*. Paris: Sirey, 1948.

———. *Le mouvement des grèves en France, 1919–1962*. Paris: Sirey,1964.

Goldring, Maurice. *L'accident*. Paris: Ed. Sociales, 1978.

Goldthorpe, John, David Lockwood et al. *The Affluent Worker*. 3 volumes. Cambridge: Cambridge University Press, 1968.

Gones, Denis. *Silence, on ferme!* Paris: Ed. Ouvrières, 1976.

Gorz, André. *Stratégie ouvrière et néocapitalisme*. Paris: Seuil, 1964.

———. *Le socialisme difficile*. Paris: Seuil, 1968.

Graham, William. *The French Socialists and Tripartism*. Toronto: University of Toronto Press, 1967.

Gravier, Jean. *Paris et le désert français*. Paris: Seuil, 1947.

Guglielmi, Jean-Louis, and Michelle Perrot. *Salaires et revendications sociales en France, 1944–1952*. Paris: Centre d'Etudes Economiques, 1953.

Guin, Yannick. *La Commune de Nantes*. Paris: Maspero, 1969.

Hamilton, Richard. *Affluence and the French Working Class*. Princeton: Princeton University Press, 1967.

Hammond, Thomas. *Lenin on Trade Unions and Revolution*. New York: Columbia University Press, 1957.

Harris, André, and Alain de Sédouy. *Voyage à l'intérieur du Parti Communiste*. Paris: Seuil, 1974.

Hobsbawm, Erik, ed. *The Italian Road to Socialism*. London: Lawrence and Wishart, 1977.

Hoffman, Stanley, et al. *In Search of France*. Cambridge: Harvard University Press, 1964.

Hoffman, Stanley, and William Andrews. *Two Decades of Gaullism*. Albany: State University of New York Press, 1980.

James, Emile. *Les comités d'entreprise*. Paris: Ed. Sociales, 1945.

Jeanneney, Jean-Marcel. *Le mouvement économique en France de 1944 à 1957*. Paris: PUF, 1958.

Joliot-Curie, Frédéric. *Cinq années de lutte pour la paix*. Paris: Ed. Défense de la Paix, 1954.

Julliard, Jacques. *La IVᵉ République*. Paris: Calmann-Levy, 1968.

Juquin, Pierre. *Libertés*. Paris: Grasset, 1975.

———. *L'actualisation à dossiers ouverts*. Paris: Ed. Sociales, 1978.

Kaes, René. *Les ouvriers français et la culture*. Paris: Dalloz, 1962.

Kergoat, Danielle. *Bulledor*. Paris: Seuil, 1975.

Kolm, Serge-Christophe. *La transition socialiste*. Paris: Cerf, 1977.

Krasucki, Henri. *Syndicats et lutte de classes*. Paris: Ed. Sociales, 1969.

_____ . *Syndicats et socialisme*. Paris: Ed. Sociales, 1972.

Kriegel, Annie. *Aux origines du communisme français*. 2 volumes. Paris: Mouton, 1964.

_____ . *Les communistes français*. Paris: Seuil, 1968.

Kriegel, Annie, and Michelle Perrot. *Le socialisme français et le pouvoir*. Paris: EDI, 1966.

Labro, Philippe. *Ce n'est qu'un début*. Paris: Ed. Premières, 1968.

Lancelot, Alain, and Gérard Adam. *Les groupes de pression*. Paris: Armand Colin, 1960.

Lannoye, Michel. *La vie sociale de l'entreprise*. Paris: Ed. Ouvrières, 1966.

Lasserre, Georges. *Le syndicalisme ouvrier en France*. Paris: Cours de l'Institut d'Etudes Politiques, 1964–1965.

Laurent, Paul. *Le PCF comme il est*. Paris: Ed. Sociales, 1978.

le Bourre, Raymond. *Le syndicalisme français dans la Ve République*. Paris: Calmann-Levy, 1959.

le Braz, Yves. *Les rejetés, l'affaire Marty-Tillon*. Paris: Table Ronde, 1974.

LeBrun, Pierre. *Questions actuelles du syndicalisme*. Paris: Seuil, 1964.

Lecler, Jean-Marie. "La position des centrales syndicales CGT, CFTC et FO à l'égard de l'unité syndicale de 1947 à 1964." Unpublished. Paris: Faculté de Droit, 1966.

Lecoeur, Auguste. *L'autocritique attendue*. Paris: Girault, 1955.

_____ . *Le partisan*. Paris: Flammarion, 1963.

_____ . *Le PCF*. Paris: Laffont, 1977

Lefebvre, Henri. *L'irruption, de Nanterre au sommet*. Paris: Anthropos, 1968.

_____ . *La somme et le reste*. 2 volumes. Paris: Le Nef, 1959.

Lefort, Claude, Edgar Morin, and Jean-Marc Coudray. *Mai 1968: la brèche*. Paris: Fayard, 1968.

Lefranc, Georges. *Les expériences syndicales en France de 1939 à 1950*. Paris: Payot, 1950.

_____ . *Le syndicalisme français*. Paris: PUF, 1965.

_____ . *Juin 1936*. Paris: Coll. Archives, 1966.

_____ . *Le mouvement syndical sous la Troisième République*. Paris: Payot, 1967.

_____ . *Le front populaire*. Paris: PUF, 1968.

_____ . *Le mouvement syndical en France, de la Libération aux événements de mai-juin 1968*. Paris: PUF, 1969.

Leites, Nathan. *On the Game of Politics in France*. Stanford, Calif.: Stanford University Press, 1962.

Lenin, Vladimir. *On Trade Unions*. Moscow: Progress, 1970.

Lesire-Ogrel, Hubert. *Le syndicat dans l'entreprise*. Paris: Seuil, 1968.

Lichtheim, George. *Marxism in Modern France*. New York: Columbia University Press, 1966.

Lille, Faculté de Droit et Sciences Economiques. *L'activité syndicale au niveau de l'entreprise*. Lille: Université de Lille, 1966.

Lorwin, Val. *The French Labor Movement*. Cambridge: Harvard University Press, 1954.

Macridis, Roy, and Bernard Brown. *Supplement to the de Gaulle Republic.* Homewood, Ill.: Dorsey Press, 1963.

Mallet, Serge. *La nouvelle classe ouvrière.* Paris: Seuil, 1963.

———. *Le Gaullisme et la gauche.* Paris: Seuil, 1964.

Marchais, Georges. *Le defi démocratique.* Paris: Grasset, 1973.

———. *Parlons franchement.* Paris: Ed. Sociales, 1977.

Marcou, Lilly. *Le Kominform.* Paris: Armand Colin, 1977.

———. *L'Internationale aprés Staline.* Paris: Grasset, 1979.

Martinet, Gilles. *La conquête des pouvoirs.* Paris: Seuil, 1968.

Marty, André. *L'affaire Marty.* Paris: Deux Rives, 1955.

Massé, Pierre. *Le Plan ou l'anti-hasard.* Paris: PUF, 1965.

Micaud, Charles. *Communism and the French Left.* London: Weidenfeld and Nicholson, 1963.

Michel, Henri. *Histoire de la Résistance.* Paris: PUF, 1950.

———. *Les courants de pensée de la Résistance.* Paris: PUF, 1962.

Minces, Juliette. *Le Nord.* Paris: Maspero, 1967.

Molina, Gérard, and Yves Vargas. *Dialogue a l'intérieur du Parti Communiste.* Paris: Maspero, 1978.

Mollet, Guy. *13 mai 1958–13 mai 1962.* Paris: Plon, 1962.

Monatte, Pierre. *Ou va la CGT?* Paris: Ed. Ouvrières, 1946.

———. *Les trois scissions syndicales.* Paris: Ed. Ouvrières, 1958.

Montluclard, Maurice. *La dynamique des comités d'entreprise.* Paris: CNRS, 1963.

Moreau, Jean-Pierre. *"Le pacte CGT-CFDT du 10 janvier 1966."* Unpublished. Université de Poitiers, 1967.

Morin, Edgar. *Autocritique.* Paris: Julliard, 1959.

Moss, Bernard. *The Origins of the French Labor Movement.* Berkeley: University of California Press, 1976.

Mothé, Daniel. *Journal d'un ouvrier.* Paris: Ed. Minuit, 1959.

———. *Militant chez Renault.* Paris: Seuil, 1965.

Mouriaux, René, and Jean Magniadas. *Les militants de la CGT.* Paris: CGT, 1973.

Naville, Pierre. *La classe ouvrière et le régime Gaulliste.* Paris: Anthropos, 1964.

Naville, Pierre, et al. *Division du travail, classe ouvrière, et syndicalisme.* Paris: CNRS, 1962.

Noirot, Philippe. *La mémoire ouverte.* Paris: Stock, 1976.

Parti Communiste Français. *Histoire du Parti communiste français (Manuel).* Paris: Ed. Sociales, 1964.

———. *Manifeste du Parti communiste français, pour une démocratie avancée, pour une France socialiste.* Paris: Ed. Sociales, 1969.

———. *Changer de cap.* Paris: Ed. Sociales, 1971.

———. *Programme commun de gouvernement.* Paris: Ed. Sociales, 1972.

———. *Traité d'économie politique (le capitalisme monopoliste d'état).* 2 volumes. Paris: Ed. Sociales, 1972.

———. *Vivre libres.* Paris: Ed. Sociales, 1975.

———. *Le socialisme pour la France.* Paris: Ed. Sociales, 1976.

Passeron, Serge. "Les minoritaires dans l'actuel CGT." Unpublished. Paris: Institut d'Etudes Politiques, 1963.

Perrin, André. *Les grèves politiques de novembre-decembre 1947.* Paris: République Moderne, 1948.

Pesquet, Henri. *Des soviets à Saclay.* Paris: Maspero, 1968.

Pfister, Thierry, and André Laurens. *Les nouveaux communistes aux portes du pouvoir.* Paris: Stock, 1977.

Pineau, Christian. *La simple vérité.* Paris: Julliard, 1961.

Poperen, Jean. *L'unite de la gauche.* Paris: Grasset, 1977.

Posner, Charles, ed. *Reflections on the Revolution in France.* Harmondsworth: Penguin, 1969.

Poulantzas, Nicos. *Les classes sociales dans le capitalisme d'aujourd'hui.* Paris: Seuil, 1972.

———, ed. *La crise de l'état.* Paris: PUF, 1977.

———. *L'état, le pouvoir, le socialisme.* Paris: PUF, 1978.

Prost, Antoine. *La CGT à l'époque du Front populaire.* Paris: Armand Colin, 1964.

Prouteau, Henri. *Les occupations d'usines en Italie et en France.* Paris: Ed. Ouvrières, 1946.

Rainville, Jean-Marie. *Condition ouvrière et intégration sociale.* Paris: Ed. Ouvrières, 1967.

Reynaud, Jean-Daniel. *Les syndicats en France.* 2nd ed. 2 volumes. Paris: Seuil, 1975.

———. *Les syndicats, les patrons et l'état.* Paris: Ed. Ouvrières, 1978.

Rieber, Alfred. *Stalin and the French Communist Party.* New York: Columbia University Press, 1962.

Rioux, Lucien. *Ou en est le syndicalisme?* Paris: Stock, 1967.

Rioux, Lucien, and René Backmann. *L'explosion de mai.* Paris: Laffont, 1968.

Robert, Jean-Louis. *La scission syndicale, 1914–1921.* Paris: PUF, 1977.

Robrieux, Philippe. *Maurice Thorez.* Paris: Fayard, 1975.

———. *Notre génération communiste.* Paris: Fayard, 1977.

Rochet, Waldeck. *Les enseignements de mai-juin.* Paris: Ed. Sociales, 1968.

———. *L'avenir du Parti communiste français.* Paris: Ed. Sociales, 1970.

Rony, Jean. *30 ans du parti.* Paris: Christian Bourgois, 1978.

Rossi, Amilcare. *Physiologie du Parti communiste français.* Paris: Ed. Self, 1948.

———. *Les communistes français pendant la drôle de guerre.* Paris: Isles d'Or, 1951.

Salini, Laurent. *Le mai des prolétaires.* Paris: Ed. Sociales, 1968.

Sartre, Jean-Paul. *Situations VI.* Paris: Gallimard, 1964.

Schwartz, Salomon. *Les occupations d'usines en France de mai et juin 1936.* Paris: Seuil, 1947.

Seale, Patrick, and Maureen McConville. *Red Flag, Black Flag.* New York: Ballantine, 1968.

Séguy, Georges. *Le mai de la CGT.* Paris: Julliard, 1972.

_____ . *Lutter*. Paris: Ed. Poche, 1978.

Sellier, François. *Stratégie de la lutte sociale*. Paris: Ed. Ouvrières, 1961.

Sellier, François, and André Tiano. *Economie du travail*. Paris: PUF, 1962.

Shulman, Marshall. "Soviet Policy in Western Europe and the French Communist Party 1949–1952." Unpublished. New York: Columbia University, 1959.

Simmons, Harvey. *French Socialists in Search of a Role*. Ithaca, N.Y.: Cornell University Press, 1970.

Stoffaës, Christian. *La grande menace industrielle*. Paris: Calmann-Lévy, 1978.

Stolvitzer, Hedvicq. "La scission de la CGT." Unpublished. Paris: Institut d'Etudes Politiques, 1957.

Suffert, Georges. *De Defferre à Mitterrand*. Paris: Seuil, 1966.

Thorez, Maurice. *La paupérisation des travailleurs français*. Paris: Ed. Sociales, 1961.

_____ . *Oeuvres choisies*. 3 volumes. Paris: Ed. Sociales, 1966.

Tiano, André, and Michel Rocard. *L'expérience française du syndicalisme ouvrier*. Paris: Ed. Ouvrières, 1956.

Tiersky, Ronald. *French Communism, 1922–1972*. New York: Columbia University Press, 1975.

Tillon, Charles. *Un procès de Moscou à Paris*. Paris: Seuil, 1971.

_____ . *On chantait rouge*. Paris: Laffont, 1977.

Tollet, André. *La classe ouvrière dans la Résistance*. Paris: Ed. Sociales, 1960.

Touchard, Jean. *Le Gaullisme, 1940–1969*. Paris: Seuil, 1978.

Touraine, Alain. *Le travail ouvrier aux usines Renault*. Paris: CNRS, 1964.

_____ . *Sociologie de l'action*. Paris: Seuil, 1965.

_____ . *La conscience ouvrière*. Paris: Seuil, 1966.

_____ . *The May Movement*. New York: Random House, 1971.

_____ . *The Post Industrial Society*. New York: Random House, 1971.

_____ . *Production de la société*. Paris: Seuil, 1973.

_____ . *Le mouvement étudiant*. Paris: Seuil, 1979.

Touraine, Alain and Olivier Ragazzi. *Ouvriers d'origine agricole*. Paris: Seuil, 1961.

Tournoux, Jean Raymond. *Le mois de mai du Général*. Paris: Plon, 1969.

Unir. *Histoire du PCF*. 3 volumes. Paris: Ed. Unir, 1962.

Vedel, Georges, ed. *La dépolitisation*. Paris: Armand Colin, 1967.

Verdier, Robert. *PS–PC*. Paris: Seuil, 1973.

Viansson-Ponté, Pierre. *Histoire de la République Gaullienne*. 2 vols. Paris: Fayard, 1971.

Vidalenc, Georges. *Aspects du mouvement syndical français*. Paris: FO, 1958.

_____ . *La classe ouvrière et le syndicalisme en France de 1789 à 1965*. Paris: FO, 1969.

Viens, Yann, et al. *La condition féminine*. Paris: Ed. Sociales, 1978.

Weber, Henri, and Daniel Bensaid. *Mai 1968: répétition générale*. Paris: Maspero, 1968.

Willard, Claude. *Socialisme et communisme français*. Paris: Armand Colin, 1967.
Willard, Claude, ed. *Le Front populaire*. Paris: Ed. Sociales, 1972.
Willard, Germaine, et al. *De la guerre à la Libération*. Paris: Ed. Sociales, 1972.
Willener, Alfred, et al. *Les cadres en mouvement*. Paris: EPI, 1969.
Williams, Philip. *Crisis and Compromise*. New York: Doubleday, 1966.
Williams, Philip, and David Goldie. *French Politicians and Elections*. Cambridge: Cambridge University Press, 1970.
Wohl, Robert. *French Communism in the Making*. Stanford, Calif.: Stanford University Press, 1966.
Zarifian, Philippe. *Inflation et crise monétaire*. Paris: Fédération Syndicale Mondiale, 1976.

INDEX

Designer:	Randall Goodall
Compositor:	Freedmen's Organization
Printer:	Edwards Brothers
Binder:	Edwards Brothers
Text:	Compugraphic English Times
Display:	Goudy Old Style

FH/MX   M/O 121 UCA
          ROSS